P9-BHX-862

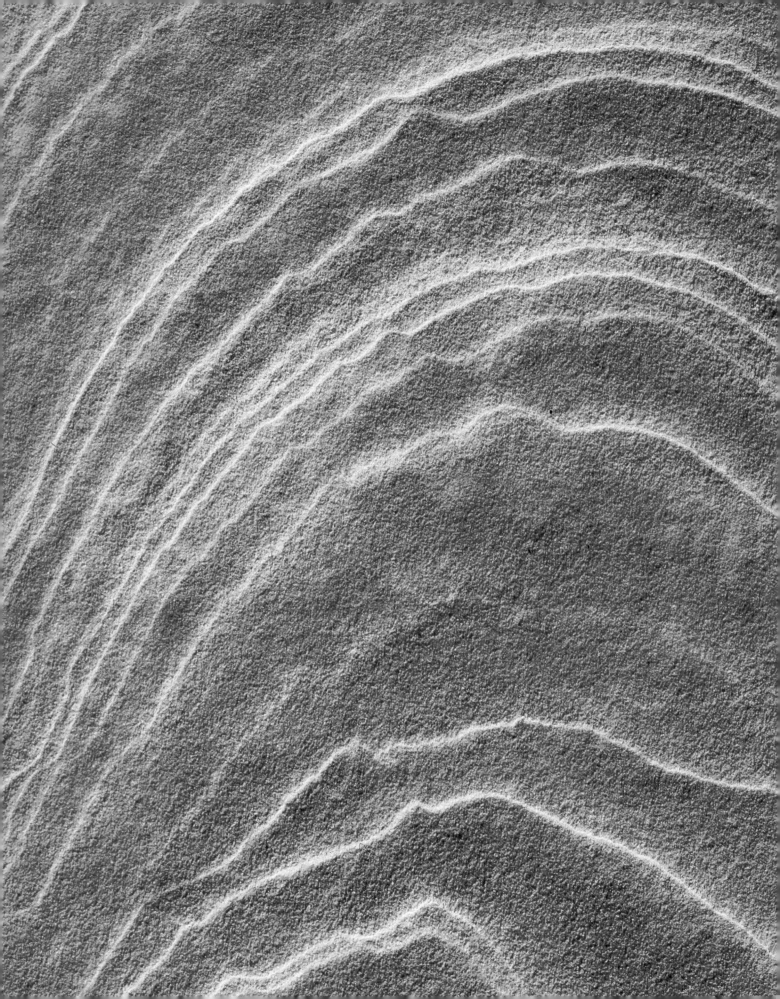

HARCOURT
SCIENCE
CALIFORNIA EDITION

Harcourt School Publishers

Orlando • Boston • Dallas • Chicago • San Diego

www.harcourtschool.com

Cover Image: This reptile is a veiled chameleon *(Chamaelo calyptratus)* They are often raised and sold as pets. In the wild, they live in the trees on the humid parts of the Arabian peninsula.

Copyright © 2000 by Harcourt, Inc.

All rights reserved. No part of this publication may be reproduced or transmitted in any form or by any means, electronic or mechanical, including photocopy, recording, or any information storage and retrieval system, without permission in writing from the publisher.

Requests for permission to make copies of any part of the work should be mailed to the following address:

School Permissions, Harcourt, Inc.
6277 Sea Harbor Drive
Orlando, FL 32887-6777

HARCOURT and the Harcourt Logo are trademarks of Harcourt, Inc.

*sci*LINKS is owned and provided by the National Science Teachers Association. All rights reserved.

Smithsonian Institution Internet Connections owned and provided by the Smithsonian Institution. All other material owned and provided by Harcourt School Publishers under copyright appearing above.

The name of the Smithsonian Institution and the Sunburst logo are registered trademarks of the Smithsonian Institution. The copyright in the Smithsonian website and Smithsonian website pages are owned by the Smithsonian Institution.

Printed in the United States of America

ISBN 0-15-317654-7

4 5 6 7 8 9 10 032 2002 2001 2000

Authors

Marjorie Slavick Frank
Former Adjunct Faculty Member at
    Hunter, Brooklyn, and Manhattan
    Colleges
New York, New York

Robert M. Jones
Professor of Education
University of Houston-Clear Lake
Houston, Texas

Gerald H. Krockover
Professor of Earth and Atmospheric
    Science Education
School Mathematics and Science
    Center
Purdue University
West Lafayette, Indiana

Mozell P. Lang
Science Education Consultant
Michigan Department of Education
Lansing, Michigan

Joyce C. McLeod
Visiting Professor
Rollins College
Winter Park, Florida

Carol J. Valenta
Vice President—Education,
    Exhibits, and Programs
St. Louis Science Center
St. Louis, Missouri
Former teacher, principal, and
    Coordinator of Science Center
    Instructional Programs
Los Angeles Unified School District
Los Angeles, California

Barry A. Van Deman
Science Program Director
Arlington, Virginia

Senior Editorial Advisor

Napoleon Adebola Bryant, Jr.
Professor Emeritus of Education
Xavier University
Cincinnati, Ohio

Program Advisors

George W. Bright
Professor of Mathematics Education
The University of North Carolina at
    Greensboro
Greensboro, North Carolina

Pansy Cowder
Science Specialist
Tampa, Florida

Robert H. Fronk
Head, Science/Mathematics
    Education Department
Florida Institute of Technology
Melbourne, Florida

Gloria R. Guerrero
Education Consultant
Specialist in English as a Second
    Language
San Antonio, Texas

Bernard A. Harris, Jr.
Physician and Former Astronaut
    (*STS 55—Space Shuttle Columbia,
    STS 63—Space Shuttle Discovery*)
Vice President, SPACEHAB Inc.
Houston, Texas

Lois Harrison-Jones
Education and Management
    Consultant
Dallas, Texas

Linda Levine
Educational Consultant
Orlando, Florida

Kenneth R. Mechling
Professor of Biology and Science
    Education
Clarion University of Pennsylvania
Clarion, Pennsylvania

Barbara ten Brink
Science Director
Round Rock Independent School
    District
Round Rock, Texas

Reviewers and Contributors

Jay Bell
K-6 Science Specialist,
    Curriculum Department
Lodi Unified School District
Lodi, California

Virginia Bergquist
Teacher, Canyon View
Irvine, California

James Cowden
Science Facilitator, Teacher's
    Academy
Chicago Public Schools
Chicago, Illinois

Kathy Franklin
Teacher, Benton Elementary
Wichita, Kansas

Katheryn Grimes
Science Specialist, K-5
Frank P. Lamping Elementary
    School
Henderson, Nevada

Lori A. Morrison
Teacher, Weldon Smith Elementary
Calallen ISD
Corpus Christi, Texas

Michael F. Ryan
Educational Technology Specialist
Lake County Schools
Tavares, Florida

Judy Taylor
Teacher, Silvestri Junior High
    School
Las Vegas, Nevada

UNIT A

LIFE SCIENCE
Interactions of Living Things

UNIT B

EARTH SCIENCE
The Changing Earth

UNIT C

PHYSICAL SCIENCE
Matter and Electricity

Extension Chapters

Introduction and References

Using Science Process Skills

When scientists try to find an answer to a question or do an experiment, they use thinking tools called the process skills. You use many of the process skills whenever you speak, listen, read, write, or think. Think about how these students used process skills to help them answer questions and do experiments.

Matthew is spending the day at the beach. He finds seashells. He carefully **observes** the shells and **compares** their shapes and their colors. He **classifies** them into groups according to their shapes.

Try This Observe, compare, and classify objects that interest you, such as rocks or leaves.

Talk About It How did Matthew use the skills of observing and comparing to classify his shells into groups?

Process Skills

Observe—use the senses to learn about objects and events

Compare—identify characteristics of things or events to find out how they are alike and different

Classify—group or organize objects or events in categories based on specific characteristics

Ling wanted to find out whether sand rubbing against rocks would cause pieces of the rock to flake off. He collected three rocks, measured their masses, and then put them in a jar with sand and water. He shook the rocks every day for a week. At the end of the week he **measured** and **recorded** the mass of the rocks and the mass of the sand and the container. He **interpreted** his data and **concluded** that rocks are broken down when sand rubs against them.

Try This Use a thermometer to measure the temperature inside and outside your classroom at the same time each day for a week. Record, display, and interpret your data to find the average indoor and outdoor temperatures for the week.

Talk About It How does displaying your data in charts, tables, and graphs help you interpret it?

Process Skills

Measure — compare an attribute of an object, such as mass, length, or capacity, to a unit of measure such as gram, centimeter, or liter

Gather, Record, Display, or Interpret Data

• gather data by making observations which are used to make inferences or predictions

• record data by writing down the observations

• display data by making tables, charts, or graphs

• interpret data by drawing conclusions about what the data shows

Caitlin wanted to know how the light switch in her bedroom worked. She decided to **use a model** to see how the electrical wires in the wall and the switch worked to turn the light on and off. She used batteries, wires, a flashlight bulb, a bulb holder, thumbtacks, and a paper clip to build her model. She **predicted** that the bulb, the wires, and the batteries had to be connected to make the bulb light. She **inferred** that the paper clip switch interrupted the flow of electricity to turn off the light. Caitlin's model verified her prediction and her inference.

Try This Make a model to show how you can light more than one bulb.

Talk About It How does using a model help you understand how electricity works to light a bulb?

Process Skills

Use a model — make a representation to explain an idea, an object, or an event, such as how something works

Predict — form an idea of an expected outcome based on observations or experience

Infer — use logical reasoning to explain events and make conclusions based on observations

Kendra wants to know which brand of paper towel absorbs the most water. She **planned and conducted a simple investigation** to find out. She chose three brands of paper towels. She poured one liter of water into each of three beakers. She put a towel from each of the three brands in a beaker for 10 seconds. She pulled the towel out of the water and let it drain back into the beaker for 5 seconds. She then measured the amount of water left in the beaker.

She **controlled variables** in her experiment by making sure each beaker contained exactly the same amount of water and that she timed each step in her experiment exactly. Based on the results of this test, she was able to tell her Dad which brand of paper towel was the most absorbent.

Try This Plan and conduct an investigation to compare different brands of a product or service that you and your family use. Identify the variables that you will control.

Talk About It Why is it important to identify and control the variables in an investigation?

Process Skills

Plan and conduct simple investigations — identify and perform the steps necessary to find the answer to a question using appropriate tools and recording and analyzing data collected

Control variables — identify and control factors that affect the outcome of an experiment so that only one variable is affected in a test

You will have many opportunities to practice and apply these and other process skills in *Harcourt Science.* An exciting year of science discoveries lies ahead!

Safety in Science

Doing investigations in science can be fun, but you need to be sure you do them safely. Here are some rules to follow.

1 **Think ahead.** Study the steps of the investigation so you know what to expect. If you have any questions, ask your teacher. Be sure you understand any safety symbols that are shown.

2 **Be neat.** Keep your work area clean. If you have long hair, pull it back so it doesn't get in the way. Roll or push up long sleeves to keep them away from your experiment.

3 **Oops!** If you should spill or break something, or get cut, tell your teacher right away.

4 **Watch your eyes.** Wear safety goggles anytime you are directed to do so. If you get anything in your eyes, tell your teacher right away.

5 **Yuck!** Never eat or drink anything during a science activity unless you are told to do so by your teacher.

6 **Don't get shocked.** Be especially careful if an electric appliance is used. Be sure that electric cords are in a safe place where you can't trip over them. Don't ever pull a plug out of an outlet by pulling on the cord.

7 **Keep it clean.** Always clean up when you have finished. Put everything away and wipe your work area. Wash your hands.

In some activities you will see these symbols. They are signs for what you need to act safely.

CAUTION
Be especially careful.

CAUTION
Wear safety goggles.

CAUTION
Be careful with sharp objects.

CAUTION
Don't get burned.

CAUTION
Protect your clothes.

CAUTION
Protect your hands with mitts.

CAUTION
Be careful with electricity.

Interactions of Living Things

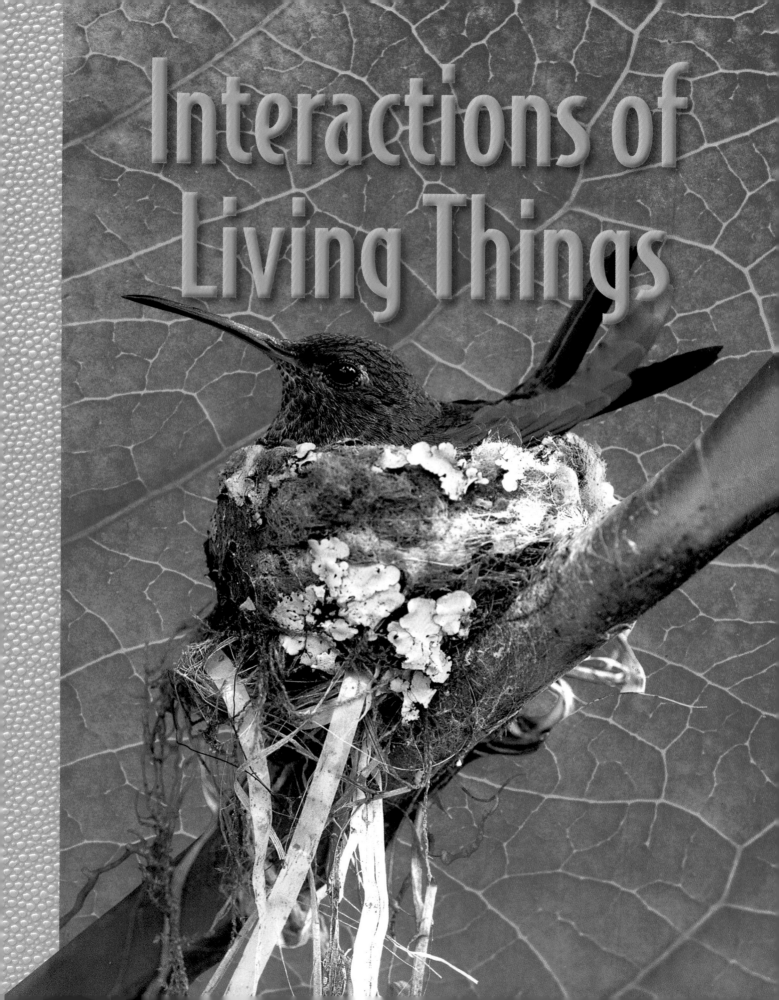

UNIT A

LIFE SCIENCE

Interactions of Living Things

Unit Project | Animal Observer

Design and make an animal feeder. Your feeder could be either for birds or for squirrels. Decide what kinds of food to provide. After you have built your feeder, use binoculars to observe it from a distance. Take notes about the animals at the feeder. You might also take photographs or draw sketches of the animals that visit your feeder and the foods they eat. Classify the birds or other animals you see. Make a bar graph to show the data you collect.

Chapter 1

Animal Growth and Adaptations

Try to think of as many kinds of animals as you can. You can probably think of a lot, and there are thousands more—all different from each other. But all animals have something in common. They all have adaptations that help them live and grow.

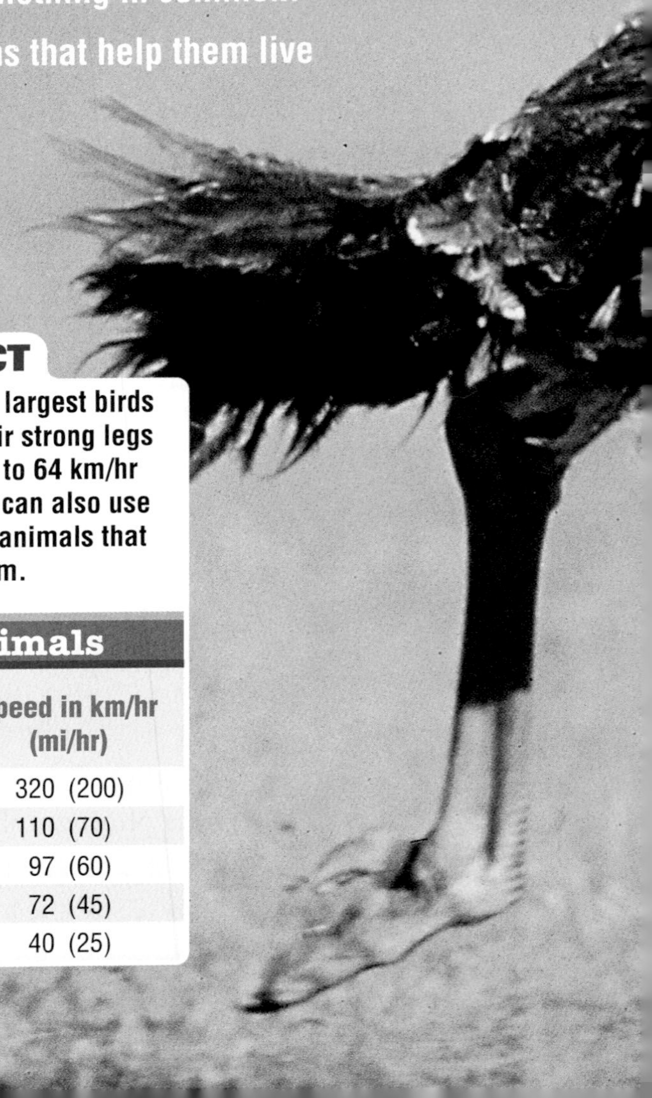

FAST FACT

Ostriches are the largest birds in the world. Their strong legs help them run up to 64 km/hr (40 mi/hr). They can also use their legs to kick animals that may threaten them.

Fast Animals

Animal	Speed in km/hr (mi/hr)
Peregrine falcon	320 (200)
Cheetah	110 (70)
Hummingbird	97 (60)
Jack rabbit	72 (45)
Dolphin	40 (25)

Vocabulary Preview

environment
climate
oxygen
shelter
metamorphosis
adaptation
camouflage
mimicry
instinct
migration
hibernation

The male seahorse gives birth! The female seahorse lays eggs in the male's pouch, and he carries them until they are born.

Scientists think that the Aldabra tortoises live longer than any other animals. It's been hard to tell because the tortoises have outlived many of the people studying them. Scientists estimate that these tortoises may live longer than 100 years!

What Are the Basic Needs of Animals?

In this lesson, you can . . .

 INVESTIGATE animal needs.

 LEARN ABOUT how animals meet their needs.

 LINK to math, writing, social studies, and technology.

◄ This tiger hunts for food in tall grasses and tropical wetlands. Food is a basic need of animals.

INVESTIGATE

Basic Needs of Mealworms

Activity Purpose Have you ever had a pet or watched animals in a zoo? Then you know that an animal has needs. Animals meet their needs in different ways. In this investigation you will make observations to help you **infer** what those needs are.

Materials
- bran meal
- spoon
- 3 shallow dishes
- plastic shoe box
- flake cereal
- water
- 10 cm square of poster board
- mealworms

Activity Procedure

1. Make a chart like the one on the next page to **record** your observations and measurements.

2. **Measure** two spoonfuls of bran meal. Put them into a shallow dish. Put it at one end of the shoe box. Count 20 flakes of cereal. Put them into another shallow dish. Put this dish at the other end of the shoe box. Put a little water in the last shallow dish. Put it in the center of the shoe box.

3. Fold about 1 cm down on opposite sides of the poster board. It should stand up like a small table. (Picture A) Put it over the water container. (Picture B)

Mealworm Observations

Condition	Location	Size and Appearance	Food Measurements	Other
One hour in dark				
Overnight in dark				
Bright sunlight				

4 Put the mealworms in the shoe box next to, but NOT in, the water. Put the lid on the box. Then put the shoe box in a dark place for an hour. Be careful not to spill anything.

5 Take the box to a dimly lit area. Open the lid, and **observe** the contents. Try to find the mealworms. **Record** your observations. Put the lid back on.

6 Put the box in a dark place overnight. Again, take the box to a dimly lit area. **Observe** the contents of the box. **Record** your observations. **Measure** the bran meal and count the cereal flakes. Record your measurements.

7 Put the box into bright sunshine for a few minutes. Does anything change? What can you **infer** from the location of the mealworms?

Picture A

Picture B

Draw Conclusions

1. What happened to the mealworms?

2. What happened to the food? Why?

3. **Scientists at Work** Scientists' explanations come partly from what they observe and partly from how they interpret those observations. What can you infer about animal needs based on your observations of the mealworms?

Investigate Further How could you find out which food the mealworms liked best? Make a prediction. Then, plan and conduct an investigation to test your prediction. Conduct multiple trials to make your results more reliable. How are your results related to your prediction?

Process Skill Tip

Observations and inferences are different. When you **observe**, you use your senses and then record information from your senses. When you **infer**, you use what you have observed to form an opinion called an inference.

A5

How Animals Meet Their Needs

FIND OUT

- five basic needs all animals have

- how some animals meet each need

VOCABULARY

environment
climate
oxygen
shelter
metamorphosis

Where Animals Meet Their Needs

Wild-animal parks are home to many kinds of animals. All the animals in these parks have some basic needs in common. You learned in the investigation that animals have basic needs for food, water, and a place to live. As you read on, you will find that animals have other needs, too.

In planning a wild-animal park, scientists include an environment for each type of animal. An **environment** (en•VY•ruhn•muhnt) is everything that surrounds and affects an animal, including living and nonliving things. All an animal's basic needs can be met in its environment.

For a wild-animal park, scientists first study each animal's natural environment and observe how the animal meets its needs. Then they can plan a similar environment for the park.

✔ **What makes up an animal's environment?**

A vulture finds its food in the desert. ▼

This desert area in Arizona is dry and has little vegetation.

When the sun is too hot, this tortoise lies in the shade or under the sand. ▶

Kangaroo rat ▶

A6

The Need for the Right Climate

People plan and build the environments in wild-animal parks. But most environments aren't made by people. Most environments are natural.

Deserts are natural land environments. In a desert, the climate is dry all year. **Climate** is the average temperature and rainfall of an area over many years. Even though deserts get very little rainfall, many plants and animals can live there.

A desert has vultures, foxes, snakes, tortoises, kangaroo rats, and other small animals. Vultures live in nests in cacti, bushes, or small trees. Kangaroo rats and foxes live in burrows in the ground.

Tortoises and kangaroo rats feed on leaves, fruits, and seeds of desert plants. Vultures, snakes, and foxes feed on other animals. Because there is little rainfall, there are few streams or lakes from which to drink. Desert animals get much of their water from the food they eat.

Different animals meet their needs in a tropical rain forest. There, the climate is wet and warm year-round. Monkeys and hummingbirds live in the trees. Jaguars, a type of large cat, hunt along the forest floor.

✔ **How are the climates of a desert and a tropical rain forest alike? How are they different?**

▲ Ocean mammals, such as this whale, come to the water's surface to breathe.

The Need for Oxygen

Animals need **oxygen**, one of the many gases in air. Many land animals get oxygen by breathing air into their lungs. Ocean mammals, such as whales and dolphins, come to the water's surface to breathe air into their lungs.

Most fish get oxygen from the water around them. Fish and many other ocean animals have body parts called gills. As water moves over the gills, the oxygen in the water passes into the fish's blood.

✔ **Where do fish get the oxygen they need?**

▲ Brown bears eat both plants and animals. This bear is trying to catch a salmon.

The Need for Food

In any environment, an animal needs energy to live and grow. For example, a hummingbird needs energy to beat its wings 70 times per second so it can fly near a flower and drink the nectar. A cheetah needs energy to run fast so it can catch its prey. Like all animals, hummingbirds and cheetahs get the energy they need from the food they eat.

All animals need food, but different animals eat different kinds of food. If you visit the plains of Africa, you may see zebras grazing on grasses, rhinos feeding on low shrubs, and giraffes nibbling leaves on the high branches of trees. Like most animals in the world, these African animals are plant eaters. Some animals, however, are meat eaters. Living among the zebras and rhinos are meat-eating lions, wild dogs, and leopards. Still other animals eat both plants and animals.

✔ **Why do animals need food?**

◄ Giraffes feed mostly on leaves high on acacia (uh•KAY•shuh) trees.

This chameleon (kuh•MEEL•yuhn) eats insects. ▶

The Need for Water

Animals also need water. They lose water by sweating, panting, or other means. That water must be replaced. Most animals replace the lost water by drinking from ponds, lakes, streams, and puddles.

Deserts, however, usually don't have bodies of water or even damp soil. Desert animals must get water in other ways. Kangaroo rats eat seeds that provide them with some water. Also, their bodies are adapted to produce water as their food is digested and used. Kangaroo rats hardly ever need to drink.

✔ **Where do animals get the water they need?**

Desert fox

Gray fox

Arctic fox

▲ Each type of fox finds shelter in its environment.

▲ These African elephants drink at watering holes to get the water they need.

The Need for Shelter

Most animals need shelter in their environment. A **shelter** is a place where an animal is protected from other animals or from the weather.

Foxes find or dig shelters in their environment. A gray fox may climb a tree to find a hollow place to hide in. An arctic fox may dig into the snow for shelter during a blizzard. Desert foxes dig connecting tunnels under the sand to protect themselves from the desert heat.

Rocks, logs, leaves—almost anything in an environment—can be a shelter for an animal. A rock may shelter a snake from the desert heat. A woodpile may shelter a field mouse from a summer storm. A rotting log on the forest floor may shelter dozens of different insects.

✔ **How does weather affect animals' needs for shelter?**

Animals and Their Young

Animals of all species need to have young. Without having young, all of a species would soon die and disappear. The young grow, become adults, and produce young of their own. Animals grow and develop in many different ways.

Insects such as butterflies lay hundreds of eggs. The eggs hatch into wormlike larvae called caterpillars. As a caterpillar grows, it *molts,* or sheds its outer skin, several times. The last time a caterpillar molts, it seals itself inside a tough shell, or *chrysalis* (KRIS•uh•lis). Inside the chrysalis the caterpillar's body slowly changes. Finally an adult butterfly breaks out of the chrysalis. This process of change from an egg to an adult butterfly is called **metamorphosis** (met•uh•MAWR•fuh•sis). Almost all insects, invertebrates that live in water, and amphibians go through some kind of metamorphosis.

Animals such as birds, fish, reptiles, and mammals do not go through metamorphosis. Instead, the young are born or hatched looking much like their parents.

Most mammals have just a few young at a time. Mammals care for their young until the young are old enough to live on their own. A koala gives birth before the young koala is fully developed. The newborn koala crawls into its mother's pouch, where it is fed and protected for six months. It then spends another six months riding on its mother's back before it is old enough to meet its own needs.

✔ **Why would an animal that has only a few young take care of them for months after birth?**

This baby penguin is asking for food from its mother. ▼

◀ Butterfly metamorphosis

4. Adult

3. Chrysalis (pupa)

2. Caterpillar (larva)

1. Egg

▲ A young koala spends six months in its mother's pouch and six months holding on to its mother's back before it can live on its own.

Summary

Animals have some basic needs in common. These include the need for the right climate and for oxygen, food, water, and shelter. Animals of a species must reproduce in order for the species to survive. Each type of animal meets its needs in its own way.

Review

1. What is an environment?
2. What five basic needs do animals have?
3. Why do animals produce young?
4. **Critical Thinking** Choose an animal and describe the shelter it needs.
5. **Test Prep** Which of the following is **NOT** a need of animals?
   - **A** food
   - **B** oxygen
   - **C** clothing
   - **D** shelter

LINKS

MATH LINK

How Many Animals? Suppose you are to report on how many animals you can find in a wooded area near your home. You count 12 snakes, 8 chipmunks, 15 squirrels, and 20 birds. Find the total number of mammals and nonmammals.

WRITING LINK

Informative Writing—Report Choose an animal, and investigate its environment and how it meets its needs. List some questions you want to answer about your animal. Use library resources, encyclopedias, or the Internet to find your answers. Then write an article for your school newspaper to report your findings.

SOCIAL STUDIES LINK

Human Shelters People build many kinds of homes. The building materials and shapes of the homes are different in different environments. Investigate one kind of home in a certain climate of the world. Explain how the climate affects the building materials and the shape of the home.

TECHNOLOGY LINK

Learn more about young animals by visiting the Smithsonian Institution Internet site.
www.si.edu/harcourt/science

How Do Animals' Body Parts Help Them Meet Their Needs?

In this lesson, you can . . .

 INVESTIGATE how the shape of a bird's beak is related to the food it eats.

 LEARN ABOUT animal adaptations, including different body parts.

 LINK to math, writing, and technology.

INVESTIGATE

Bird Beaks and Food

Activity Purpose Different birds have different types of beaks. A hummingbird's beak is long and straight. A hawk's beak is short and hooked. The tools in this investigation stand for beaks of different sizes and shapes. You will **use a model** to find what kind of "beak" works best for picking up and "eating" different foods.

Materials
- chopsticks or 2 blunt pencils
- pliers
- clothespin
- spoon
- forceps
- plastic worms
- cooked spaghetti
- cooked rice
- raisins
- birdseed
- peanuts in shells
- water in a cup
- small paper plates

▼ In what ways are these pictures of chopsticks and this bird's beak alike?

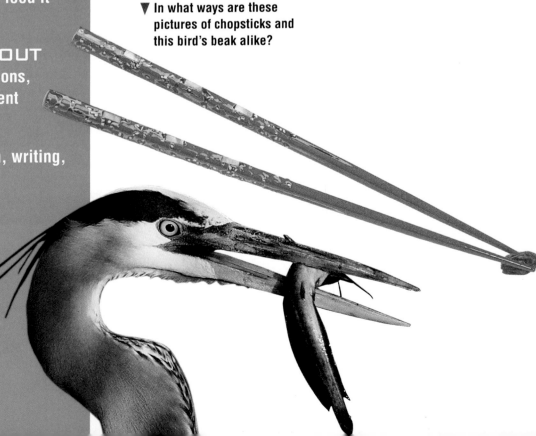

Activity Procedure

Bird Food and Beak Observations

Food	Best Tool (Beak)	Observations

1 Make a chart like the one above.

2 Put the tools on one side of the desk. Think of the tools as bird beaks. For example, the pliers might be a short, thick beak.

3 Put the rest of the materials on the other side of the desk. They stand for bird foods.

4 Put one type of food at a time in the middle of the desk. Try picking up the food with each beak. (Picture A)

5 Test all of the beaks with all of the foods. See which beak works best for which food. **Record** your observations in your chart.

Picture A

Draw Conclusions

1. Which kind of beak is best for picking up each food? Which is best for crushing seeds?

2. By **observing** the shape of a bird's beak, what can you **infer** about the food the bird eats?

3. **Scientists at Work** Scientists often **use models** to help them test ideas. How did using models help you test ideas about bird beaks?

Investigate Further Find a book about birds. Identify real birds that have beaks like the tools you used in this investigation. Make a booklet describing each beak type and how birds use it to gather and eat food. Include your own pictures of the beaks and of the matching foods each beak can best gather and eat.

Process Skill Tip

Observing many kinds of real birds would be difficult to do in your classroom. **Using models** of birds' beaks makes it easier to infer how real beaks work.

Animal Adaptations: Body Parts

A Closer Look at Bird Beaks

FIND OUT

- ways birds are adapted to meet their needs
- other types of animal adaptations

VOCABULARY

adaptation
camouflage
mimicry

Finches on the Galápagos Islands in the Pacific Ocean look very much alike. However, their beaks are different in size and shape. Scientists observed and recorded information about where the finches lived, the shapes of their beaks, and their food sources. Scientists noted that some finches eat seeds, others eat fruit, and still others eat insects.

Scientists used the evidence they gathered just as you did in the investigation. They inferred that the differences in the finches' beaks are adaptations to the kinds of foods the finches eat. An **adaptation** is a body part or behavior that helps an animal meet its needs in its environment. The scientists saw that the seed eaters have thick, heavy beaks. The fruit eaters have short, stubby beaks. The insect eaters have sharp, pointed beaks.

✔ **How does having a thick, heavy beak help a bird eat seeds?**

The house finch uses its short, stubby beak to eat fruit. ▼

▲ The European goldfinch eats insects with its sharp, pointed beak.

A Darwin's finch uses its thick, heavy beak to crack open large seeds. ▼

▲ An osprey's talons (TAL•uhnz), or claws, are adapted for catching and carrying its prey.

Other Bird Adaptations

Like finches, all other birds have beaks that help them get food from their environment. Birds also have many other adaptations that help them live. These include the size of an owl's eyes and the shape of a hawk's claws. Although birds have the same basic needs, they have different adaptations that help them meet their needs in different ways.

Feathers keep birds warm and dry and help them fly. Feathers are very light, and they give a bird's body a smooth surface over which air flows easily. Another adaptation for flying is hollow bones. A bird's bones are filled with air pockets. These make a bird especially light.

But not all birds fly. Some flightless birds have adaptations for running. The ostrich's long legs and two-toed feet allow it to run at speeds up to 64 kilometers (about 40 mi) per hour. Some water birds don't fly or run. Penguins are the largest group of flightless water birds. As you can see in the picture, their bodies have adaptations for moving in water. Almost everything about a bird's body, from its beak to its feet, is an adaptation that helps it meet its needs.

✓ **How do strong claws help a hawk meet its need for food?**

Penguins use their wings as flippers and their feet for steering. They can swim underwater as fast as 35 kilometers (about 22 mi) per hour. That's about the fastest you can pedal a bicycle. ▶

Body Coverings

Every animal's body covering is an adaptation that helps the animal survive. You have learned that feathers protect birds and help them fly. The fur or hair that covers most mammals helps keep them warm. Some mammals have sharp hairs that are adaptations for protection. Others have whiskers—stiff hairs that have adapted as sense organs. Many fish are covered with scales. The scales help protect the fish from disease and from other animals that live in the water. A reptile's scales protect it from injury and from drying out. The scales on a snake overlap to form a smooth covering that helps the snake move.

✔ **What are three different kinds of body coverings?**

▲ Both pictures show the same porcupine fish. Which shows the fish trying to scare away predators?

◀ The hairs of a polar bear's thick fur are actually clear, not white. They allow light to get to the bear's dark skin, helping the bear stay warm in the cold Arctic climate.

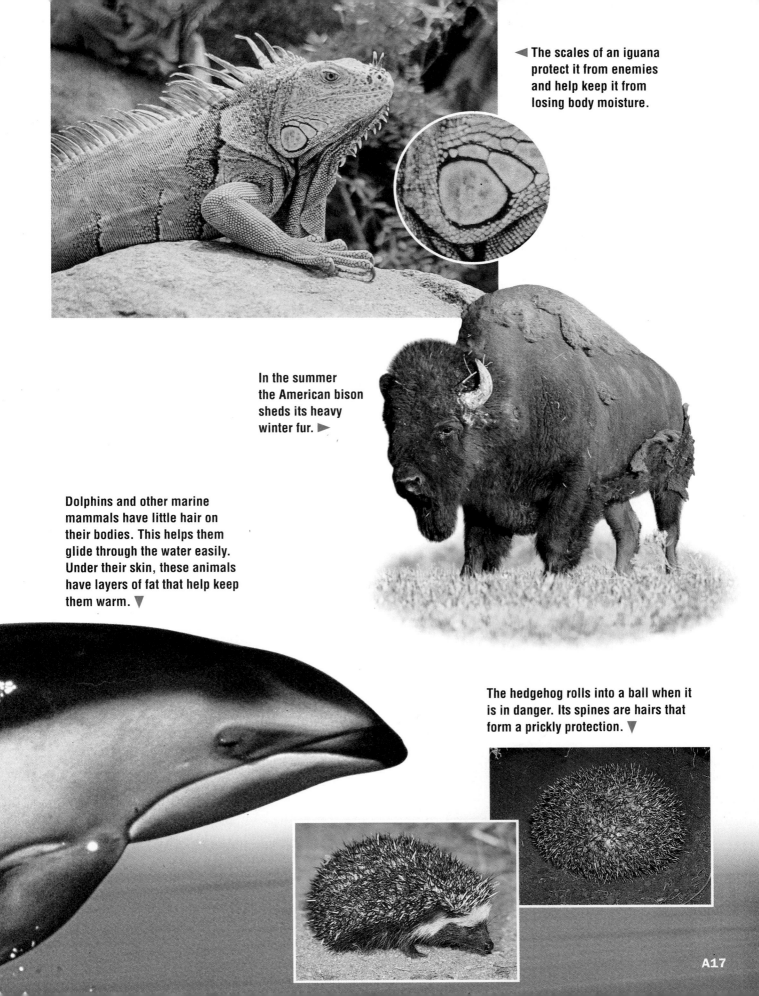

◄ The scales of an iguana protect it from enemies and help keep it from losing body moisture.

In the summer the American bison sheds its heavy winter fur. ►

Dolphins and other marine mammals have little hair on their bodies. This helps them glide through the water easily. Under their skin, these animals have layers of fat that help keep them warm. ▼

The hedgehog rolls into a ball when it is in danger. Its spines are hairs that form a prickly protection. ▼

A17

Color and Shape

The snowshoe hare is white in winter and brown in summer. Its changing fur color makes the hare difficult for other animals to hunt because the hare blends in with its environment. The hare's color is an example of camouflage. **Camouflage** (KAM•uh•flahzh) is an animal's color or pattern that helps it blend in with its surroundings. Camouflage is an adaptation that helps an animal hide.

Many animals have body coverings and shapes that are camouflage. For example, a tiger's fur is striped. The stripes help the tiger blend in with the light and shadows of the tall grass in its environment. Toads—with their bumpy, brownish skin—look like pebbles on the forest floor. A chameleon's color changes to match its surroundings.

The dark skin on an alligator's back makes it blend into the swamps where it lives.

▲ A chameleon's skin can change color in minutes. This form of camouflage enables the chameleon to blend in with the tree in which it waits for food.

Mimicry (MIM•ik•ree) is an adaptation in which an animal looks very much like another animal or an object. The viceroy butterfly is a good example of mimicry. It looks like the monarch butterfly, which tastes bad to birds. Birds often mistake the viceroy for a monarch and leave it alone. The walking stick is another example of mimicry. The walking stick, an insect, would be easy for birds to catch and eat. But because it looks so much like a twig, birds often overlook it.

✔ **How is a viceroy butterfly a mimic?**

▲ The body covering of a snowshoe hare is brown during the summer. In winter a thick coat of white fur covers the hare's body.

A18

Summary

Animals have adaptations, which enable them to meet their needs. Adaptations include body coverings and the shapes, sizes, and colors of body parts.

Review

1. List three bird adaptations.
2. Choose an animal. What needs of the animal can be met by its body covering?
3. Choose an animal you know about. Give three examples of how its adaptations help it meet its needs.
4. **Critical Thinking** How are mimicry and camouflage different? How are they alike?
5. **Test Prep** Which adaptation would best help a hawk catch a mouse?
   - **A** talons
   - **B** camouflage
   - **C** hollow bones
   - **D** feathers

Why do you think this insect is called a walking stick? ▶

MATH LINK

Accurate Drawings Choose a bird to research. Draw a life-size picture of the bird viewed from the side. Use a ruler to help you make accurate measurements. Paint or color the bird to show what it looks like. Cut out the bird, and compare it to the birds your classmates drew. Decide how to order the birds by size.

WRITING LINK

Informative Writing—Explanation Choose an animal to "interview." Write a list of questions you could ask the animal. Include questions about how it meets its basic needs and which of its adaptations are especially helpful. Research the animal to find answers to your questions. Using your interview notes, write an article for your school newspaper explaining how the animal meets its needs.

TECHNOLOGY LINK

Learn more about reptile body adaptations by visiting the Smithsonian Institution Internet site.
www.si.edu/harcourt/science

LESSON 3

How Do Animals' Behaviors Help Them Meet Their Needs?

In this lesson, you can . . .

INVESTIGATE a behavior of some butterflies that helps them survive.

LEARN ABOUT other animal behaviors that are adaptations.

LINK to math, writing, social studies, and technology.

INVESTIGATE

Monarch Butterfly Travel

Activity Purpose Monarch butterflies cannot live through cold winters. From observations, scientists know that the butterflies travel south for the winter. To discover where the butterflies go and the paths they take to get there, scientists have tagged some of the butterflies. The tags let the scientists track the butterflies as they fly between their summer and winter homes. In this investigation you will learn where the butterflies go during the cold winter months.

Materials

- outline map of North America
- 2 pencils of different colors

Activity Procedure

1. Label the directions north, south, east, and west on your map.

2. During the summer many monarch butterflies live in two general areas. Some live in the north-eastern United States and around the shores of the Great Lakes. Others live along the south-western coast of Canada and in the states of Washington and Oregon. Locate these two large general areas on your map. Shade each area a different color. (Picture A)

◄ Monarch butterfly

Picture A

Picture B

3 At summer's end large groups of monarchs gather and travel south for the winter. Most of those east of the Rocky Mountains fly to the mountains of central Mexico. But some of these butterflies make their way to Florida. Butterflies west of the Rocky Mountains fly to sites along the California coast. All these areas have trees where the butterflies can rest, temperatures that are cool yet above freezing, and water to drink. Find these areas on your map. Shade each winter area the same color as the matching summer area. Then use the right color to draw the most direct route from north to south over land. (Picture B)

Draw Conclusions

1. **Compare** the climate where the monarch butterflies spend the summer with the climate where they spend the winter.

2. What can you **infer** about how the behavior of the butterflies helps them meet their needs?

3. **Scientists at Work** Scientists use maps and graphs to **communicate** data and ideas visually. How does making a map of butterfly movements help you understand where monarchs travel?

Investigate Further Many kinds of birds, fish, and mammals travel to different places when the seasons change. Research the travel route of one of these animals. Use a map to show the route.

Process Skill Tip

Sometimes the best way to **communicate** what you have learned is to use a graphic, a visual display such as a map, rather than words.

Animal Adaptations: Behaviors

Instincts

FIND OUT

- some instincts that help animals meet their needs

- two examples of learned behavior

VOCABULARY

instinct
migration
hibernation

In the investigation, you learned that monarch butterflies fly south for the winter. They go to places where they have the food and climate they need to survive. Their *behavior*, or action, of flying south is not something they have learned. It is an instinct. An **instinct** (IN•stingkt) is a behavior that an animal begins life with. Instincts are adaptations that help animals meet their needs.

✓ **What instinct do monarch butterflies have?**

Migration

Like the monarch butterfly, some other animals travel long distances to meet their needs. For example, female Atlantic green turtles go to Ascension Island in the South Atlantic Ocean to lay their eggs. They bury the eggs in the sand on the beach. After hatching, the young turtles move toward the ocean. Then they swim toward feeding areas along the coast of Brazil, more than 1000 kilometers (about 620 mi) away. When the female turtles become adults, they return to Ascension Island to lay their eggs. The turtles do not learn from other turtles where the feeding areas are or how to get to Ascension Island. They know by instinct where to go. Scientists hypothesize that the turtles are able to use Earth's magnetic field to guide them as they swim.

The Atlantic green turtle's instinct for travel to Ascension Island is an example of migration. **Migration** (my•GRAY•shuhn) is the movement of a group of one type of animal from one region to another and back again. It is a behavioral adaptation.

Many birds migrate to environments where there is food and a good climate. For instance, the pectoral sandpiper travels from northern Canada to southern South America each fall. These birds return to Canada in the spring when the weather in Canada warms up.

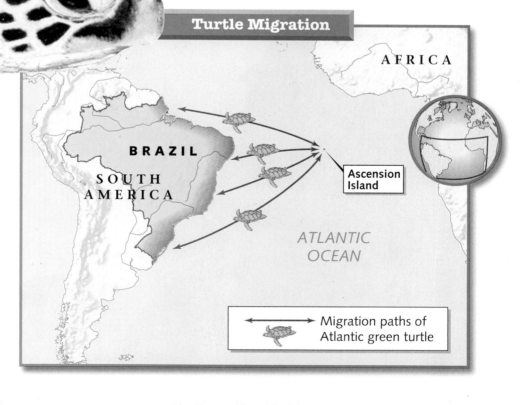

Turtle Migration

AFRICA

BRAZIL

SOUTH AMERICA

Ascension Island

ATLANTIC OCEAN

Migration paths of Atlantic green turtle

◄ Instinct guides this Atlantic green turtle to and from nesting grounds on Ascension Island.

Some animals have an instinct to migrate to places where their young can survive. Gray whales spend the summer in areas where they can find food easily—near the North Pole. In the winter they migrate to the warm waters off Mexico, where they give birth to their young.

Pacific salmon also migrate before producing their young. Salmon hatch from eggs in rivers and streams. Then they swim to the ocean, where they spend most of their lives. When these salmon are ready to produce young of their own, they migrate to the same stream where they hatched.

✔ **Name some animals that migrate.**

▲ These birds migrate each year. In the fall, they fly south. In the spring, they return to the north to lay their eggs and raise their young.

▼ Pacific salmon attempt to leap over whatever is in their way as they travel upstream to the place where they were hatched.

Hibernation

Not all animals have the instinct to migrate as winter brings colder temperatures and a lack of food. Instead, some animals adapt to these changes by hibernating. **Hibernation** (hy•ber•NAY•shuhn) is a period when an animal goes into a long, deep "sleep." An animal prepares to hibernate by eating extra food and finding shelter. During hibernation the animal's body temperature drops and its breathing rate and heartbeat rate fall. As a result, the animal needs little or no food. The energy it does need comes from fat stored in its body.

The ground squirrel is an animal that hibernates. As winter approaches, the squirrel goes into an underground nest. Within a

▲ Many North American bats hibernate in caves or rocky places.

few hours, its body temperature drops to 15°C (about 59°F), and its heartbeat rate and breathing rate fall. Before long, the squirrel is taking only about four breaths per minute.

✔ **How does an animal's body change during hibernation?**

THE INSIDE STORY

Normal	Hibernation

▲ A ground squirrel prepares to hibernate by eating extra food and building a nest.

86°F — 30°C

Body temperature

Heartbeats per minute

Heartrate

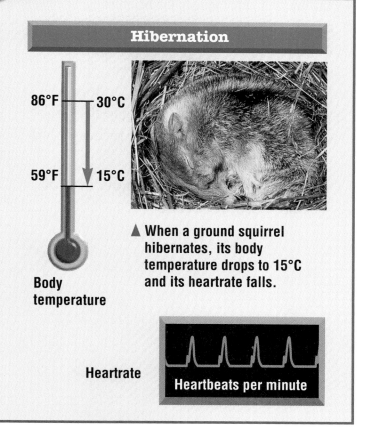

86°F — 30°C

59°F — 15°C

Body temperature

▲ When a ground squirrel hibernates, its body temperature drops to 15°C and its heartrate falls.

Heartrate

Heartbeats per minute

Learned Behaviors

Some animal behaviors are not instincts. They are learned. For instance, adult tigers are excellent hunters, but tigers aren't born knowing how to hunt. Tiger cubs learn to hunt by watching their mothers hunt and by playing with other tiger cubs.

Chimpanzees, too, learn many behaviors that help them survive. Chimps use sounds to communicate with one another. A loud call is a warning. A soft grunt is a happy sound. Young chimps learn the meanings of the sounds by observing the adults in their environment. Observation also helps a young chimp learn how to build a leafy nest for sleeping and how to use a stone to crack open a nut.

Some animals are difficult to study, so we know less about them. For example, the humpback whale makes sounds that can be heard for many kilometers under water. Scientists think that males might use these "songs" to attract females or to tell other males to stay away. But is the act of singing an instinct? Or does a whale learn a song by listening to the songs of other whales? Scientists are trying to find out.

✔ **What animals do you know of that can learn behaviors?**

The chimpanzee's loud cry warns other chimps of possible dangers. ▼

This mother cheetah will teach her cubs to hunt. ▶

▲ Humpback whales make sounds that can be heard many kilometers away under water.

Summary

Animals behave in ways that enable them to meet their needs. The behaviors are adaptations to their environments. Some of the behaviors are instincts. Others are learned.

Review

1. How is an instinct different from a learned behavior? Give an example of each.

2. What is migration? How does migration help an animal meet its needs? Give an example.

3. What is hibernation? How does hibernation help an animal meet its needs? Give an example.

4. **Critical Thinking** Suppose a dog barks when a stranger comes close to its home. Suppose it also barks when asked to speak. Which behavior is probably learned? Which is instinct? Explain your answers.

5. **Test Prep** An animal's body temperature drops for a long period when it is —

   A migrating
   B sleeping
   C hibernating
   D hunting

LINKS

MATH LINK

Measurement Use a globe and a map to measure the migration path of monarch butterflies from Minneapolis, Minnesota, to Mexico City. How is measuring different on the globe and on the map?

WRITING LINK

Narrative Writing—Personal Story Suppose you are an animal that migrates in the spring and fall. Tell what kind of animal you are, where you live in the summer, and where you spend the winter. For your teacher, make a log of the things you might do and see as you travel.

SOCIAL STUDIES LINK

Migration Barriers Study the needs and migration behaviors of deer. Think of ways that people might make it difficult for deer to migrate. Make a large drawing showing the deer's migration routes and any barriers that may be built or caused by people living nearby. Explain your drawing in writing.

TECHNOLOGY LINK

To learn more about instincts, watch the video *Monarch Migration* on the **Harcourt Science Newsroom Video** in your classroom video library.

ROBOT
Roaches and Ants

Scientists are finding new uses for insects—both real insects and mechanical ones.

Roaches for Research

Most people think of roaches as pests, and they want to get rid of them. But scientists in Japan are raising these insects. Hundreds of roaches are grown in plastic bins in a laboratory at Tokyo University. Because the American cockroach is harder to kill and bigger than other species, the scientists have chosen it for their experiments.

For some of the roaches, surgery is done to take off their wings and antennae. Then the roaches are fitted with tiny backpacks, weighing about 3 grams ($\frac{1}{10}$ oz). Cockroaches can

Cockroach wearing a control backpack

carry up to 20 times their own weight, and the backpacks are only about twice a roach's weight. Each backpack has tiny wires that guide the roach. Electricity from the wires makes the roach jump forward or backward or turn left or right.

Small Is Beautiful

Japanese scientists hope to use these specially equipped insects as tiny explorers. For example, with a microcamera added to the pack, a roach might crawl through rubble. It could be guided to search for people trapped during a fire or an earthquake. The roaches also could go into other places that are too small or dangerous for people.

There are still problems for scientists to solve. Although the roaches may live for several months, they may stop responding to the electricity. Also, scientists are still studying the nervous systems of roaches to decide on the best place to attach the wires.

Ant Attack!

If you don't like the idea of a living robot roach, what about artificial ants? At the Massachusetts Institute of Technology, scientists are building microrobots. Each tiny robot is only about the size of a walnut. But it has 17 different *sensors,* devices for observing its environment.

The robot ants are being programmed to mimic, or act like, real members of an ant colony. They can hunt for food, pass messages to one another, and play games such as tag and follow the leader. The designers of the ants hope that the robots someday will help doctors. They might also just help with simple tasks around the home.

In England, another group of researchers is also trying to make robots that mimic ants. They hope to use the robots to inspect bundles of wire inside telephone cables. The ants could find which sections of cable are used least. Then system managers could route calls to those sections. This would avoid overuse of some phone lines.

With this kind of microtechnology, we may someday think of roaches and ants as friends, not pests!

Think About It

1. What insects or insect behaviors do you know about that might be useful for technology?
2. How would it be useful for robot roaches to look for survivors of earthquakes or fires?

WEB LINK:
For Science and Technology updates, visit the Harcourt Internet site.
www.harcourtschool.com/ca

Careers   Entomologist

What They Do
Entomologists study the ecology, life cycles, and behavior of the more than $1\frac{1}{2}$ million species of insects. Most entomologists work for state agriculture departments, universities, or industry. Some study how to protect crops and other materials from insect damage. Others study how to protect helpful insect species.

Education and Training   Most entomologists have a college degree in entomology or biology. Many have a Ph.D. in entomology.

Jane Goodall

ANIMAL BEHAVIORIST

"Chimpanzees have given me so much. The long hours spent with them in the forest have enriched my life beyond measure. What I have learned from them has shaped my understanding of human behavior, of our place in nature."

Probably the most famous animal behaviorist of all time, Jane Goodall has spent most of her life studying wild chimpanzees. She set up her camp in the Gombe Stream Game Preserve in Tanzania in 1960. Over the next 35 years, Dr. Goodall and her team of researchers made important observations of chimpanzee behavior and ecology. One of her most important discoveries was that chimpanzees can make and use tools. Before this discovery, people believed that only humans could make tools.

At first Dr. Goodall had trouble finding wild chimpanzees to study. The animals were very shy and tended to avoid people.

When she did spot a family group, she had to observe them from a distance, with binoculars. After more than a year, the chimps got used to

her presence. Then she could observe them up close. In time, Dr. Goodall was able to distinguish individual chimpanzee personalities and gave each chimp a name. She gave chimps within each family group different names that started with the same letter.

Today Dr. Goodall travels around the world giving lectures about her experiences at Gombe. She also speaks to school groups about "Roots and Shoots," an environmental education program for young people.

THINK ABOUT IT

1. Why was finding out that chimpanzees can make tools an important discovery?

2. Why do you think it took Dr. Goodall so long to get close to the chimps?

GOMBE PRESERVE

AFRICA

TANZANIA

Indian Ocean

Building a Bird's Nest

How do birds construct their nests?

Materials

- large paper plate
- small branches, twigs, leaves
- string or yarn
- purchased feathers (optional)
- mud

Procedure

1. Build a bird's nest on a plate. Place your branches, twigs, leaves, string, and feathers in a way that makes the nest a sturdy shelter. Use the mud like glue.

2. Share your building methods with a classmate.

Draw Conclusions

Was it easy or hard to build a sturdy nest? What body parts and behaviors do you think help birds build their nests?

Earthworm Instincts

What is an earthworm instinct for keeping safe?

Materials

- black paper
- white paper
- scissors
- tape
- baking pan, 9 in. × 13 in.
- water
- earthworm

Procedure

1. Cut black paper to fit the bottom of one half of the baking pan. Cut white paper to fit the other half. Line the bottom of the pan with the pieces of paper.

2. Tape a black paper lid over the black-paper half of the pan to make a "cave."

3. Moisten the paper in the bottom of the pan. Put the pan in a well-lighted place. Put an earthworm on the white side of the pan. Predict where the earthworm will move. Justify your prediction based on cause and effect.

4. Observe the earthworm for 5 minutes. Record your observations.

5. Repeat Steps 3 and 4 two more times.

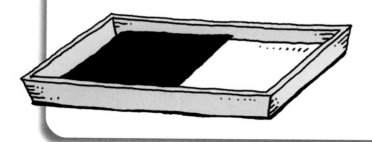

Draw Conclusions

Why do you think the earthworm moved as it did? How do you think its movement is related to instinct?

Animal Observation

How do two animals meet their needs?

Materials
- two different small animal pets such as a fish and a dog or cat

Procedure

1. Observe each animal closely for five minutes. Pay special attention to how each animal is meeting its needs.

2. Describe each animal and how it moves. Make a drawing to show the animal in its environment.

3. Identify any special body part adaptations that help the animal meet its needs.

4. Observe the animals again at a different time of day.

Draw Conclusions

How did the two animals meet their needs for food, water, and oxygen? How were the animals alike? How were they different?

Vertebrate Observation

How many vertebrates can you spot?

Materials
- calendar
- poster board
- colored pencils

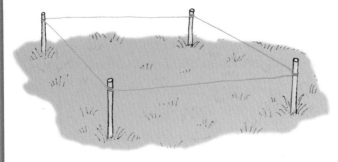

Procedure

1. Choose a time of day and a location that you can watch closely every day for a week.

2. Observe your location each day at the same time for one-half hour. Record all the vertebrates you observe during that time.

3. On the poster board draw a picture of each vertebrate you observe. Classify the vertebrates.

Draw Conclusions

How many different groups of vertebrates did you observe? If you wanted to observe fish and amphibians, what location might you choose?

Seeking Shelter

What kind of environment do sowbugs prefer?

Materials
- wide shoebox with a lid
- sheet of construction paper
- scissors
- 8–10 sowbugs
- dry soil
- water
- tape
- flashlight

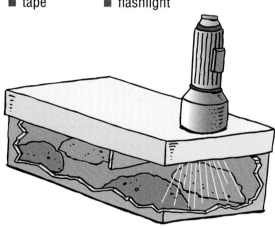

Procedure

1. Tape a paper divider to the top of the box. Cut it so the sowbugs can crawl under it.

2. Arrange four areas of soil, each covering one-fourth of the bottom of the box. Dampen one area on each side of the divider.

3. Cut a hole in the center of one end of the lid. Balance the lighted flashlight over the hole.

4. Place the sowbugs on the lighted side of the box. Leave the box and return after 30 minutes.

Draw Conclusions

Which of the four environments do the sowbugs prefer? Where do you think you would find sowbugs in nature?

Earthworm Movement

How do earthworms move?

Materials
- earthworm
- sandpaper
- square of vinyl tile
- hand lens

Procedure

1. Place the vinyl tile and the sandpaper next to each other.

2. Set the earthworm on the sandpaper. Use the hand lens to watch it move. Sketch what you see.

3. Set the earthworm on the vinyl tile. Use the hand lens to watch it move. Sketch what you see.

Draw Conclusions

Which body parts do earthworms use to move? Do earthworms move more quickly over a smooth surface or a rough surface? Why do you think that is?

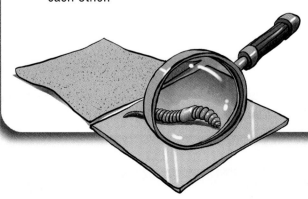

A33

Chapter 1 Review and Test Preparation

Vocabulary Review

Use the terms below to complete the sentences. The page numbers in ( ) tell you where to look in the chapter if you need help.

environment (A6)   camouflage (A18)
climate (A7)   mimicry (A18)
oxygen (A7)   instinct (A22)
shelter (A9)   migration (A23)
metamorphosis (A10)   hibernation (A25)
adaptation (A14)

1. The body changes that a butterfly goes through as it grows from an egg into an adult are called ____.

2. An adaptation in which an animal looks like an object or another animal is ____.

3. A place such as a burrow where an animal can protect itself is a ____.

4. A body part or behavior that enables an animal to meet its needs is called an ____.

5. The average temperature and rainfall of an area make up ____.

6. ____ enables an animal to blend in with its surroundings.

7. A period when an animal goes into a long, deep sleep is called ____.

8. A behavior such as migration that an animal does not have to learn is an ____.

9. The movement of a group of one type of animal from one region to another is ____.

10. Everything that surrounds and affects an animal is its ____.

11. Some animals meet their need for ____ by breathing.

Connect Concepts

Use the Word Bank to complete the graphic organizer below.

adaptations
camouflage
food
instincts
learned
needs
oxygen
shelter
water

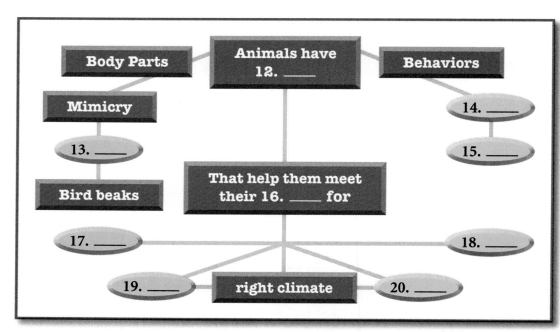

Body Parts — Animals have 12. ____ — Behaviors

Mimicry

13. ____

14. ____

15. ____

Bird beaks

That help them meet their 16. ____ for

17. ____

18. ____

19. ____   right climate   20. ____

Check Understanding

Write the letter of the best choice.

21. When a winter storm is coming, animals often look for —
  A drinking water
  B a partner
  C shelter
  D an open area

22. A bird's hollow bones help the bird ____ more easily.
  F fly   H hop
  G heal   J eat

23. When preparing to hibernate, animals must —
  A grow a thinner coat
  B lose weight
  C eat extra food
  D breathe faster

Use the photos below to answer Questions 24–25.

24. What process is shown here?

25. Explain the changes going on.

Critical Thinking

26. Rabbits have large ears. Infer how this adaptation helps rabbits meet their needs.

27. Because humans can think, they can adapt to new environments by making things or changing behaviors. Describe how your life would change if you moved to a place where the climate was very different from where you live now.

Process Skills Review

28. How did you use your observations of the mealworms in Lesson 1 to **infer** about animals' needs?

29. **Compare** tools and birds' beaks.

30. Which is more useful for **communicating** information about migration routes—a data table or a map? Explain your answer.

Performance Assessment

Animal Plan

Work with a partner. Design and make a model of an animal that has adaptations for living in a desert. Explain how these adaptations would help the animal meet its needs.

Chapter

Vocabulary Preview

carbon dioxide
nutrient
photosynthesis
symmetry
transpiration
taproot
fibrous root
germinate
spore
tuber

Plant Growth and Adaptations

If you went into your schoolyard, how many different plants could you find? Even if your schoolyard is paved, there are probably plants growing in the cracks in the cement or along the edges of the yard. There are many different kinds of plants. But all plants need the same basic things to live and grow.

FAST FACT

Some living things work together. Ants defend the bullhorn acacia from other insects, mammals, and even other plants. In return, the plant provides food for the ants!

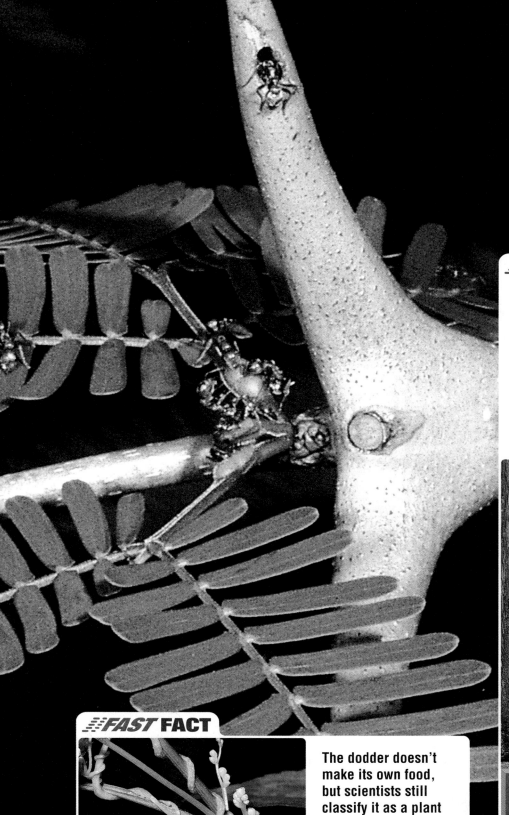

Some of the oldest known living things are trees. Plants that live for a long time have adaptations that help protect them from dangers in the environment. The thick, spongy bark of the giant sequoia protects it from being damaged by insects. The insects eat the bark instead of the inner wood.

How Long Some Plants Live

Plant	Oldest Individual Known
Bristlecone pine	5,000 years
Giant sequoia	2,500 years
Saguaro cactus	200 years

The dodder doesn't make its own food, but scientists still classify it as a plant because it produces flowers and seeds. The dodder meets its needs by getting food, water, and nutrients from other plants.

What Do Plants Need to Live?

In this lesson, you can . . .

INVESTIGATE the effect of light on plants.

LEARN ABOUT what plants need to live.

LINK to math, writing, social studies, and technology.

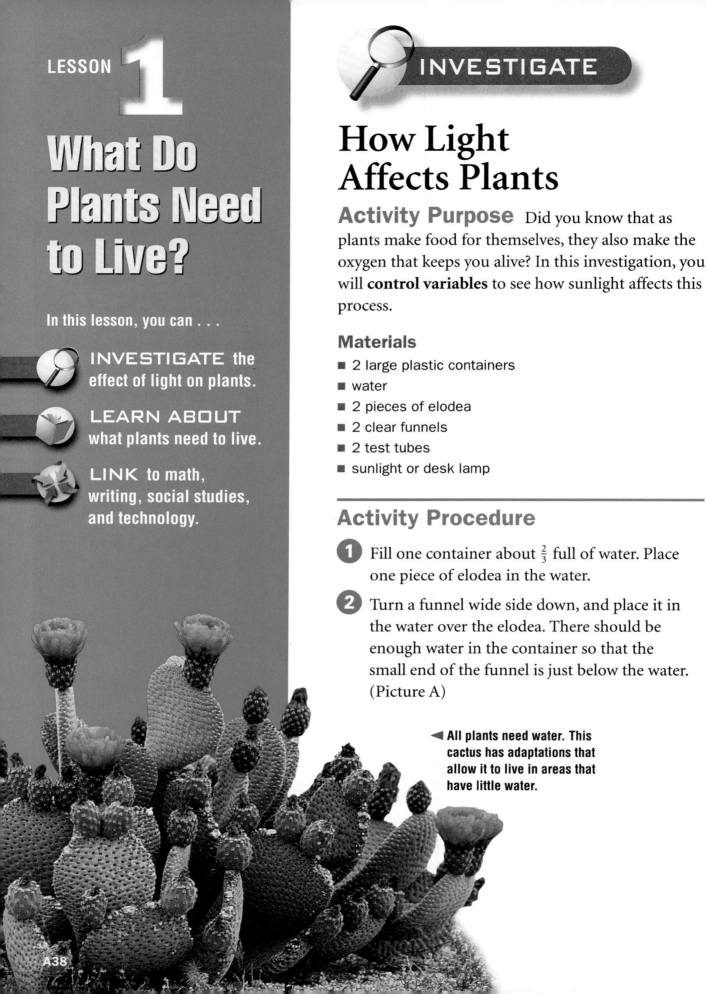

◄ All plants need water. This cactus has adaptations that allow it to live in areas that have little water.

How Light Affects Plants

Activity Purpose Did you know that as plants make food for themselves, they also make the oxygen that keeps you alive? In this investigation, you will **control variables** to see how sunlight affects this process.

Materials

- 2 large plastic containers
- water
- 2 pieces of elodea
- 2 clear funnels
- 2 test tubes
- sunlight or desk lamp

Activity Procedure

1 Fill one container about $\frac{2}{3}$ full of water. Place one piece of elodea in the water.

2 Turn a funnel wide side down, and place it in the water over the elodea. There should be enough water in the container so that the small end of the funnel is just below the water. (Picture A)

Picture A

Picture B

3 Fill a test tube with water. Cover the end with your thumb and turn the tube upside down. Place the test tube over the end of the funnel. Allow as little water as possible to escape from the tube. (Picture B)

4 Repeat Steps 1–3 using the second container, funnel, piece of elodea, and test tube.

5 Set one container of elodea in sunlight or under a desk lamp. Set the other in a dark place such as a closet.

6 After several hours, **observe** the contents of each container.

Draw Conclusions

1. **Compare** the two test tubes. What do you **observe**?

2. One test tube is now filled partly with a gas. What can you **infer** about where the gas came from?

3. **Scientists at Work** Scientists **control variables** to learn what effect each condition has on the outcome of an experiment. What one variable did you change in this investigation? Which variables were the same in both containers?

Investigate Further Repeat the activity with the plant placed in light. Use a graduate instead of a test tube. Measure the volume of air in the graduate every 15 minutes for an hour. Predict the volume of air in two hours. Conduct multiple trials to test your prediction. Make a line graph of your data. Based on your graph, how fast do plants produce oxygen?

> **Process Skill Tip**
>
> A variable is a condition that can be changed. When you **control variables** in an experiment, you change only one condition. You keep all other conditions the same.

Life Support for Plants

Basic Needs

FIND OUT

- four basic needs of plants
- how plants make food

VOCABULARY

carbon dioxide
nutrient
photosynthesis

Plants are living things. They have many of the same needs as animals. They use energy from food to grow. They use gases from the air. They need water and the right climate. But there is one big difference between plants and animals—plants can make their own food.

To live, a plant needs four things from its environment—air, nutrients, water, and light. Air provides a plant with **carbon dioxide** (KAR•buhn dy•AHKS•yd), a gas breathed out by animals. There is plenty of this gas in the air. Soil provides most plants with needed nutrients. **Nutrients** (NOO•tree•uhnts) are substances, such as minerals, that all living things need to grow. A plant gets water from rain. Some of the water is taken in by the plant's leaves. Most of the water, however, is taken in by roots, which get it from rain-soaked soil. A plant can get enough light if it is not too shaded. Though some plants do well in shade, no plant can live in total darkness.

In the investigation, you saw that light affects how a plant gives off oxygen. Oxygen is given off as plants make food. Light provides the energy for the food-making process.

✔ **What four things do plants need to live?**

▼ These flowers are healthy. They are growing in clean air. They also are receiving plenty of water, nutrients from the soil, and sunlight.

Making Food

A plant makes its own food by a process that is called **photosynthesis** (foht•oh•SIN•thuh•sis). *Photo* means "light" and *synthesis* means "putting together." Photosynthesis takes place in a plant's leaves. Light is trapped by chlorophyll, the material that makes a leaf green. The energy from the light starts the food-making process. Without light, plants would not get the food they need to live and grow.

Carbon dioxide and water are the two main materials that the plant combines to make food. The food made is sugar. The leaves take in carbon dioxide, and the roots take in water. The water travels up tubes in the stem to the leaves. The leaves then use the energy from light to put together the carbon dioxide and water to make sugar. Oxygen is a waste product of photosynthesis. It is given off by the leaves.

✔ **What does a plant need to carry out photosynthesis?**

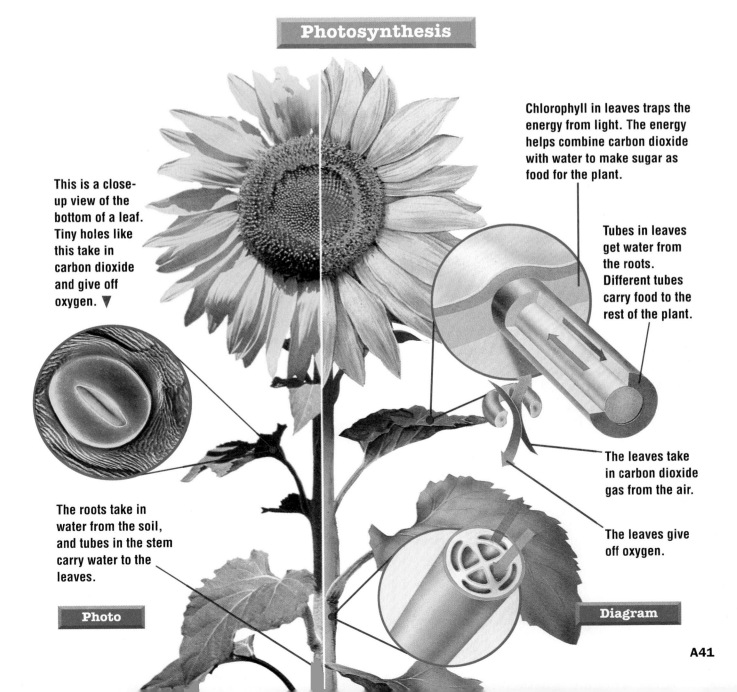

Photosynthesis

This is a close-up view of the bottom of a leaf. Tiny holes like this take in carbon dioxide and give off oxygen. ▼

The roots take in water from the soil, and tubes in the stem carry water to the leaves.

Chlorophyll in leaves traps the energy from light. The energy helps combine carbon dioxide with water to make sugar as food for the plant.

Tubes in leaves get water from the roots. Different tubes carry food to the rest of the plant.

The leaves take in carbon dioxide gas from the air.

The leaves give off oxygen.

Photo

Diagram

A41

The waterlily's leaves float on the water's surface to take in sunlight. Its roots are in the soil at the bottom of the pond. ▶

Adaptations for Different Environments

Plants live all over Earth's surface. Like animals, plants have adaptations that help them live in different climates and conditions.

Most of the plants that you've seen live on land. Some plants, however, have adaptations that allow them to live in water. For example, waterlilies live in some ponds and lakes. They grow from soil below the water. Sunlight filters through the water to reach the young waterlily. The plant's stems grow toward the surface, taking along the leaves, which are rolled up like tubes. At the surface

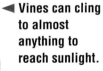

◀ Vines can cling to almost anything to reach sunlight.

the leaves unroll to form flat pads. They are then ready to take in sunlight and carbon dioxide. The roots take in water and nutrients from the muddy bottom. The long stems move the materials back and forth between the leaves and the roots. In this way, all the waterlily's needs are met.

Vines have a different type of stem adaptation that helps them meet their needs. Vines often grow on forest floors, where the light is dim. To reach sunlight, vines have long stems with adaptations for clinging to other objects for support. These adaptations help vines climb fences, walls, rocks, and even other plants.

Plants in the desert have adaptations for living with little water. Just as a plant can't live without light, it can't live without water. Desert soil is dry and hard. It may be months, even years, between rain showers in some deserts. Cacti have roots that grow near the surface of the ground where they can collect any rainwater quickly. They also have thick stems in which they store water to use during dry periods.

✔ **How do stems that are adapted for climbing help vines meet their needs?**

▲ This barrel cactus has a thick stem that stores water.

Summary

Plants need air, nutrients, water, and light to live. Their leaves make food through photosynthesis. Plants have adaptations to help them meet their needs in different settings.

Review

1. What are the four things that plants need to live?
2. What provides the energy for photosynthesis to take place?
3. What adaptations do cacti have for life in the desert?
4. **Critical Thinking** What would happen if there were no carbon dioxide in the air?
5. **Test Prep** Which of the following provides most plants with nutrients?
   - **A** air
   - **B** water
   - **C** soil
   - **D** sunlight

LINKS

MATH LINK

Using Graphs Keep track of the heights of two plants that were given different amounts of water for two weeks. Use *Graph Links* or another computer graphing program to make a bar graph to show how water amounts affected the plants.

WRITING LINK

Informative Writing—Compare and Contrast For a younger child, compare ways that plants live in the wild and in homes. Describe how plants in both places meet their needs. In what ways do they meet their needs differently?

SOCIAL STUDIES LINK

History A plant conservatory (kuhn•SER•vuh•tawr•ee) is a building where unusual plants are grown and displayed. Use library reference materials to find out more about conservatories. Choose a conservatory, and write a short report about when and why it was built. Include in your report pictures of plants found in the conservatory.

TECHNOLOGY LINK

Learn more about growing conditions for plants by viewing *Bloomin' Business* on the **Harcourt Science Newsroom Video** in your classroom video library.

LESSON 2

How Do Leaves, Stems, and Roots Help Plants Live?

In this lesson, you can . . .

 INVESTIGATE how plants "breathe."

 LEARN ABOUT different parts of plants.

 LINK to math, writing, art, and technology.

How Plants "Breathe"

Activity Purpose It sounds strange to say that plants "breathe." But they do. They need to exchange gases as animals do. In this investigation you will look for evidence that a plant breathes through its leaves.

Materials
- leafy potted plant
- petroleum jelly
- 2 clear plastic bags
- twist ties

Activity Procedure

1 Make a chart like the one below.

2 Put a thin layer of petroleum jelly on both the top and bottom surfaces of a leaf on the plant. (Picture A)

3 Put a plastic bag over the leaf. Gently tie the bag closed. Do this just below the place where the leaf attaches to the stem. (Picture B)

Plant Leaf	Observations
Leaf with petroleum jelly	
Leaf with no petroleum jelly	

◄ Wild orchids grow in many parts of the world. Where are the roots, stems, and leaves on this orchid?

Picture A

Picture B

④ Put a plastic bag over a second leaf and seal it. Do not put any petroleum jelly on this leaf.

⑤ Put the plant in a place that gets plenty of light, and water it normally.

⑥ After two days, **observe** the two leaves. **Record** your observations on your chart.

Draw Conclusions

1. **Compare** the two plastic bags. What do you **observe**?

2. What can you **infer** from what you **observed** in this investigation?

3. **Scientists at Work** Scientists often **compare** objects or events. Comparing allows the scientists to see the effects of the variables they control. Compare the leaves you used in this investigation. What can you **infer** about the effect of the petroleum jelly?

Investigate Further Find out where gases are exchanged in a leaf. This time, coat the top side of one leaf and the bottom side of another leaf. Tie a plastic bag over each leaf. What do you **observe**? What explanation can you **infer**?

Process Skill Tip

When you **compare** objects or events, you look for ways they are alike. You also look for ways they are different.

The Functions of Plant Parts

FIND OUT

- **how leaves, stems, and roots help plants live**
- **unusual adaptations plants have**

VOCABULARY

symmetry
transpiration
taproot
fibrous root

Leaves

The leaves of different plants can be very different in shape and size. All leaves, however, work to help plants live. There are two main types of leaves—needles and broad leaves. Most conifers, trees such as pine and spruce, and many cacti have needles. Needle-shaped leaves help prevent water loss. Most other plants have broad leaves. Broad leaves are wide and flat. Beech, oak, and maple trees have broad leaves. So do rosebushes and English ivy.

An interesting characteristic of most leaves is that they have symmetry. An object that has **symmetry** (SIM•uh•tree) can be divided into two parts that look the same. Each half of a leaf is a mirror image of the other.

You already know that leaves carry on photosynthesis. In the investigation, you saw that moisture forms as a leaf "breathes." The water that formed inside the uncoated leaf's bag was caused by transpiration. **Transpiration** (tran•spuh•RAY•shuhn) is the giving off of water by plant parts. As the sun heats a leaf, it causes water to become a gas called water vapor. The waxy surface of most leaves keeps water from escaping, but water vapor can escape from tiny holes in the leaves. These are the same holes where gases are exchanged during breathing.

✔ **What is transpiration?**

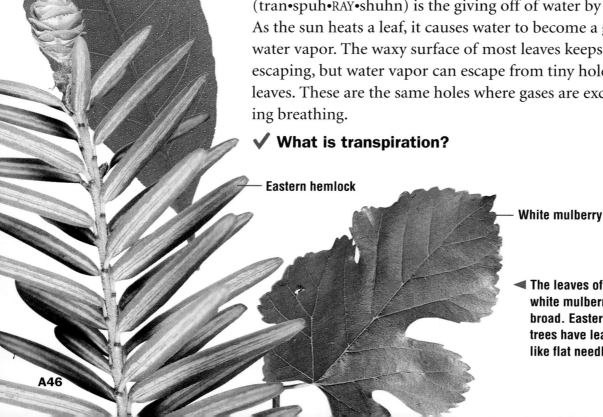

— Lemon

— Eastern hemlock

— White mulberry

◀ The leaves of lemon and white mulberry trees are broad. Eastern hemlock trees have leaves shaped like flat needles.

Stems

Stems support plants and give them shape. They also contain tubes that move water and minerals from the roots and take food from the leaves to all parts of the plant. Stems also store water and food.

Many plant stems, such as those of garden flowers, are soft and flexible, or easy to bend. They have a thin, waxy covering that protects them. Most plants with this kind of stem are small and live for only one growing season. When the next season starts, they must grow again from seeds or from the plant's roots.

Other plants have stiff, woody stems. Woody stems are hard and thick. They have a layer of bark that protects them. Each year, woody stems grow thicker and sometimes taller. Plants with these tough stems can live many years. Trees and shrubs have woody stems.

✔ **Which type of plant usually grows for only one season?**

▲ The manzanita has a woody stem.

The Texas bluebonnet has a flexible stem. ▶

▲ A long, thick taproot firmly holds a dandelion in the ground. The taproot reaches deep into the ground.

Shallow-growing fibrous roots hold this marigold in the soil. ▶

Roots

Roots form the third main part of vascular plants—plants that have tubes. Most roots are underground and hold plants in the soil. Roots also take in water and nutrients that plants need for photosynthesis. Some roots store food made by leaves.

Roots have adaptations to help plants meet their needs. Some plants have taproots. A **taproot** is one main root that goes deep into the soil. If you have ever tried to pull up a dandelion, you know how well taproots hold plants in place. Smaller roots branch off from the taproot. Tiny root hairs that take in water and nutrients grow from the taproot.

A plant with **fibrous** (FY•bruhs) **roots** has many roots of the same size. Fibrous roots grow long but not deep. The fibrous roots also have root hairs that take in water and nutrients from the soil. Grass has fibrous roots.

✔ **Cacti have roots that are close to the surface of the soil. Which type of roots are they?**

Unusual Adaptations

You may have read science-fiction stories about human-eating plants. Plants don't really eat humans, but some of them do eat meat. Some plants that grow in poor soils have leaf adaptations that let them trap and eat insects. Such plants still make their own food. Insects just provide needed nutrients that may be missing in the soil.

The Venus' Flytrap

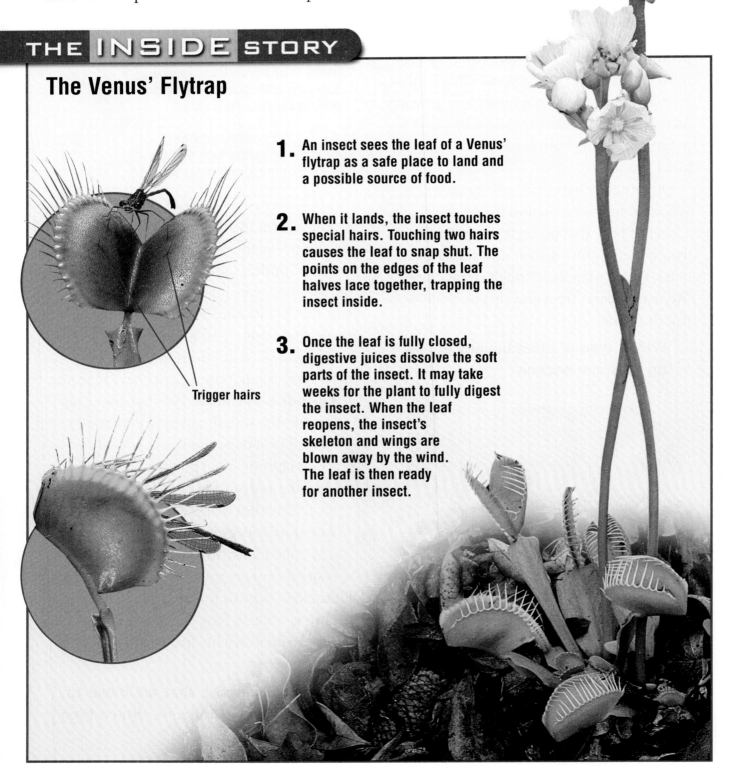

Trigger hairs

1. An insect sees the leaf of a Venus' flytrap as a safe place to land and a possible source of food.

2. When it lands, the insect touches special hairs. Touching two hairs causes the leaf to snap shut. The points on the edges of the leaf halves lace together, trapping the insect inside.

3. Once the leaf is fully closed, digestive juices dissolve the soft parts of the insect. It may take weeks for the plant to fully digest the insect. When the leaf reopens, the insect's skeleton and wings are blown away by the wind. The leaf is then ready for another insect.

Some meat-eating plants have a smell that attracts their prey. Insects that land on them become trapped by a sticky surface or fall into a pool of liquid and drown. Then the plant's digestive juices dissolve the insect. Sundews and cobra lilies catch their prey in these ways. Other meat-eating plants have active traps with parts that move. The pictures on the facing page show how a Venus' flytrap works.

✔ **How do adaptations for trapping insects help some plants meet their needs?**

Summary

Plants have leaf, stem, and root adaptations that help them meet their needs. Some plants have parts that trap and digest insects to get needed nutrients.

Review

1. What are the two types of leaves? What is one unusual leaf adaptation?

2. What is the main difference between the two types of stems?

3. Which parts of roots take in nutrients for a plant?

4. **Critical Thinking** Moisture from leaves is produced by transpiration. Why can you use the presence of moisture as evidence that a plant is exchanging gases, or "breathing"?

5. **Test Prep** An insect is to a meat-eating plant as a _____ is to a human.
   A helper
   B drink of water
   C candy bar
   D vitamin pill

LINKS

MATH LINK

Sorting Leaves Collect leaves of different shapes and sizes. Make a Venn diagram by overlapping two circles made of yarn. Place leaves in your diagram by ways they are alike and ways they are different.

WRITING LINK

Narrative Writing—Story Science fiction writers often take an ordinary fact of nature and exaggerate it. Making a Venus' flytrap into a human-eating plant is an example. Think of a plant adaptation that interests you. Exaggerate the facts, and write a short story for a classmate.

ART LINK

Symmetry Get a broad leaf from a tree. Cut the leaf in half along the large vein that runs down the middle. Stand a mirror on edge along the cut side of a leaf half. When you look in the mirror, does the leaf appear whole? Tape your leaf part down on white paper. Carefully draw an identical but opposite side to make the leaf look whole.

TECHNOLOGY LINK

Learn more about garden plants from all over the world by visiting the National Museum of Natural History Internet site.
www.si.edu/harcourt/science

LESSON

3

How Do Plants Reproduce?

In this lesson, you can . . .

 INVESTIGATE how plants grow from seeds.

 LEARN ABOUT plant life cycles.

 LINK to math, writing, social studies, and technology.

Seedling Growth

Activity Purpose It's not often that you can see a seed start to grow into a plant. This process is usually hidden by soil until the tiny stem grows above the ground. In this investigation, you will **observe, measure,** and **compare** the growth of two types of seeds.

Materials

- 2 paper towels
- small, clear jar or cup
- alfalfa seed
- bean seed
- water
- hand lens
- yarn
- ruler

Activity Procedure

1 Fold a paper towel, and place it around the inside of the jar.

2 Make the second paper towel into a ball, and place it inside the jar to fill the space.

3 Place the alfalfa seed about 3 cm from the top of the jar, between the paper-towel lining and the jar's side. You should be able to see the seed through the jar.

4 Place the bean seed in a similar position on the other side of the jar. (Picture A)

5 Pour water into the jar to soak the towels completely.

6 Set the jar in a sunny place, and leave it there for five days. Be sure to keep the paper towels moist.

◄ New raspberry bushes can grow from seeds. The seeds are inside the berries.

Picture A

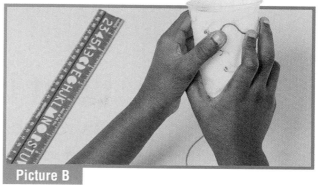

Picture B

Seed Growth

	Alfalfa		Bean	
	Size	Other Observations	Size	Other Observations
Day 1				
Day 2				

7 Make a chart like the one above.

8 Use the hand lens to **observe** the seeds daily for five days. **Measure** the growth of the roots and shoots with the yarn. Use the ruler to measure the yarn. **Record** your observations on your chart. (Picture B)

Draw Conclusions

1. What plant parts grew from each seed?

2. **Compare** the growth of the roots and shoots from the two seeds. Did they grow to be the same size? Did they grow at the same rate?

3. **Scientists at Work** Scientists take a lot of care to **measure** objects the same way each time. Think about how you measured the plants. How do you know your measurements were accurate?

Investigate Further Plant each of the seedlings in soil. Give the seeds the same amounts of water and light. Continue **observing** and **recording** information about your plants for a month. Make a drawing of your plants each week. Identify and label the parts of the plants. Make a graph of your measurements. Based on the graph, how fast did the plants grow?

Process Skill Tip

One way to compare objects accurately is to **measure** them. An instrument such as a ruler or a balance is used to measure. A scientist often repeats measurements to make sure that they are as accurate as possible.

Plant Life Cycles

Plants from Seeds

FIND OUT

- ways plants reproduce
- how seeds are spread

VOCABULARY

germinate
spore
tuber

Have you ever planted seeds in a garden? Seeds form in the cones of conifers. Seeds also form in the flowers of flowering plants. When a flower dries up and falls away, fruit forms around the young seeds. The fruit protects the seeds. Inside each seed is a tiny plant and the food it needs to start growing.

Seeds are the first part in a flowering plant's life cycle. To begin to grow, seeds need warmth, water, and air. Most seeds don't get what they need, so they don't grow. When a seed has its needs met, it **germinates** (JER•muh•nayts), or sprouts. Seedlings that sprout in soil may keep growing. They grow to become adult, or mature, plants. The mature plants form flowers.

Animals such as bees, birds, and bats feed on nectar, a sweet liquid in the flowers. This spreads pollen and helps flowers form seeds.

✔ **What do most seeds need to begin to grow?**

Life Cycle of a Plant

A plant's life cycle usually repeats itself year after year. The warm, moist climate of some regions sometimes speeds up the cycle.

Birds carry seeds in their beaks and on their feathers. ▼

The Spread of Seeds

Fruit falling to the ground is just one way seeds get to the soil. Animals play a role, too. For example, birds eat the fruit from plants. The seeds pass through their bodies and end up far away from the parent plants. Squirrels gather and eat nuts such as walnuts. When there are many walnuts, squirrels bury some to be eaten later. In the spring a few walnuts that were forgotten germinate and become young trees.

Wind and water also spread seeds. Dandelion seeds are light. The fruit is the fluffy part. When the seeds are ready, the wind carries the fluffy fruit away. Large seeds such as those from coconut and mangrove trees can float in water to shores far away from the parent plants.

Some seeds, such as those of beggar's-lice, stick to things. Animals that brush against these plants carry away the seeds in their fur. In the same way, humans carry the seeds on their clothing.

✔ **Describe a seed that can be carried by the wind.**

Seeds of beggar's-lice have tiny hooks that stick to fur, hair, and clothing. ▼

Milkweed seeds are carried away by wind. ▼

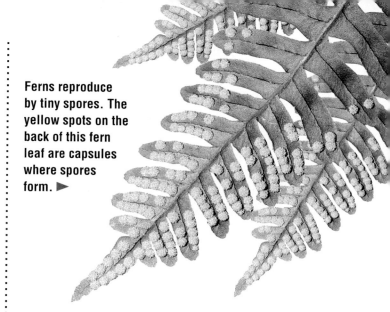

Ferns reproduce by tiny spores. The yellow spots on the back of this fern leaf are capsules where spores form. ▶

Plants from Spores

Not all plants have flowers that form fruits and seeds. Some plants grow from spores. **Spores** (SPOHRZ) are tiny cells. Spores are much smaller than seeds. In fact, most spores are made of only one cell and can be seen only with a microscope.

Spores are like seeds in some ways. Like seeds, spores contain food. And some spores have thick walls that allow them to stay inactive for months. They can be carried by wind, water, and animals.

Spores grow in capsules, or small cases. You may have seen ferns with tiny brown or yellow dots on the underside of their leaves. The dots are capsules and the spores are inside.

When spores are mature, the capsules dry up and open. Spores are then released into the air where they scatter. Spores germinate if they land where conditions are good. But the tiny plants that begin to grow are not complete. Adult plants form only after two different parts of these tiny plants join. Mature spore-making plants grow from the joined parts.

✔ **How are spores spread?**

New Plants from Old

Growing plants from seeds and spores can take a long time. Some plants have adaptations that let them make new plants in other ways.

A spider plant sends out buds on a type of stem called a runner. Buds are immature, or young, plant shoots. When these buds touch the ground, they form roots and begin to grow.

Tulips grow from bulbs. A bulb is a kind of bud that grows underground. Bulbs can be split into pieces. Each piece can grow into a new plant. You may have helped someone plant bulbs in the fall to have flowers the next spring.

Some plants grow from a piece of stem put in water. Many people who grow plants indoors start new ones by cutting off a branch of the stem. Then they trim off lower leaves and put that piece in water. New roots grow from it. The new stem with roots is planted in soil.

People have come up with ways to join two or more different plants to make a new plant. The process is called *grafting*. To graft plants, people attach a cut stem of one plant to a slice in the stem of another plant. The joined stem uses the roots of the other plant to get water and nutrients.

Grafting is used to make a new plant with the good characteristics of each plant. For example, branches of different apple trees can be joined to the trunk of another tree. The tree then grows apples that have more desirable flavors and sizes.

The spider plant sends out runners with buds attached. ▼

Three different branches were grafted to one trunk. That is why this small tree has three different colors of flowers. ▶

Potato tubers develop "eyes," each of which can make a new plant. ▶

Potatoes are **tubers** (TOO•berz), or swollen underground stems. Tubers are often dug up to eat. They also can be cut into pieces and planted. Each piece of a potato that has a bud, or "eye," can make a new plant.

✓ **What process ends with a "new and improved" plant?**

Summary

Plants reproduce by seeds and spores. Many plants can also grow from buds, bulbs, tubers, and stem pieces. Seeds are spread by falling fruit, animals, wind, and water.

Review

1. What must both seeds and spores do before they begin to grow in soil?
2. What are two ways that animals help spread seeds?
3. Spider plants, tulips, and potatoes can grow from seeds. How are their other ways of reproducing alike?
4. **Critical Thinking** If you had a leafy plant with damaged roots, how might you start a new plant?
5. **Test Prep** Which part of a flowering plant protects seeds?
   A flowers
   B fruit
   C capsules
   D birds

LINKS

MATH LINK

Using Fractions Wrap 10 bean seeds and 10 corn seeds in a moist paper towel. Seal them in a plastic bag for a week. What fraction of each seed group sprouts? Why might this information be important to a gardener?

WRITING LINK

Expressive Writing—Poem Haiku is a form of Japanese poetry. Haiku are often written about a season, such as fall. Write a haiku for a family member about what plants are like during your favorite season.

SOCIAL STUDIES LINK

Grains Around the World All grains are seeds. Many grains are important food sources. Find out which grains are eaten in different parts of the world. Use a world map to show which grains are grown in different areas of the world.

TECHNOLOGY LINK

Learn more about growing plants under different conditions–on a computer screen! Try *Do You Have a Green Thumb?* on **Harcourt Science Explorations CD-ROM.**

Superveggies

Researchers have found ways to make eating your vegetables more appealing.

Why Improve Vegetables?

"No dessert until you've finished your vegetables!" If you've ever heard those words, there's good news for you! Researchers at Texas A&M University are working on superveggies. These vegetables are better-tasting

BetaSweet carrots

than many well-known vegetables. They also have more of some nutrients. So people who eat only a few vegetables will still get plenty of nutrients. Superveggies also may prevent or fight diseases such as cancer and heart disease. Many different vegetables are being tested. They include onions, potatoes, peppers, corn, broccoli, cabbage, tomatoes, leeks, and Brussels sprouts.

A Sweet Success

A big success story is the BetaSweet carrot. It is sweeter and crisper than regular carrots, and its color is maroon! It has extra beta carotene (BAYT•uh KAIR•uh•teen), which your body changes to vitamin A. Eating just one-third of a BetaSweet carrot would meet your daily need for beta carotene.

Dr. Leonard M. Pike is the scientist who is heading research at the Vegetable Improvement Center at Texas A&M. He first got the idea for a maroon carrot in 1989. He saw carrots grown from Brazilian seeds. These carrots had maroon patches mixed in with the carrots' normal orange color. He began trying to design a carrot that had more flavor and nutrition.

New Veggies on the Horizon

Another new veggie to watch for is a cucumber that's orange inside! This special cucumber tastes like other cucumbers. But like BetaSweets, it also gives you a higher level of vitamin A.

How would you like a rose-colored onion with a mild flavor? These onions are meant to be eaten raw. Cooking destroys some of the important nutrients that make them look and taste different.

Researchers are also working on types of peppers that will have more vitamin C than an orange. Specially marked bell peppers and chili peppers may be in grocery stores soon. So be sure to "eat your superveggies"!

Think About It

1. If you could ask scientists to improve the nutrition, flavor, or color of certain fruits or vegetables, which ones would you choose?

2. One-third of a BetaSweet carrot gives you all of one nutrient you need for a day. In the future, people might need less of all foods to get all needed nutrients. Do you think people will eat less food? Explain.

WEB LINK:
For Science and Technology updates, visit the Harcourt Internet site.
www.harcourtschool.com/ca

Careers   Genetic Engineer

What They Do   A genetic engineer in agriculture works with plants to make them stronger or more healthful. For example, a genetic engineer might find a gene that helps a plant live for a while without water.  That gene might be put into other plants to make them stronger, too. Genetic engineers also work with animals.

Education and Training   People who want to be genetic engineers study biology in college. They must learn about cell division and DNA. Most get advanced college degrees in genetics and plant or animal sciences.

Mary Agnes Meara Chase

BOTANIST

"If it were not for grasses, the world would never have been civilized."

Agnes Chase devoted her life to the study of grasses. She worked as a botanist (BAH•tuhn•ist), a scientist who studies plants, for the United States Department of Agriculture (USDA). She collected and described over 10,000 species of grasses. Early in her career, Chase made sketches of plants. She also helped write a book called *The Manual of Grasses.*

To a botanist, grasses include more than what grows in a front yard or at a park. Grasses also include grains such as rice, wheat, oats, rye, hay, and corn. Sorghum, bamboo, and sugar cane are also grasses. All these grasses are food for animals and for people. They provide building material and sugar. They also build up the land and prevent soil erosion. At the USDA, Chase helped scientists experiment with crops. The scientists wanted to develop nutritious plants that also resisted disease.

Chase often traveled to collect plants. She visited Europe twice and traveled to Mexico and Puerto Rico to study grasses and get samples. After she retired, Chase went to Venezuela

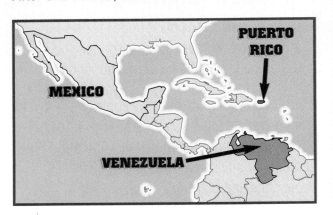

because its government asked for her help in collecting and studying grasses. While there, she encouraged students from South America to come to the United States to study. Some of the students who did come lived at her home in Washington, D.C.

Chase wrote over 70 different books and magazine articles. She kept on working, without pay, after she retired. She was in charge of the National Herbarium at the Smithsonian Institution. She eventually donated her personal collection to the Smithsonian Institution.

THINK ABOUT IT

1. What grasses do you eat regularly?
2. What features of grasses make them useful to people?

Plant Colors

What dyes do plants contain?

Materials

- dry yellow onion skins
- dry red onion skins
- pot
- water
- hot plate
- white cotton cloth
- string
- oven mitt

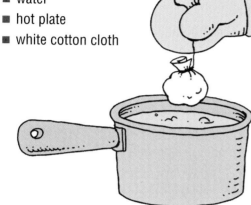

Procedure

1. An adult will boil each color of onion skins in water for about 20 minutes.

2. Tightly tie the cotton cloth into bunches with the string. Leave a length of string that you can use to hold the cloth.

3. Using an oven mitt, hold the string and put the cloth into one of the pots of hot onion water for about 5 minutes. Let the cloth cool. Then unwrap it and let it dry.

Draw Conclusions

What color did the cloth turn? Compare your cloth to one that was dyed with different colored onion skins. Why are the cloths different?

Identifying Trees

How can you identify trees?

Materials

- 3 zip-top bags, each containing leaves, bark, and seeds from a different type of tree
- paper
- colored pencils

Procedure

1. Observe the contents of each plastic bag.

2. For each bag, make a page that someone else could use to identify the tree without seeing the bag. Include any sketches or descriptions you think are important.

Draw Conclusions

What plant parts are in the bags? What other tree parts could be used to identify a tree? Compare your pages to the key or guidebook your teacher gives you. Try to name each tree.

Plants from Spores

How does a fern reproduce from spores?

Materials

- fern with spore cases that have turned dry and brown
- pot of potting soil with peat moss
- plastic wrap
- saucer of water

Procedure

1. Sprinkle the spores over the soil, and cover the pot with plastic wrap.

2. Move the pot to a light but not sunny location. Place the pot in the saucer.

3. Keep water in the saucer.

4. When the ferns are 2.5–4 cm tall, move clumps of them to their own pots.

Draw Conclusions

How does fern reproduction differ from reproduction in other plants with which you are familiar? In what ways do you think that having spores has helped ferns survive?

Growth and Touch

How do vines wrap around supports?

Materials

- clear plastic cup lined with a paper towel
- water
- 4 morning glory or moonflower seeds
- 4 pencils
- masking tape

Procedure

1. Wet the paper towel, and slip the seeds between the towel and the cup.

2. Put the cup in a warm, lighted place, and keep the towel moist.

3. Wait two to three weeks, until the seeds sprout and the stems reach the top edge of the cup.

4. Tape the pencils to the outside of the cup, as shown.

Draw Conclusions

When a stem reached a pencil, which side grew faster—the inside part touching the pencil or the outside part not touching the pencil? How does this behavior help the seedlings survive? In what direction are the seed roots growing? How does this help the seedling survive?

Traveling Water

How does water move through moss?

Materials

- small plate of dry sphagnum moss
- shallow container of water
- green food coloring
- hand lens

Procedure

1. Color the water by adding green food coloring.

2. Gently pull out a strand of moss. Make sure one end remains attached to the rest of the moss.

3. Put the end of the strand in the container of water, as shown.

4. Using the hand lens, observe what happens.

Draw Conclusions

How do you know the water has entered the moss? How did the water enter and spread through the moss?

Plant Stems

How does water move through celery?

Materials

- fresh celery stalk with leaves
- plastic knife
- two containers
- water
- red food coloring
- blue food coloring
- paper towels
- hand lens

Procedure

1. Trim 1 cm from the end of the celery stalk. Split the celery lengthwise from the middle to the trimmed end. Don't cut the stalk completely in half.

2. Fill each container halfway with water. Add 15 drops of red food coloring to one container and 15 drops of blue to the other.

3. Place the containers side by side, and place one of the cut stalk ends in each container.

4. Observe the celery every 15 minutes for an hour. Remove the stalk, and dry it with the towels. Use the hand lens to observe the cut ends.

Draw Conclusions

Where did the water travel in the stalk? How do you know? How is this different from the way water traveled in the moss?

Chapter 2 Review and Test Preparation

Vocabulary Review

Use the terms below to complete the sentences. The page numbers in ( ) tell you where to look in the chapter if you need help.

carbon dioxide (A40)   **taproot** (A47)

nutrient (A40)   **fibrous roots** (A47)

photosynthesis (A41)   **germinate** (A52)

symmetry (A46)   **spores** (A53)

transpiration (A46)   **tuber** (A55)

1. Water loss due to evaporation is ____.

2. Carrots have a ____, a single main root that grows deep into the soil.

3. *Sprout* is another word for ____.

4. Animals breathe out a gas called ____.

5. A substance a plant needs in order to grow is a ____.

6. The way a plant makes food is ____.

7. A root system that has many roots of the same size is made up of ____.

8. Potatoes have a swollen underground stem called a ____.

9. Tiny reproductive cells of ferns are ____.

10. An object with ____ can be divided into two or more parts that look the same.

Connect Concepts

Use the terms in the Word Bank to complete the concept map.

carbon dioxide   **fibrous roots**

nutrients   **photosynthesis**

taproots

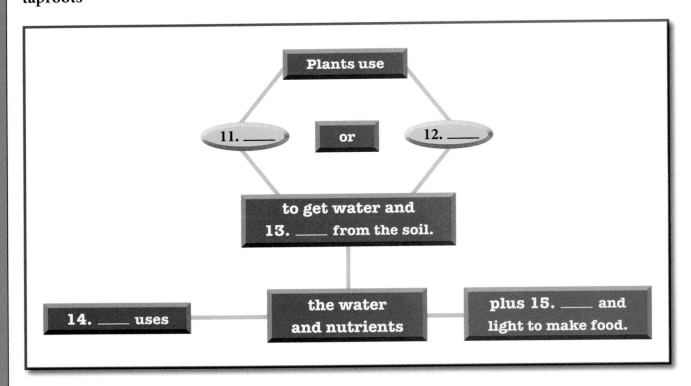

Plants use

11. ____   or   12. ____

to get water and 13. ____ from the soil.

14. ____ uses   the water and nutrients   plus 15. ____ and light to make food.

Check Understanding

Write the letter of the best choice.

16. A plant with a thick stem for storing water would probably grow in the —
    A ocean   C forest
    B mountains   D desert

17. Transpiration by plants could help form —
    F carbon dioxide
    G symmetry
    H rain clouds
    J oxygen

18. A seed eaten by a bird —
    A cannot grow
    B will probably make the bird sick
    C may become several seeds
    D may germinate far from where it was eaten

19. Which process can end with a "new and improved" plant?
    F grafting
    G cutting up tubers
    H placing cuttings in water
    J splitting apart bulbs

20. Which of the following terms does **NOT** belong with the others?
    A seed   C spore
    B flower   D fruit

Critical Thinking

21. Why do you think photosynthesis is one of the most important processes on Earth?

22. The fact that plants have many ways to spread seeds can cause problems for gardeners. Why is this?

Process Skills Review

23. You want to find out if a certain plant grows best in a hot, warm, or cool climate. What **variables** should you **control?** What variable will you **test?**

24. You want to buy a new pair of shoes. What are three shoe features you could **compare?**

25. You need to **measure** how fast a friend can run 25 meters. What two measuring instruments would you need?

Performance Assessment

Arctic Plant

The Arctic is very cold. The water and soil there are frozen most of the year, and the growing season is very short. Design and draw a plant that could live in the Arctic. Label the adaptations your plant has that help it live in this harsh climate. How would it reproduce?

Living Things Interact

When poet John Donne wrote "No man is an island," he was talking about how people need and depend on other people. In fact, almost every living thing on Earth needs and depends on other living things. We are all part of the biosphere, Earth's life zone.

Vocabulary Preview

individual	food web
population	energy
community	pyramid
ecosystem	competition
habitat	symbiosis
niche	producer
consumer	food chain
endangered	decomposer
threatened	extinct

FAST FACT

There are more than 750 endangered species of plants and animals, like this manatee, in the United States.

Endangered Species	
Type	Number
Mammals	55
Birds	74
Fish	65
Other animals	126
Plants	434

FAST FACT

In 1859 a settler released a few rabbits in Australia. Within a few years, millions of rabbits were competing for food with native birds and mammals. Although the rabbits have done well, some of these native Australian animals are now extinct.

FAST FACT

Most islands would have no plants or animals if they didn't arrive from other places. For example, the islands of Hawai'i are the most isolated islands on Earth. The native plants and animals that live there somehow reached the islands from the mainland of Central America.

What Are Ecosystems?

In this lesson, you can . . .

INVESTIGATE a local environment.

LEARN ABOUT how organisms live together in an ecosystem.

LINK to math, writing, literature, and technology.

Prairie dogs live in large groups, called colonies. They feed on prairie plants. ▼

INVESTIGATE

The Local Environment

Activity Purpose   All living organisms interact with one another and with their environment. The environment includes all the nonliving things in an area, such as weather, soil, and water. In this investigation you will **observe** a local environment and note the interactions that occur in that environment.

Materials

- garden gloves
- meterstick
- 4 wooden stakes
- string
- hand lens
- aluminum pan
- wet paper towels
- garden trowel
- toothpick

CAUTION

Activity Procedure

1 **CAUTION** **Wear garden gloves to protect your hands**. Your teacher will send you to a grassy or lightly wooded area near your school. Once you are there, use the meterstick to **measure** an area of ground that is 1 m^2 (1 m $\times$ 1 m). Push a stake into each corner of the plot. Tie the string around the stakes. (Picture A)

2 Before observing the plot, **predict** what living organisms and nonliving things you might find in this environment. **Record** your prediction.

3 **Observe** the plot carefully. Use the hand lens to look for small things in the plot. **Record** your observations by making lists of the living organisms and the nonliving things in this environment.

4 Sit back and continue to **observe** the plot for a while. Look for living organisms, such as insects, interacting with other organisms or with the environment. Describe and **record** any interactions you observe.

5 Put wet paper towels in the aluminum pan, and use the garden trowel to scoop some soil onto them. Use a toothpick to sift through the soil. Be careful not to injure any living organisms with the toothpick. (Picture B)

6 **Record** what you **observe**, especially any interactions. Then return the soil to the plot of ground.

Picture A

Draw Conclusions

1. How did what you **predicted** compare with what you **observed**?

2. What did you **observe** that showed living organisms interacting with one another or with the environment?

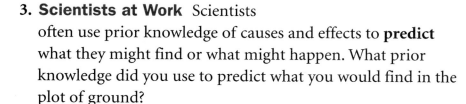

Picture B

3. **Scientists at Work** Scientists often use prior knowledge of causes and effects to **predict** what they might find or what might happen. What prior knowledge did you use to predict what you would find in the plot of ground?

Investigate Further Sometimes you can **infer** what interactions are occurring in an environment by **observing** what's in that environment. Choose an environment near your home or school. Observe what kinds of organisms live there, and infer how they interact with one another and with the environment.

Process Skill Tip

Scientists use what they already know to **predict** what they might find or what might happen. Careful observation also helps make a prediction more than a guess.

Ecosystems

Organisms and Their Environment

The living organisms you observed in the investigation may stay in that small plot of land as long as the physical environment provides everything they need to survive. The physical environment includes all the nonliving things in an area, such as soil, weather, landforms, air, and water.

A single organism in an environment is called an **individual**. One grasshopper in a field is an individual. Individuals of the same kind living in the same environment make up a **population**. All the grasshoppers in a field are the grasshopper population. All the populations of organisms living together in an environment make up a **community**. A community may include many different populations. Each community interacts with its physical environment. Together, a community and its physical environment make up an **ecosystem**.

✔ **What are the two parts of an ecosystem?**

FIND OUT

- about the parts of an ecosystem
- how the environment affects living organisms in an ecosystem

VOCABULARY

individual
population
community
ecosystem
habitat
niche

An individual caribou (KAR•uh•boo) (left) is part of a caribou population (right). Many plant and animal populations make up a community. The community interacts with the environment to make an ecosystem.

Habitats and Niches

Every population has a place where it lives in an ecosystem. This is its **habitat**. Think of a habitat as a neighborhood, and think of a community as the residents of that neighborhood. You might spot a golden eagle on a rocky mountain slope or near an open field that has tall trees around it. These areas are part of the golden eagle's habitat.

Many different populations can share a habitat. But each population has a certain role, or **niche** (NICH), in its habitat. For example, during the day eagles soar high above open ground, hunting for small animals such as mice. Great horned owls share the golden eagle's habitat, and they also hunt mice. But owls hunt at night. Because of their different hunting habits, golden eagles and great horned owls have different niches in the same habitat.

In a healthy ecosystem, populations are interdependent. That is, they depend on each other for survival. For example, great horned owls eat mice, which may eat the seeds of one type of plant. Since eagles help keep the mouse population from getting too large, the plant population never dies out. In a similar way, the mice control the size of the owl population. If there are too many owls and not enough mice for them to eat, some of the owls will die.

In addition, the interactions of plants and animals help keep the balance of carbon dioxide and oxygen in the atmosphere. Plants and animals also give off water. This is an important part of the water cycle.

✔ **What is a niche?**

Red fox

Ground squirrel

Limiting Factors

The environment largely determines what type of ecosystem will develop in an area. Soil conditions, temperature, and rainfall help determine what plants will grow. Cactus plants, for example, have adaptations for living in desert conditions. A desert environment has very little rain, and much of it drains away quickly in the sandy soil. But the shallow roots of cactus plants take in water quickly when it is available.

The kinds and numbers of plants in an ecosystem determine what animals will live there. Where there are only a few plants, the populations of animals that depend on plants for food are small.

Caribou, for example, graze on the few plants that grow in the cold Arctic ecosystems. Caribou must space themselves out, moving in small herds, or groups, from place to place to find enough food.

The amount of food—or any limited resource—in an ecosystem affects the size of

Sandy desert soil has few nutrients and doesn't hold water. High temperatures and little rainfall mean that relatively few plants live in deserts. ▼

Southern Vermont/ Brattleboro

■ Precipitation   **Month**   — Temperature

Southern Arizona/ Tucson

■ Precipitation   **Month**   — Temperature

▲ The soil of eastern forests has a lot of organic matter. This type of soil holds water well and supports many organisms. Moderate temperatures and plenty of rain allow a variety of plants to grow.

a population. For example, one area may have enough food to support 100 caribou. Another area of the same size but with fewer plants may be able to support only 50 caribou. The *population density,* or number of animals in a certain area, is greater for the first area than it is for the second.

✔ **What is population density?**

Summary

Individuals of the same species make up a population. Populations of different organisms live together in a community. Communities of organisms together with the physical environment make up an ecosystem. Each organism in a habitat has its own niche. Limiting factors, such as the amount of food, affect population density.

Review

1. What is the relationship of a population to a community?

2. What is an ecosystem?

3. Use the data on page A70. How much warmer is it in June in the southern Arizona desert ecosystem than it is in the forest ecosystem of southern Vermont?

4. **Critical Thinking** The environment determines the ecosystem of an area. What things in the environment where you live determine your local ecosystem?

5. **Test Prep** Nonliving things that affect the organisms living in an ecosystem include weather, landforms, and —

   A habitat
   B niche
   C soil
   D population

LINKS

MATH LINK

Population Density A scientist studied the habitat of a certain spider. She counted the number of spiders living in a field. On one hectare of a sunny, open section, she found 80 spiders. On one hectare of a shady, heavily wooded section, she found 10 spiders. How many times as great was the population density of spiders in the open area compared with the shady area?

WRITING LINK

Informative Writing—Narration Write a narration for a nature video about an ecosystem with which you are familiar. Before you begin your narration, make an outline of the living and nonliving things in the ecosystem.

LITERATURE LINK

What's a Penguin Doing in a Place Like This? by Miriam Schlein (Millbrook, 1998) tells how these interesting animals have adapted to a tropical ecosystem, which is very different from that of Antarctica. Read the book and share with your classmates how penguins came to live in this ecosystem.

TECHNOLOGY LINK

Learn more about ecosystems by visiting the Harcourt Learning Site.

WELCOME TO
THE
LEARNING
SITE

www.harcourtschool.com/ca

LESSON 2

How Does Energy Flow Through an Ecosystem?

In this lesson, you can . . .

INVESTIGATE what eats what in ecosystems.

LEARN ABOUT how energy is transferred in an ecosystem.

LINK to math, writing, literature, and technology.

A hawk gets the energy it needs from eating this field mouse. ▼

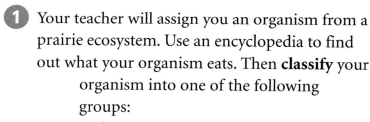

INVESTIGATE

What Eats What in Ecosystems

Activity Purpose All animals must eat to survive. The energy from food is needed for all life processes. Some animals eat plants, and some eat other animals. Any food energy that isn't used by an animal is stored in its body tissue. When an animal is eaten, this stored energy is passed on to the animal that eats it. In this investigation you will **classify** and **order** organisms to see what eats what in a prairie ecosystem.

Materials

- index cards
- markers
- pushpins
- bulletin board
- yarn

Activity Procedure

1. Your teacher will assign you an organism from a prairie ecosystem. Use an encyclopedia to find out what your organism eats. Then **classify** your organism into one of the following groups:
   - plants
   - plant-eating animals
   - meat-eating animals
   - animals that eat both plants and meat
   - animals that eat dead organisms

2. Use markers to draw your organism or write its name on an index card.

Picture A

Picture B

3 Your teacher will now assign you to a class team. Each team will have at least one organism from each group listed in Step 1. With your teammates, **order** your team's cards to show what eats what in a prairie ecosystem. (Picture A)

4 When your team's cards are in order, pin them in a line on the bulletin board. Connect the cards with yarn to show what eats what—both within your team's group of organisms and between those of other teams. (Picture B)

Draw Conclusions

1. When your team put its cards in **order**, what kind of organism was first?

2. How would you **classify** the organism that came right after the first organism?

3. **Scientists at Work** When scientists **classify** things that happen in a particular order, it helps them understand how something works. Look again at your team's cards on the bulletin board. Could you classify or order them in any other way to explain what eats what in an ecosystem?

Investigate Further Find out what eats what in another ecosystem. Then make a drawing to show the flow of energy and matter in that ecosystem. Share your drawing with the class.

Process Skill Tip

When you **classify** things, you can better see relationships among them. For example, you may notice that plants are always first in an ecosystem. Seeing the order of the other organisms in an ecosystem helps you figure out each organism's niche.

How Energy Is Transferred in an Ecosystem

FIND OUT

- how living things get the energy they need
- why energy is lost in the transfer between organisms

VOCABULARY

producer
consumer
food chain
decomposer
food web
energy pyramid

Living Things Need Energy

Cells get the energy they need from food. In the investigation you saw that animals eat plants or other organisms to get energy. The sun provides the energy for almost every ecosystem on Earth. Plants, or **producers**, use sunlight to make the food they need from carbon dioxide and water.

As all other organisms do, plants use food energy to grow and reproduce. Any energy not needed is stored in roots, stems, and leaves. All life in an ecosystem depends on producers to capture the energy of the sun, change it into living tissue, and pass it on to other organisms. All other organisms in an ecosystem community must eat to get the energy they need. So the animals in a community are **consumers**.

✔ **Why do all animals in a community depend on producers?**

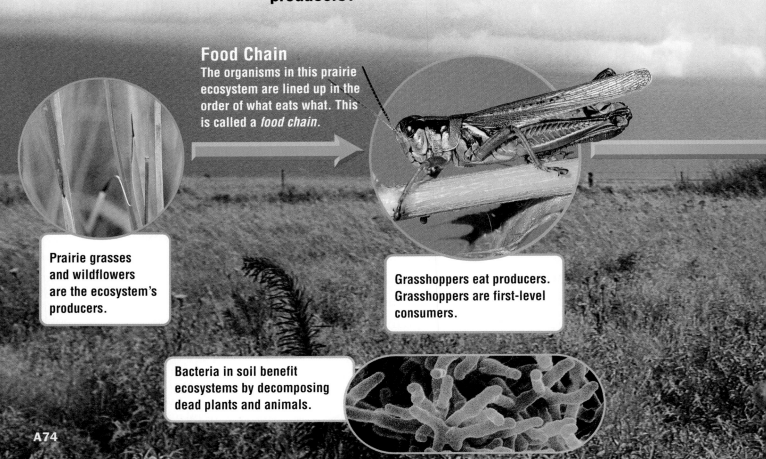

Food Chain
The organisms in this prairie ecosystem are lined up in the order of what eats what. This is called a *food chain*.

Prairie grasses and wildflowers are the ecosystem's producers.

Grasshoppers eat producers. Grasshoppers are first-level consumers.

Bacteria in soil benefit ecosystems by decomposing dead plants and animals.

Food Chains

Energy and matter are passed through communities by way of food chains. A **food chain** shows how the consumers in an ecosystem are connected to one another according to what they eat. A food chain has several levels. At the base of every food chain are the producers—usually plants. Consumers make up all the other levels. First-level consumers, called *herbivores,* eat the producers. Second-level consumers, called *carnivores,* eat first-level consumers. Third-level consumers eat second-level consumers, and so on. Each level of consumer eats organisms from the level below it.

Identifying the organisms and their levels in a food chain can help you understand how energy moves through an ecosystem. For example, energy and matter in a grass plant may become part of a grasshopper's body. The grasshopper uses some of the energy and stores the rest.

If a snake eats the grasshopper, it consumes, or uses up, the energy stored in the grasshopper's body. In this way energy moves up through each level of the food chain, from producer to first-level consumer, to second-level consumer, and so on.

Decomposers, such as mushrooms, bacteria, and some insects, are consumers that break down and recycle the tissues of dead organisms. They use some nutrients from the dead tissue as food. What matter decomposers don't use becomes part of the soil. Soil that has a lot of nutrients helps plants grow. In this way decomposers connect both ends of a food chain.

✔ **What kind of food does a first-level consumer eat?**

Snakes eat grasshoppers. Snakes are second-level consumers.

Hawks eat snakes. This makes hawks third-level consumers.

Decomposers, such as these mushrooms, get energy by recycling dead organisms.

A Prairie Food Web

A food web shows the relationships between many different food chains in a single ecosystem. Prairie grass, for example, is a producer in several food chains. In one, bison eat the grass. Since few bison are eaten by carnivores, the food chain is short. But prairie grass is also eaten by mice, which in turn are eaten by snakes. And the snakes may be eaten by hawks. A food web shows how organisms may be part of several food chains at the same time. What food chains could you make from these prairie organisms?

1. Needle-and-thread grass
2. Purple coneflower
3. Bison
4. White prairie clover
5. Side-oats grama grass
6. Swainson's hawk
7. Black-eyed Susan
8. Painted lady butterfly
9. Fairy ring mushroom
10. Buffalo grass
11. Thirteen-lined ground squirrel
12. Grass spider
13. Dung fly
14. Bullsnake
15. Field cricket
16. Western harvest mouse
17. Two-striped grasshopper

Energy Pyramids

In the food chains of most ecosystems, there are many more producers than there are consumers. Producers use about 90 percent of the food energy they make during photosynthesis for their life processes. Only 10 percent of the energy is stored in plant tissue. When a consumer eats the plant tissue, it uses about 90 percent of the plant's stored food energy to stay alive. It stores the other 10 percent in its body tissue. This huge loss of stored food energy occurs at each level in a food chain. An **energy pyramid** shows the amount of energy available to pass from one level of a food chain to the next.

Remember, only 10 percent of the energy at any level of a food chain is passed on to the next higher level. Since less energy is available to organisms higher up the food chain, there are usually fewer organisms at these levels. High-level consumers, such as wolves, have relatively small populations. There is not enough energy available to support a large population of wolves.

The size of each level of an energy pyramid is related to the sizes of the populations at that level. The producer population is usually the largest, since it provides energy for all consumer levels in the pyramid.

✔ **How much of the food energy that is taken in by an organism is used for its own life processes?**

Energy Pyramid

◄ **Third-level consumers** Hawks are at the top of this energy pyramid. They eat snakes. There are few hawks because most of the energy has been used at lower levels of the pyramid.

hawk

◄ **Second-level consumers** There are far fewer snakes than grasshoppers. This is because grasshoppers use 90 percent of the food energy they get for their own life processes.

snakes

◄ **First-level consumers** Since plants use 90 percent of the food energy they produce, there are fewer grasshoppers than there are grasses and other plants.

grasshoppers

◄ **Producers** Producers, such as grasses and other plants, form the base of an energy pyramid.

grass

▲ Vultures are called *scavengers*. They feed on the bodies of dead animals.

Summary

Producers use sunlight to make their own food energy. Consumers eat other organisms to get energy. A food chain may have several levels of consumers. Food webs show feeding relationships among several food chains. All organisms use most of the food energy they take in for themselves. Only 10 percent of the energy is passed on to organisms in the next higher level of an energy pyramid.

Review

1. In most ecosystems, what kinds of organisms are producers?
2. What benefit do decomposers provide for an ecosystem?
3. What is any organism that eats another organism called?
4. **Critical Thinking** Think of three things you like to eat. What level consumer are you for each of the foods you chose?
5. **Test Prep** Organisms at the bottom of an energy pyramid are always —
   A plant eaters
   B producers
   C hunters
   D scavengers

LINKS

MATH LINK

Percents Only 10 percent of the total energy at one level in a food chain is available to organisms in the next higher level. How much of the energy in grass is available to a snake that eats an insect that eats the grass?

WRITING LINK

Persuasive Writing—Opinion Some scientists suggest that if humans ate more producers and fewer consumers, more food could be produced for less money. Write a paragraph in which you support this opinion with facts you learned in this lesson. Then share your paragraph with your classmates.

LITERATURE LINK

Who Eats What? Food Chains and Food Webs by Patricia Lauber (HarperCollins, 1996) describes the interactions of plants and animals in different kinds of ecosystems. Read it to add to what you've learned in this lesson.

TECHNOLOGY LINK

Learn more about the flow of energy in an ecosystem by investigating *Prairie Dog Town* on the **Harcourt Science Explorations CD-ROM.**

LESSON **3**

How Do Organisms Compete and Survive in an Ecosystem?

In this lesson, you can . . .

INVESTIGATE how body color helps animals survive.

LEARN ABOUT the ways in which organisms compete.

LINK to math, writing, literature, and technology.

INVESTIGATE

Body Color

Activity Purpose An animal's physical characteristics, such as its body color, may give it a better chance of survival. For example, the body colors of many animals blend with their background. A green grasshopper in a grassy field may be nearly invisible to hungry snakes. In this investigation you will **gather data** and then **infer** how body color can help animals survive.

Materials

- colored acetate sheets: red, blue, green, yellow
- hole punch
- large green cloth
- clock with second hand

Activity Procedure

1 Copy the table on page A81. Use the hole punch to make 50 pieces from each of the acetate sheets. These colored acetate pieces will stand for insects that a bird is hunting. (Picture A)

2 **Predict** which color would be the easiest to find in grass. Predict which would be the hardest to find. **Record** and justify your predictions.

3 Spread the cloth on the floor. Your teacher will randomly scatter the acetate "insects" over the cloth.

◄ Rattlesnakes eat kangaroo rats, limiting the size of the rat population in this desert ecosystem.

Number of Insects Found

	Red	Blue	Green	Yellow
Hunt 1				
Hunt 2				
Hunt 3				
Total				

Picture A

4 Each member of the group should kneel at the edge of the cloth. You will each try to pick up as many colored acetate "insects" as you can in 15 seconds. You must pick them up one at a time. (Picture B)

5 Total the number of acetate pieces of each color your group collected. **Record** the data in the table.

6 Put aside the "insects" you collected. Repeat Step 4 two more times. After each 15-second "hunt," **record** the number of acetate pieces of each color your group collected. After the third hunt, total each column.

Picture B

Draw Conclusions

1. Look at the data you **recorded** for each hunt. What color of acetate was collected least? Were the results of each hunt the same, or were they different? Explain.

2. **Compare** the results with what you **predicted**. Do the results match your prediction? Explain.

3. **Scientists at Work** Scientists often **gather data** before they **infer** a relationship between things. Based on the data you gathered, what can you infer about the survival chances of brown-colored insects in areas where grasses and leaves turn brown in the fall?

Investigate Further Many insects have a body shape that allows them to blend in with their background. **Hypothesize** about what body shape might help an insect hide in a dead tree. Then **plan and conduct a simple investigation** to test your hypothesis. Include multiple trials in your plan.

Process Skill Tip

You can better **infer** relationships between things after you **gather data**. When scientists infer a relationship, they often conduct another experiment to gather more data.

Ways in Which Organisms Compete

Competition for Limited Resources

FIND OUT

- **how organisms compete for and share resources**
- **what symbiosis is**
- **how instincts and learned behaviors help animals survive**

VOCABULARY

competition
symbiosis

Food is a resource, and animals have different ways of getting resources. Because most ecosystems have limited supplies of resources, there may be **competition**, or a contest, among organisms for these resources.

All organisms in a community compete in some way for resources. In the investigation you saw that body color may help some animals survive by making them nearly invisible to *predators*—animals that hunt them. Other animals use patterns of body color, or *camouflage* (KAM•uh•flahzh), to sneak up on *prey*—animals they hunt. Camouflage helps these animals compete for limited food resources. Animals also compete for water and shelter. Plants compete for water and sunlight.

Deer compete with each other for food, especially in winter.

Moray eels compete for shelter— a hole in a coral reef.

In dry months, fish compete for water in a swamp "gator hole."

A82

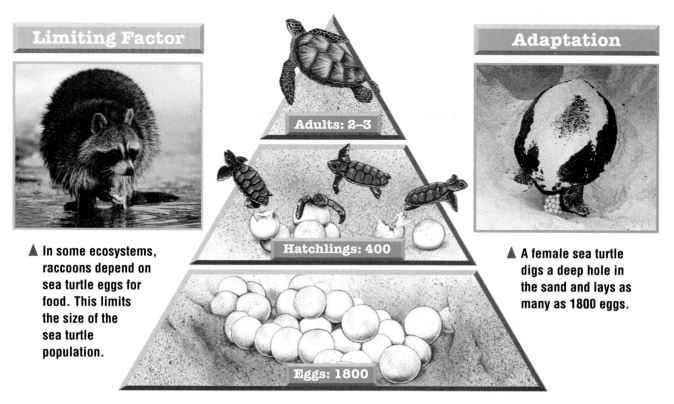

Limiting Factor

▲ In some ecosystems, raccoons depend on sea turtle eggs for food. This limits the size of the sea turtle population.

Adults: 2–3

Hatchlings: 400

Eggs: 1800

Adaptation

▲ A female sea turtle digs a deep hole in the sand and lays as many as 1800 eggs.

▲ For every 1800 sea turtle eggs that are laid, only 400 will hatch. Only 2 or 3 of the hatchlings will live to become adults.

Every organism has adaptations that help it compete for resources. For example, a cheetah's speed allows it to hunt and capture prey such as zebras and antelopes. Yet cheetahs, too, are limited by competition. Hyenas hunt prey in large packs. A pack of hyenas may chase away a single cheetah feeding on a zebra and then eat the zebra themselves. This adaptation—hunting in packs—helps hyenas compete with cheetahs.

If an organism competes successfully for resources, it is more likely to survive and reproduce. However, a balance usually exists between competing organisms, such as cheetahs and hyenas. Both compete for the same food resource, but each animal wins the contest often enough to survive.

✔ **What are two resources that organisms may compete for?**

Sharing Resources

Sea turtle eggs provide food for raccoons, while newly hatched sea turtles provide food for shorebirds. Although they share a resource, raccoons and shorebirds have different niches in the community.

In some communities animals live together and share resources. For example, many different herbivores eat the plants growing on the African plains. Giraffes eat from the higher branches of trees, antelopes eat from the middle branches, and rhinos eat from the lower branches.

At the same time, zebras and several other kinds of animals graze on the grasses. The reason the animals can all feed together is that they do not directly compete with each other. During a drought, when food is scarce, some animals will have to find other food supplies, or many will die.

Some trees provide food for several kinds of birds. All the birds eat insects, but in different parts of the tree.

The Blackburnian warbler spends more than half its feeding time eating insects at the top of the tree.

The bay-breasted warbler eats insects from the middle of the tree.

Myrtle warblers also eat insects. But they feed near the bottom of the tree.

Resources are shared in many ecosystems, including those in your own neighborhood. A single tree may be a habitat for hundreds of animals. Some animals, such as insects, may eat the leaves or bark of the tree, or they may lay their eggs in or on the tree. Birds may nest near the middle of the tree and eat the insects.

The tree at the left has three different kinds of warblers. Although the birds all feed on insects, they don't compete with each other for food. One kind of warbler feeds only in the top of the tree, while another feeds mainly in the middle branches. The third warbler feeds in the lower branches and along the tree's trunk.

In addition to the warblers, many other animals may find niches in the tree. Owls may sleep all day in the tree's upper branches and then sit on those same branches at night to watch for prey in a nearby field. Woodpeckers looking for insects may make holes in the tree's trunk. Then a squirrel may fill the holes with seeds or pine cones as part of its winter food supply. All of these animals share one resource, the tree, which provides them with food and shelter.

✔ **Why don't warblers compete for food, even though they all eat insects in the same tree?**

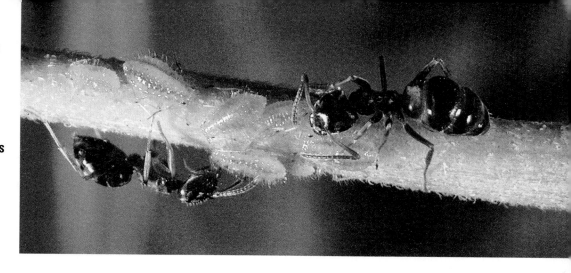

Ants herd aphids to fresh leaves where the aphids can feed and the ants can defend them against predators. When an ant rubs an aphid with its antennae, the aphid gives off a sweet juice that the ant eats. ▶

Symbiosis

Different kinds of organisms often live closely together for most or all of their lives. A long-term relationship between different kinds of organisms is called **symbiosis** (sim•bee•OH•suhs).

Symbiosis may benefit both organisms, or it may benefit one organism but not the other. A relationship where both organisms benefit is called *mutualism*. For example, bacteria live inside termites. The bacteria help the termite digest wood. The benefit is mutual. The termites get nutrients and the bacteria get food and shelter.

The relationship between flowers and bees is also an example of mutualism. Flowers produce nectar that bees eat. While the bees feed on the nectar, they pollinate the flowers.

One kind of African tree is protected by a mutual relationship with stinging ants. The ants live in the tree's large, hollow thorns and eat a sweet liquid the tree produces. Whenever another animal lands on or brushes up against the tree, the ants attack and often can sting the invader to death. The tree provides the ants with food and shelter, while the ants protect the tree.

✔ **What is symbiosis?**

◀ Many kinds of coral live in symbiosis with tiny, one-celled yellow-brown algae. The corals get photosynthesis products from the algae. From the corals, the algae get shelter and access to sunlight. Corals without beneficial algae usually grow too slowly to build large reefs.

Parasitism

Another type of symbiosis is *parasitism* (PAIR•uh•suh•tih•zuhm). In parasitism, one organism gains energy at the expense of the other. The organism that benefits is called a *parasite* (PAIR•uh•syt), and the other organism is called the *host*. Mosquitoes and ticks are common parasites. They feed on blood from warm-blooded animals, such as birds, deer, and people. Usually, a parasite harms its host. Some parasites eventually kill their hosts.

Parasites have body-part adaptations for feeding on other living things. Female mosquitoes have needlelike mouth parts for drilling through skin and sucking blood. In fact, these mouth parts are so small and sharp that you may not notice a bite until it starts to itch.

Sea lampreys are snakelike parasite fish that feed on saltwater fish and animals. First, a lamprey attaches itself to a fish by means of a sucker. Then it rasps a hole in the fish's skin or scales to feed on the fish's blood and other body fluids. This feeding just weakens larger fish, such as sharks, but it can kill smaller fish and animals.

There are also plant parasites. Mistletoe is a plant parasite that grows high up in trees. Its leaves carry out photosynthesis as the leaves of other plants do. However, it uses its roots to draw nutrients from the host tree, not from the soil.

✓ **What is the symbiotic relationship between a parasite and its host?**

▲ **Mistletoe forms a globe-shaped mass of leaves in an oak tree.**

This lamprey is feeding on a carp. ▼

▲ This mosquito is drawing blood from its host.

Summary

Organisms may compete for limited resources in an ecosystem. The sizes of certain populations are limited by the amount of resources available. Sometimes organisms share resources, and sometimes they form relationships with other organisms.

Review

1. Why does a female sea turtle lay more than a thousand eggs at a time?
2. How might the number of oak trees in a park affect the number of squirrels that can live there?
3. What resources are sometimes shared by squirrels and certain birds?
4. **Critical Thinking** Why do you think parasites rarely kill their hosts quickly?
5. Which of the following would **NOT** limit a population of squirrels?

   A hawk population
   B number of acorns
   C grass height
   D available water

LINKS

MATH LINK

Interpreting Tables Look at the table. By how much did the population grow between 1650 and 1850? By how much might it grow between 1850 and 2050?

Year	Human Population
1650	0.5 billion
1850	1 billion
1930	2 billion
1980	4.5 billion
2050	14 billion (projected)

WRITING LINK

Expressive Writing—Poem Choose an animal you are familiar with, and write a poem about it for your class. Moving from head to tail, begin each line of the poem with the name of a body part of that animal. Then describe how the part helps the animal survive.

LITERATURE LINK

What Do You Do When Something Wants to Eat You? by Steven Jenkins (Houghton Mifflin, 1998) describes how behaviors help animals survive. Read and share with your class what you learn.

TECHNOLOGY LINK

Learn more about animal relationships by visiting the Harcourt Learning Site.
www.harcourtschool.com/ca

WELCOME TO THE LEARNING SITE

LESSON 4

What Is Extinction and What Are Its Causes?

In this lesson, you can . . .

INVESTIGATE
vanishing habitats.

LEARN ABOUT
extinction and its causes.

LINK to math, writing, literature, and technology.

◄ Hunting and habitat destruction have almost caused the extinction of wolves in the United States.

INVESTIGATE

Vanishing Habitats

Activity Purpose Changing conditions in an ecosystem may cause problems for plants and animals. Populations may decline, or become smaller. They may even disappear. In this investigation you will **use numbers** to **infer** how loss of habitat could lead to the decline of animal populations in a South American rain forest.

Materials

- globe or world map
- calculator
- graph paper
- graphing calculator or computer (optional)

Rain Forest Area and Human Population in Ecuador				
Year	1961	1971	1981	1991
Rain Forest (square km)	173,000	153,000	No data	112,000
Population (in millions)	5.162	7.035	No data	10.782

Activity Procedure

1 Locate Ecuador, a country in South America, on the globe or world map. (Picture A)

2 Study the table above. It shows the size of Ecuador's rain forests and the size of its human population between 1961 and 1991.

3 **Calculate** and **record** the changes in rain-forest area for each of the periods shown (1961–1971 and 1971–1991). Then calculate and record the changes in the population size for the same periods.

Picture A

Picture B

4 Using graph paper and a pencil, a graphing calculator, or a computer, make a double-bar graph that shows changes in forest area and population size for these periods. (Picture B)

Draw Conclusions

1. **Compare** the two sets of data in the double-bar graph. What relationship, if any, do you **observe** between the growth of the human population and the amount of rain forest in Ecuador?

2. Based on the **data collected**, what can you **infer** about the size of Ecuador's human population and the area of its rain forests in 1981?

3. According to the data, what do you **predict** the size of the rain forests in Ecuador will be in 2001 if the human population increases at the same rate as it has in the past?

4. **Scientists at Work** Scientists often **interpret data** to help them **infer** what may happen. If the size of the rain-forest habitat keeps getting smaller, what can you infer about the populations of animals that live there?

Investigate Further Research the changes in the size of the human population over several decades in your area. Then make a graph of the changes. **Infer** how these changes in the human population might have affected animal populations in your area.

Process Skill Tip

Interpreting data about changes in habitat size can help you **infer** what effects these changes might have on populations living there.

Extinction and Its Causes

Population Decline

FIND OUT

- how changes in the environment may lead to the decline or extinction of populations
- how humans can help endangered populations

VOCABULARY

extinct
endangered
threatened

You observed in the investigation how an increase in human population may be related to a decrease in the size of an ecosystem. Loss of habitat causes a decline in population numbers of many organisms in a community.

Most declines in populations are caused by human activity. In the United States, hunting led to declines in the populations of bison, alligators, and wolves. Importing nonnative, or *exotic,* organisms into the country has brought in diseases that kill native populations. Building new roads, homes, and businesses also reduces the size of natural habitats, causing declines in many populations.

Natural events that change the environment—such as floods, fires, or droughts—also cause populations to decline. An erupting volcano or a strong hurricane may destroy habitats. A drought may kill producers in a food chain, which then causes consumer populations to decline. However, most natural changes are temporary, and healthy populations usually survive. But that is often not the case with changes caused by human activity.

✓ **Give two reasons why populations decline.**

Ivory is prized in many parts of the world. Even though selling ivory is illegal in every country, some people still kill elephants for their ivory tusks, shown at the right. ▼

◄ The government of China has set aside a protected habitat for pandas. This hasn't totally solved the problem, however, since pandas need a large habitat to survive.

Extinction Is Forever

A population of organisms can survive only if there are enough individuals to produce healthy offspring. If there are fewer than 50 individuals, the population is not likely to survive. As a result, some organisms become **extinct**. That is, the last individual in the population dies, and the organism is gone forever.

A number of natural processes cause extinction. Through all of Earth's history, disasters have resulted in the extinction of organisms. The extinction of dinosaurs is probably the best-known example. Natural processes usually cause the extinction of several species every thousand years or so. Today, however, habitat destruction causes the rate of extinction to be about 1000 times faster than normal. Scientists know of at least 50 kinds of birds and 75 kinds of mammals that have become extinct in the past 200 years.

Island organisms are especially in danger of extinction. If an organism lives only on one island, any change to its habitat may cause the organism to die out.

Organisms that have populations spread out over several areas have a better chance of avoiding extinction. Because of the islands' distance from other land areas, more species have become extinct in Hawai'i than in any other state.

For decades people in the United States have been working to reduce extinction. In 1973 Congress passed the Endangered Species Act. The act lists organisms according to how small their populations are.

Organisms listed as **endangered** have populations so small that they are likely to become extinct if steps to save them aren't taken right away. Places like state and national wildlife refuges protect endangered birds, mammals, reptiles, coral reefs, and plants.

Organisms listed as **threatened** are likely to become endangered if they are not protected. Threatened organisms, such as alligators, are protected by strict hunting laws. And some threatened organisms, such as bison, have been brought back into areas where there were once large populations.

✔ **What is the biggest cause of extinction today?**

Extinct, Endangered, and Threatened Animals of the United States

Extinct	Endangered	Threatened
Caribbean monk seal	Jaguarundi	American alligator
Mexican grizzly bear	Ridley's sea turtle	Bald eagle
Passenger pigeon	Florida manatee	California sea otter
Steller's sea cow	Mexican wolf	Peregrine falcon
Carolina parakeet	Whooping crane	Brown pelican
Tacoma pocket gopher	Florida panther	American bison
Arizona cotton rat	American crocodile	Spotted owl
Kansas bog lemming	California condor	Sandhill crane

In the 1800s there were billions of passenger pigeons in the United States. On September 1, 1914, the last one, named Martha, died at the Cincinnati Zoo in Ohio. ►

Success Stories

During the 1940s people began using a poison called DDT to kill insects. It had many harmful effects on the environment that lasted a long time. One effect was the weakening of bald eagles' eggshells. Fewer and fewer offspring hatched, and the bald eagle population began to decline. Bald eagles were listed as endangered in the 1960s. In 1972 the Environmental Protection Agency made the use of DDT illegal. Scientists began raising bald eagles in captivity and releasing them back into the wild. Others worked to save and improve the habitats of bald eagles. Slowly, over many years, the bald eagle population has increased. Although still threatened, the bird that is our national symbol is no longer endangered.

In 1998 another endangered bird, the peregrine falcon, was removed from the endangered list. Like the bald eagle, the peregrine falcon population also declined as a result of DDT use. The falcon was listed as endangered in 1970. By 1975 there were only 324 pairs in the entire country. A program of saving and restoring habitats began. Today there are more than 1600 pairs of peregrine falcons in the wild.

A species that may or may not escape extinction is the California condor. The condor is a large scavenger whose natural habitat is open, hilly areas of southern California. In 1982, when scientists began breeding condors in captivity, only 30 birds were known to exist in the wild. Captive breeding is difficult, but some chicks hatched, grew to adulthood, and were released into the wild. Scientists still aren't sure if the California condor population will recover in its few remaining habitats near the crowded cities of Los Angeles and San Diego.

✔ **What two birds were successfully removed from the endangered list?**

◄ California condor chicks are cared for with a hand puppet that looks like a condor. This helps chicks learn to recognize and trust their own kind instead of humans.

◄ California condors weigh as much as 45 kg (about 100 lb) and have wing-spans of about 3 m (10 ft).

Summary

When the last individual dies, an organism is extinct. Extinction occurs naturally, but certain human activities result in a high rate of extinction among the world's plants and animals. An organism is endangered or threatened when its population is too small. People have saved some organisms from extinction.

Review

1. Name a natural cause of decline in a population.
2. How is a threatened organism different from an endangered one?
3. How many living individuals are there in a population that is extinct?
4. **Critical Thinking** Think of an animal or plant in your state. What changes in the environment could cause it to become threatened or endangered? Give specific examples.
5. **Test Prep** It is impossible for an endangered organism to recover if —
   A its habitat is restored
   B its population is too small
   C hunting is stopped
   D it is bred in captivity

LINKS

MATH LINK

Estimate When peregrine falcons were first listed as endangered in 1975, there were about 325 pairs in the United States. When the birds were removed from the endangered list in 1998, there were about 1600 pairs. Estimate how many times more peregrine falcon breeding pairs there were in 1998 than in 1975.

WRITING LINK

Persuasive Writing—Opinion Should endangered organisms be protected? Are some organisms more important than others? Write an essay giving your opinion on this subject.

LITERATURE LINK

There's Still Time: The Success of the Endangered Species Act by Mark Galan (National Geographic, 1998) and *Back to the Wild* by Dorothy H. Patent (Gulliver, 1998) are two interesting and informative books about endangered organisms. Read one of these books. Then tell your classmates about it.

TECHNOLOGY LINK

Learn more about saving endangered animals by viewing *Yellowstone Wolves* on the **Harcourt Science Newsroom Video** in your classroom video library.

THE NEW ZOOS

What if you were well fed and had a comfortable home but had nothing to do all day? At first you might really enjoy it, but pretty soon you would get bored. Zoo animals get bored, too, and often they show it. The big cats pace back and forth, and the chimps just loaf around, picking at their food and watching the people.

"Natural" Environments

Zoo animals need enriched environments that not only imitate their natural habitats but also give them the chance to behave as they would in the wild. Animal experts have come up with some clever ideas for keeping zoo animals happier and, as a result, healthier.

In the wild, chimpanzees use twigs to pry termites out of mounds. So the Lowry Park Zoo in Tampa, Florida, built their chimps some artificial termite mounds and filled them with honey and jelly. The chimps spend hours using twigs to scoop out their treats.

On African savannas, giraffes walk many miles each day to find baobab leaves to eat. At Disney's Animal Kingdom in Orlando, Florida, an imaginative system of mechanical baobab trees keeps the animals

This chimp is using a twig as a tool to get insects out of this tree.

This polar bear needs a big pool to stay healthy.

moving. Artificial branches with real leaves spring out of a tree trunk, and the giraffes walk to them to eat. An hour later a branch pops out of another tree some distance away, and the giraffes are on the move again.

Since lions are hunters, the Animal Kingdom freezes large chunks of meat inside blocks of ice. When a lion pounces on its "prey," the slippery ice block shoots away, and the lion has to chase it down.

Enriched Play

At the Central Park Zoo in New York, Gus the polar bear now swims in a bigger pool. Zoo officials also added some big plastic floats that look like icebergs for Gus to climb on. The floats are always moving because Gus makes waves when he swims, so the bear's environment keeps changing, too.

Orangutans at the National Zoo in Washington, D.C., travel hand over hand just as they do through the trees in the rain forest. Surprisingly, they swing directly over visitors' heads on thick cables 13.5 m (about 45 ft) up in the air. The apes are free to come and go as they please from the Ape House. They cross the open space above a visitors'

walkway on their way to a new play center called the Think Tank.

In the enriched environments of these zoos, animals behave more as they would in the wild. Experts hope that more zoos will develop ways to enrich their environments to keep their animals alert, healthy, and happy.

THINK ABOUT IT

1. How do the new zoo environments help meet animals' needs?
2. Suppose you ran a zoo. Make a list of some ways you would keep the animals happy and healthy. Be creative!

WEB LINK:
For science and technology updates, visit The Learning Site.
www.harcourtschool.com/ca

Careers   Zoo Guide

What They Do Zoo guides take visitors on tours and may also work in school outreach programs. Some guides may also help in the gift shop or with animal care and grounds work.

Education and Training People wishing to be zoo guides need at least a high school diploma and should have taken courses in biology and other sciences. Zoos provide more training in working with the animals, leading tours, and keeping visitors safe.

Dorothy McClendon
MICROBIOLOGIST

Dorothy McClendon works for the U.S. Army Tank Automotive Command (TACOM) in Warren, Michigan. She's not a soldier, however. She's a microbiologist. A microbiologist studies microorganisms—living things too small to be seen without a microscope—such as fungi and bacteria.

Most microorganisms do not cause disease. In fact, many are harmless or even beneficial. For example, they are found in the digestive systems of most animals, including humans. People have learned how to make microorganisms work for them in many ways, such as in making cheese and in cleaning up oil spills. However, microorganisms can also be harmful to humans. Some cause disease. Others cause foods to spoil and materials to decay.

Ms. McClendon is a specialist known as an industrial microbiologist. She is in charge of research on microorganisms for the army. Her job is to develop ways to keep microorganisms from breaking down fuel oil and other materials

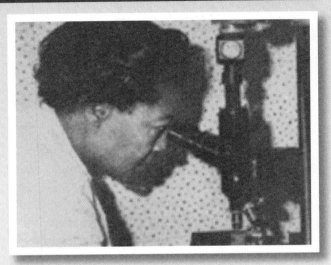

the army stores. She is now working on the development of a new fungicide, a chemical that will kill fungi. It must do the job without being harmful to people.

Ms. McClendon was born in Louisiana and moved to Detroit, Michigan, where she became interested in science as a student in high school. She went on to major in biology in college and took advanced science courses at several universities. Before becoming a microbiologist, she was a teacher in Arizona and Arkansas.

THINK ABOUT IT

1. How are some microorganisms harmful to humans?
2. Why might it be difficult to develop a chemical that kills fungi but doesn't harm humans?

A microscopic fungus

Feast on This!

How does an animal's diet affect the environment?

Materials

- sanitized owl pellet
- forceps
- toothpicks
- hand lens
- black paper
- glue

Procedure

1 Use the forceps and toothpicks to separate the materials in the owl pellet.

2 Sort the materials. Group together bones that look the same.

3 Reconstruct the skeletons on the black paper. When you are satisfied that all the bones are arranged correctly, glue the skeletons to the paper.

Draw Conclusions

How many skeletons did you find in the pellet? If an owl throws up one pellet a day, how many animals does the owl eat in a year? If all the owls were removed from an ecosystem, what would happen to the population of prey animals?

Pyramids

Is lunch like an energy pyramid?

Materials

- food-guide pyramid
- energy pyramid

Procedure

1 Put the food-guide pyramid next to the energy pyramid. Compare them.

2 Look at today's menu from the school cafeteria. See if it also makes a pyramid according to the recommendations of the food-guide pyramid.

Draw Conclusions

How are the energy pyramid and the food-guide pyramid alike? Does the cafeteria menu meet the recommendations of the food-guide pyramid? What level consumers are people?

Chapter 3 Review and Test Preparation

Vocabulary Review

Use the terms below to complete the sentences. The page numbers in ( ) tell you where to look in the chapter if you need help.

individual (A68)
population (A68)
community (A68)
ecosystem (A68)
habitat (A69)
producers (A74)
extinct (A91)
endangered (A91)
threatened (A91)

food web (A76)
energy pyramid (A78)
competition (A82)
symbiosis (A85)
niche (A69)
consumers (A74)
food chain (A75)
decomposers (A75)

1. Green plants are ____, or organisms that make their own food.

2. A ____ is the role a population has in its habitat.

3. Dead organisms are broken down by ____.

4. An ____ is a single member of a ____.

5. A population that begins to decline may be listed as ____.

6. An organism is ____ when all individuals are dead.

7. A ____ consists of all the populations of organisms in an ____.

8. A ____ shows the feeding relationships among food chains.

9. Organisms take part in ____ for the limited amount of resources in an ecosystem.

10. An ____ shows the amount of energy available at each level of a food chain.

11. Different kinds of organisms sharing a long-term, close relationship is called ____.

12. Organisms that eat other living things to survive are called ____.

13. Producers will always be the first organisms in any ____.

14. An ____ organism, such as a California condor, is at risk of becoming extinct.

15. The prairie is a ____ for animals such as snakes, hawks, bison, and mice.

Connect Concepts

Put the letter of each organism in the correct level of the Energy Pyramid.

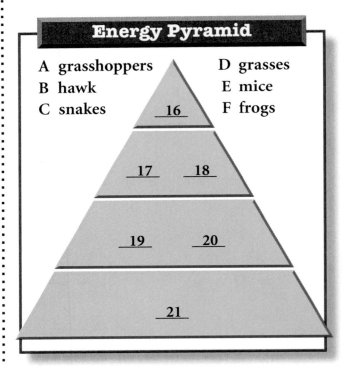

Energy Pyramid

A grasshoppers
B hawk
C snakes
D grasses
E mice
F frogs

16
17   18
19   20
21

Check Understanding

22. When a large volcano erupts, tons of dark ash often stay in the sky for months. If the ash blocks enough sunlight, producers will not be able to —
  A decompose dead organisms
  B perform photosynthesis
  C prey on consumers
  D none of the above

23. Habitat destruction is a major cause of —
  F extinction   H instinct
  G competition   J symbiosis

24. Organisms at the top of a food chain are predators and —
  A producers   C first-level consumers
  B herbivores   D carnivores

25. The oxpecker bird stands on the back of an ox and eats insects off the ox's back. Both the bird and the ox benefit. This relationship is called —
  F competition
  G learned behavior
  H parasitism
  J mutualism

26. If humans do not help endangered populations, the organisms are likely to become —
  A instinct   C threatened
  B extinct   D communities

Critical Thinking

27. Some people place bird feeders in their yards. What effect do you think this has on the bird populations of the local ecosystem?

28. What would be the effect of destroying most or all of the plants in an ecosystem?

29. Why do you think the rate of extinction in an ecosystem is important to other organisms in the ecosystem, including people?

Process Skills Review

30. Wildlife experts know that wolves hunt and eat elk. What would wildlife experts **predict** about the elk population of Yellowstone National Park if all the wolves were killed? Explain.

31. Terns are shorebirds. When one tern's nest is attacked, all the terns in the area gather together and fight the predator. What can you **infer** about how this behavior helps terns survive?

32. A sundew is a green plant that traps and digests live insects. Do you think scientists would **classify** this plant as a consumer or as a producer? Explain.

Performance Assessment

Lunch Line

Choose one kind of food you like to eat, for example, cheeseburgers or pizza. On a sheet of paper, trace each ingredient in the food back to its source. Then make a poster that shows where the ingredients come from.

Biomes

You probably know that part of this country is desert, part is grassland, and part is forest. And you probably know that these areas normally aren't mixed together. Each area developed where favorable conditions for it existed.

Vocabulary Preview

biome
climate zone
intertidal zone
near-shore zone
open-ocean zone
estuary

≡*FAST* FACT

Wheat is the most important food crop of the grasslands. If all the wheat produced in the world were put into freight cars, the train would be more than 160,900 km (about 100,000 mi) long.

FAST FACT

A doubling of the human population requires a doubling of food production. It took 80 years for the human population to double from 1 billion to 2 billion. It took 45 years for the population to double from 2 billion to 4 billion. From the table, when do you infer the population will reach 8 billion?

Earth's Population	
Year	Number of People
10,000 B.C.	3,000,000
8000 B.C.	5,000,000
A.D. 1	200,000,000
1650	500,000,000
1850	1,000,000,000
1930	2,000,000,000
1975	4,000,000,000
2000	6,000,000,000

FAST FACT

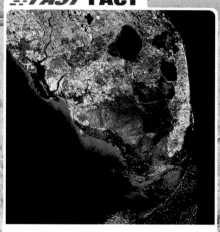

Landsat satellites are used to make maps like this one of south Florida. Scanners on these satellites measure wavelengths of reflected sunlight. This helps scientists identify water, soil, rock, and plants in the area mapped. Landsat maps also help people decide the best way to use the mapped land.

What Are Land Biomes?

In this lesson, you can . . .

INVESTIGATE biomes and climates.

LEARN ABOUT Earth's biomes.

LINK to math, writing, social studies, and technology.

Biosphere 2, near Tucson, Arizona, is a research center in which scientists have modeled several North American biomes. ▼

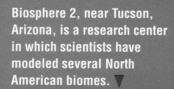

INVESTIGATE

Biomes and Climates

Activity Purpose   The plants and animals where you live are adapted to live there. In North America there are six large-scale ecosystems called *biomes*. Each biome has characteristic plants and animals adapted to conditions there. In this investigation you will prepare one map of North American biomes and one of North American *climate zones*.

Climate zones are areas in which the long-term weather patterns are similar. Then you will **compare** the maps and **draw conclusions** about relationships between biomes and climate zones.

Materials

- map of North American climate zones
- map of North American biomes
- markers or colored pencils

Activity Procedure

1 On the map of North American climate zones, color the different climates as shown in the first chart on page A103. (Picture A)

2 On the map of North American biomes, color the biomes as shown in the second chart on page A103.

3 **Compare** the green areas on the two maps. How does the area with a warm, wet climate compare to the area of tropical rain forest? Compare other biomes and climate zones that are colored alike.

Picture A

North American Climate Zones		
Area	**Climate**	**Color**
1	More than 250 cm rain; warm all year	green
2	75–250 cm rain or snow; warm summer, cold winter	purple
3	20–60 cm rain or snow; cool summer, cold winter	blue
4	10–40 cm rain or snow; warm summer, cold winter	orange
5	Less than 10 cm rain; hot summer, cool winter	yellow
6	250 cm snow (25 cm rain); cold all year	brown

Draw Conclusions

1. How do areas on the climate map **compare** to areas shown in the same color on the biome map?

2. **Observe** the maps. If an area is too wet to be a desert but too dry to be a forest, what biome would you expect to find there?

3. **Order** the biomes from wettest to driest.

4. **Scientists at Work** When scientists **compare** sets of data, they can **draw conclusions** about relationships between the data sets. Conifers are the dominant plants of the taiga. Broad-leaved trees are the dominant plants of the deciduous forest. What conclusions can you draw about the water needs of conifers compared to those of broad-leaved trees?

Investigate Further Use a computer to make a chart showing the climates of the six biomes and a map combining climate zones and biomes.

North American Biomes		
Area	**Biome**	**Color**
A	Tropical rain forest	green
B	Deciduous forest	purple
C	Taiga	blue
D	Grassland	orange
E	Desert	yellow
F	Tundra	brown

Process Skill Tip

When scientists **compare** two different sets of data, they can sometimes find relationships between the data sets.

Land Biomes

Earth's Biomes

FIND OUT

- about the Earth's biomes

- what determines the organisms of a biome

- how plants and animals are adapted to living in a biome

VOCABULARY

biome
climate zone

Suppose you suddenly found yourself in a region far from your home. The first thing you would probably be aware of is the weather. Is it hotter or colder than where you live? Is it wetter or drier? Later you might be aware of the plant and animal life. How is it different from the plant and animal life in your region?

You would be in a new biome. A **biome** is a large-scale ecosystem. Its climate and the plants and animals adapted to living in that climate are what make it different from other biomes. As you saw in the investigation, biomes roughly match up with climate zones. A **climate zone** is a region in which yearly patterns of temperature, rainfall, and the amount of sunlight are

The photographs show a little bit of each biome.

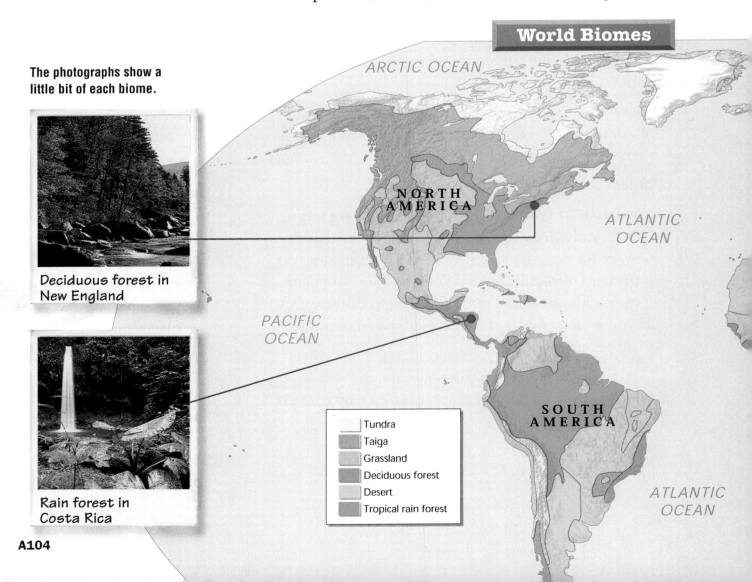

Deciduous forest in New England

Rain forest in Costa Rica

World Biomes

ARCTIC OCEAN

NORTH AMERICA

ATLANTIC OCEAN

PACIFIC OCEAN

SOUTH AMERICA

ATLANTIC OCEAN

	Tundra
	Taiga
	Grassland
	Deciduous forest
	Desert
	Tropical rain forest

A104

similar throughout. Wind patterns, land-forms, and closeness to large bodies of water help determine climate zones.

Earth has six major types of biomes: tropical rain forest, deciduous forest, grassland, desert, taiga (TY•guh), and tundra. Each type of biome occurs in several places on Earth. For example, North America, South America, Africa, Asia, and Australia all have desert biomes. All plants and animals that live in deserts have adaptations for living in dry climates. However, a certain organism may live only in a particular desert biome. For instance, lizards live in both Australian and North American deserts. But the collared lizard lives only in North America, while the frilled lizard lives only in Australia.

Differences also occur within biomes. All the plants and animals living in a biome may have similar adaptations for the climate of that biome. But different areas of the biome may have different plants and animals. One reason for these differences is that climate is not the only factor that affects what lives in a certain place. The type of soil, for example, helps determine which plants will grow well. The plant life, in turn, helps determine the kinds of animals that can live there.

✔ **What biome do you live in?**

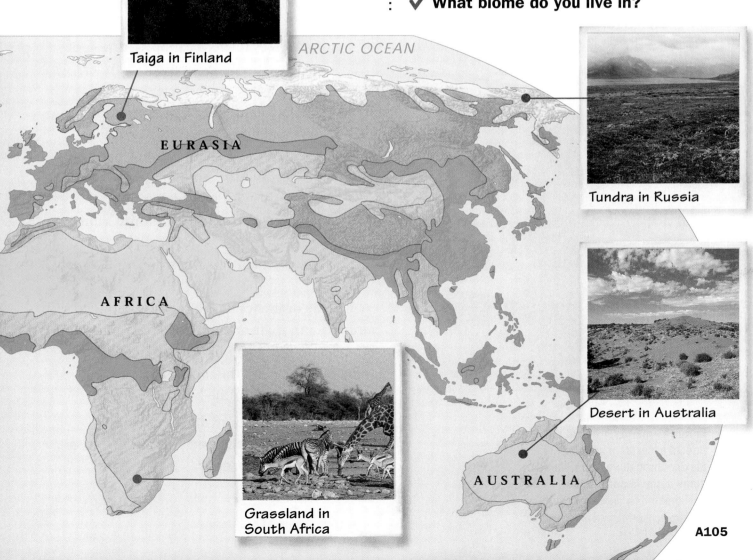

Taiga in Finland

ARCTIC OCEAN

EURASIA

AFRICA

Tundra in Russia

Desert in Australia

AUSTRALIA

Grassland in
South Africa

A105

Tropical Rain Forests

You can get an idea of what it feels like to be in a tropical rain forest by walking through a greenhouse. Tropical rain forests are found near the equator. There, Earth receives direct sunlight most of the year, so temperatures are always warm. The climate of tropical rain forests is also very wet. It rains almost every day.

The strong sunlight and warm, wet climate provide ideal growing conditions for a variety of plants. Tropical rain forests have about half of all the different kinds of plants on Earth. This amazing diversity, or variety, of life is one of the characteristics of tropical rain forests.

Producers in a rain forest are found in three layers. The tallest trees form the upper layer. Slightly lower, a second layer of trees forms a canopy, or roof, of leaves and tree branches. Under the canopy are a few shorter trees and many vines, orchids, and ferns. Very few plants live on the rain-forest floor because very little sunlight gets down through the thick canopy.

A tropical rain forest's animal life is just as diverse as its plant life. Many animals spend most of their lives in the branches of the canopy. Reptiles, amphibians, mammals, insects, fish, and birds all do well in a rain forest. The food webs they form are the most varied and complicated of all of the biomes.

✔ **What factors contribute to the diversity of plant and animal life in a tropical rain forest?**

Tucanette

In North America, tropical rain forests occur from southern Mexico through Panama, on many of the islands in the Caribbean Sea, and in Hawai'i.

Deciduous Forests

The forests of New England are famous for their autumn colors. The leaves of many trees turn red, orange, and yellow before they drop. These broad-leaved trees are deciduous—they shed their leaves each year. They are the dominant plants in deciduous forests. This biome occurs where there are moderate temperatures and moderate amounts of rainfall. Every continent except Africa and Antarctica has deciduous forests.

The varying amounts of sunlight Earth's surface receives at different times of the year cause changes of seasons in deciduous forests. The seasonal changes, in turn, cause a yearly cycle of plant growth. Warm temperatures in the spring and summer allow plants to grow and bloom. During the winter, temperatures often fall below freezing. The growing season in deciduous forests lasts about six months.

Several layers of plants can be found in deciduous forests. The tallest trees—oaks, maples, and hickories—form a thin canopy of leaves. Unlike the tropical rain forest, the deciduous forest lets enough sunlight get through the canopy to allow a layer of small trees and shrubs. Mosses, lichens, and ferns grow beneath the shrubs.

The different layers of plants provide a variety of habitats for animals. Many species of insects and birds live in the canopy. Rabbits, skunks, deer, and chipmunks are plant eaters of the forest floor. Toads, salamanders, and snakes also live on the forest floor. Foxes, coyotes, hawks, and a few other small carnivores prey on the herbivores.

✔ **What characteristic of deciduous forest trees is most obvious?**

Whitetail deer

Deciduous forests in North America occur mostly from southeastern Canada through the mountains of northern Georgia and west to the Mississippi River.

Grasslands

Imagine a sea of grass rippling in the wind like ocean waves. No matter which way you turn, you see tall grasses stretching away to the horizon. This is what you might see in the prairies, or grasslands, of North America. The temperatures are moderate, rainfall is light, and various grasses are the dominant plants. Grasslands are found on all continents except Antarctica.

Grasses have several adaptations that help them live without much rain. Their long, slender leaves allow little water loss. Their roots grow just below the surface of the soil, and they spread out to take in much of the rain that does fall. The few trees that grow in grasslands are usually found along streams and rivers, where they can get more water.

A number of small animals, such as rabbits, prairie dogs, gophers, badgers, rats, mice, snakes, and insects, live in grasslands. Herds of larger herbivores, such as deer, pronghorn, and bison, are also found in North American grasslands.

Grasslands play a major role in world agriculture. Thousands of farmers grow wheat, corn, rice, and other grains, all of which are types of grass. These grasses are used to make animal feed, bread, flour, and cereal. North American grasslands produce so much food that they are sometimes called the breadbasket of the world. Grasslands are also used to graze herds of livestock, such as cattle and sheep, which provide most of the animal products people eat.

✔ **How are grasses adapted to the grassland climate?**

Burrowing owl

North American grasslands stretch from central Canada through Texas and into Mexico.

Deserts

If you ever watch old westerns on TV, you know what a desert looks like. And if you visit the Sonoran Desert in Arizona, you will find that it's just as it looks in movies. The sun is always shining, it doesn't rain very often, and the soil and air are both very dry. Because deserts have little or no water, only a few kinds of plants can grow there.

Most deserts are very hot on summer days, but temperatures can drop below freezing on winter nights. Some deserts have no bodies of water at all. In others, streams or lakes form after a few heavy rainstorms, but they don't last long. All desert organisms have adaptations to extremes in temperature and very little water.

Desert plants have adaptations that help them conserve water. The cactus plants of North American deserts store water in their thick leaves or stems. Their roots lie close to the surface of the soil, so they can quickly absorb water from the occasional rains. Unlike the cactus, desert bushes such as the mesquite (mes•KEET) and the creosote (KREE•uh•soht) don't store water. Instead, their roots grow up to 15 m (about 50 ft) long to reach underground water.

Desert animals are also adapted to a dry climate. Reptiles, such as snakes and lizards, have tough, scaly skins that help prevent water loss. Some small mammals get all the water they need from the plants they eat. Most desert animals hide during the heat of the day. They come out to hunt for food at night, when it is cooler.

✔ **How are desert organisms adapted to a dry climate?**

Jackrabbit

Deserts in North America reach from the interior of southwestern Canada through northern Mexico.

Taiga

You can travel for miles in the taiga and see nothing but evergreen trees. The taiga is a forest of needle-leaved evergreens that extends in a broad belt across Eurasia and North America. Taiga winters are too long for most deciduous trees to survive. A few deciduous trees do grow in the taiga, but only around lakes and streams.

Evergreens, which include pines, firs, spruces, and hemlocks, are adapted to the taiga. The most important adaptation is their needlelike leaves. A waxy covering protects needles from the cold and limits the amount of water loss. And evergreens don't shed their needles all at once, so they can make food all year.

Unlike deciduous forests, the taiga has only two layers. The trees form an almost solid canopy. The forest floor is always covered with a thick mat of dead, dry needles. Even during a heavy rain, most water is caught and held in the canopy. Mosses and lichens are usually the only plants that grow below the canopy, either on the forest floor or on the trunks of the trees.

Insects, mammals, and birds all live in the taiga. The diversity of life, however, changes from season to season. Mosquito and fly populations increase during the summer months, and insect-eating birds return from the south. Owls, warblers, and woodpeckers live in the taiga year-round. Snowshoe hares, porcupines, and mice also live there year-round. Lynxes, weasels, and wolves prey on these other mammals. Bears may also live in the forest, eating nuts, leaves, and small animals.

✔ **Name two differences between deciduous forests and the taiga.**

Canada lynx

The taiga in North America stretches from Alaska across central Canada to the Atlantic Ocean.

Tundra

The tundra is a rolling plain that spreads across Greenland and the most northern areas of Eurasia and North America. It also covers the southern tip of South America and a small part of Antarctica.

Low temperatures and long winters in the tundra prevent trees from growing. Only smaller plants that send out roots in dense, shallow mats are able to survive on the tundra. Permafrost, a layer of permanently frozen soil just below the surface, is the reason larger plants cannot survive. In the spring, the surface of the ground above the permafrost begins to thaw. A few small plants grow in this layer of muddy, thawed ground. They grow low to the ground, away from the strong, drying winds.

The tundra is a region of dramatic seasonal changes. Because of its distance from the equator, the sun is rarely seen in the fall and winter. In most of the tundra, it disappears below the horizon in the fall and does not rise again for several months. Many animals, such as birds, caribou, and musk ox, migrate into the taiga for the winter. Animals that remain, like the arctic fox and arctic hare, have thick white coats that help them blend in with the snowy landscape.

In contrast, the sun shines all the time in summer. The constant light allows the tundra plants to sprout, grow, and bloom in only a few weeks. Herds of caribou and musk ox return to graze, and birds come back to their summer nesting grounds.

✔ **How are tundra plants adapted to the cold climate?**

Grizzly bear

In North America the tundra is limited to northern Alaska and Canada, and to the higher peaks of the Rocky Mountains.

A111

Comparing Biomes

Starting at the poles, as you move toward the equator, biomes occur in this order: tundra, taiga, deciduous forest, grassland or desert, and tropical rain forest.

Biomes are in this order because the corresponding climate zones occur in this order. At the equator the sun is directly overhead most of the year, and the number of hours of daylight varies only a little. Because the climate zone near the equator receives more solar energy than other zones, it is warmer. It is also wetter, so it provides a climate in which tropical rain forests can grow.

As you move from the equator toward the poles, each climate zone receives a little less energy from the sun. Near the poles, sunlight reaches Earth at a sharp angle during the summer. No sunlight reaches those areas during the winter. Since little solar energy is available in these cold climate zones, tundra develops.

In temperate climate zones, there are different biomes, depending on the amount of water available. Temperate zones near oceans or other large bodies of water may have enough moisture for deciduous forests, while temperate zones farther from water may have only enough moisture for grasslands.

Variations in landforms also affect climate. High elevations, such as the Rocky Mountains, have local climates that result in taiga on their slopes and tundra on their peaks. When the wind forces moist air up over a mountain, the air cools, and any moisture condenses into clouds. The moisture then falls to Earth as rain or snow. By the time the air reaches the side of the

Waialeale in Hawai'i is the world's wettest place, receiving about 1150 cm (about 450 in.) of rain a year. ▼

Amount of Rainfall	
Biome	**Yearly Precipitation**
Tropical rain forests	250 cm (about 100 in.)
Deserts	10 cm or less (about 4 in.)
Grasslands	10–40 cm (about 4–16 in.)
Deciduous forests	75–250 cm (about 30–100 in.)
Taiga	20–60 cm (about 8–24 in.)
Tundra	25 cm (about 10 in.)

The Atacama Desert in northern Chile is the world's driest place. Some areas receive no rain for as long as 20 years at a time. ▼

mountain away from the wind, it is very dry. This dry area is called a *rain shadow*. Many deserts occur in the rain shadows of large mountain ranges.

✔ **Why does a certain type of biome occur only within a certain climate zone?**

Summary

The major land biomes are tropical rain forest, deciduous forest, grassland, desert, tundra, and taiga. The climate of each biome is unlike that of any other biome. Climate is affected by the amount of sunlight received, the amount of moisture, and the kinds of landforms. The coldest climate zones are near the poles, and the warmest zone is near the equator. Plants and animals show adaptations to the climate of their particular biome.

Review

1. In what order do biomes occur, from the poles to the equator?
2. How are areas within the same biome alike? How might they differ?
3. How is a tropical rain forest different from the taiga?
4. **Critical Thinking** The map of Earth's major biomes shows sharp borders between different biomes. Would you find this to be true if you traveled from one biome to another? Explain.
5. **Test Prep** The biome with the greatest diversity of plants and animals is the —

    A desert
    B tropical rain forest
    C deciduous forest
    D taiga

LINKS

MATH LINK

Calculate Large areas of the world's tropical rain forests are cut down each year. In Brazil alone, about 13,820 km^2 were cut down in 1990. At that rate, how much will have been cut from 1991 through 2000?

WRITING LINK

Informative Writing—Friendly Letter Write a letter to a relative who lives in a different biome. Describe the biome of your area, and ask the person to describe the biome of his or her area.

SOCIAL STUDIES LINK

Read Maps Work alone or with a partner. Write down one set of coordinates (latitude and longitude). Then locate those coordinates on a map or globe. Write down the name of the continent and the country or the ocean. Then find out what the climate is like and which biome occurs there.

TECHNOLOGY LINK

Learn more about the variety of life in a tropical rain forest by viewing *Rainforest Diversity* on the **Harcourt Science Newsroom Video** in your classroom video library.

LESSON 2

What Are Water Ecosystems?

In this lesson, you can . . .

INVESTIGATE life in a pond community.

LEARN ABOUT three different water ecosystems.

LINK to math, writing, social studies, and technology.

The green heron is a consumer in several freshwater ecosystems. ▼

Life in a Pond Community

Activity Purpose Lakes, rivers, ponds, and oceans are all water ecosystems. In Lesson 1 you learned about the producers and consumers in each land biome. In this investigation you will **observe** some organisms in a pond community and **infer** whether they are producers or consumers.

Materials
- Microslide Viewer
- Microslide set of pond life
- Microslide set of ocean life

Alternate Materials
- pond water
- hand lens
- dropper
- slide
- coverslip
- microscope

Activity Procedure

1. Put the "Pond Life" Microslide in the Microslide Viewer. **Observe** the first photograph, which shows the fish and plants found in a pond. **Record** your observations by making a drawing and writing a short description of these organisms. You may use the information on the Microslide card to help you with your description. (Picture A)

A114

2 The other photographs in the set show microscopic life in a pond. **Observe** each of the organisms. Then **record** your observations by making a drawing and writing a short description of each organism. (Picture B)

3 **Classify** each of the organisms as producer or consumer. **Record** this information on your drawings and in your descriptions.

Picture A

4 Now put the "Marine Biology" Microslide in the Microslide Viewer. **Observe** each of the organisms, but don't read the information on the Microslide card yet. **Predict** which of the organisms are producers and which are consumers. Justify your prediction.

5 Now read the information on the Microslide card to see if your predictions were correct.

Picture B

Draw Conclusions

1. **Compare** the two sets of organisms. Which pond organism was similar to the coral polyp? Which marine organisms were similar to the algae?

2. In what way were all the producers alike?

3. **Scientists at Work** Scientists often explain relationships between organisms using **inferences** based on **observations** of the organisms in their natural habitats. Think about your observations of pond life and ocean life. What organisms in a pond community have the same position in a pond food chain as zooplankton has in an ocean food chain?

Investigate Further Now that you have observed photographs of pond organisms, use the materials in the *Alternate Materials* list to **observe** a drop of water from a pond or other water ecosystem. Then **classify** as producers and consumers the organisms you observe. See page R5 for tips on using a microscope.

Process Skill Tip

Before you can **infer** a relationship between two organisms, you need to carefully **observe** the organisms in their natural habitats.

A115

Water Ecosystems

FIND OUT

- about three types of water ecosystems
- about adaptations of plants and animals to the ecosystems in which they live

VOCABULARY

intertidal zone
near-shore zone
open-ocean zone
estuary

Life in Water

Living things are found in almost every body of water on Earth. Although there are many water ecosystems, they can be classified into three main types. Saltwater ecosystems include oceans and seas. Freshwater ecosystems include streams, rivers, lakes, and ponds. There are also *brackish*-water ecosystems—where salt water and fresh water mix.

Just as organisms of the various land biomes are adapted to conditions in their particular ecosystems, so are organisms living in water. Sunlight, for example, can reach to a depth of only about 200 m (about 660 ft). So plants can't grow below this depth. The amount of oxygen in the water is another limiting factor. Oxygen gets into water from the water's contact with air at its surface. In deep water, organisms must have adaptations that allow them to survive with less oxygen.

✔ **What are the three types of water ecosystems?**

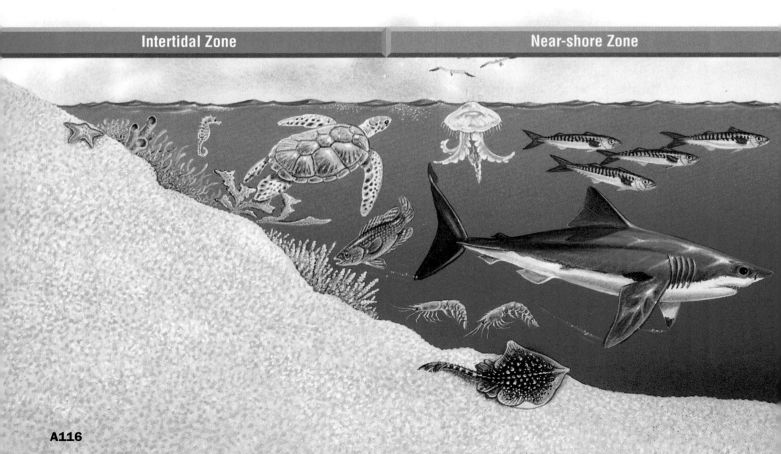

Intertidal Zone   Near-shore Zone

Saltwater Ecosystems

Varieties of saltwater ecosystems exist because of differences in sunlight, nutrients in the water, the temperature of the water, and the movement of the water. Organisms in the ocean have adaptations to help them survive in their ecosystems.

At the ocean's edge, waves constantly lap at the shore and tides rise and fall each day. In this area, called the **intertidal zone**, the tide and the churning waves provide a constant supply of oxygen and nutrients that living organisms need. Animals of the intertidal zone, such as starfish, sea urchins, clams, and crabs, can live both in water and in moist sand.

Beyond the breaking waves, the **near-shore zone** extends out to waters that are about 180 m (about 600 ft) deep. Rivers that empty into the ocean provide most of the nutrients for this zone. The water is calm in this zone, and the temperature doesn't change much. Schools of fish, including anchovies, cod, and mackerel, feed on the large numbers of algae growing there. Organisms such as oysters and worms, which live on the ocean floor in this zone, rely on the steady "rain" of dead organisms from above for their food. This is because producers can live only as far down as sunlight reaches.

The **open-ocean zone** includes most of the ocean waters. In this zone the water is very deep, but most organisms live near the surface. Trillions of microscopic algae make up *phytoplankton* (FY•toh•plangk•tuhn), the beginning of the open-ocean food chain. Tiny herbivores, which make up *zooplankton* (ZOH•oh•plangk•tuhn), graze on the algae. Small fish eat the zooplankton and, in turn, are eaten by larger carnivores, such as sharks.

✔ **Name the three ocean zones.**

Open-ocean Zone

Beneficial microscopic algae are the beginning of the open-ocean food chain.

Few organisms live in the depths of the open-ocean zone, where it is dark and cold. Note: Diagram not to scale.

0 m–30 m

30 m–200 m

deeper than 200 m

A117

Freshwater Ecosystems

Lakes, ponds, streams, rivers, some marshes, and swamps are all freshwater ecosystems. The plants and animals in these ecosystems are adapted to life in fresh water only. They can't survive in salt water. Freshwater plants include duckweed, waterlilies, cattails, and many different grasses. There are also many kinds of algae in fresh water. Trout, bass, catfish, frogs, crayfish, and turtles are a few of the more common freshwater animals.

THE INSIDE STORY

Life in a Pond

On a hot summer day, a pond is a busy world of plants and animals that make up many complex food webs.

1. The roots of water plants are in the bottom of the pond.
2. When frogs are tadpoles, they feed on tiny pond plants, but as adults they catch insects.
3. Water striders, whirligig beetles, and mosquito larvae live at the surface of the water.
4. Turtles and small fish, such as bluegills, swim through the pond and feed on minnows and insects.
5. Bottom feeders and burrowing animals, such as snails, worms, and insect larvae, live in the bottom mud.
6. Birds may not live in the pond, but they go there to nest or to find food and water.
7. Microscopic organisms feed on the plants.

Water temperature and the speed at which the water moves, if it moves at all, determine the kinds of organisms that live in a freshwater ecosystem. In streams and rivers, the water moves fast. Fewer plants and animals live in fast-moving water than in still water such as lakes and ponds. The plants and animals that do live in rivers often have adaptations for anchoring themselves to the bottom. Algae attach themselves to rocks. Insects and crayfish often live under rocks.

✔ **What two factors determine the kinds of organisms living in fresh-water ecosystems?**

Estuaries

Brackish water is a mixture of fresh water and salt water. Brackish water is usually found in an **estuary**, a place where a fresh-water river empties into an ocean. At the mouth of the river, the water contains huge amounts of nutrients and organic matter. They make estuaries the most productive ecosystems on Earth. Salt marshes and mangrove swamps are two types of estuaries.

All estuaries have changing water conditions. At high tide, salty ocean water flows into the estuary. At low tide, estuaries are filled with fresh water or they become exposed, muddy flats. Organisms in estuaries have adaptations that allow them to survive in both fresh water and salt water.

Except for the slow rise and fall of tides, estuary waters are calm and still. The water is always fairly shallow, and sunlight easily reaches the bottom. These factors, along with the large amounts of nutrients, make estuaries ideal habitats for many plants and animals. Two-thirds of all the fish and shellfish harvested along the east coast of the United States depend on estuaries for their

▲ Mangroves grow along the coasts of Florida, Mexico, Central America, and other tropical areas.

survival. Oysters, mussels, and shrimp feed on plants and decaying plant matter. They then become food for fish and birds.

The young of many fish and shellfish also start their lives in the calm, sunlit waters of estuaries. There is plenty of food, and the young animals are safe from large predators that can't live in brackish water.

The importance of estuaries wasn't noticed for many years. Besides their role as a water habitat, they also help prevent

Tall grasses are the main plants in salt marshes. These plants are able to live in brackish water because they get rid of salt through pores in their leaves. ▼

coastal flooding and the erosion of shore-lines. Now that people recognize both their beauty and their importance, the remaining estuaries may be saved from fill-and-build practices that have destroyed many of these remarkable ecosystems.

✔ **What adaptations must all estuary organisms have?**

Summary

Water ecosystems occur in fresh water, salt water, and brackish water. Water organisms have adaptations to help them survive in their particular ecosystems. Saltwater ecosystems are the intertidal zone, the near-shore zone, and the open-ocean zone. Freshwater ecosystems occur in rivers, ponds, lakes, streams, some marshes, and swamps. Estuaries are brackish-water ecosystems where rivers empty into oceans.

Review

1. What factors determine the kinds of organisms that can live in a saltwater ecosystem?
2. What might be one adaptation of an organism that lives in a river?
3. Where do many shellfish and ocean fish spend the first part of their lives?
4. **Critical Thinking** Why are estuaries critical to both land and sea?
5. **Test Prep** The ocean zone that is the deepest is the —
   A near-shore zone
   B intertidal zone
   C open-ocean zone
   D estuary

LINKS

MATH LINK

Circle Graphs Use a computer to make a circle graph based on the information below. It shows how much of Earth's water is salt water, ice water, and fresh water.

97 percent—salt water (oceans)
 2 percent—ice (glaciers and icecaps)
 1 percent—fresh water

WRITING LINK

Narrative Writing—Story Write a story about what life might be like in a coastal town. Describe the role that the ocean plays in your life and the lives of the townspeople. Then read your finished story to your classmates.

SOCIAL STUDIES LINK

Mangroves Perhaps the greatest value of mangrove swamps is their role as coastal protectors. But in some parts of the world, people cut mangroves and use the wood for fuel. Find out where mangroves are being destroyed and what is being done to protect them.

TECHNOLOGY LINK

Learn more about ocean ecosystems by visiting the National Museum of Natural History Internet site.
www.si.edu/harcourt/science

"SEE" FOOD

Scientists are now using a satellite to study ocean food chains. Images from this satellite provide valuable information about microscopic organisms that are the key to life in the oceans.

Links in a Chain

Life in the oceans—like life on land—depends on organisms that use energy from sunlight to produce food. These microscopic producers are the first link in the food chains that connect all living things.

In the ocean, the primary producers are floating algae called phytoplankton. In Greek, *phyto* means "plant" and *plankton* means "drifting." Phytoplankton are no bigger than a pinhead. Tiny consumers called zooplankton (drifting animals) eat the phytoplankton. Larger animals, such as shrimp and small fish, eat the zooplankton, adding another link to the ocean food chain. Larger fish eat the smaller ones, and the chain gets longer. The last link includes the ocean's largest predators, such as sharks and killer whales. It also

A SeaWiFs image

Phytoplankton

includes humans looking for seafood dinners. But all these meat eaters would go hungry without the phytoplankton.

Phytoplankton grow in the warm, sunlit upper layers of the ocean. Changes in wind and weather can change the ocean's currents. The warm waters where phytoplankton grow best can shift location by hundreds of kilometers. When this happens, the animals—including humans who want to find the ocean's best fishing spots—must move.

An Eye in the Sky

Scientists have a new tool to help them find the places where phytoplankton are growing. It's a satellite called SeaWiFS, which stands for Sea-viewing Wide Field Sensor. SeaWiFS orbits more than 640 km (about 400 mi) above Earth. It senses the color of ocean water. Ocean water with a healthy growth of phytoplankton is greener than surrounding water. Images from SeaWiFS can also show where pollution is damaging the ocean's food chains.

SeaWiFS surveys the entire planet every 48 hours. It can scan an entire ocean in less than one hour. "What SeaWiFS can see in one minute would take a decade to measure using ships," says a scientist who helped develop the satellite.

SeaWiFS helps scientists keep track of Earth's ocean "gardens." This allows them to help people plan to take advantage of the oceans' living resources without upsetting the balance that keeps them healthy and productive.

THINK ABOUT IT

1. Why are phytoplankton important?
2. How do satellites make it easier to observe ocean resources?

WEB LINK:
For science and technology updates, visit The Learning Site.
www.harcourtschool.com/ca

Careers Ecologist

What They Do
Ecologists study the relationships between living things, such as phytoplankton, and their environments.

Education and Training People
wishing to become ecologists should study subjects such as botany, zoology, and chemistry in college. They should also do a lot of research outdoors, where they can see how plants and animals react to changes in their environment.

Alissa J. Arp

ECOLOGICAL PHYSIOLOGIST

"Although the average person may not think that what happens at the bottom of the ocean or in the stinky environment of a mud flat is of particular importance, clearly there are some very unique and unusual animals in these habitats."

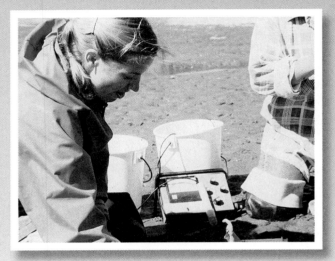

How can tube worms live in a zone of crushing pressure 7000 meters (about 23,000 ft) below sea level? How do clams live in the untreated sewage released into the ocean by some coastal cities? Why doesn't sulfur, a chemical normally poisonous to animals, kill black abalone? These are questions that Alissa J. Arp tries to answer.

Dr. Arp is an ecological physiologist. She studies marine animals that live under harsh conditions. She tries to learn how these animals can live in toxic chemicals, extremely cold tempera-

tures, and total darkness. Her research takes her from polluted mud flats along the coast to cracks in the crust of the ocean floor. To reach these sea vents, where sulfurous water bubbles out into the near-freezing blackness, she dove in the U.S. Navy's deep-sea submarine, *Sea Cliff*.

Some of Dr. Arp's research may be important for humans. For example, animals who live in toxic chemicals have adaptations to get rid of the poisons. Humans may be able to use some of these animals to clean up polluted environments.

Currently Dr. Arp is a professor of biology and director of the Romberg Tiburon Center for Environmental Studies at San Francisco State University. Dr. Arp uses her position as a professor and research director to inspire young women to consider careers in science.

THINK ABOUT IT

1. How are the animals that Dr. Arp studies able to survive in toxic chemicals?
2. How might Dr. Arp's research be used to help humans living in industrial areas?

Deep-sea vent

Land Biomes

What adaptations do animals from land biomes show?

Materials

- terrarium
- bedding
- water bottle
- food
- small animal: hamster, mouse, snake, or lizard

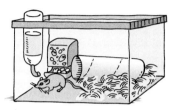

Procedure

1. Set up the terrarium to meet the needs of the animal.

2. Observe the animal in this environment for several days.

Draw Conclusions

What needs did you provide for the animal? What adaptations does the animal have for living in a land biome? What is the natural environment of the animal? How does the terrarium compare to the natural environment?

Water Ecosystems

What interactions occur in water ecosystems?

Materials

- bucket
- collecting net
- large jar or aquarium
- air pump

Procedure

1. With an adult, visit a stream or pond in your community.

2. Use the bucket and the collecting net to scoop up sand, water, water plants, and water animals.

3. Transfer the materials and organisms to the jar or aquarium.

4. Set up the air pump, and observe the water ecosystem.

Draw Conclusions

List all the living and nonliving things in the ecosystem. How do the living things interact with each other? How do the living things and nonliving things interact?

Chapter 4 Review and Test Preparation

Vocabulary Review

Use the terms below to complete the sentences. The page numbers in ( ) tell you where to look in the chapter if you need help.

biome (A104)
climate zone (A104)
intertidal zone (A117)
near-shore zone (A117)
open-ocean zone (A117)
estuaries (A120)

1. The ____ extends out into the ocean to a depth of about 180 m (600 ft).

2. A ____ is defined by its climate and the plants and animals that are adapted to that climate.

3. Most animals that live in the ____ can live both in water and in moist sand.

4. The deepest part of the ocean is the ____.

5. A ____ is a region with similar yearly patterns of temperature, rainfall, and sunlight.

6. ____ occur where fresh water and salt water mix.

Connect Concepts

Complete the chart using the choices below.

- Rivers and streams
- Near-shore zone
- Organisms are adapted to live in rapidly moving water.
- Intertidal zone
- Brackish water
- Estuaries such as saltwater marshes and mangrove swamps.
- Many organisms can live both in water and in moist sand.
- In deep water, the lack of oxygen can be a factor.
- Open-ocean zone

Water Ecosystems	Characteristics
Fresh water	
7. ____	8. ____
Lakes and ponds	9. ____
Salt water	
10. ____	11. ____
12. ____	Light reaches much of this zone, allowing plants to grow.
13. ____	Most organisms live close to the surface, where light reaches.
14. ____	Areas where salt water mixes with fresh water
15. ____	Organisms can survive in salt water and fresh water.

Check Understanding

Write the letter of the best choice.

16. The biome that has a frozen layer of ground year-round is the —
    A taiga   C tundra
    B deciduous forest   D polar region

17. A biome is **NOT** characterized by —
    F its plants   H its climate
    G its animals   J its location

18. The biome where you would find the greatest number of tree species is the —
    A deciduous forest   C desert
    B tropical rain forest D grasslands

19. A water ecosystem that has brackish water is —
    F the near-shore zone
    G a river
    H the open-ocean zone
    J a mangrove swamp

20. An example of a freshwater biome is —
    A an estuary   C a pond
    B a taiga   D a tundra

21. Factors that affect water ecosystems include —
    F the amount of sunlight
    G the amount of oxygen
    H the temperature
    J all of the above

Critical Thinking

22. Since the Aswan Dam was built on the Nile River in Egypt, the waters of the Nile no longer reach the sea. How do you think that has affected the estuary at the river's mouth?

23. Deciduous beech and oak trees grow in the lowest regions of the Alps, a moun-tain range in Europe. Higher up, only conifers such as fir and pine grow. Even higher, tundra is found. What do you think causes this series of biomes?

Process Skills Review

24. Explain what you would need to **observe** in an area to determine which biome it is part of.

25. Write a brief paragraph in which you **compare** the climate and plant and animal life found in a desert and in a tropical rain forest.

Performance Assessment

Biome Mystery

Cut a sheet of paper into about 10 or more pieces. On each piece, write a biome clue or a water ecosystem clue. Write the name of the biome or water ecosystem on the back. Clues might be the name of a plant or animal that lives only in that biome or ecosystem, where on Earth the biome is found, the name of one water ecosystem, and so on. A list of clues might include the following: blue whale (ocean), pond (fresh-water ecosystem), biome near the equator (tropical rain forest), and so on. Exchange your collection of clues with a classmate and challenge each other to guess the answers.

Vocabulary Preview

succession
pioneer plants
climax community
pollution
acid rain
conserving
reduce
reuse
recycle
reclamation
wetlands

Protecting and Preserving Ecosystems

The eastern third of the United States was once covered with forests. Today it is covered with cities. Large parts of the western United States are deserts. But many of the deserts are now green with lawns and golf courses. Ecosystems change—especially when humans live there. Luckily there are places where natural ecosystems still exist.

FAST FACT

Yellowstone National Park was the world's first national park. In the United States, about 10.5 percent of the land is protected in parks and wilderness areas. But some countries have even larger percentages of protected land.

Protected Lands	
Country	**Percentage**
Venezuela	22.2
Bhutan	19.8
Chile	19.8
Botswana	17.4
Panama	16.9
Namibia	12.7

Between 25,000 years ago and 10,000 years ago, huge glaciers covered the northern half of North America. As the ice melted, it left deposits of large rocks and thousands of lakes.

FAST FACT

Every year about 60,000 km² (23,000 mi²) of Earth becomes desert. That's an area about the size of West Virginia.

1

How Do Ecosystems Change Naturally?

In this lesson, you can . . .

INVESTIGATE how a pond changes over time.

LEARN ABOUT how ecosystems change.

LINK to math, writing, art, and technology.

This lone plant growing in a crack in the lava is a pioneer for a new ecosystem. ▼

INVESTIGATE

How a Pond Changes

Activity Purpose In any ecosystem small changes occur every day. Those small changes some-times lead to big changes over time. In this investigation you will **make a model** of a pond ecosystem. You will **observe** some of the changes that occur in a pond ecosystem over time.

Materials

- plastic dishpan
- potting soil
- water
- duckweed
- birdseed
- camera (optional)

Activity Procedure

1 Spread a layer of potting soil about 5 cm deep in the dishpan. Now bank the soil about 10 cm high around the edges of the dishpan. Leave a low spot, with about 1 cm of soil, in the center of the pan. (Picture A)

2 Slowly pour water into the low area of the pan until the water is about 4 cm deep. You may have to add more water as some of it soaks into the soil. Place some duckweed on the "pond."

3 Sprinkle birdseed over the surface of the soil. Don't worry if some of the seed falls into the water. Do not water the seed. Take a photograph or draw a picture to **record** how your pond looks. Put your pond model in a sunny window. (Picture B)

Picture A

Picture B

4. After three or four days, **measure** and **record** the depth of the water. Take another photograph or draw another picture. Then sprinkle more birdseed over the soil. Water the soil lightly.

5. After three or four more days, **observe** how your pond has changed. **Measure** and **record** the depth of the water. **Compare** your observations with the photographs you took or the pictures you drew.

Draw Conclusions

1. Describe any changes in the pond during the week. How did the depth of the water change?

2. **Compare** the changes in your model with those in a real pond. How are they the same? How are they different?

3. **Scientists at Work** By **observing** the changes that occur when they **use models**, scientists can **infer** changes that might occur in nature. From what you observed in your model, what do you infer might happen to a real pond over time?

Investigate Further An actual pond ecosystem has a greater diversity of plants and animals than your model. **Make a model** that includes a greater variety of living things.

Process Skill Tip

It is difficult to **observe** how an ecosystem changes, since these changes often occur over long periods of time. However, you can **use models** to **infer** changes that might take place.

A131

Natural Succession

Primary Succession

In the investigation you observed the changes that occur in a pond ecosystem. All ecosystems—both water and land—change constantly. Small changes in climate, in soil conditions, or in plant and animal populations can change an ecosystem. Gradual change in an ecosystem—sometimes occurring over thousands of years—is called **succession**.

There are two types of succession. The first is *primary succession*. This type of succession occurs on bare, newly formed land. New land forms in a number of ways. Volcanic islands emerge from the sea. Glaciers melt, uncovering new land. **Pioneer plants** are the first plants to invade a bare area. Their sprouting and growth begins the process of succession. At the edge of a pond, for example, the roots of duckweed trap tiny bits of soil. As the duckweed dies and decays, more matter is added to the soil. Eventually, there is enough soil for a second community of plants, such as reeds and cattails, to take over. Over time the pond ecosystem grows smaller, and a land ecosystem takes its place.

FIND OUT

- what happens in the stages of succession
- what happens to an ecosystem after a natural disaster

VOCABULARY

succession
pioneer plants
climax community

As a glacier melts, rock that was covered with ice for thousands of years is exposed. ▼

Lichens, shown at the right, and small plants such as fireweed are common pioneer plants on glacier soil.

Glacier Bay, Alaska, is like a giant outdoor laboratory for studying primary succession. For the past 250 years, the glaciers have been melting and receding northward—leaving behind deposits of rock. The rock nearest the glaciers has been exposed for only a few days. Walking south—away from the glaciers and toward the bay—is like walking through time. As you walk, you pass through older stages of succession.

The first stage is the pioneer-plant stage. Pioneer organisms such as lichens—combinations of algae and fungi—grow nearest the glacier. As they die, their decaying matter adds nutrients to the ground. After a few years, a thin layer of soil forms and mosses take over. This is the second stage of succession, the *mossy stage*. Bits of organic matter and bird droppings become trapped in the dense moss. They add more nutrients to the slowly deepening soil.

Farther south, soil conditions have continued to improve. Grasses and flowering plants have taken root. A *grassy stage* is the third stage of succession. Farther still, the soil has become deep enough and rich enough to support the growth of alder and willow trees. Alders and willows gradually make the soil more acidic—producing favorable conditions for spruce trees to grow. The tall spruce trees begin to crowd out the alders as you continue south.

A spruce and hemlock forest makes up the **climax community**, the last stage of succession. If there are no disasters, such as volcanoes or fires, a climax community may stay the same for thousands of years. In the northeastern United States, the climax community is a deciduous forest. A prairie is the climax community in areas of the Midwest.

✔ **What are the first and last stages of primary succession?**

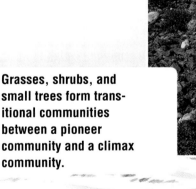

Grasses, shrubs, and small trees form transitional communities between a pioneer community and a climax community.

After 250 years, a climax community of spruce and hemlock has developed.

Secondary Succession

On May 18, 1980, Mount St. Helens erupted in Washington state. The eruption was one of the most violent ever recorded in North America. It blanketed the surrounding land with a thick layer of ash and mud. However, *secondary succession*, the return of a damaged ecosystem to its natural climax community, soon began.

Under the ash and the mud were seeds and living roots. Rains washed away some of the ash, allowing the seeds and roots to sprout. Winds blew in more seeds, some of which sprouted and grew. By the summer of 1981, the slopes of the once-barren mountain blazed with pink fireweed flowers. In the fall, the dying fireweed helped to enrich the soil. As soil conditions improved, shrubs began to grow. Today a community of shrubs dominates the area. This community will probably last at least 20 more years. However, fir trees have already started to grow. They are a sign that a climax community of fir and hemlock trees is returning.

Forest fires burned much of Yellowstone National Park in 1988. Fires are another type of natural disaster that changes ecosystems. However, unlike volcanic eruptions, fires actually speed up the process of secondary succession.

▲ Shock waves from the 1980 eruption leveled the fir trees near Mount St. Helens. Secondary succession is already well underway.

Because of fires in Yellowstone National Park, a patchwork of new meadows and a mix of old and young forests exists. This mixture of plant life provides habitats for a variety of animals. ▼

The Yellowstone fires quickly burned the dead leaves and branches on the forest floor, releasing nutrients into the soil. After the fire, meadows of grasses sprouted in the rich soil. After a few years, a forest of lodgepole pines began growing, blocking out sunlight and gradually replacing the meadows. In the shade of the lodgepoles, a new climax community of spruce and fir has already started growing.

✔ **How are some forest fires helpful?**

Summary

The slow change of an ecosystem is called succession. Primary succession occurs on new, barren land. First, hardy pioneer plants grow. Eventually, most ecosystems reach a stable stage, called the climax community. Secondary succession occurs after a natural disaster has damaged an ecosystem.

Review

1. Describe the four stages of succession that occur after a glacier recedes.
2. What might you expect to find on Mount St. Helens 20 years from now?
3. Where would you find the pioneer stage of succession around a pond?
4. **Critical Thinking** How does a community of pioneer plants produce changes that cause its own destruction?
5. **Test Prep** The most stable stage of succession is the —
   A grassy community
   B pioneer stage
   C climax community
   D mossy stage

LINKS

MATH LINK

Succession Time Line After a glacier recedes, it takes 50 years for thick stands of alders to appear. It takes 120 more years for a dense forest of spruce to replace the alders, and another 80 years for the climax community, a spruce-hemlock forest, to appear. Make a time line, beginning in 1750, of these stages of succession. Include historical events on your time line.

WRITING LINK

Persuasive Writing—Request Some people believe that forest fires in national parks should be put out to save the natural beauty of the parks. Others believe that fires should be allowed to burn because they benefit the natural ecosystems. Write a letter to the head ranger of a nearby national or state park. Ask the ranger to send you information about the fire policy in that park.

ART LINK

Succession Draw a series of pictures showing the stages of succession of abandoned fields in your area. Include in your drawings the plants and animals associated with each stage.

TECHNOLOGY LINK

Learn more about succession by visiting this Internet site.
www.scilinks.org/harcourt

How Do People Change Ecosystems?

In this lesson, you can . . .

INVESTIGATE how chemical fertilizers can affect an ecosystem.

LEARN ABOUT how some human activities affect ecosystems.

LINK to math, writing, art, and technology.

INVESTIGATE

How Chemical Fertilizer Affects a Pond

Activity Purpose Many people use chemical fertilizers on their fields, gardens, and lawns to help plants grow. However, not all of the fertilizer stays where it is put. Rain washes some of it into ponds, lakes, rivers, and streams. In this investigation you will **observe** what happens to pond water when fertilizer is added to it.

Materials

- marker
- 4 jars or cups with lids
- pond water
- liquid fertilizer
- dropper

Activity Procedure

1 Use the marker to label the jars 1, 2, 3, and 4. (Picture A)

2 Fill the jars with pond water.

3 Put 10 drops of liquid fertilizer in Jar 1, 20 drops in Jar 2, and 40 drops in Jar 3. Don't put any fertilizer in Jar 4. (Picture B)

◀ Trash that isn't disposed of properly can be harmful to wildlife.

Picture A

Picture B

4 Put the lids on the jars. Then place the jars in a sunny window.

5 **Observe** the jars every day for two weeks. **Record** your observations.

Draw Conclusions

1. What differences did you **observe** among the jars? Which jar had the most plant growth? Which had the least plant growth? How could you tell?

2. As organisms die and decay, they use up the oxygen in the water. Which cup do you **infer** will eventually have the least oxygen?

3. When water ecosystems are contaminated by fertilizer, fish and other animal populations begin to die off. Why do you think this happens?

4. **Scientists at Work** When scientists **identify and control variables**, they can **observe** the effects of one variable at a time. What variable were you observing the effect of in this investigation? What variables did you control?

Investigate Further Some fertilizers have chemicals to kill weeds. **Predict** how using these fertilizers affects a lawn. **Plan and conduct an investigation** with multiple trials to test your prediction. How are your results related to your prediction?

> **Process Skill Tip**
>
> When you **identify and control variables**, you can **observe** the effects of one variable at a time.

How People Change Ecosystems

FIND OUT

- how human activity changes ecosystems
- where pollution comes from and how it affects ecosystems

VOCABULARY

pollution
acid rain

Damaging Ecosystems

In the investigation you observed the way one human activity—using chemical fertilizers—can change an ecosystem. People can change ecosystems in three ways. Some changes are beneficial, or good; some are detrimental, or bad; and some are neutral, or neither bad nor good. Often changes are detrimental. For example, some of the richest soil in the world is in the mid-western United States and Canada, where there were once grass-land ecosystems. At one time there were several kinds of grasses and many different kinds of wildflowers. They supported a large variety of animal populations, including bison, deer, antelope, and prairie chickens. Now fields of corn, wheat, barley, and oats have replaced most of the natural producers. The diversity, or variety, of life has been greatly reduced.

Farming is vital to human survival. But a growing human population increases the demand for food. This demand results in methods of agriculture that include the use of many different

Chemical pesticides are sprayed on crops to kill insects. These pesticides may harm surrounding ecosystems. ▼

This thick green blanket of algae, called an *algal bloom*, was caused by chemical fertilizers running off nearby farmland. ▼

Areas with a lot of acid rain

Areas with some acid rain

Areas where plants are very sensitive to acid rain

▲ Winds can cause acid rain to fall far from the source of the pollution.

▲ This forest has been killed by acid rain.

chemicals. The use of these chemicals can damage ecosystems.

In addition to farming, other human activities damage natural ecosystems. In growing human communities, for example, people build new roads, homes, schools, and shopping centers. New construction damages and often destroys natural habitats.

Getting natural resources to make things also damages ecosystems. Many things people use today are made of wood or paper. To make wood and paper products, people cut down trees. Cutting entire forests damages ecosystems and destroys habitats.

Making things also produces wastes. And many wastes are harmful and difficult to get rid of. Some waste products damage ecosystems by killing organisms and break-

ing food chains. Any waste product that damages an ecosystem is called **pollution**.

Burning fossil fuels produces some of the most damaging pollution—air pollution and acid rain. Energy stations, some factories, and motor vehicles give off gases that include nitrogen oxides and sulfur dioxide. When water vapor in the air mixes with these gases, nitric acid and sulfuric acid form. The acids condense into clouds and fall to Earth as **acid rain**.

Many trees are damaged by acid rain, and some die from it. Acid rain also damages crops and destroys soil. Runoff from acid rain can kill plants and animals in lakes. Scientists estimate that about 4 percent of the lakes in North America are too acidic for fish to live in.

If ecosystems are not damaged too severely, some of them can slowly recover. A cut forest, for example, can become a forest ecosystem again through succession.

✔ **How does the making of things damage ecosystems?**

Catastrophic Changes

Some human activities can cause catastrophic (kat•uh•STRAHF•ik) changes to an ecosystem—changes so great that the ecosystem cannot recover. For example, one way to get rock and mineral resources from the ground is by strip mining. In this process, all the topsoil and overlying rock layers are removed until the resource is reached. Strip mining destroys all the communities and many of the nonliving parts of an ecosystem, such as streams and ponds.

Since 1977, however, the United States has required that all strip-mined areas be restored to their original condition. In most cases the soil is replaced, and forests or grasslands are replanted. In other cases the mine pits are turned into lakes. However, many older strip-mined areas have not been restored.

Catastrophic changes can also occur when highways, subdivisions, and shopping malls are built on small or fragile ecosystems. Large-scale construction projects often destroy habitats completely. Even when they don't, they often change conditions so much that natural communities can't survive. Some kinds of ecosystems, such as wetlands, are in danger of disappearing completely.

It is impossible for humans to be part of an ecosystem and not affect it. But people can live in ways that do less damage to natural ecosystems. You will find out more about some of those ways in Lesson 3.

✔ **What is a catastrophic change to an ecosystem?**

The Kennicott copper mine in Utah is the largest strip mine in the world. ▼

▲ In many areas people drain wetlands to build subdivisions and shopping centers.

Summary

Human activity has a huge effect on natural ecosystems. People need land for homes and natural resources to make things. These activities can damage ecosystems and cause pollution. Damaged ecosystems sometimes recover slowly, but catastrophic changes often destroy them.

Review

1. What human activities damage ecosystems?

2. What is acid rain?

3. Why is it difficult to recover land that has been strip-mined?

4. **Critical Thinking** Why do you think desert ecosystems are rarely affected by catastrophic changes?

5. **Test Prep** Acid rain is **NOT** caused by —
   A cars
   B energy stations
   C factories
   D farming

LINKS

MATH LINK

Ordering Acidity is measured on a scale called a pH scale, with 0 being the most acidic and 14 being the least acidic. Each whole unit of the scale stands for an increase or decrease of ten times in acidity. Order the items in the list below from least acidic to most acidic.

lemon juice	2.3	vinegar	3.3
distilled water	7.0	acid rain	4.3
human blood	7.4	sea water	8.0

WRITING LINK

Informative Writing—Compare and Contrast Think of an ecosystem that has been changed by human activity. Write a paragraph in which you compare and contrast the appearance of the ecosystem before and after the change.

ART LINK

Collage Make a collage of items that you think symbolize our modern lifestyle. Cut photographs out of old magazines, or draw pictures of the items. Include pictures of ecosystems that might be changed to produce the items.

TECHNOLOGY LINK

Learn more about damage to forest ecosystems by visiting the National Air and Space Museum Internet site.
www.si.edu/harcourt/science

How Can People Treat Ecosystems More Wisely?

In this lesson, you can . . .

INVESTIGATE what happens to trash in a landfill.

LEARN ABOUT using resources wisely.

LINK to math, writing, social studies, and technology.

Using beach crossovers is an easy way to treat a fragile ecosystem wisely. ▼

KEEP OFF DUNES
UNLAWFUL TO DISTURB DUNES OR VEGETATION
FLORIDA STATUTE 161Q253

INVESTIGATE

What Happens in a Landfill

Activity Purpose Do you know what happens to your trash once it's picked up? Most of it is taken to a landfill. There it is combined with the trash of everyone else in your community. In this investigation you will **make a model** of a landfill to find out what happens to trash.

Materials
- plastic gloves
- newspaper
- small pieces of trash, such as aluminum foil, tissues, plastic bags, Styrofoam cups, potato peels, bones, and apple cores
- shoe box
- plastic wrap
- potting soil
- tray
- measuring cup
- water
- watering can

CAUTION

Activity Procedure

1. Make a chart listing ten different items of trash. Allow space in your chart to **record** observations you will make later.

2. **CAUTION** **Put on the plastic gloves**. Spread newspaper on your work surface. Choose the ten items of trash listed on your chart to put in the model landfill. Lay the trash on the newspaper. (Picture A)

3. Now prepare the model landfill. First, line the shoe box with plastic wrap. Then put a layer of potting soil on the bottom of the box.

Picture A

Picture B

4 Take the pieces of trash from the newspaper, and place them on top of the soil. Then cover the trash completely with another layer of soil. (Picture B)

5 Set the model landfill on the tray. Use the watering can to sprinkle the soil each day with 50 mL of water.

6 After two weeks, put on plastic gloves and remove the top layer of soil. **Observe** the items of trash, and **record** your observations.

Draw Conclusions

1. Did you **observe** anything starting to decay? What items decayed the most? What items decayed the least?

2. Things that decay are said to be *biodegradable*. What items in your trash are biodegradable?

3. **Scientists at Work** Scientists often **draw conclusions** based on observations made while **using a model**. From your observations of a model landfill, what conclusions can you draw about using paper trash bags instead of plastic trash bags?

Investigate Further Nonbiodegradable items often are removed from trash before it is collected. Use your knowledge of cause and effect to **predict** how quickly trash in a landfill would decay if it were all biodegradable. Justify your prediction. **Make a model** to test your prediction. How are your results related to your prediction?

Process Skill Tip

Observations made while **using a model** can help you **draw conclusions** about real-world situations.

Using Resources Wisely

Reduce, Reuse, and Recycle

FIND OUT

- how to reduce your use of resources and how to recycle or reuse resources
- what landfills are

VOCABULARY

conserving
reduce
reuse
recycle

To help people treat ecosystems more wisely, scientists research and plan ways to protect ecosystems from catastrophic changes. To support these plans, governments pass laws to prevent strip mining, pollution, and overdevelopment. All new cars, for example, must have *catalytic converters,* devices that change some of the poisonous exhaust gases into carbon dioxide and water. New cars must also be more efficient—that is, they need to be able to go farther on less gasoline.

Changing human habits that damage ecosystems is just as important as passing new laws. Everyone can help protect ecosystems by saving, or **conserving**, resources. The three *Rs*—*reduce, reuse,* and *recycle*—are ways of conserving resources.

Reduce means to cut down on the use of resources. For example, appliances like clothes dryers, water heaters, and air

Reducing, reusing, and recycling are three ways to conserve resources and protect ecosystems. ▼

Recycle

Reduce

Reuse

conditioners use huge amounts of electricity. Using them wisely reduces the need for energy resources such as coal. Reducing the need for coal saves ecosystems from being destroyed by strip mining. Using appliances wisely also protects ecosystems by reducing air pollution. The burning of coal to make electricity is one of the main causes of acid rain.

Reuse means not to throw away items that can be used again. For example, cups and plates that can be washed and used again produce less waste than disposable ones. Reusing items also saves the resources needed to make new products.

Reusing also means using items for different purposes. For example, you can wash out milk cartons and juice bottles and use them as planters or bird feeders. You can also give to a resale shop toys or clothes you have outgrown. Buying used items saves resources, reduces pollution, and protects ecosystems.

Recycle means to recover a resource from an item and to use the recovered resource to make a new item. Many resources can be conserved by recycling. Aluminum, glass, and paper can be ground up or melted down and then used over and over again. Recycling saves energy as well as resources. It takes less energy to make an item out of recycled material than it does to make the same item out of raw resources. Like reducing and reusing, recycling protects ecosystems from damage or destruction.

✔ **What are the three ways of conserving resources and protecting ecosystems?**

Today anyone can help protect ecosystems.

A145

Landfills

What can't be recycled or reused usually goes to a landfill. Years ago, trash was either burned or dumped into a huge hole in the ground. These open dumps attracted birds, rats, and insects. When it rained, water filtered through the trash, carrying harmful chemicals into the groundwater. Today most open dumps have been replaced by landfills like the one shown here.

A landfill starts as a large hole in the ground. Unlike an open dump, the bottom and sides of a landfill are layered with heavy clay soil or plastic sheets. This helps keep harmful liquids from getting into groundwater.

Large trucks haul in the trash. Each layer of trash is flattened. Then it is covered with at least 15 cm (about 6 in.) of soil. This helps keep away insects and other animals.

Summary

Governments have passed many laws to reduce pollution and to protect ecosystems. However, people can also do things to protect ecosystems. For example, they can conserve resources using the three *R*s. That is, people can reduce the use of resources, reuse as many items as possible, and recycle. What cannot be reused or recycled should go to landfills.

Review

1. Explain the three *R*s of conserving resources.
2. What is a landfill?
3. How have cars become less harmful to ecosystems?
4. **Critical Thinking** What can people do to reduce the amount of coal burned to produce electricity?
5. **Test Prep** Catalytic converters —
   - **A** reduce the air pollution from factory smokestacks
   - **B** change some exhaust gases into carbon dioxide and water
   - **C** reduce the amount of carbon dioxide in the air
   - **D** change water into oxygen and carbon dioxide

LINKS

MATH LINK

Calculate The average American family throws away about 6.5 kg (14.3 lb) of trash each day. That's 4.5 billion kg (about 10 billion lb) of trash per week for all Americans. How many kilograms of trash does the average family produce each year? How many kilograms of trash are produced by all Americans?

WRITING LINK

Informative Writing—Report Research an environmental "tradeoff," a choice between two actions. For example, which is better for the environment, using disposable baby diapers or using cloth diapers? Cloth diapers don't fill up landfills, but cleaning them uses more water and energy. Report your findings to your class.

SOCIAL STUDIES LINK

Earth Day The first Earth Day was observed in 1970. Interview a parent, an older neighbor, or a teacher to find out how your community has changed since then. Use a tape recorder or video camera to record the interview. Then write a report.

TECHNOLOGY LINK

Learn more about trash disposal by visiting the Harcourt Learning Site. **www.harcourtschool.com/ca**

WELCOME TO THE LEARNING SITE

How Can People Help Restore Damaged Ecosystems?

In this lesson, you can . . .

INVESTIGATE how waste water can be cleaned.

LEARN ABOUT restoring damaged ecosystems.

LINK to math, writing, social studies, and technology.

How Waste Water Can Be Cleaned

Activity Purpose Fifty years ago, most waste water was dumped directly into rivers, lakes, or other large bodies of water. But waste water can cause great damage to ecosystems. It contains pollutants such as harmful organisms and poisonous chemicals. Now waste water from homes and factories is treated before it is released into the environment. Treatment removes pollutants from the water. In this investigation you will **experiment** with a process that filters pollutants from waste water.

Materials

- plastic jar with lid
- spoon
- soil
- water
- paper clip
- 6 paper cups
- marker
- ruler
- gravel
- sand
- charcoal

Activity Procedure

1 Put several spoonfuls of soil in the jar. Then fill the jar with water and put the lid on. (Picture A)

2 Shake the jar for 15 sec. Then put the jar aside for about 5 min. A process called *sedimentation* is taking place in the jar. It is the first step in waste-water treatment. **Observe** the water in the jar. **Record** your observations.

3 Unbend the paper clip. Use it to punch 10 small holes each in the bottoms of 3 paper cups. Using the marker, label the cups *A*, *B*, and *C*.

◀ A simple way to help restore damaged ecosystems is to provide food for some of the animal populations.

Picture A

Picture B

4 Using the spoon, put a 2.5-cm layer of gravel in Cup A. Put a 2.5-cm layer of sand and then a 2.5-cm layer of gravel in Cup B. Put a 2.5-cm layer of charcoal, then a 2.5-cm layer of sand, and finally a 2.5-cm layer of gravel in Cup C. (Picture B)

5 Put each cup with holes inside a cup without holes. Label the outer cups *A, B,* and *C* to match the inner cups. Then carefully pour equal amounts of water from the jar into the inner cups. Try not to shake the jar as you pour. A process called *filtering* is taking place in the cups. It is the second step in waste-water treatment.

6 Separate each set of cups, allowing all the water to drain into the outer cups. **Observe** the water in the outer cups. **Record** your observations.

Draw Conclusions

1. What did you **observe** happening during sedimentation?

2. What combination of materials filtered the water best?

3. What materials do you **infer** might not be filtered out of waste water?

4. **Scientists at Work** Scientists must **identify and control variables** when they **experiment**. In a real waste-water treatment plant, what variables might affect the filtering process?

Investigate Further **Plan and conduct a simple investigation**, using water that is "polluted" with food coloring. Decide what equipment you will need. Conduct multiple trials and test several different kinds of filters.

> **Process Skill Tip**
>
> You can **identify and control variables** more easily when you **experiment** with a model of a large or complex system.

Restoring Ecosystems

FIND OUT

- how ecosystems are being reclaimed
- what you can do to help restore natural ecosystems

VOCABULARY

reclamation
wetlands

Rivers

In the investigation you experimented with the best way to filter muddy water. By experimenting on a larger scale, scientists have developed more effective ways to treat waste water. This has helped to restore water ecosystems that had been polluted. In the 1960s, for example, the Hudson River, which flows from the Adirondack Mountains to New York Harbor, was dangerously polluted. Today, all waste water must be treated before being released into the river. The river is much cleaner now, and fish and wildlife populations have increased in size. The Hudson River ecosystem has been partly restored.

The process of restoring a damaged ecosystem is called **reclamation** (rek•luh•MAY•shuhn). Within the past 20 years, reclamation has occurred in many places. However, restoring most ecosystems takes a long time and a tremendous amount of work. For example, in many freshwater ecosystems, the bodies of fish contain high levels of poisons called PCBs. When carnivores eat these fish, PCBs enter their bodies. And when the fish die and decompose, the PCBs reenter the water. In this way poisons can remain in an ecosystem for many years, passing from one organism to another.

This wetland in California was built to filter waste water. ▼

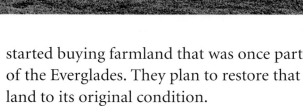

Sometimes it isn't practical to restore natural ecosystems. The park at the right and the fountain above were once landfills. The lands have been adapted to new useful purposes.

Wetlands

Scientists have only recently learned the importance of saltwater marshes, mangrove swamps, and mud flats. These water ecosystems, called **wetlands**, provide habitats for marine organisms. They also act as natural filters that purify water. But 80 percent of the wetlands in the United States are already gone.

Scientists are now working on ways to protect the remaining wetlands and to restore damaged water ecosystems. The Florida Everglades, a mixture of marshes and mangrove swamps, once covered more than 1.6 million hectares (about 4 million acres). It covers only half that much area today. Since 1983 scientists have been working with the state of Florida and the Save Our Everglades program to help preserve the remaining ecosystem. They have also started buying farmland that was once part of the Everglades. They plan to restore that land to its original condition.

Scientists are also experimenting with ways to replace ecosystems that have already been destroyed. In 1986 the city of Arcata, California, completed construction of an artificial wetland. The wetland is used in the city's waste-water treatment.

Arcata's waste water is treated first by sedimentation and filtration. Then the water flows into two treatment marshes. The marshes contain plants that filter out most of the remaining pollutants. Only after this final filtering does the city's waste water flow into the ocean. Many wetland animals now live in the marshes, making this artificial environment a complete ecosystem.

✔ **Why are wetlands such important ecosystems?**

Your Own Back Yard

Local governments and civic organizations across the country are helping to restore natural ecosystems in schoolyards, public parks, and back yards. In midwestern states, for example, many people are replacing their lawns with grasses and flowers found in the area's original prairie ecosystem. Traditional lawns require the use of fertilizers and pesticides. As you have learned, fertilizers can get into groundwater, and pesticides can kill birds and other animals. Prairie lawns are a beneficial change because they need little attention once they are established. And unlike traditional lawns, prairie lawns attract a wide variety of birds, butterflies, and other wildlife.

What was the natural ecosystem like in the area where you live? Have parts of it been saved or reclaimed? Reclaiming an ecosystem takes a lot of research, money, and time. The first steps in the process of reclamation are to learn about the causes of habitat loss and to investigate ways to restore native plants.

The bluebonnet, a prairie wildflower, is the state flower of Texas. In the spring, the bright-blue blossoms cover large areas of the Texas prairie. ▼

Members of the Lady Bird Johnson Wildflower Center, in Texas, conduct research on native plants.

But there are many little things that people can do to attract wildlife to an area. Planting a variety of wildflowers and native shrubs will provide food and shelter for birds, butterflies, and other small animals. Building a small pond will attract wildlife searching for water. The pond will also provide a habitat for frogs and insects.

✓ **How can people help to restore ecosystems in their own back yards?**

Summary

Reclamation is the restoring of a damaged ecosystem. Complete reclamation takes years of research and effort. The ecosystems that are still left must first be saved from destruction. Experimenting with new ways to restore ecosystems is also important. Reclaiming ecosystems takes the efforts of many people in an area.

Review

1. Name three types of wetlands.
2. How can research help to restore ecosystems?
3. What can people do to help restore ecosystems?
4. **Critical Thinking** Explain why government action may be needed to save or restore ecosystems.
5. **Test Prep** The recovery of natural ecosystems that have been damaged by human activity is called —

   A restoration
   B reclamation
   C recovery
   D reinstatement

LINKS

MATH LINK

Graphing Design and conduct a survey to determine people's interest in restoring a natural ecosystem in your area. Find out what people know about the original ecosystem and whether or not they are interested in restoring it. Also ask how much time they would be willing to commit each week. Compile the results of your survey, and summarize those results in a bar graph. You may want to use a computer program such as *Graph Links* to make your graph.

WRITING LINK

Expressive Writing—Poem Write a poem about the reclamation of a damaged ecosystem. Describe how the area looks, smells, feels, and sounds. Then read your poem to your class.

SOCIAL STUDIES LINK

National Park System Since 1872 the National Park Service has established more than 330 parks. Find out how the park system tries to meet people's needs while preserving the environment. Report your findings to your class.

TECHNOLOGY LINK

Learn more about restoring natural ecosystems by viewing *Prairie Restoration* on the **Harcourt Science Newsroom Video** in your classroom video library.

Major Events in Environmental Awareness

The Industrial Revolution, which began in England in the 1700s and then spread to Europe and the United States, resulted in dramatic changes to the natural environment. Air, water, and land became more and more polluted, and Earth's natural resources were used much more rapidly. With these changes, some people began to develop a greater sense of responsibility for the environment.

Environmental Awareness Begins

In 1789 Englishman Gilbert White, often called the "father of ecology," wrote what is considered to be the first ecology book. In his book, White described the plants and animals of the English countryside.

By the mid-1800s the Industrial Revolution was in full swing on the east coast of the United States. At the same time, westward expansion of the country threatened to destroy the remaining wilderness areas. In 1872 President Ulysses S. Grant established the world's first national park—Yellowstone National Park.

A Book Sparks a Movement

Through the first half of the 1900s, the United States became more urban and more industrialized. Manufacturing plants dumped many kinds of pollutants into the environment. Farmers used large amounts of chemicals to kill insect pests and weeds. In 1962 Rachel Carson published *Silent Spring*, in which she told that the use of

The History of Environmental Awareness

1872
The first national park is established.

1908
The Grand Canyon becomes a national monument.

100 B.C.	A.D. 1700	A.D. 1800	A.D. 1900

100 B.C.
The Chinese develop a natural insecticide made from dried flower parts.

1789
Gilbert White publishes the first ecology book,
The Natural History and Antiquities of Selborne.

1962
Rachel Carson publishes *Silent Spring*.

DDT—a pesticide—was also killing birds, particularly the bald eagle. She also wrote that poisons in the environment can affect all living things, including people.

Laws that Protect

Largely because of Rachel Carson's work, the government and people of the United States began taking pollution seriously. Many laws were passed to control it. In 1972 Congress passed a law banning the use of DDT. In 1973 the Endangered Species Act was passed. This law helped save threatened and endangered wild plants and animals from extinction. Since then many more environmental laws have been passed, both in the United States and in countries around the world.

Many environmental problems affect the whole planet and require the cooperation of all nations to solve them. For example, in the late 1970s, scientists found that chemicals used in refrigerators and air conditioners destroy the atmosphere's protective ozone layer. Scientists from many nations met to find ways to help stop ozone destruction. The result was the development of new chemicals for refrigeration that do not destroy ozone.

Today the major environmental concern is global warming. Many scientists hypothesize that excess carbon dioxide, released into the air by the burning of fossil fuels, is raising the temperature of the atmosphere. If this hypothesis is correct, the world faces a great challenge, since modern societies depend on the burning of fossil fuels for industry and transportation.

THINK ABOUT IT

1. What started people thinking about ways to save the environment?

2. Why is environmental protection a worldwide problem?

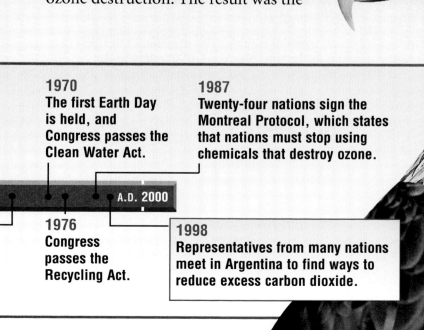

The bald eagle, America's national bird, was saved from extinction when Congress banned the use of DDT in 1972.

1970
The first Earth Day is held, and Congress passes the Clean Water Act.

1987
Twenty-four nations sign the Montreal Protocol, which states that nations must stop using chemicals that destroy ozone.

A.D. 2000

1976
Congress passes the Recycling Act.

1998
Representatives from many nations meet in Argentina to find ways to reduce excess carbon dioxide.

A155

Raman Sukumar

CONSERVATIONIST

"Many species are claimed to be flagships for conservation. But no species can make stronger claim to this than the Asian elephant. If the tiger is the spirit of the jungle, the elephant is its body."

Raman Sukumar is deputy chairperson of the Asian Elephant Specialist Group of the World Conservation Union. He is one of the world's leading authorities on Asian elephants. His work involves planning conservation strategies and finding ways to resolve conflicts between human and elephant use of the same land. He knows that unless these conflicts can be resolved, Asian elephants will not survive in the wild.

Mr. Sukumar believes deeply in the importance of protecting the Asian elephant. "Elephants are beloved locally and globally," he says. Mr. Sukumar stresses that the protection of the elephant will also help to preserve other species living in the elephant's habitat. "Elephants prosper in large forests that are home to a great number of plant and animal species," he says.

Mr. Sukumar first became interested in a career in conservation when he was in high school. It wasn't until college, however, that he began to study elephants. Since that time Mr. Sukumar has spent nearly two decades observing elephants in the wild to better understand their way of life.

Mr. Sukumar currently lives in India with his wife and daughters. Like many scientists, he uses the Internet to stay connected with colleagues around the world.

THINK ABOUT IT

1. What will happen to Asian elephants if conflicts over land use are not resolved?
2. Why will Mr. Sukumar's work help to preserve many other organisms in the Asian elephant's habitat?

Asian elephant at work

Acid Rain

How does acid rain affect art objects?

Materials

- chalk
- paper clip
- modeling clay
- vinegar
- dropper

Procedure

1. Using the paper clip as a tool, carve the piece of chalk into a sculpture.

2. Place your sculpture on a base of clay.

3. Using the dropper, drop vinegar onto your sculpture and observe what happens.

Draw Conclusions

What effect does the vinegar, an acid, have on your sculpture? Chalk is similar to the limestone and marble of real art objects. What do you infer is happening to art objects around the world because of acid rain?

Powerful Plants

How can plants reclaim a damaged ecosystem?

Materials

- 2 small clay pots
- potting soil
- 6 bean seeds
- water
- flour

Procedure

1. Fill both pots half-full of soil. Plant three bean seeds in each pot, and water them with equal amounts of water.

2. Mix the flour and water until it forms a thick batter.

3. Pour the batter into one pot, covering the soil and completely filling the space between the soil and the top of the pot.

4. Place both pots in a warm, sunny place. Water the soil of the uncovered pot when it feels dry.

5. Observe the pots every day for two weeks.

Draw Conclusions

Which pot is the control? What do you observe about the plants in the experimental pot? Where have you noticed plants growing in similar conditions in your neighborhood? How do plants help reclaim damaged ecosystems?

Chapter 5 Review and Test Preparation

Vocabulary Review

Use the terms below to complete the sentences. The page numbers in ( ) tell you where to look in the chapter if you need help.

succession (A132)
pioneer plants (A132)
climax
  community (A133)
pollution (A139)
acid rain (A139)

conserving (A144)
reduce (A144)
reuse (A145)
recycle (A145)
reclamation (A150)
wetlands (A151)

1. When you _____, you recover a resource from an item and use the resource to make a new item.

2. A spruce and hemlock forest is a final stage of succession, or a _____.

3. Reducing, reusing, and recycling are three ways of _____ resources.

4. If you cut down on the resources you use, you _____. If you _____ items, you use them for new purposes.

5. Primary _____ occurs on new, barren land, such as the land exposed by a receding glacier.

6. When pollutants such as nitrogen oxides and sulfur dioxide combine with water vapor and condense, _____ results.

7. Plants that grow during the first stage of succession are called _____.

8. The _____ of the Hudson River ecosystem has brought life back to the river, but it is not yet complete.

9. Untreated waste water, PCBs, and fertilizers form _____ that damages ecosystems.

10. Mangrove swamps, mud flats, and salt-water marshes are all types of _____.

Connect Concepts

Choose items from the list below to fill in the spaces in the concept map.

A an increase in population
B following the three *Rs*
C catastrophic changes
D succession after a glacier, fire, or volcanic eruption
E researching ways to restore habitats
F pollution and acid rain
G passing laws that punish polluters

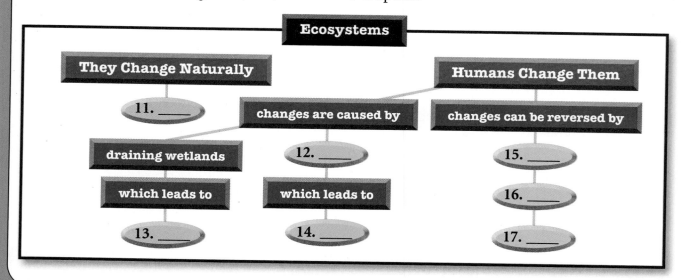

Check Understanding

Write the letter of the best choice.

18. The last stage of succession is called —
    A the pioneer stage
    B the climax community
    C the third stage
    D the full-forest stage

19. An example of a pioneer plant is the —
    F hemlock tree   H fireweed
    G willow tree   J spruce tree

20. The causes of acid rain do **NOT** include —
    A pollution from cars
    B pollution from factories
    C pollution from energy stations
    D pollution from waste water

21. The three *R*s are —
    F refuse, reduce, and recycle
    G replace, recycle, and reuse
    H reduce, reuse, and recycle
    J reward, refuse, and reduce

22. The reclamation of ecosystems does **NOT** include —
    A passing laws like the Clean Water Act
    B civic projects like the Save Our Everglades program
    C research to find new ways to restore ecosystems
    D misusing resources

Critical Thinking

23. A pond is dug in an area where a deciduous forest is the climax community. If the pond is left alone, how will it change?

24. In what ways do you think your actions might affect an ecosystem?

25. Explain how reducing the amount of hot water you use could help to save an ecosystem.

Process Skills Review

26. Suppose you are sent to a river to find out whether it is polluted or not. How would you make your observations? Would you use any instruments to help you **observe**? What would you look for?

27. In Lesson 1 you made a pond model to study succession in a pond ecosystem. Suppose you wanted to find out whether the same thing happens in a river ecosystem. Describe how you could **make a model** of a river ecosystem.

28. Describe how you could **experiment** to test how well a certain fertilizer works in sandy soil, in red clay soil, and in black potting soil. What other **variables** would you need to **identify and control**? What problems might you encounter?

Performance Assessment

Algae Growth

In one jar, fertilizer was added to distilled water. The same amount of fertilizer was added to pond water in another jar. The jars were then put in a sunny spot and left undisturbed for two weeks. What variable was changed in this experiment? What variables were controlled? Predict which jar will have more growth. Explain. Then observe the two jars and draw conclusions.

Unit Project Wrap Up

Here are some ideas for ways to wrap up your unit project.

Write a Project Guide

Make a guide to tell others what you learned about the animals that visited your feeder. Explain how you built your feeder, so someone else could build one, too!

Display at a Science Fair

Make a display about your project for a school science fair or curriculum fair. Prepare a written report describing the procedure you used and your results. On a poster, display the data you collected. You can also display photographs and sketches of the animals that visited your feeder.

Make a Video Presentation

Ask someone to videotape you as you describe the results of your project. Show your videotape to others for review.

Investigate Further

How could you make your project better? What other questions do you have about animals? Plan ways to find answers to your questions. Use the Science Handbook on pages R2-R9 for help.

The Changing Earth

UNIT B

EARTH SCIENCE

The Changing Earth

Unit Project

Earth-Sample Collection

Collect samples of rocks, minerals, and fossils in your area. Record where you find each sample. Plan ways to sort, identify, and label the samples in your collection. Use reference materials to make notes about your samples. Find out what the samples show about the geology of your community.

Chapter 1

Vocabulary Preview

landform
weathering
erosion
deposition
mass movement
crust
mantle
core
plate
magma
volcano
earthquake
fault
continental drift
Pangea
fossil

Changes to Earth's Surface

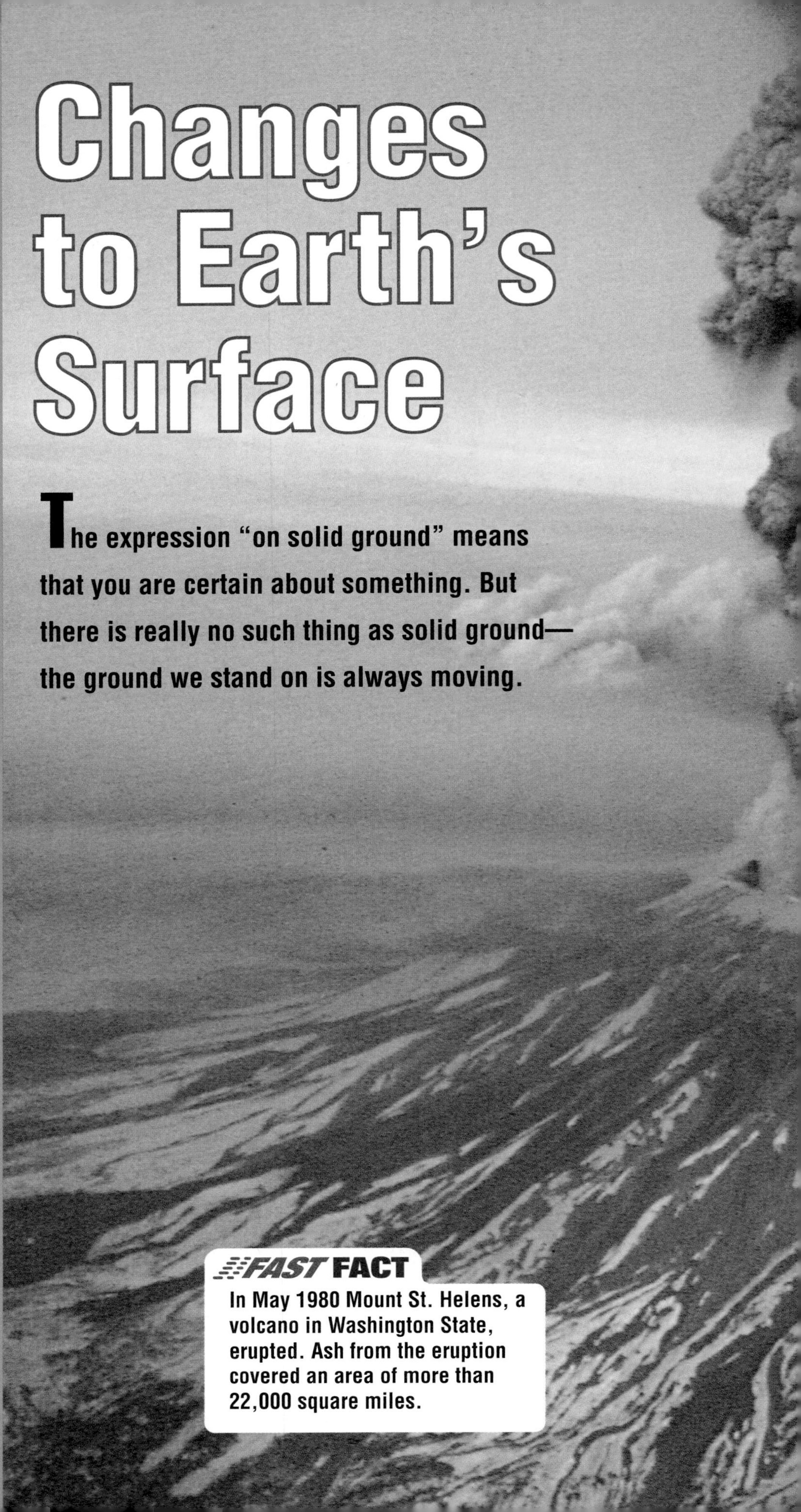

The expression "on solid ground" means that you are certain about something. But there is really no such thing as solid ground—the ground we stand on is always moving.

FAST FACT

In May 1980 Mount St. Helens, a volcano in Washington State, erupted. Ash from the eruption covered an area of more than 22,000 square miles.

There are more than half a million earthquakes every year. Most occur at the bottom of the ocean and are too small to be felt. Only about 1000 earthquakes a year cause any damage.

Mauna Kea, a dormant volcano on the island of Hawai'i, is one of the tallest mountains in the world. From the floor of the Pacific Ocean it rises 9750 m (about 32,000 ft) to sea level and 4205 m (13,796 ft) above sea level, for a total height of nearly 14,000 m (about 46,000 ft). By comparison, Mount Everest is 8848 m (about 29,000 ft) high.

What Processes Change Landforms?

In this lesson, you can .

INVESTIGATE how water cuts through sand.

LEARN ABOUT how wind, water, and ice shape landforms.

LINK to math, writing, social studies, and technology.

▼ Sand carried by wind can carve desert rock into unusual shapes.

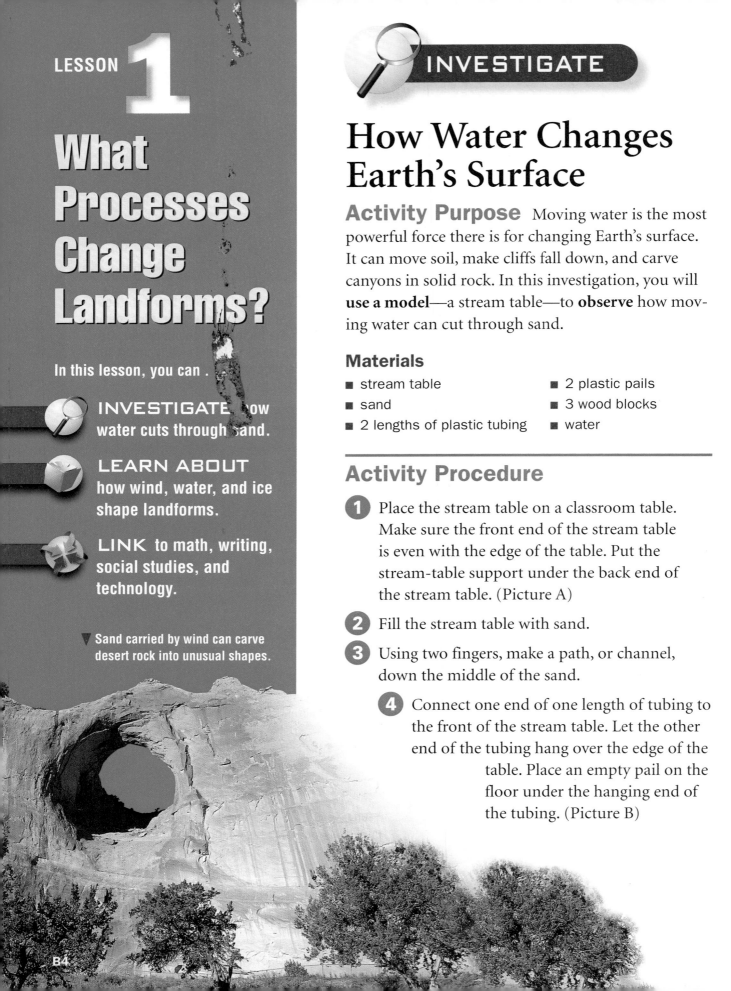

How Water Changes Earth's Surface

Activity Purpose Moving water is the most powerful force there is for changing Earth's surface. It can move soil, make cliffs fall down, and carve canyons in solid rock. In this investigation, you will **use a model**—a stream table—to **observe** how moving water can cut through sand.

Materials

- stream table
- sand
- 2 lengths of plastic tubing
- 2 plastic pails
- 3 wood blocks
- water

Activity Procedure

1 Place the stream table on a classroom table. Make sure the front end of the stream table is even with the edge of the table. Put the stream-table support under the back end of the stream table. (Picture A)

2 Fill the stream table with sand.

3 Using two fingers, make a path, or channel, down the middle of the sand.

4 Connect one end of one length of tubing to the front of the stream table. Let the other end of the tubing hang over the edge of the table. Place an empty pail on the floor under the hanging end of the tubing. (Picture B)

Picture A

Picture B

5 Place the other pail on two wood blocks near the raised end of the stream-table channel. Fill this pail $\frac{3}{4}$ full of water.

6 Put the second length of tubing into the pail of water and fill it with water.

7 Seal one end of the tube and take that end from the pail. To start the water flowing, lower that end and unseal it.

8 **Observe** any changes the water makes to the sand in the stream table. **Record** your observations.

9 Place the third wood block on top of the support under the stream table. Repeat Steps 7 and 8.

Draw Conclusions

1. In which setup was the speed of the water greater?

2. In which setup did you **observe** greater movement of sand from the channel?

3. **Scientists at Work** Scientists infer explanations based on **observations**. What can you infer about how water can change land based on your observations of the stream table?

Investigate Further Use your knowledge of cause and effect to **predict** what would happen if you replaced the sand with soil. **Plan and conduct** multiple trials to test your prediction.

Process Skill Tip

When you use your eyes to notice how the sand looks before and after water flows through it, you **observe** a change. Careful observations are important in science.

Changes to Earth's Surface

Changing Landforms

FIND OUT

- how Earth's crust is broken down into soil
- how water, wind, and ice change landforms

VOCABULARY

landforms
weathering
erosion
deposition
mass movement

Earth's surface is changing all around you. Rivers wear away rock and produce deep canyons. Waves eat away at sea cliffs, turning them into beach sand. Glaciers scrape away the tops of mountains, and winds carrying sand grind away desert rock. Earth's **landforms**, physical features on its surface, might seem as if they never change, but they do.

In the investigation, you saw how the force of flowing water can move sand. Forces such as flowing water, waves, wind, ice, and even movements inside the Earth are constantly changing landforms. Sometimes the changes happen fast enough for you to observe. For example, a volcano might erupt suddenly and blow away a mountaintop, or a powerful hurricane might sweep away a sandy beach. But most changes to Earth's landforms happen so slowly that you cannot observe them directly. Sometimes you can see only the results of past changes.

✔ **What are some of the forces that change landforms?**

◀ Thousands of years of rain and wind shaped these landforms in Utah's Monument Valley.

Flowing water cuts into riverbanks and carries away soil. ▼

◀ The pounding of ocean waves slowly wears away rocky cliffs.

This satellite photo shows the delta the Mississippi River has built in the Gulf of Mexico. ▶

Water

Much of Earth's surface is made of rock. The shaping of landforms starts when weathering wears away rock. **Weathering** is the process of breaking rock into soil, sand, and other tiny pieces, or particles, called *sediment.* Water is an important agent, or cause, of weathering.

Water weathers rock in several ways. Fast-flowing rivers can carve deep canyons in rock. Arizona's Grand Canyon, carved by the action of the Colorado River, is 1.6 km (about 1 mi) deep. Also, ocean waves can weather cliffs and cause them to fall into the sea. Water can weather rock in other ways, too. When it rains, water seeps into tiny holes, or pores, and cracks in rock. If this water freezes, it expands, breaking the rock. Rain that becomes acidic because of pollution can dissolve rock. And flowing water tumbles rocks against each other, breaking them into smaller pieces and smoothing their edges.

After weathering has broken rock into sediment, erosion and deposition move the sediment around and leave it in new places. **Erosion** (ee•ROH•zhuhn) is the process of moving sediment from one place to another. **Deposition** (dep•uh•ZISH•uhn) is the process of dropping, or depositing, sediment in a new location.

Water is not only an important agent of weathering but also the chief agent of erosion. Water can erode great amounts of sediment. At the shore, sediment from weathered cliffs is eroded by waves and deposited as new sand on beaches. Rainfall

TOP
Deltas form as rivers slow down and deposit sediment at their mouths.

CENTER
As the delta builds, the river separates into smaller channels.

BOTTOM
The number of channels continues to increase. Each one becomes a place where sediment is deposited.

erodes sediment and carries it into rivers and streams. Rivers pick up the sediment and move it downstream. Most rivers deposit sediment in flat areas along their banks. These *flood plains,* as they are called, can become rich agricultural areas. Some rivers deposit sediment in broad areas at their mouths. These areas of new land are called *deltas.* The Mississippi River delta is one of the largest in the world.

✔ **What is the difference between weathering and erosion?**

B7

Wind

Wind is another agent of weathering and erosion. Have you ever seen a machine called a sandblaster? It uses a powerful jet of air containing sand to clean building surfaces. In a similar way, wind can carry bits of rock and sand that weather rock surfaces. Wind also moves sediment from place to place. If the wind blows hard, it can erode a lot of sediment.

In dry areas like the American Southwest, wind erosion has shaped some of the world's most unusual landforms—rocks that look like tables, arches, or columns. Wind erodes dry sediment more easily than it erodes particles of soil or damp rock. And there is little plant life in dry areas to hold sediment in place.

Wind erosion can also blow sand into large mounds called *dunes*. Huge dunes as much as 100 m (about 325 ft) high form in some deserts. Many sandy beaches have long lines of dunes on their land side. Beach dunes are built by the constantly blowing sea breezes. They help protect the land behind them during storms.

✔ **How does wind erosion change landforms?**

Ice

Ice in the form of glaciers can also change landforms. *Glaciers* are thick sheets of ice, formed in areas where more snow falls during the winter than melts during the summer. Glaciers seem to stand still, but they actually move. Because of a glacier's great size and weight, it erodes everything under it. Glaciers erode sediment from one place and deposit it in another.

There are two kinds of glaciers. *Valley glaciers* are found in high mountain valleys. They flow slowly down mountainsides, eroding the mountains under them and forming U-shaped valleys. This forms a special soil called glacial till. So, this soil can show places where glaciers traveled in the past.

Continental glaciers cover large areas of Earth. They cover almost all of Greenland and Antarctica today. But thousands of years ago, when the climate was colder, continental glaciers covered Europe, Canada, and the northern United States.

✔ **What are glaciers?**

The Athabasca Glacier recedes about 13 m (43 ft) each year. During the past 100 years, it has receded about 1.6 km (1 mi). ▶

Dunes form where an obstacle, such as a plant or a rock, causes wind to slow and deposit the sand it is carrying. ▼

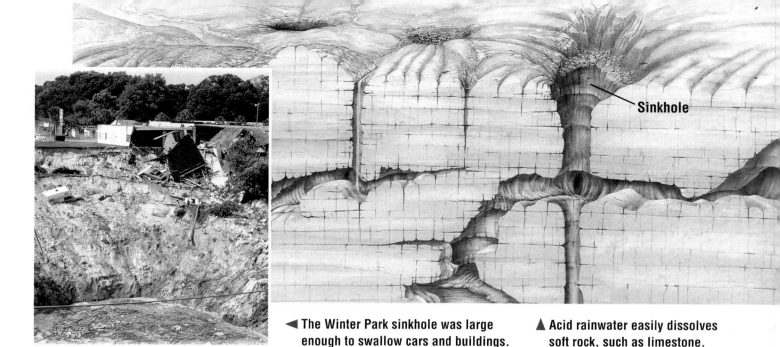

◄ The Winter Park sinkhole was large enough to swallow cars and buildings.

▲ Acid rainwater easily dissolves soft rock, such as limestone.

Sinkhole

Mass Movement

During the winter of 1997–1998, heavy rains fell on much of the California coast. One night, families living in a small canyon heard a loud noise. When they went outside to see what had happened, they discovered that a mound of mud had slid down the steep sides of the canyon, covering part of a house. This mudslide occurred when a mass of soil that was full of water moved rapidly downhill.

A mudslide is one type of mass movement. **Mass movement** is the downhill movement of rock and soil because of gravity. Mass movements, such as mudslides and landslides, can change landforms quickly. Mudslides move wet soil. Landslides move dry soil. Landslides occur when gravity becomes stronger than the friction that holds soil in place on a hill. The soil falls suddenly to the bottom of the hill.

Another type of mass movement—one that occurs slowly, as you might guess from its name—is called *creep*. Creep occurs when soil moves slowly downhill because of gravity. Creep is so slow that changes in landforms are hard to observe directly. The land may move only a few centimeters each year. But over time, creep can move fences, utility poles, roads, and railroad tracks.

One day in 1981, in the city of Winter Park, Florida, an area of land suddenly collapsed, or fell in on itself. The hole swallowed houses, swimming pools, and businesses, including a car dealership. Today there is a lake where there was once dry land. The process that led to the formation of the Winter Park sinkhole is different from that of other types of mass movement.

A sinkhole is a large hole in the ground that opens suddenly. Sinkholes form after rock under the surface has dissolved or become weak. Sinkholes often appear in areas of limestone rock, because limestone dissolves easily. Rain seeping into the ground combines with carbon dioxide from the air to form a weak acid called *carbonic acid*. Carbonic acid dissolves limestone, forming huge holes. When enough rock has dissolved, land over the weakened area collapses.

✔ **What is mass movement?**

New Landforms

Erosion and deposition can change landforms or produce new ones. Rivers can deposit sediment that builds deltas. They can also change their path, or course, producing new lakes on wide flood plains.

Glaciers are major forces for forming new landforms. As the glaciers of the last Ice Age moved forward, they pushed mounds of rock and soil in front of them. When the glaciers melted, they left behind at their lower ends long ridges of soil and rock, called *terminal moraines*. Long Island and Cape Cod are terminal moraines. They mark the leading edge of the glacier that covered much of North America.

New islands can be formed by volcanic eruptions. Underwater volcanoes increase their height by depositing melted rock and ash. In time, they break through the sea surface as islands. The Hawaiian Islands formed in this way. Almost constant eruptions of Kilauea add daily to the size of the island of Hawai'i. Another volcano, now growing slowly on the ocean floor east of Hawai'i, will one day become the island of Hohonu.

✔ **What new landforms are created by erosion and deposition?**

Old, slow-moving rivers form broad loops. ▼

The loops can become so broad that they meet. ▼

Because the river follows the shortest route, its flow cuts off the loop. The old loop forms a crescent-shaped body of water called an *oxbow lake*. ▼

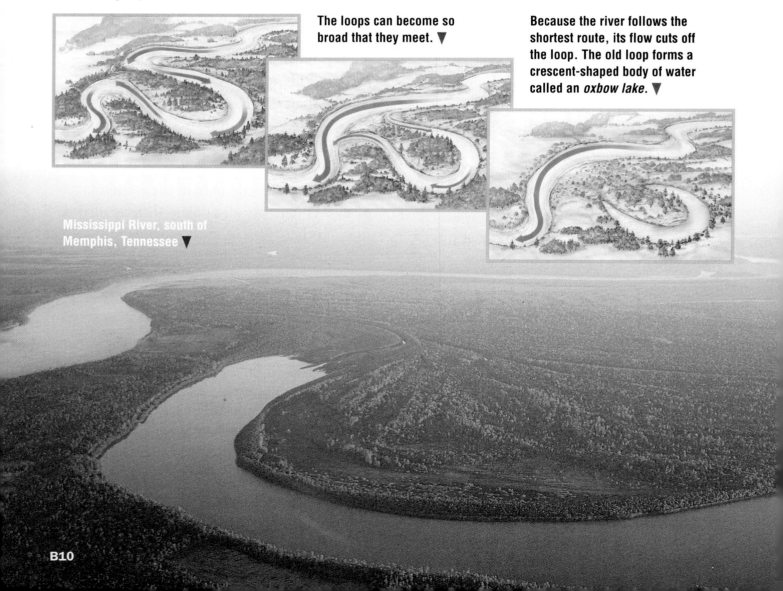

Mississippi River, south of Memphis, Tennessee ▼

Summary

Weathering breaks down the rock of Earth's surface into soil, sand, and other small particles. Agents of erosion, such as water, wind, and ice, change Earth's landforms by moving rock and soil. Water can carve canyons and deposit sediment to form deltas. Wind can form sand dunes. Ice can carve U-shaped valleys and leave landforms such as terminal moraines. Even forces within the Earth, such as volcanoes, can produce new landforms.

Review

1. What is erosion?
2. What is deposition?
3. What forces cause erosion and deposition?
4. **Critical Thinking** Why is weathering so important to life on land?
5. **Test Prep** A type of mass movement is a —
   A glacier
   B delta
   C mudslide
   D terminal moraine

LINKS

MATH LINK

Glacier Size The Aletsch Glacier in Europe is 80 km^2. Malaspina Glacier in Alaska measures 1344 km^2. The Grinnell Glacier in Montana is about 2 km^2. Use a computer, if possible, to make a bar graph that compares these glaciers.

WRITING LINK

Informative Writing—Description Erosion can cause beautiful landforms. Suppose you are hiking through an area with much wind or ice erosion, such as Yosemite or Bryce Canyon National Park. Use reference materials to find out more about the area. Then write a story for your teacher describing your hiking trip. Identify landforms caused by erosion and tell how they formed.

SOCIAL STUDIES LINK

Topographic Maps Topographic maps use symbols and colors to represent landforms. These maps can tell you how the land looks—if you know how to read them. At the library, look for a topographic map of the area where you live. What kinds of symbols are used to show water, wetlands, and deserts?

TECHNOLOGY LINK

Learn more about landscapes and erosion by visiting this Internet site.
www.scilinks.org/harcourt

LESSON 2

What Causes Mountains, Volcanoes, and Earthquakes?

In this lesson, you can . . .

 INVESTIGATE the structure of Earth.

 LEARN ABOUT what forms mountains and volcanoes.

 LINK to math, writing, literature, and technology.

Volcanoes release melted rock from deep inside Earth. ▼

INVESTIGATE

Journey to the Center of Earth

Activity Purpose If you could slice Earth in half, you would see that it has several layers. Of course, you can't slice Earth in half, but you can make a model of it. In this investigation you will **make a model** that shows Earth's layers.

Materials

- 2 graham crackers
- 1 small plastic bag
- disposable plastic gloves
- 1 spoon
- 1 jar peanut butter
- 1 hazelnut or other round nut
- freezer
- plastic knife

Activity Procedure

1 Put the graham crackers in the plastic bag. Close the bag and use your hands to crush the crackers into crumbs. Then set the bag aside.

2 Put on the plastic gloves. Use the spoon to scoop a glob of peanut butter from the jar and put it in your gloved hand. Place the nut in the center of the peanut butter. Cover the nut with more peanut butter until there is about 2.5 cm of peanut butter all around the nut. Using both hands, roll the glob of peanut butter with the nut at its center into a ball. (Picture A)

Picture A

Picture B

3. Open the bag of crushed graham crackers, and roll the peanut butter ball in the graham cracker crumbs until the outside of the ball is completely coated.

4. Put the ball in the freezer for about 15 minutes. Remove the ball and cut into your model with the plastic knife. **Observe** the layers inside. You might want to take a photograph of your model for later review. (Picture B)

Draw Conclusions

1. The peanut butter ball is a model of Earth's layers. How many layers does Earth have in this model?

2. Which layer of Earth do the crushed graham crackers represent? Why do you think your model has a thick layer of peanut butter but a thin layer of graham cracker crumbs?

3. **Scientists at Work** Scientists can see and understand complex structures better by **making models** of them. What does the model show about Earth's layers? What doesn't the model show about Earth's layers?

Investigate Further Some geologists, scientists who study the Earth, say that Earth's center is divided into a soft outer part and a hard inner part. How could you **make a model** to show this?

Process Skill Tip

You cannot see Earth's layers. So **making a model** helps you understand how they look in relation to each other. In this activity, you need to cut open the model to see the layers.

Mountains, Volcanoes, and Earthquakes

Earth's Interior

FIND OUT

• how mountains form

• what causes volcanoes and earthquakes

VOCABULARY

crust
mantle
core
plate
magma
volcano
earthquake
fault

As the model you made in the investigation showed, Earth is not a solid ball of rock. It has three distinct layers. We live on Earth's crust. The **crust** is the outer layer, and it is made of rock. Earth's crust is very thin compared to the other layers. If Earth were the size of a chicken's egg, the crust would be thinner than the egg's shell.

The **mantle** is the layer of rock beneath Earth's crust. Just under the crust, the rock of the mantle is solid. But the mantle is very hot. This makes the lower part of the mantle soft, like melted candy. No one has ever been to the mantle, but hot, soft rock from the lower mantle sometimes reaches Earth's surface through volcanoes.

The **core** is the center layer of Earth. It is Earth's hottest layer. The core can be divided into two parts: an outer core of liquid, or *molten,* iron and an inner core of solid iron. Even though the core is very hot, great pressure at the center of Earth keeps the inner core solid.

✔ **What parts of Earth are solid rock?**

Separating plates

Crust

Mantle

Core

B14

Earth's Crust Moves

Earth's surface is not a single piece of rock. Instead, it is made up of many plates. **Plates** are rigid blocks of crust and upper mantle rock. Most of North America, Greenland, and the western half of the North Atlantic Ocean are on the North American plate. Part of California and most of the Pacific Ocean make up the Pacific plate. There are 12 major plates in all. Earth's plates fit together like the pieces of a jigsaw puzzle.

Although these plates are enormous, they actually float on the soft rock of the mantle. Pressure and heat within the Earth produce currents in the soft rock of the mantle. As the mantle moves, the plates floating on it move, too.

Plate movement is very slow—only a few centimeters each year. But because plates are right next to each other, the movement of one plate affects other plates. Some plates push together. Some pull apart. Other plates slide past each other. As plates move around, they cause great changes in Earth's landforms.

Where plates collide, energy is released, and new landforms are produced. On land, mountains rise and volcanoes erupt. South America's Andes Mountains are a result of the Nazca and South American plates colliding. On the ocean floor, deep trenches form.

As plates pull apart on land, valleys dotted with volcanoes develop. Africa's Great Rift Valley was formed by the African and Arabian plates pulling apart. The rift, or crack, will one day result in a complete separation of part of eastern Africa from the rest of the continent. Where plates pull apart under the sea, ridges and volcanoes form. This spreading forms new sea floor at the ridges.

When plates scrape and slide past each other, they shake Earth's surface. Along the San Andreas (an•DRAY•uhs) fault in California, the Pacific plate is moving past the North American plate. The plates rub and shake as they grind past each other, causing earthquakes.

✔ **What are Earth's plates?**

Colliding ocean plates

Colliding continental plates

The Himalayas formed as the Indian plate pushed into the Eurasian plate. The plates are still pushing together, and the mountains are still getting taller.

Mountain Formation

Mountains are Earth's highest landforms. They form as the crust folds, cracks, and bends upward because of the movements of Earth's plates.

Most of the highest mountains form where continental plates collide. As the plates push together, their edges crumple and fold into mountains. The Himalayas (him•uh•LAY•uhz), Earth's highest mountain range, formed this way.

At some places, continental and oceanic plates collide. Because continental rock is less dense than seafloor rock, the continental plate moves up and over the oceanic plate. The Cascade Mountains, near the Pacific Ocean, formed this way.

Mountains do not form only at the edges, or boundaries, of plates. Some mountains form where pressure from movement at the boundaries pushes a block of rock upward. The Grand Tetons (TEE•tahnz) of Wyoming rise straight up from the flat land around them.

In some places, plates pull apart, and magma from below rises into the gaps that are produced. **Magma** is hot, partially molten rock that forms in the Earth's upper mantle. Where it rises and solidifies, it forms

long chains of mountains under the ocean. These mountains are called *mid-ocean ridges*. The Mid-Atlantic Ridge is Earth's longest mountain range. It separates the North American and Eurasian plates in the North Atlantic and the South American and African plates in the South Atlantic.

✔ **How do most of the highest mountains form?**

Volcanoes

You have read that most volcanoes form at plate boundaries. A **volcano** is a mountain formed by lava and ash. *Lava* is magma that reaches Earth's surface. *Ash* is small pieces of hardened lava.

Chains of volcanoes form where a continental plate and an oceanic plate collide. The edge of the oceanic plate pushes under the edge of the continental plate. The leading edge of the oceanic plate melts as it sinks deep into the mantle. The melted rock becomes magma that forces its way up between the plates. The volcanoes of the Cascades, such as Mount St. Helens, formed this way.

Sometimes volcanoes form in the middle of plates, over unusually hot columns of magma. The magma melts a hole in the plate and rises through the hole, causing a volcanic eruption. The Hawaiian Islands are the tops of a chain of volcanoes that formed in the middle of the Pacific plate. As the Pacific plate continues moving over this hot spot, new volcanoes and new islands form. The big island of Hawai'i, with its active volcano, Kīlauea, is the youngest island in the chain. Kure Atoll, an extinct volcano 2617 km (about 1625 mi) to the northwest, is the oldest.

✔ **What is a volcano?**

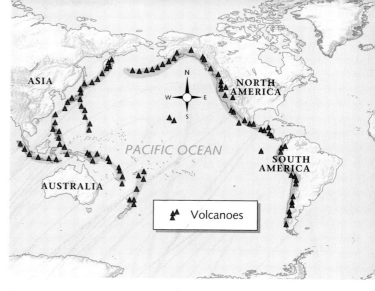

▲ Many volcanoes are located at plate boundaries around the Pacific plate. That's why this area is called the Ring of Fire.

THE INSIDE STORY

Volcanoes

Volcanoes take on their characteristic shapes as lava and ash build up around their openings, or *vents*.

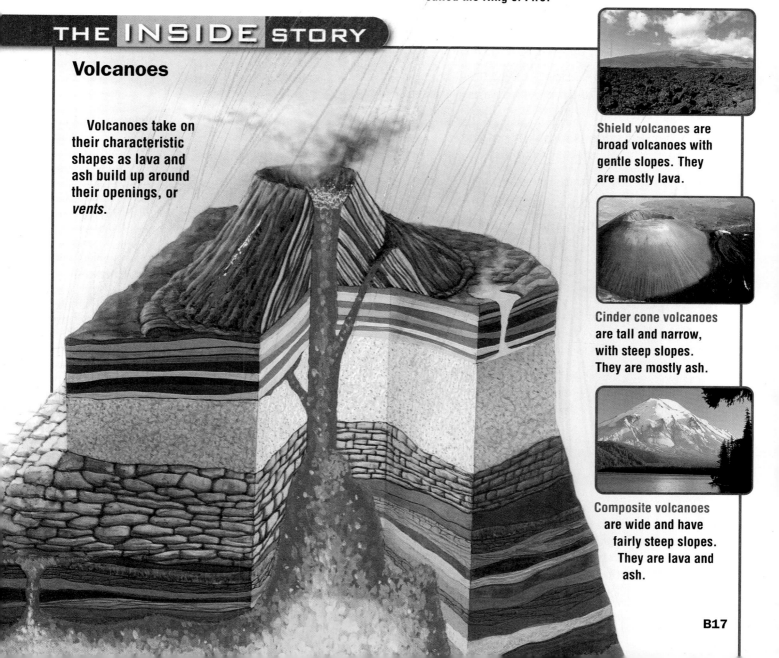

Shield volcanoes are broad volcanoes with gentle slopes. They are mostly lava.

Cinder cone volcanoes are tall and narrow, with steep slopes. They are mostly ash.

Composite volcanoes are wide and have fairly steep slopes. They are lava and ash.

In 1964 a large earthquake hit Anchorage, Alaska. Streets split open, bridges collapsed, and houses slid downhill toward the sea.

Earthquake center, or *focus*

Fault

Earthquakes

On March 27, 1964, thousands of people in Anchorage, Alaska, were shaken as the ground rocked under them. A strong earthquake, possibly the most powerful one ever recorded, knocked down houses, broke up roads, and cut water, gas, and power lines all over the area.

An **earthquake** is a shaking of the ground caused by the sudden release of energy in Earth's crust. The energy released as plates crush together, scrape past each other, or bend along jagged boundaries can cause great damage. Earthquakes are very common. Nearly a million of them occur each year. However, most are too small to be felt or to cause damage.

Many earthquakes occur along the boundaries of the Pacific plate. Earthquakes also occur along faults in the crust. You have read that Earth's crust can bend or break in the middle of a plate as forces press in on it. These breaks can form **faults**, or places where pieces of the crust move.

An earthquake sends out energy in the form of *seismic* (SYZ•mik) *waves*. Seismic waves are like ripples that form on a pond when a stone is tossed in. Scientists measure and record seismic waves on an instrument called a *seismograph* (SYZ•muh•graf). These measurements can then be used to compare the relative strengths of earthquakes.

✔ **What is an earthquake?**

Major Earthquakes		
Magnitude	**Year**	**Location**
9.1	1964	Alaska
8.9	1933	Japan
8.4	1946	Japan
8.2	1976	China
8.1	1979	Indonesia
8.1	1985	Mexico
6.9	1989	California
6.8	1994	California

▲ The Richter scale is used to measure relative strengths, or *magnitudes,* of earthquakes. On this scale an earthquake with a magnitude of 7.5, for example, is 32 times more powerful than an earthquake with a magnitude of 6.5.

◄ Sudden movement along a fault can cause an earthquake.

Summary

Earth has three layers: the crust, the mantle, and the core. Rock of the crust and upper mantle makes up plates that fit together like puzzle pieces. Earth's plates collide, pull apart, and slide past each other. Most mountains and volcanoes form at plate boundaries. Many earthquakes also occur at plate boundaries.

Review

1. Describe three ways in which Earth's plates interact.
2. What is magma and where does it come from?
3. How do volcanoes form where oceanic and continental plates collide?
4. **Critical Thinking** Assume that the overall size of Earth's crust stays the same. If one plate is pushing away from the plate next to it on one side, what must be happening at the boundary with another plate on the opposite side?
5. **Test Prep** Many strong earthquakes are caused by —
   A plates sliding past each other
   B lava flowing down the side of a volcano
   C plates spreading apart
   D hot magma

LINKS

MATH LINK

Earthquake Magnitudes Each whole number on the Richter scale represents a force 32 times as strong as the next lower number. An earthquake of magnitude 7 is 32 times as strong as one of magnitude 6. How many times as strong is an earthquake of magnitude 8 compared with an earthquake of magnitude 5?

WRITING LINK

Informative Writing—Explanation The 1980 explosion of Mount St. Helens was a very powerful volcanic eruption. Find pictures in books and magazines of Mount St. Helens before, during, and after the eruption. Write captions for the pictures to explain what happened. Share your photo essay with your class.

LITERATURE LINK

Eruption *Volcano: The Eruption and Healing of Mount St. Helens* by Patricia Lauber (Bradbury Press, 1986) explains how and why Mount St. Helens erupted. It also describes the destruction the eruption caused, and how the land has since recovered.

TECHNOLOGY LINK

Learn more about volcanoes by viewing *Ring of Fire* and *Volcano Hunters* on the **Harcourt Science Newsroom Video** in your classroom video library.

3

How Has Earth's Surface Changed?

In this lesson, you can . . .

INVESTIGATE the movement of continents.

LEARN ABOUT how Earth's surface has changed over time.

LINK to math, writing, art, and technology.

◀ Over millions of years, these trees have turned to stone.

INVESTIGATE

Movement of the Continents

Activity Purpose Earth's surface 100 million years ago probably looked much different than it does today. In the last lesson, you read that Earth's surface is made up of plates that move. In this investigation, you will **make a model** to find out how Earth's surface might have looked before these plates moved to their present locations.

Materials

■ 3 copies of a world map
■ scissors
■ 3 sheets of construction paper
■ glue
■ globe or world map

Activity Procedure

1 Cut out the continents from one copy of the world map.

2 Arrange the continents into one large "super-continent" on a sheet of construction paper. As you would with a jigsaw puzzle, arrange them so their edges fit together as closely as possible. (Picture A)

3 Label the pieces with the names of their present continents, and glue them onto the paper.

4 Use a globe or world map to locate the following mountains: Cascades, Andes, Atlas, Himalayas, Alps. Then draw these mountains on the supercontinent.

Picture A

Picture B

5 Use your textbook to locate volcanoes and places where earthquakes have occurred. Put a *V* in places where you know there are volcanoes, such as the Cascades. Put an *E* in places where you know that earthquakes have occurred, such as western North America.

6 Repeat Steps 1–5 with the second copy of the world map, but before gluing the continents to the construction paper, separate them by about 2.5 cm. That is, leave about 2.5 cm of space between North America and Eurasia, between South America and Africa, and so on. (Picture B)

7 Glue the third world map copy onto a sheet of construction paper. Then place the three versions of the world map in order from the oldest to the youngest.

Draw Conclusions

1. Where do the continents fit together the best?

2. Where are most of the mountains, volcanoes, and earthquake sites in relation to the present continents? Why do you think they are there?

3. **Scientists at Work** Scientists **use models**, such as maps, to better understand complex structures and processes. How did your models of Earth's continents help you **draw conclusions** about Earth's past? What limitations did your models have?

Investigate Further **Hypothesize** about the fact that the continents do not fit together exactly. Then **plan and conduct a simple investigation** to test your hypothesis.

Process Skill Tip

It is impossible to actually see Earth's surface as it looked millions of years ago. But by **using a model**, you can **draw conclusions** about how it may have looked.

How Earth's Surface Has Changed

FIND OUT

- **how Earth's surface features have changed over millions of years**
- **how fossils help scientists to learn about plants and animals of the past**

VOCABULARY

continental drift
Pangea
fossil

Continental Drift

From evidence like the models you used in the investigation, scientists infer that Earth's surface has not always looked the way it does today. The surface is constantly changing because of continental drift. **Continental drift** is the theory of how Earth's continents move over its surface.

According to the theory, about 225 million years ago, all of the land on Earth was joined together in one "supercontinent" called **Pangea** (pan•JEE•uh). Evidence suggests that about 200 million years ago, Pangea broke into two big continents. The southern one, Gondwana, contained all the land that is now in the Southern Hemisphere. The northern continent, Laurasia, contained land that would become North America and Eurasia. Finally, Gondwana and Laurasia broke into smaller land masses, forming the continents we know today.

Since the continents are still moving, you might infer that the surface of Earth will be very different 200 million years from now. The Atlantic Ocean is getting wider, pushing Europe and North America apart. The Pacific Ocean is getting smaller. And Australia is moving north.

✔ **What is the theory of continental drift?**

Continental Drift

200 million years ago
Pangea begins to break apart.

100 million years ago
Gondwana breaks into smaller continents earlier than Laurasia does.

Today
Earth's surface may look even different in the future.

The Rock Record

If you were floating down the Colorado River through the deepest part of the Grand Canyon, shown at the right, you would be looking up at layers of sedimentary rock nearly 2 billion years old! *Sedimentary rock* is rock formed from sediments that have cemented together. The Grand Canyon is a mile-deep slice into Earth's history, cutting through 20 different layers of sediment.

The sedimentary rocks of the canyon contain a fossil record of Earth's organisms from its earliest history to the present. **Fossils** are the remains or traces of past life found in sedimentary rock. Scientists study fossils to find out how life on Earth has changed.

Scientists also depend on the fact that some things will always be the same. Processes that produced features like the Grand Canyon are still occurring today. Running water still erodes sedimentary rock layers, and new layers of sedimentary rock are still forming.

From the position of sedimentary rock layers, scientists can infer the relative ages of the rocks. Younger rock layers are found on top of older rock layers. Some of the oldest rock layers on Earth are near the bottom of the Grand Canyon.

The walls of the Grand Canyon contain rock from only the earliest stages of Earth's history. Erosion has worn away more recent rock. If you stand on the canyon's north rim, you are standing on rock that is about 250 million years old.

✔ **Why is looking at the Grand Canyon like looking at Earth's history?**

The youngest rocks are at the top of the canyon walls.

The oldest rocks are at the bottom of the canyon.

B23

How Fossils Show Changes

Fossils show us that life on Earth has not always been the same as it is now. Dinosaurs once roamed Earth, as did large, elephantlike animals called *woolly mammoths.* Scientists have drawn conclusions about these creatures from what they left behind—whole mammoths frozen in ice and fossilized bones and teeth of dinosaurs.

Most fossils, however, are not the actual remains of once-living organisms. Instead, they are traces left behind when dead plants and animals decayed or dissolved. When sediment buries an organism, it can produce a mold or cast as the sediment hardens into rock. A mold forms when underground water dissolves the organism, leaving only its shape behind in the rock. If minerals fill the empty space and harden, the fossil becomes a cast—like a dinosaur egg.

In addition to showing what kinds of organisms lived on Earth long ago, fossils also show that Earth's surface was different than it is today. Scientists have found fossils of sea organisms in rock at the tops of high mountains. They infer that those areas were once under water. Scientists use fossil evidence to support the theory of continental drift. Fossils of similar plants and animals have been found in Africa, South America, India, and Australia. This means that these widely separated continents must have been joined at one time.

✓ **How are fossils used to show changes?**

Fossil dinosaur bones have been found in relatively young rock layers.

Fossil fish were found in rock layers much older than those containing dinosaur bones.

Trilobites (TRY•loh•byts) were unusual animals. We know of their existence only because of the fossils they left behind.

There are not many fossils from the earliest era. That is because organisms did not yet have hard body parts, such as bones, shells, and teeth, which fossilize easily.

▲ Scientists called *paleontologists* study fossils to learn about life of the past.

Summary

Earth's continents once were joined to form a supercontinent called Pangea. Pangea broke apart and, over millions of years, the continents drifted to their present locations. Fossils, the remains and traces of dead organisms, show what Earth's life was like in the past. They also show that Earth's surface has changed.

Review

1. What was Pangea?
2. How old are the oldest rocks of the Grand Canyon?
3. How do we know that Earth's life was different in the past?
4. **Critical Thinking** Why is the Grand Canyon important to scientists studying Earth's past?
5. **Test Prep** The Southern continent that existed 200 million years ago was called —

   A Gondwana   C Laurasia
   B Precambria   D Eurasia

 # LINKS

 ### MATH LINK

Geologic Time Scale Research Earth's history. Then make a chart showing the relative lengths of the various eras and periods. Your chart should show how long each era and period lasted and how long ago each occurred. Draw the chart to scale. For example, if an era lasted for half the time of Earth's history, it should cover half the chart.

 ### WRITING LINK

Informative Writing—Compare and Contrast You learned that Earth's continents were once in different places. Where will they be in the future? Research what a map of the world might look like 100 million years from now. Then compare and contrast this map with a current map in a report for your teacher.

 ### ART LINK

Past Life Look for illustrations of what Earth's surface might have looked like thousands, or even millions, of years ago. Compare what you find with the way Earth's surface looks today.

 ### TECHNOLOGY LINK

Learn more about changes to Earth's surface by visiting the National Air and Space Museum Internet site.
www.si.edu/harcourt/science

Exploring Earth's Surface from Space

Newly released satellite images of the ocean floor are making scientists question old theories about the processes that change Earth's surface.

Satellite Secrets

Until recently, information collected by a U.S. government Geosat satellite was top secret. Now data gathered by this satellite has been released, and geologists are excited. However, they say it will take about ten years to analyze the satellite's images of Earth's geologic processes.

If you've ever sailed on the ocean, you probably couldn't tell that the water bulges up in certain places. It does this because of gravity. Rock on the ocean floor has a gravitational pull on the water around it. The more rock, the stronger the pull. The stronger the pull, the more the water bulges up. A 2000-m (about 6562-ft) underwater volcano causes a water bulge of about 2 m (6.6 ft).

Many of the volcanoes under the Pacific Ocean were discovered by gravity imaging.

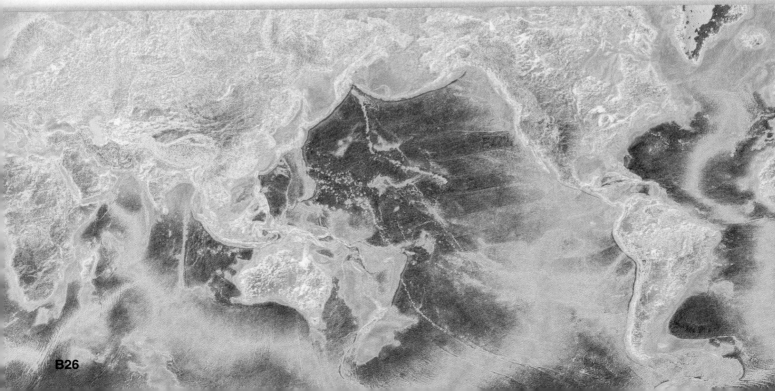

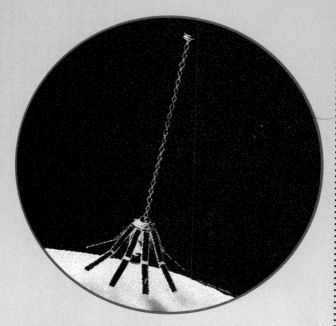

This drawing shows a Geosat circling Earth.

Sensitive equipment on board a Geosat can measure these bulges from space. By measuring the surface of the ocean very precisely, the satellite produces clear gravity images of volcanoes, mountain ranges, plains, and other "landforms" on the ocean floor.

New Data Shakes Up Old Theories

Many areas of the ocean floor had never been surveyed before. About half of the underwater volcanoes shown by the Geosat's gravity imaging had not been known to exist. Gravity images of water bulges are also making scientists question old theories about how volcanic island chains form.

The old theory, called the "hot spot" model, said that there are hot areas in Earth's mantle. As Earth's plates pass slowly over a hot spot, a long line of volcanoes forms. Each new volcano in the line is younger than the one just before it.

But the hot spot model can't explain some of the newly discovered volcano chains. For example, the Pukapuka Ridges, which extend for thousands of kilometers east of Tahiti, seem to have erupted all at the same time. Rock samples from different parts of the chain are all the same age.

Scientists are arguing about what these new discoveries mean in terms of the old theories about hot spots being correct. Many agree that the hot spot model may be wrong. All agree that there is much work ahead to develop more accurate theories based on this Geosat data.

THINK ABOUT IT

1. How does gravity imaging work?
2. Why do you think oil companies might be interested in gravity images?

WEB LINK:
For science and technology updates, visit The Learning Site.
www.harcourtschool.com/ca

Careers — Satellite Technician

What They Do
Satellite technicians work as part of a team that plans, constructs, launches, and operates satellites. They may also work at control stations to receive and monitor data transmissions from satellites.

Education and Training A person wishing to become a satellite technician needs training in electronics, computer sciences, and communications systems.

Kia K. Baptist

GEOSCIENTIST

"A key to being a scientist is to be unafraid to ask questions and unafraid that there may not be answers."

Kia Baptist can see what lies below Earth's surface. She is a geoscientist who works for an oil company. Her job is to help find oil and natural gas resources by finding clues in different kinds of data.

Ms. Baptist collects seismic data by creating small "earthquakes" in rock. Then she analyzes the sound signals that return and uses them to map the rock formations and structures underground.

Ms. Baptist also analyzes geochemical data to learn the chemical nature of the rock. This tells her what kind of rock it is, how old it is, and whether there is oil present. This information, along with computer technology, allows her to give advice to the oil companies on specific locations where oil and natural gas may be found.

Looking for clues is natural for Ms. Baptist. As a child growing up in Baltimore, Maryland, she was a mystery solver. She decided she wanted to help solve the mysteries of space by becoming an astronaut. Several times she worked as an intern at NASA, learning all she could about astronomy and physics. She took courses in many areas of science, believing that knowing about all branches of science would help her do her best work in one. When she began to study geology and chemistry, she realized her true interest lay in those areas. She hasn't stopped studying the Earth since then.

Ms. Baptist gives good advice to young scientists. She says, "Part of the process of science is attacking a problem and trying to find answers, but don't be intimidated if you don't find answers right away. Just keep learning."

THINK ABOUT IT

1. How could analyzing seismic data give clues about where oil is located?

2. Why is it important to know the specific location of oil?

Sedimentary rock layers

Model Earth

How can you model Earth's layers?

Materials

- rounded objects, such as

  an apple   a tennis ball

  an avocado   an orange

  a peach   a plum

  a hard-boiled egg   plain chocolates, or

  a nectarine   chocolate-covered
  peanuts

Procedure

❶ Make two columns on a sheet of paper.

❷ Label one column "Does Model Earth's Layers." Label the other column "Does Not Model Earth's Layers."

❸ Decide what characteristics an object must have to model Earth's layers.

❹ Examine each object. Then write the name of the object in the appropriate column.

Draw Conclusions

What characteristics must an object have to model Earth's layers? Which parts of the objects in the "Does Model Earth's Layers" column represent Earth's layers? What other objects can you think of that model Earth's layers?

Featuring Earth

How do landforms change?

Materials

- apple
- tape measure
- pan
- hotpad
- oven

Procedure

❶ Measure the circumference of the apple.

❷ Place the apple in a pan and, using the hot pad, put the pan in the oven and bake it for one hour at 300°F.

300° OVEN

❸ Your teacher or another adult will remove the apple from the oven. Allow it to cool, and measure it again.

❹ Observe the features of the baked apple.

Draw Conclusions

In some ways, baked apples are a good model of how Earth's landforms change. Compare the circumference of the apple before and after you baked it. What happened to the peel as the apple cooled? What layer of Earth does the peel represent? What "landforms" can you identify on the apple peel? In what ways is the apple *not* a good model of Earth's changing landforms?

Chapter 1 Review and Test Preparation

Vocabulary Review

Use the terms below to complete the sentences. The page numbers in ( ) tell you where to look in the chapter if you need help.

landform (B6)
weathering (B7)
erosion (B7)
deposition (B7)
mass movement (B9)
crust (B14)
mantle (B14)
core (B14)
plate (B15)
magma (B16)
volcano (B16)
earthquake (B18)
fault (B18)
continental drift (B22)
Pangea (B22)
fossils (B23)

1. An _____ is a sudden release of energy in Earth's _____, causing the ground to shake.

2. A rigid block of Earth's crust and upper mantle rock is a _____.

3. A _____ is a physical feature on Earth's surface, such as a mountain or valley.

4. The remains or traces of past life found in Earth's crust are called _____.

5. Hot, soft rock from Earth's lower mantle is _____.

6. A _____ is a break in Earth's crust, along which pieces of the crust move.

7. _____ is the process of breaking rock into soil, sand, and other particles called sediment.

8. Lava is magma that reaches Earth's surface through an opening, called a _____, in Earth's crust.

9. The downhill movement of rock and soil because of gravity is _____.

10. The _____ is the layer of rock beneath Earth's crust.

11. The theory that the continents move over Earth's surface is _____.

12. _____ is the supercontinent that held all of Earth's land 225 million years ago.

13. _____ is the process of moving sediment from one place to another, and _____ is the process of dropping, or depositing, sediment in a new location.

14. The _____ is the center of Earth.

Connect Concepts

Use the Word Bank to complete the sentences.

deltas   beaches   tables   sinkholes   terminal moraines
arches   canyons   dunes   floodplains

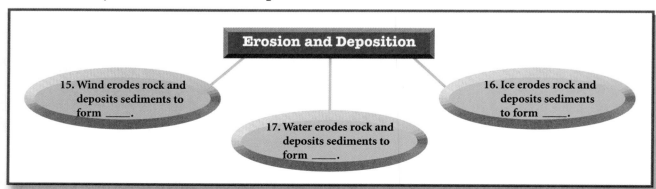

Erosion and Deposition

15. Wind erodes rock and deposits sediments to form _____.

17. Water erodes rock and deposits sediments to form _____.

16. Ice erodes rock and deposits sediments to form _____.

Check Understanding

Write the letter of the best choice.

18. Beginning with the outermost layer,
    Earth's layers are the —
    A crust, magma, and core
    B crust, mantle, and core
    C core, mantle, and crust
    D core, magma, and crust

19. Gondwana and Laurasia were formed
    by —
    F continental drift
    G erosion
    H deposition
    J earthquakes

20. Which of the following was **NOT** an
    ancient continent?
    A Pangea
    B Laurasia
    C Gondwana
    D Cenozoa

Critical Thinking

21. Explain why water erodes Earth's surface
    more than wind does.

22. If the mantle were solid rock, what fea-
    ture would not form on Earth's surface?
    Explain.

23. Scientists have found many fossils of
    past life. Are fossils still being formed
    today? Explain.

Process Skills Review

24. What can you **observe** about these
    pieces of rock that shows you which
    one has been weathered and moved
    by water?

25. How might you **make a model** of a
    volcano?

Performance Assessment

Plate Boundaries

Identify the three types of plate boundaries at A, B, and C in the illustration
below. Explain what is happening at each
boundary.

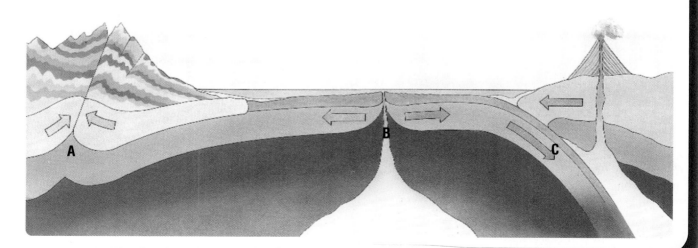

Chapter 2

Vocabulary Preview

mineral
streak
hardness
luster
rock
igneous rock
sedimentary rock
metamorphic rock
rock cycle

Rocks and Minerals

Rocks and minerals are all around you. The ground you walk on every day is made of rocks and minerals. They are in the soil. They are the gems that sparkle in jewelry. The Earth itself is made mostly of rocks and minerals.

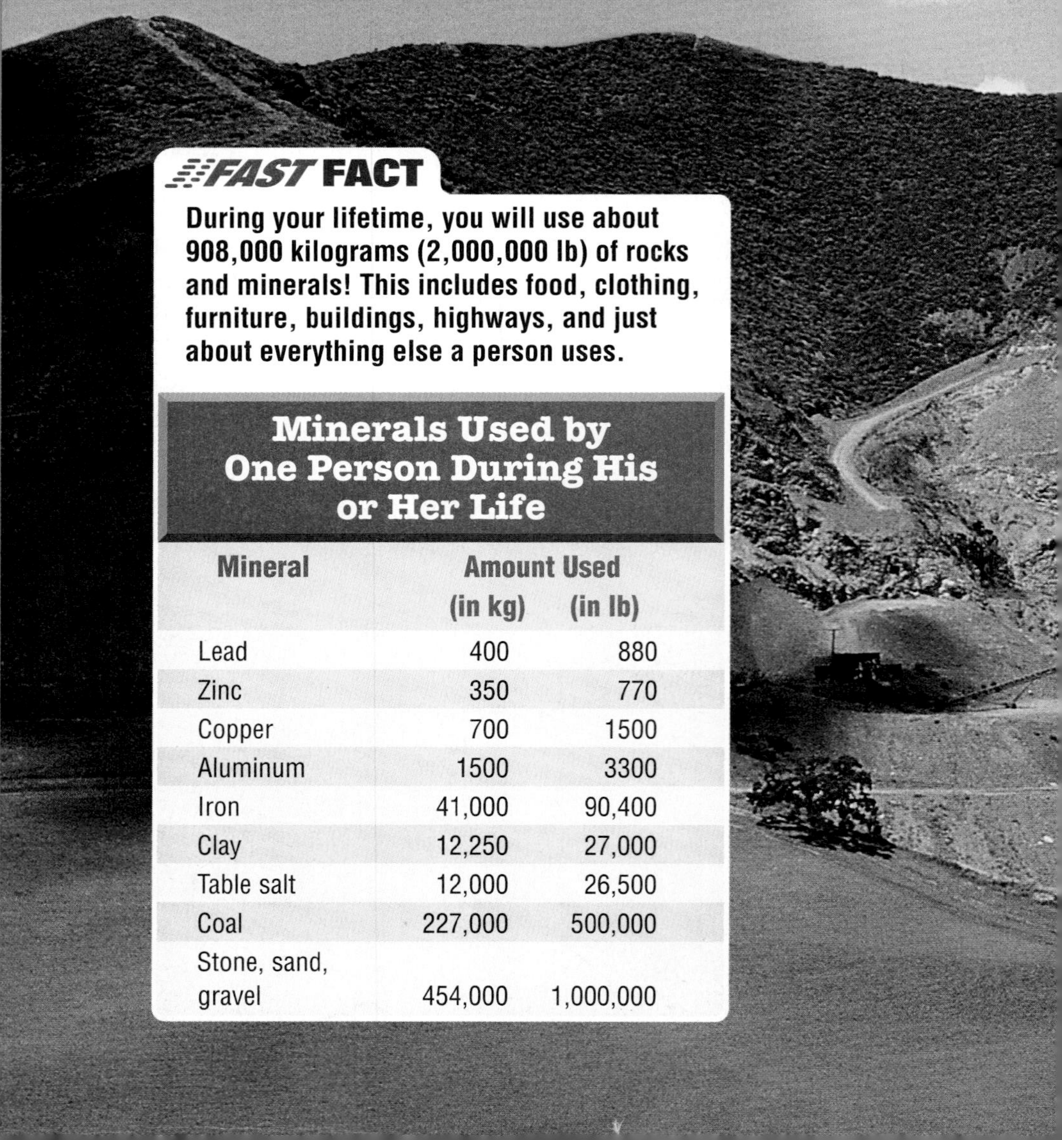

FAST FACT

During your lifetime, you will use about 908,000 kilograms (2,000,000 lb) of rocks and minerals! This includes food, clothing, furniture, buildings, highways, and just about everything else a person uses.

Minerals Used by One Person During His or Her Life

Mineral	Amount Used (in kg)	(in lb)
Lead	400	880
Zinc	350	770
Copper	700	1500
Aluminum	1500	3300
Iron	41,000	90,400
Clay	12,250	27,000
Table salt	12,000	26,500
Coal	227,000	500,000
Stone, sand, gravel	454,000	1,000,000

All the gold known in the world would fit in a cube measuring about 18 meters (60 ft) on each side! But a little bit goes a long way. Twenty-eight grams (1 oz) of gold can be flattened into a thin sheet covering about 28 square meters (300 sq ft). That's enough to cover one-fourth of a tennis court!

These pictures show equal weights of gold and salt. In ancient times, salt was so precious that it was traded ounce for ounce for gold! If you worked hard and you were "worth your salt," you were paid a "salary." This word meant "money for buying salt"!

This gravel quarry provides gravel for roads and buildings.

What Are Minerals?

In this lesson, you can . . .

INVESTIGATE mineral properties.

LEARN ABOUT how minerals form and how we use them.

LINK to math, writing, social studies, and technology.

INVESTIGATE

Mineral Properties

Activity Purpose Chalk leaves a mark on a chalkboard because the board is harder than the chalk. Hardness is a property, or characteristic, of minerals, such as the calcite (KAL•syt) that makes up chalk. In this investigation you will **observe** that a mineral can be scratched by some things but not by other things. You will also test other mineral properties and then **classify** minerals by their properties.

Materials

- 6 labeled mineral samples
- hand lens
- streak plate
- copper penny
- steel nail

CAUTION

Activity Procedure

1. Copy the chart shown on page B35.

2. Use the hand lens to **observe** each mineral. Describe the color of each sample. **Record** your observations in the chart. (Picture A)

3. Use each mineral to draw a line across the streak plate. (Picture B) What color is the streak each made? **Record** your observations.

4. **CAUTION** Use caution with the nail. It is sharp. Test the hardness of each mineral by using your fingernail, the copper penny, and the steel nail. Try to scratch each mineral with each of these items. Then try to scratch each sample with each of the other minerals. **Record** your observations in the chart.

◄ A mineral can be different colors. Tourmaline (TOOR•muh•lin) can be pink, purple, green, black, or the mix of colors called watermelon, shown here. Tourmaline is often used in jewelry.

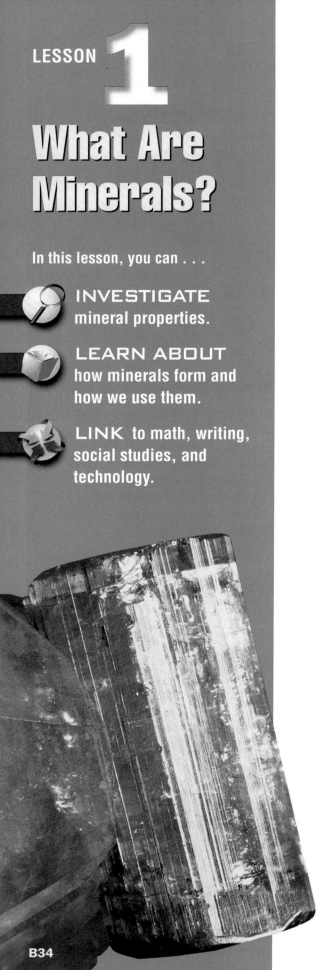

Picture A

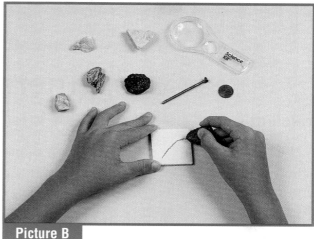

Picture B

Mineral Sample	Color of the Mineral Sample	Color of the Mineral's Streak	Things That Scratch the Mineral
A			
B			
C			

5 **Classify** the minerals based on each property you tested: color, streak, and hardness. Make labels that list all three properties for each mineral.

6 **Identify** the mineral samples by using the properties you tested and the table of diagnostic properties on pages R10-R11.

Draw Conclusions

1. How are the minerals you tested different from each other?

2. Which of the minerals you tested is the hardest? Explain your choice.

3. **Scientists at Work** Scientists **classify** things so it is easier to study them. How do you think scientists classify minerals?

Investigate Further Obtain five other unknown mineral samples. Determine the hardness, color, and streak of each. **Identify** the minerals by using the table of diagnostic properties on pages R10-R11.

Process Skill Tip

When you **classify** things, you put them into groups based on ways they are alike. Organizing things in this way can make it easier to learn about them. Often, you can classify the same group of objects in many ways.

B35

Minerals

How Some Minerals Form

FIND OUT

- what minerals are
- how to identify minerals
- how minerals are used

VOCABULARY

mineral
streak
luster
hardness

To be a mineral, a material must have certain features. A **mineral** (MIN•er•uhl) is always a solid material with particles arranged in a repeating pattern. This pattern is called a crystal (KRIST•uhl). Almost all minerals are made from material that was never alive. Also, true minerals form only in nature. They are not made in a laboratory.

Minerals form in many ways. Some minerals, such as diamond, form in Earth's mantle. There, high heat and pressure change carbon into hard, sparkling crystals called diamond. Diamonds have many uses. Some are cut and shaped to make jewelry. Most are used on cutting tools such as drills and saws.

Other minerals, such as calcite, can form at or near Earth's surface. Some calcite forms in the ocean when calcium, oxygen, and carbon combine in sea water. Some ocean animals form calcite shells or other body parts. Calcite also forms as water evaporates in limestone caves.

Water also plays a role in forming other minerals. Galena crystals form when hot, mineral-rich water moves slowly through cracks in Earth's crust, mixing with other minerals before it cools and evaporates.

▲ Calcite is a mineral found in chalk.

✔ **What are some features a material must have to be called a mineral?**

◄ This shiny mineral is galena (guh•LEE•nuh), which is made of lead and sulfur. Galena crystals often form cubes.

The first compass needles were made from a mineral called magnetite. Magnetite is magnetic, as shown by the nail stuck to the sample. ▼

Mica is a mineral that splits easily into thin, clear sheets. ▼

Some Mineral Properties

You saw in the investigation that one property of a mineral is streak. **Streak** is the color of the powder left behind when you rub a mineral against a white tile called a streak plate. Usually the streak is the same color as the mineral. Chalcopyrite (chal•koh•PY•ryt), however, looks like shiny gold but has a black streak.

Luster (LUHS•tuhr) describes the way the surface of a mineral reflects light. Some minerals look shiny, like aluminum foil looks. These minerals have a *metallic* luster. Others look dull or dark. These minerals have a *nonmetallic* luster. The sparkling appearance of a diamond is known as a *brilliant* luster.

Hardness is a mineral's ability to resist being scratched. Mohs' hardness scale, shown at the right, lists minerals that have hardnesses from 1 to 10. A mineral with a higher number on the scale can scratch a mineral with a lower number.

✔ **Which minerals on Mohs' hardness scale can be scratched by quartz?**

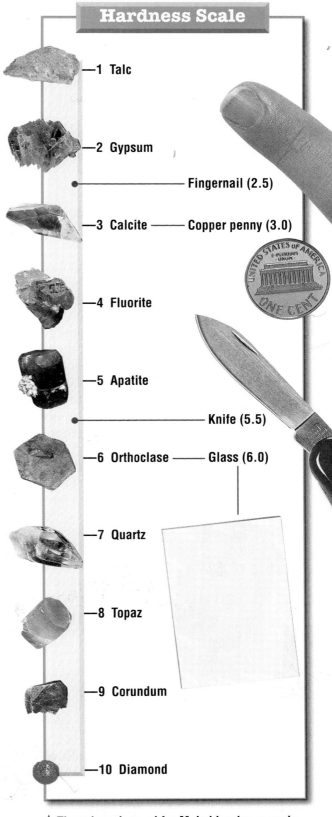

Hardness Scale

—1 Talc

—2 Gypsum

Fingernail (2.5)

—3 Calcite —— Copper penny (3.0)

—4 Fluorite

—5 Apatite

Knife (5.5)

—6 Orthoclase —— Glass (6.0)

—7 Quartz

—8 Topaz

—9 Corundum

—10 Diamond

▲ The minerals used for Mohs' hardness scale are shown above on the left. When scientists don't have all these with them, they often use the materials above on the right to test for hardness.

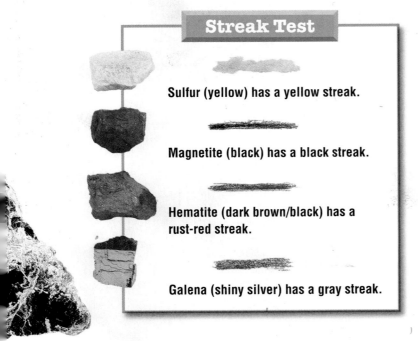

Streak Test

Sulfur (yellow) has a yellow streak.

Magnetite (black) has a black streak.

Hematite (dark brown/black) has a rust-red streak.

Galena (shiny silver) has a gray streak.

How We Use Minerals

Some minerals can be used in nearly the same form they have in nature. They don't need much refining, or processing to remove other materials. For example, silver and copper can be used to make musical instruments, electric wire, and jewelry. Gypsum can be used to make plaster and wallboard. Graphite is used in pencils. Halite, or table salt, can be used to flavor and preserve foods.

Pure silver is a very soft metal. It has a hardness of about 2 on the Mohs' hardness scale. Because it is so soft, it can be shaped easily. It also can be mixed with other metals to make beautiful jewelry or to cover musical instruments, such as this fluegelhorn.

Hematite is a mineral made of iron and oxygen. It has a hardness of 5 to 6.5 on the Mohs' hardness scale. Hematite is an important source of the iron used to make steel. Steel beams are used to make tall buildings strong.

Diamond is the hardest natural substance found on Earth. It has a hardness of 10 on Mohs' hardness scale. Some diamonds are used to make beautiful jewelry. Diamonds that are not good enough for jewelry are used on drills that dig deep into Earth's crust. The small cylinders all along the edges of this drill are industrial diamonds. They're hidden under the silver paint.

Some minerals are not useful in their natural form. They must be refined to be useful. The mineral cuprite (KOOP•ryt) is made of copper and oxygen. After cuprite is refined, the copper is used in making pennies, pots and pans, and water pipes.

✔ **What are five uses of minerals?**

Summary

Some minerals form in Earth's mantle, and others form at or near Earth's surface. Minerals can be identified by their properties. Some mineral properties are streak, hardness, and luster. People use minerals in many ways.

Review

1. List three features a material must have to be a mineral.
2. What is mineral hardness?
3. Name six ways people use minerals.
4. **Critical Thinking** You have a sample of an unknown mineral. It can scratch fluorite but not quartz. What is its approximate hardness?
5. **Test Prep** Which of the following minerals is the hardest?
   A diamond
   B apatite
   C topaz
   D talc

LINKS

MATH LINK

Measure the Mass Collect six different mineral samples that are all about the same size. Use a balance to find the mass of each sample. Record each value in a table. Explain why minerals that are about the same size may have very different masses.

WRITING LINK

Expressive Writing—Poem A birthstone is the gem that stands for a particular month. Find a list of the birthstones for all the months, and make a poster about them. Draw a color picture of each gem next to its name. Write a poem for a family member about your birthday month and birthstone.

SOCIAL STUDIES LINK

Go West! Find out why so many Americans in the mid-1800s risked their lives riding west in covered wagons or sailing around Cape Horn to get to California. Make a map of the routes they took. Add pictures of what they did in California.

TECHNOLOGY LINK

Learn more about the mineral gold by viewing *Gold Mining* on the **Harcourt Science Newsroom Video** in your classroom video library.

What Are Rocks?

In this lesson, you can . . .

 INVESTIGATE different kinds of rocks.

 LEARN ABOUT how rocks form.

 LINK to math, writing, physical education, and technology.

 **INVESTIGATE**

Identifying Rocks

Activity Purpose Have you ever helped make chocolate chip cookies? If so, you know that you put ingredients in a bowl, mix them, spoon the mixture onto a cookie sheet, and then bake it in an oven. The heat in the oven causes the ingredients to change and stick together to form something new—cookies. Some rocks form in a similar way. In this investigation you will **observe** some rocks and **classify** them by the ways they formed.

Materials

- 5 labeled rock samples
- hand lens
- dropper
- vinegar
- safety goggles
- paper plate
- paper towels

 CAUTION

Activity Procedure

1 Make a chart like the one shown on page B41.

2 Use the hand lens to **observe** each rock. What color or colors is each rock? **Record** your observations in your chart.

◀ Wind-blown sand and rain carved away bits of rock to form this arch in Arches National Park, Utah.

Rock Sample	Color	Texture	Picture	Bubbles When Vinegar Added
1				
2				
3				
4				
5				

3 Can you see any grains, or small pieces, making up the rock? Are the grains very small, or are they large? Are they rounded, or do they have sharp edges? Do the grains fit together like puzzle pieces? Or are they just next to one another? **Record** your observations under *Texture* in your chart. Draw a picture of each rock in the *Picture* column.

4 **CAUTION** **Put on your safety goggles.** Vinegar bubbles when it is dropped on the mineral calcite. Put the rock samples on the paper plate. Use the dropper to put a few drops of vinegar on each rock. **Observe** what happens. **Record** your findings. (Picture A)

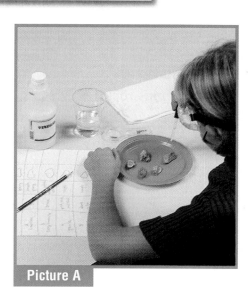
Picture A

5 **Classify** your rocks into two groups based on how the rocks are alike.

Draw Conclusions

1. What properties did you use to **classify** your rocks?

2. How does your classification system **compare** with those of two other students?

3. **Scientists at Work** One way scientists **classify** rocks is by how they formed. Choose one rock and explain how you think it might have formed.

Investigate Further Take a walk around your school or neighborhood. Using your **observations**, list at least three ways people use rocks. Based on your **observations**, what rocks do you infer are found commonly in your area?

Process Skill Tip

Classifying is a way to study a large number of objects. You **classify** by grouping things, based on how they are alike. For rocks, their size, shape, color, and what has happened to them are all things that can be alike.

Types of Rocks

Igneous Rocks

FIND OUT

- **how rocks form**
- **how people use rocks**

VOCABULARY

rock
igneous rock
sedimentary rock
metamorphic rock

Earth is made mostly of rocks. A **rock** is material made up of one or more minerals. But unlike minerals, rocks are not crystals. Like minerals, some rocks form at or near Earth's surface. Others form deep in the crust or in Earth's middle layer, the mantle. There are many different kinds of rocks. But they all can be classified into three groups based on how they formed.

Rocks that form when melted rock hardens are called **igneous** (IG•nee•uhs) **rocks**. In Chapter 1 you learned that lava is melted rock that reaches Earth's surface through a volcano. Lava cools and hardens before large mineral crystals have time to form. Rocks formed from lava have small mineral pieces and are called *fine-grained*. Usually their mineral crystals can be seen only with a microscope.

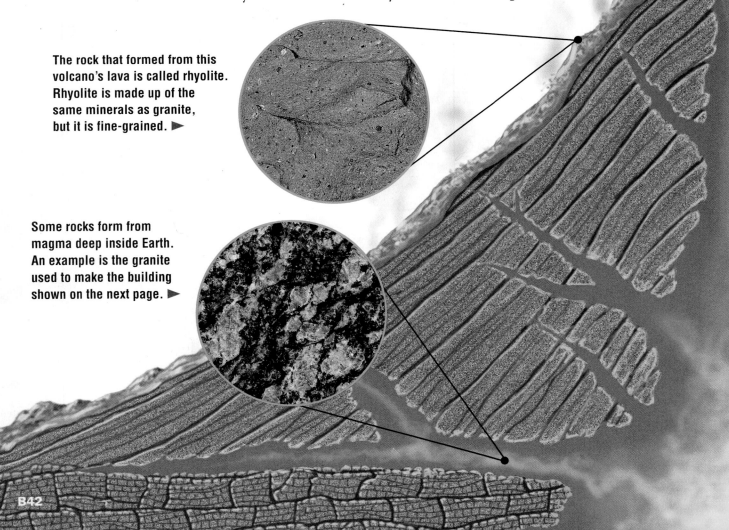

The rock that formed from this volcano's lava is called rhyolite. Rhyolite is made up of the same minerals as granite, but it is fine-grained. ▶

Some rocks form from magma deep inside Earth. An example is the granite used to make the building shown on the next page. ▶

▲ Basalt

▲ Gabbro

▲ Pumice

▲ Obsidian

Melted rock that stays below Earth's surface is called magma (MAG•muh). Magma cools and hardens slowly. Its minerals can form large grains that are easy to see. Igneous rocks formed from slowly cooling magma are called *coarse-grained*.

Basalt (buh•SALT) is the most common igneous rock that forms from lava at Earth's surface. Basalt is a dark, greenish-black rock made up mostly of the minerals feldspar (FELD•spar) and pyroxene (py•RAHKS•een). Gabbro (GAB•roh) is an igneous rock that is also made up mostly of these two minerals. But gabbro has larger mineral grains than basalt. That's because gabbro forms inside Earth instead of at Earth's surface.

Pumice (PUHM•ihs) is another igneous rock. The tiny holes in pumice are caused by gases escaping from the lava as it cools. Pumice feels rough and scratchy. Obsidian (uhb•SID•ee•uhn) also forms from lava. The lava cools so quickly that the rock looks like black glass. When obsidian breaks, sharp edges form.

Granite is a common igneous rock that forms when magma cools slowly beneath Earth's surface. Most granite is made up of large grains of feldspar, quartz, and mica (MY•kuh). These mineral grains are joined together tightly, making granite a strong rock that lasts for a long time.

✔ **What are igneous rocks?**

◀ Granite is an igneous rock often used for building. Brookings Hall at Washington University in St. Louis is made of unpolished pink granite blocks.

Sedimentary Rocks

Rocks are broken down into smaller pieces by weathering. Weathering is caused by many things. At Earth's surface the actions of wind, water, ice, and plant roots cause weathering.

After rocks are weathered into small pieces, blowing winds, flowing water, gravity, or slow-moving glaciers often move the pieces to other places. The movement of weathered rock pieces from one place to another is erosion.

When erosion is caused by water, over time the rock pieces drop to the bottoms of streams, rivers, or lakes. The material that is dropped is called *sediment*. Over a long time, layers of sediments can form **sedimentary** (sed•uh•MEN•ter•ee) **rock** as they are squeezed and stuck together.

Most sediments are dropped by moving water when it slows down, such as when a river or stream enters a lake. The largest pieces of weathered rock are dropped first. Conglomerate (kuhn•GLAHM•er•it) is a type of sedimentary rock that can form from these larger pieces. The pieces in a conglomerate can be as big as boulders or as small as peas. In a conglomerate, the pieces are round and smooth. Most conglomerates form in shallow water.

Smaller sediments are carried farther by the water and dropped later. Siltstone is one type of rock made up of smaller sediments.

Limestone is a fine-grained sedimentary rock. It is made up mostly of the mineral calcite. Most limestone forms in oceans, sometimes from seashells. A few kinds of limestone form in lakes.

Many sedimentary rocks form in bodies of water like this stream. Sedimentary rocks may contain fossils. This happens when shells, bones, or other remains of once-living organisms are buried in sediment layers.

▲ Conglomerate

▲ Limestone

▲ Sandstone

▲ Shale

Sandstone is another kind of sedimentary rock. Sandstones, as you might guess from their name, are made up of bits of rocks and minerals the size of sand grains. Nearly all sandstones are made up mostly of the mineral quartz.

Some sandstones are fine-grained. They feel smooth when you touch them. Other sandstones are coarse-grained. They feel rough against your skin. Sandstones can form in water or on land.

Shale is a fine-grained sedimentary rock made of very small sediments. The sediments in most shales are so small that you can see them only with a strong hand lens. Some shale sediments are so small that you can see them only with a microscope.

✔ **What processes help form sedimentary rocks?**

THE INSIDE STORY

Crossbedding

1. Many sandstones are *crossbedded*. Crossbeds begin to form when wind blows sand grains in one direction for a long time. The grains pile up until the piles become so steep that sand begins to drop off the top edge. These sand piles, or dunes, will become the first rock layer.

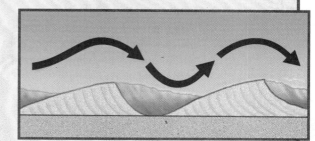

2. Over time, more sand covers the first layer. This new sand keeps the first layer from moving. Sand blown by the wind keeps filling the gaps between dunes.

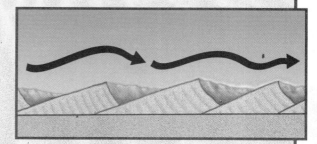

3. When the wind changes direction, the next sand layer is put down at a different angle. As the wind keeps changing direction, new layers are put down at different angles. The rock layers that form from the sand layers will show these changes in wind direction.

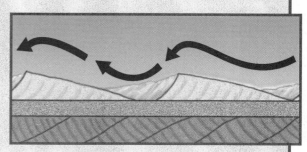

Metamorphic Rocks

High heat and great pressure can change the texture of rock—the way it looks and feels. They can also change the form of the minerals that make up the rock. These changed rocks are called **metamorphic** (met•uh•MAWR•fik) **rocks**. Metamorphic rocks can form from any kind of rock—sedimentary, igneous, or even other metamorphic rocks.

Some metamorphic rocks form when mountains are built up. Schist (SHIST) and gneiss (NYS) are two examples. Schist has wavy lines. It splits easily into layers. Gneiss forms when schist is heated and squeezed more. Gneiss often has bands of light and dark minerals.

Marble is another metamorphic rock. Marble forms when limestone is squeezed and heated. Artists often use marble to make statues. It also is used in buildings.

Slate is a metamorphic rock that forms when shale is under great pressure. Like shale, slate has layers. In the past, people used slate to make chalkboards for schools. Slate tiles are sometimes used to cover roofs.

Quartzite forms from sandstone when heat melts the sand grains together. Quartzite usually has a milky color. Other minerals in the sandstone can give quartzite a gray or pink color.

✔ **How do metamorphic rocks form?**

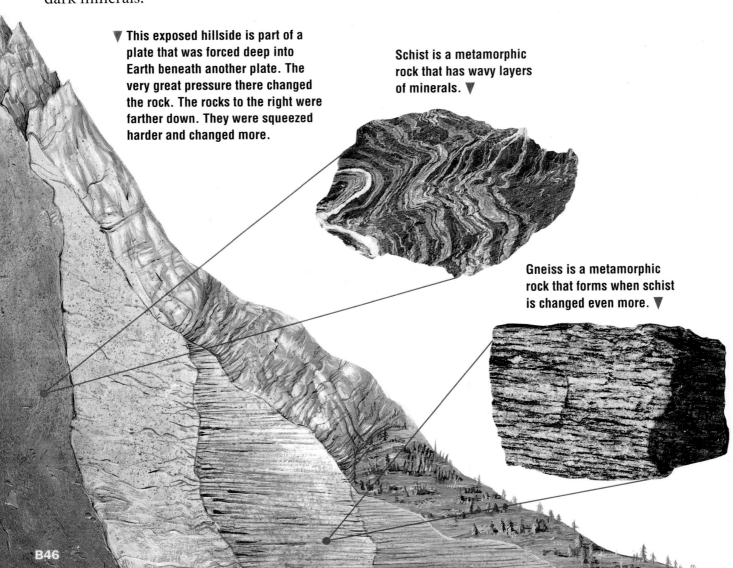

▼ This exposed hillside is part of a plate that was forced deep into Earth beneath another plate. The very great pressure there changed the rock. The rocks to the right were farther down. They were squeezed harder and changed more.

Schist is a metamorphic rock that has wavy layers of minerals. ▼

Gneiss is a metamorphic rock that forms when schist is changed even more. ▼

Slate is a metamorphic rock that can be split into thin sheets. Slate pieces are used to cover roofs on houses.

Summary

Rocks are made up of one or more minerals. Rocks are classified by the way they form. Igneous rocks form when magma or lava cools and hardens. Sedimentary rocks are usually made of pieces of rock that have been squeezed and stuck together. Metamorphic rocks form when heat and pressure change rocks.

Review

1. What are rocks?
2. How are rocks classified?
3. In which type of rock are fossils found?
4. **Critical Thinking** You find a rock that is made of small grains. How can you tell whether it is igneous or sedimentary?
5. **Test Prep** Which kind of rock is granite?

   A igneous
   B metamorphic
   C layered
   D sedimentary

LINKS

MATH LINK

Make a Graph A lake has three rivers flowing into it. Each river deposits 1 centimeter of sediment in one year. How deep will the sediments be after 10 years? If the lake is a meter deep, when will it be completely filled by sediment?

WRITING LINK

Informative Writing—Narration Use library reference materials to find out about the Navajo Sandstone crossbeds. Then write a story for your teacher describing the area while the crossbeds were forming.

PHYSICAL EDUCATION LINK

Rock Climbing Use library reference materials to find out the equipment needed for safe rock climbing. Make a list of safety rules for the sport of rock climbing. Tell how rock types affect climbing rules.

TECHNOLOGY LINK

Learn more about rock types by visiting this Internet site.
www.scilinks.org/harcourt

What Is the Rock Cycle?

In this lesson, you can . . .

INVESTIGATE how rocks can change.

LEARN ABOUT ways in which rocks change.

LINK to math, writing, technology, and other areas.

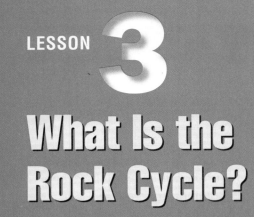

INVESTIGATE

The Rock Cycle

Activity Purpose Do you recycle aluminum cans? After the recycling truck takes away the cans, they go through many changes before they become new products. In this investigation you will **make a model** to show how Earth's natural processes can change rocks.

Materials

- small objects—pieces of aquarium gravel, fake jewels, and a few pennies
- 3 pieces of modeling clay, each a different color
- 2 aluminum pie pans

Activity Procedure

1. The small objects stand for minerals. Press the "minerals" into the three pieces of clay. Each color of clay with its objects stands for a different igneous rock.

2. Now suppose that wind and water are weathering and eroding the "rocks." To **model** this process, break one rock into pieces (sediments) and drop the pieces into one of the pie pans (a lake). (Picture A)

◄ Giant's Causeway in Ireland began to form when lava quickly cooled and shrank to form basalt. Over many years, water and ice weathered the rock to form these spectacular, six-sided columns.

Picture A

Picture B

3 Drop pieces from the second rock on top of the first rock layer. Then drop pieces of the third rock on top of the second layer. Press the layers together by using the bottom of the empty pie pan. What kind of rock have you made?

4 Squeeze the "sedimentary rock" between your hands to warm it up. What causes the rock to change? Which kind of rock is it now? (Picture B)

Draw Conclusions

1. How did the igneous "rocks" change in this investigation?

2. What might weathering and erosion do to a metamorphic rock?

3. **Scientists at Work** Scientists often **make a model** to help them understand processes that occur in nature. What process did your hands represent in Step 4 of the activity?

Investigate Further Tell how you could change this model to show igneous rocks that formed from magma and igneous rocks that formed from lava. What knowledge of cause and effect did you use to change the model?

> **Process Skill Tip**
>
> If you **make a model**, you can often understand a natural process that is hard to observe. Because rocks change over a long time, it's hard to see the changes happening.

How Rocks Change

Processes That Cause Change

FIND OUT

- about processes that change rocks
- how rocks change over time

VOCABULARY

rock cycle

Rocks are always changing. However, the changes usually happen so slowly that you would never notice them. It can take thousands of years for a rock to weather and erode. It can take many more years for the eroded pieces to be changed into sedimentary rock.

You learned in Lesson 2 that high heat and pressure can change rocks. Sometimes the rocks get hot enough to melt completely. When this melted rock cools and hardens, it has changed from metamorphic to igneous. It usually takes many years for rock to be buried deep enough inside Earth to melt.

A rock can begin as one type and be changed many times. You made a model of these changes in the investigation. Instead of a few minutes, however, changes can take many thousands of years. Some part of the first rock, however, will still be there after each change.

✔ **How does weathering affect rock?**

Follow the blue arrows to learn about the changes that might happen to one rock. ▼

◄ Basalt forms when lava quickly cools and hardens at Earth's surface. Basalt is the most common igneous rock on Earth.

Wind or rain carries the weathered pieces of basalt to the river. The river carries the pieces downstream. As they move, they bump into one another. Jagged edges are slowly rounded off. ▼

Tree roots weather the basalt by growing into the rock and breaking it into pieces. Freezing and thawing and rain also weather the rock. ►

B50

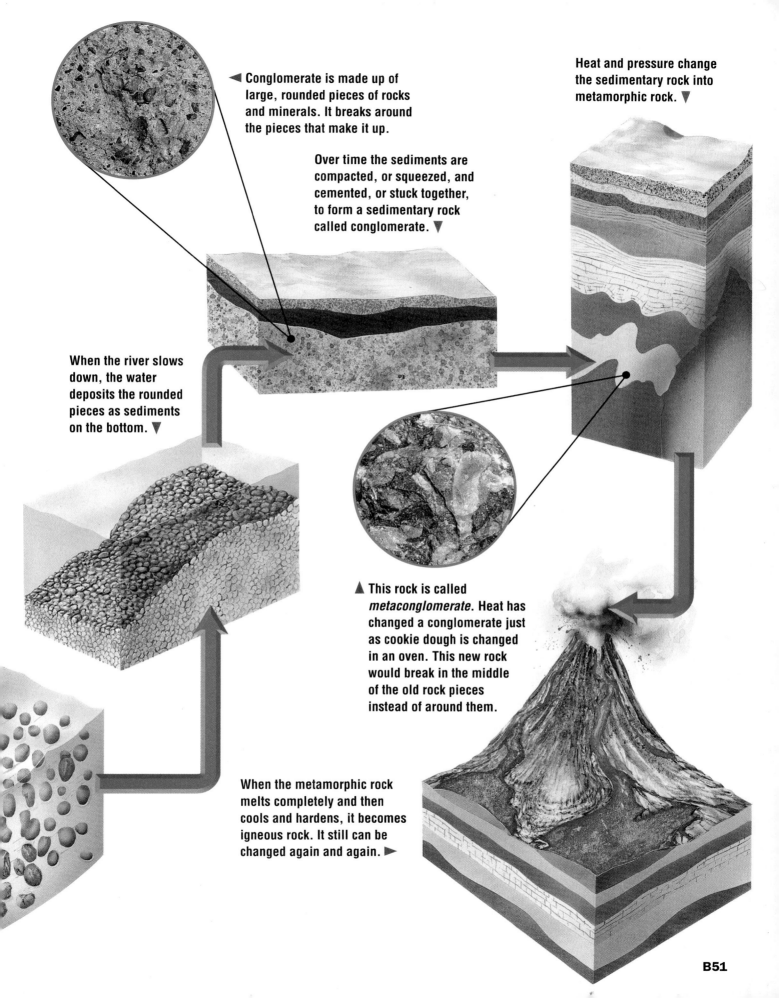

Conglomerate is made up of large, rounded pieces of rocks and minerals. It breaks around the pieces that make it up.

Heat and pressure change the sedimentary rock into metamorphic rock. ▼

Over time the sediments are compacted, or squeezed, and cemented, or stuck together, to form a sedimentary rock called conglomerate. ▼

When the river slows down, the water deposits the rounded pieces as sediments on the bottom. ▼

This rock is called *metaconglomerate*. Heat has changed a conglomerate just as cookie dough is changed in an oven. This new rock would break in the middle of the old rock pieces instead of around them.

When the metamorphic rock melts completely and then cools and hardens, it becomes igneous rock. It still can be changed again and again. ▶

B51

The Rock Cycle

The diagram below and on the next page shows the never-ending rock changes that are called the **rock cycle**. Notice that many arrows lead out from each rock type. This shows that there is more than one path through the rock cycle.

As rocks move through the rock cycle, the materials that make them up are used over and over. Look at the diagram. Try to find where rocks are squeezed. Also notice where sticking together might take place, where rocks melt, and where rocks are under heat and pressure. As you study the diagram, remember that all these processes take a very long time.

✔ **How can a metamorphic rock be changed into a different metamorphic rock?**

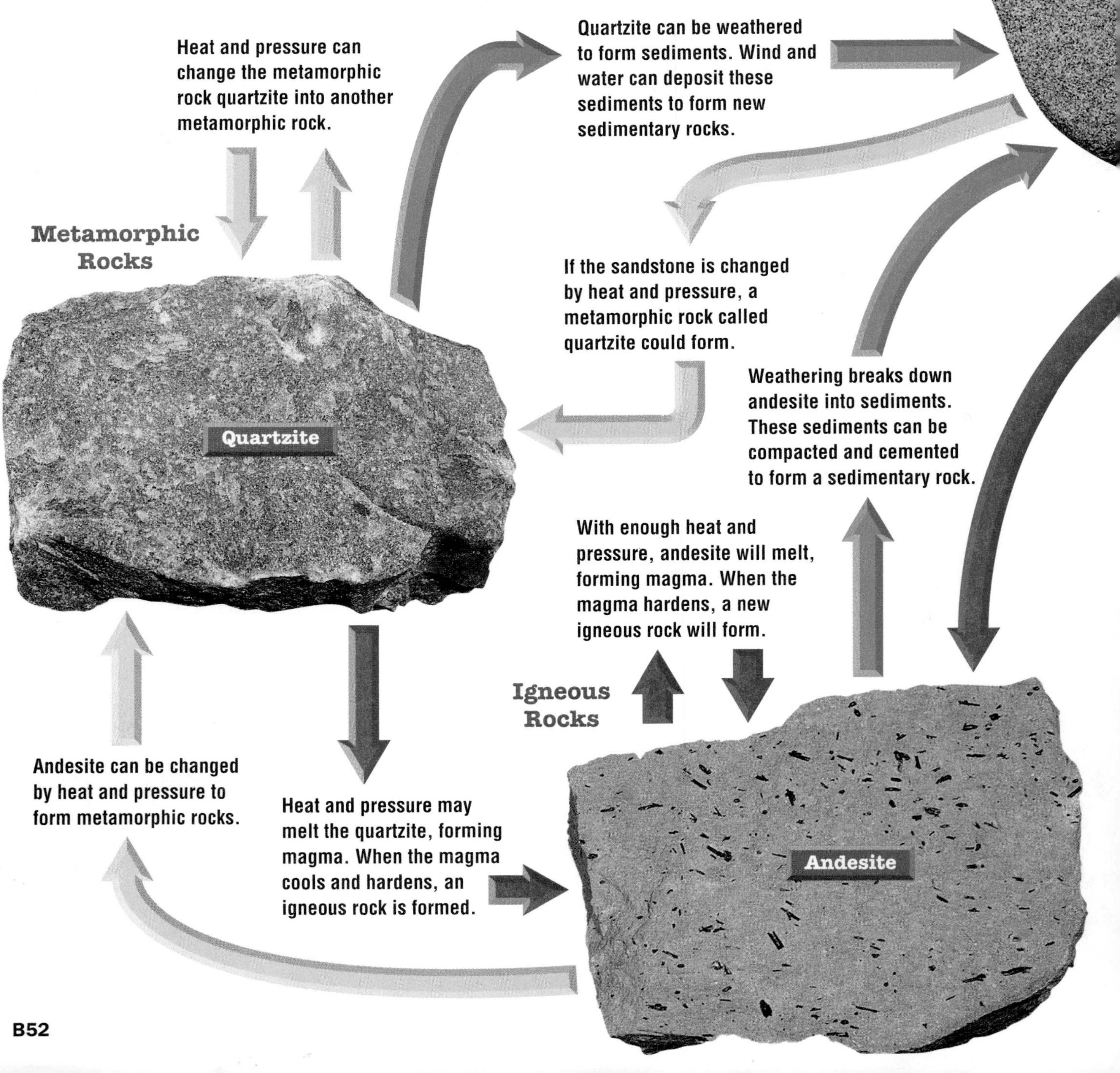

Heat and pressure can change the metamorphic rock quartzite into another metamorphic rock.

Metamorphic Rocks

Quartzite

Quartzite can be weathered to form sediments. Wind and water can deposit these sediments to form new sedimentary rocks.

If the sandstone is changed by heat and pressure, a metamorphic rock called quartzite could form.

Weathering breaks down andesite into sediments. These sediments can be compacted and cemented to form a sedimentary rock.

With enough heat and pressure, andesite will melt, forming magma. When the magma hardens, a new igneous rock will form.

Igneous Rocks

Andesite can be changed by heat and pressure to form metamorphic rocks.

Heat and pressure may melt the quartzite, forming magma. When the magma cools and hardens, an igneous rock is formed.

Andesite

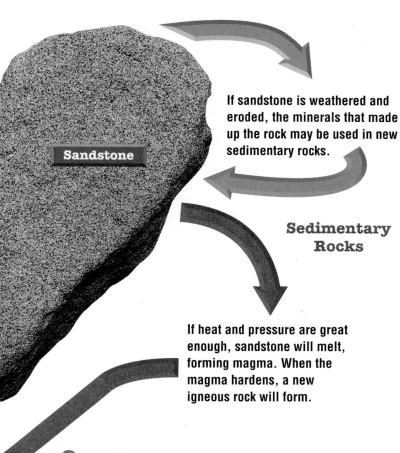

Sandstone

If sandstone is weathered and eroded, the minerals that made up the rock may be used in new sedimentary rocks.

Sedimentary Rocks

If heat and pressure are great enough, sandstone will melt, forming magma. When the magma hardens, a new igneous rock will form.

Summary

Rocks change from one kind to another in the rock cycle. Some of the processes in the rock cycle are weathering, erosion, melting, compaction, and cementation.

Review

1. What is the rock cycle?
2. What part do volcanoes play in the rock cycle?
3. What is one thing that can change a rock to metamorphic rock?
4. **Critical Thinking** How might a sandstone change into another sandstone?
5. **Test Prep** What starts the change from an igneous rock to a sedimentary rock?
   A heat
   B pressure
   C melting
   D weathering

LINKS

MATH LINK

How Long Did It Take? A layer of sedimentary rock is 5 meters thick. The layer was laid down at the rate of 1 centimeter per year. How many years did it take to form?

WRITING LINK

Narrative Writing—Story For a younger child, tell about the "life" of a rock from the rock's point of view. Tell where the rock has been. Tell where it will go. Make sure the rock has been changed into each type of rock at least once.

SOCIAL STUDIES LINK

Building Materials Use library references to find out why some types of rocks are most often used as building materials in your city. Make a model or poster to show what you learned.

LITERATURE LINK

Everybody Needs a Rock Read the book *Everybody Needs a Rock* by Byrd Baylor. Make a list of rules to follow to find your own special rock.

TECHNOLOGY LINK

Visit the Harcourt Learning Site for related links, activities, and resources.
www.harcourtschool.com/ca

WELCOME TO THE LEARNING SITE

DIAMOND COATINGS

Perhaps you've seen a ring that holds a diamond—a sparkling natural mineral. But did you know that diamonds can be made? These artificial diamonds aren't made for jewelry but for use by scientists and in factories.

ARTIFICIAL DIAMONDS

In nature, diamonds form when carbon is kept at very high pressures and temperatures. It may take millions of years for the diamonds to reach Earth's surface. To make artificial diamonds, scientists imitate the natural process. They use enormous pressures and temperatures to make diamonds in a much shorter time than in nature. However, these diamonds are usually plain-looking and very small. These artificial diamonds have been made since the 1950s.

CVD

Now a new, easier way to make artificial diamonds has been found. It takes high temperature but not high pressure. The new method uses simple hydrocarbons (HY•droh•kar•buhnz). These are materials made of the elements hydrogen and carbon.

Scientists heat these materials to very high temperatures. At these temperatures the materials become gases. When the gases cool, they form a thin layer of diamond crystals. This process is called chemical vapor deposition, or CVD. The thin layers of hard diamond crystals are used to protect softer materials.

A thin coating of artificial diamond can protect metal parts. Examples are airplane wings and parts of automobile engines. The coating makes the parts last longer. A thin diamond coating also lowers friction and improves speed. Perhaps someday golf clubs and racing boats will have diamond coatings.

◀ This microscope photograph shows a diamond crystal growing on a metal surface.

Researchers also have removed the wire after it was coated. This leaves behind a very small, hollow diamond tube. These tubes might be used as fiber optic wires for computers, or they could be very fine needles for use by doctors and surgeons.

Think About It

1. Why would people want to make artificial diamonds?
2. Why is chemical vapor deposition useful?

WEB LINK:
For Science and Technology updates, visit the Harcourt Internet site.
www.harcourtschool.com/ca

SEND ME A WIRE

A group of scientists in England is working to develop diamond-coated wires and fibers. The coating adds very little weight but makes the coated materials much stronger. For example, the metal tungsten (TUHNG•stuhn) is too heavy to use as wire for some jobs. But a thin, lightweight wire coated with diamond would work as well as a thicker, heavier, uncoated wire.

Careers	Organic Chemist

What They Do
Organic chemists work with materials containing the element carbon, such as hydrocarbons. These materials include plastics as well as animal and vegetable matter. Organic  chemists develop new products or test them. Some organic chemists teach high school or college chemistry.

Education and Training Organic chemists have at least a four-year college degree. Most have a master's degree or a Ph.D.

Mack Gipson, Jr.

STRUCTURAL GEOLOGIST

Dr. Mack Gipson grew up on a farm in South Carolina. He helped with farm work and was interested in nature. In junior high, he read a book about Earth and began to wonder how rocks were formed and what caused Earth's layers.

After finishing college with degrees in science and mathematics, Gipson became a high school teacher. He was drafted into the U.S. Army and trained as a radio technician. While he was with the army in Germany, he decided to go back to school and study geology. He decided he wanted to work outdoors as a geologist rather than spend all day indoors teaching.

One of Dr. Gipson's jobs in college was to test core samples. A core sample shows layers of soil and rock from underground. To get a core sample, a long metal tube is drilled into the ground.

Builders test core samples to make sure the ground can withstand the weight of a building or road. Gipson tested core samples for the building of runways at O'Hare International Airport in Chicago. He also studied rock layers near coal mines in Illinois.

After graduating from the University of Chicago, Dr. Mack Gipson stayed to help study samples of rock and clay from the ocean floor. This study helped scientists learn about how the oceans have changed over time.

Dr. Gipson founded the Department of Geological Sciences at Virginia State University. In addition to teaching, he has done studies for the National Aeronautics and Space Administration (NASA). He studied pictures of pyramidlike mountains on Mars. He concluded that the pictures show extinct volcanoes eroded by the wind.

THINK ABOUT IT

1. How might studying a core sample show how much weight the ground could safely support?

2. What skills do you think are needed to study worlds far from Earth?

Geologists studying core samples

Growing Crystals

How are minerals left behind by evaporation?

Materials

- plastic gloves
- safety goggles
- apron
- 1 tablespoon of laundry bluing
- 1 tablespoon of water
- 1 tablespoon of ammonia
- 1 tablespoon of table salt
- plastic cup
- plastic spoon
- sponge
- plastic bowl
- food coloring

Procedure

CAUTION Be sure to wear gloves, safety goggles, and an apron.

1. Mix the bluing, water, ammonia, and salt in the plastic cup. Stir gently until the salt has dissolved.

2. Place the sponge in the bowl. Pour the mixture over the sponge. Throw away the cup.

3. Sprinkle 4 drops of food coloring over the sponge. Wait one day.

Draw Conclusions

Observe the sponge. Does it change? What is forming?

Weathering Rock

How can you model weathering by using chalk?

Materials

- 2 pieces of chalk
- plastic jar with lid
- water
- strainer

Procedure

1. Break each piece of chalk into about three pieces. Put all the chalk pieces except one into the jar.

2. Pour water into the jar until the chalk is covered. Put the lid on the jar. Make sure it is tightly sealed. Shake the jar for about 5 minutes to "weather" the chalk.

3. Pour the water through the strainer to get the chalk pieces.

4. Predict how larger and smaller pieces of chalk will be weathered. Conduct multiple trials to test your prediction. How are your results related to your prediction?

Draw Conclusions

Compare the strained pieces to the chalk that was left out. What happened? Why? Compare this model to real rocks, weathering, and erosion. How are they alike? How are they different?

Chapter 2 Review and Test Preparation

Vocabulary Review

Use the terms below to complete the sentences. The page numbers in ( ) tell you where to look in the chapter if you need help.

mineral (B36)   **sedimentary rock** (B44)
streak (B37)   **metamorphic rock** (B46)
hardness (B37)   **rock cycle** (B52)
luster (B37)
rock (B42)
igneous rock (B42)

1. A natural, nonliving, solid material that has particles in a repeating pattern is a ____.

2. A ____ is made up of one or more minerals.

3. Limestone is a form of ____.

4. The ____ is the repeating of changes from one kind of rock to another over time.

5. A ____ is a rock changed by heat and pressure.

6. Melted rock cools and hardens to form ____.

7. The color of the powder left behind when you rub a mineral on a white porcelain plate is called the mineral's ____.

8. ____ is a mineral property that describes the way light reflects from the mineral's surface.

9. A mineral's ability to resist being scratched is its ____.

Connect Concepts

Fill in the blanks with the correct terms from the Word Bank.

color   **luster**   **Mohs' hardness scale**
hardness   **streak**

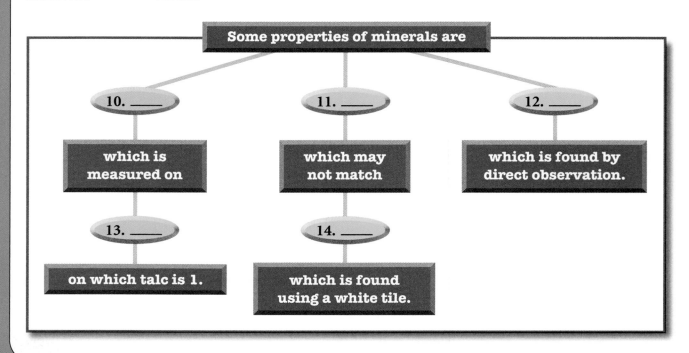

Some properties of minerals are

10. ____ — which is measured on — 13. ____ — on which talc is 1.

11. ____ — which may not match — 14. ____ — which is found using a white tile.

12. ____ — which is found by direct observation.

Check Understanding

Write the letter of the best choice.

15. A rock forms in layers of small pieces. It is a ____ rock.
    - A sedimentary
    - C igneous
    - B mineral
    - D metamorphic

16. Mohs' hardness scale is used to identify a mineral's —
    - F color
    - H streak
    - G luster
    - J hardness

17. If you describe a mineral as being shiny, you are describing the property of —
    - A streak
    - C hardness
    - B luster
    - D color

18. A rock that has been changed by pressure and heat is called a ____ rock.
    - F sedimentary
    - G metamorphic
    - H igneous
    - J metallic

19. When wind or water breaks a rock into smaller pieces, the process is called —
    - A weathering
    - C igneous
    - B hardness
    - D schist

20. Which of the following minerals is the hardest on Mohs' hardness scale?
    - F talc
    - H diamond
    - G gypsum
    - J quartz

21. Rocks change over time from one type to another. This process is called —
    - A type changing
    - B the rock cycle
    - C erosion
    - D melting

22. Particles in minerals form regular patterns called —
    - F crystals
    - H conglomerates
    - G layers
    - J shells

Process Skills Review

23. Based on the **model** you made of the rock cycle, what might happen to the "rock" if you made it hot enough to melt?

24. Why do scientists **classify** minerals?

25. How do scientists **classify** rocks?

Critical Thinking

26. How can a metamorphic rock be changed into an igneous rock?

27. Describe the path of a rock through the rock cycle.

Performance Assessment

Mineral Tests

Work with a partner. Use the hand lens to take a closer look at five mineral samples. Make a chart showing all the properties of each mineral. Tell how you tested for each property. Use the table on pages R10–R11 to identify the minerals.

Chapter 3

Vocabulary Preview

humus
fertile
soil conservation
contour plowing
strip cropping
terracing

Soil—A Natural Resource

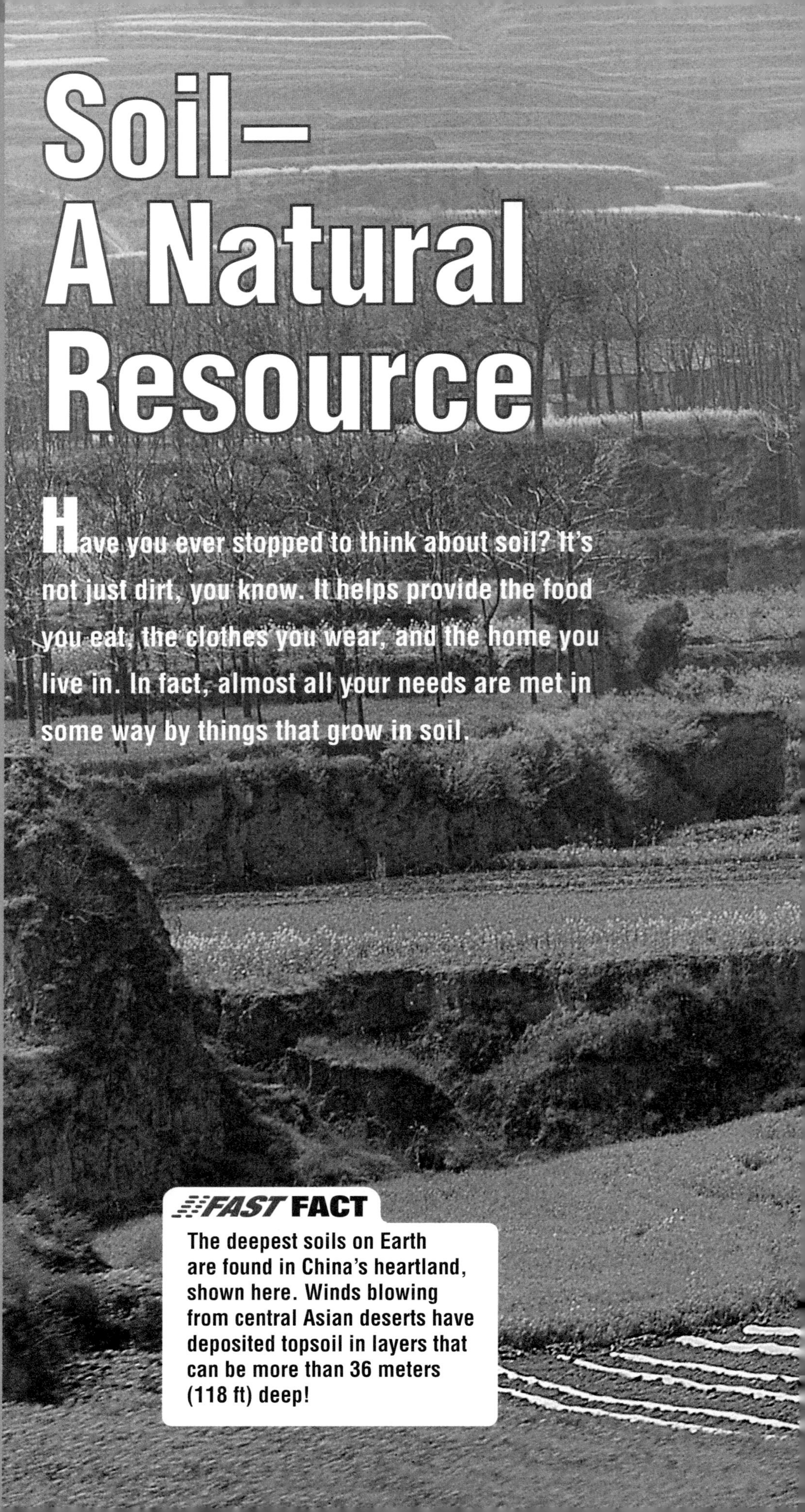

Have you ever stopped to think about soil? It's not just dirt, you know. It helps provide the food you eat, the clothes you wear, and the home you live in. In fact, almost all your needs are met in some way by things that grow in soil.

FAST FACT

The deepest soils on Earth are found in China's heartland, shown here. Winds blowing from central Asian deserts have deposited topsoil in layers that can be more than 36 meters (118 ft) deep!

A square meter of soil might look like just a lot of dirt. But if you dig, you'll find thousands of living things in the soil.

Springtails

Things Living in Soil

Animal	Average Number in a Square Meter
Earthworms	100
Slugs and snails	100
Millipedes	500
Springtails	10,000

≡FAST FACT

Humans aren't the only animals that grow crops. Attini ants plant and care for fungus gardens. The fungi are microorganisms that provide the ant colony with an important benefit—all its food!

How Does Soil Form?

In this lesson, you can . . .

 INVESTIGATE the layers of soil.

 LEARN ABOUT soil formation.

 LINK to math, writing, art, and technology.

INVESTIGATE

Soil Layers

Activity Purpose Have you ever taken time to look at soil? You may be surprised to know that soil is actually a mixture of different-sized particles. In this investigation you will **observe** soil to see its parts as it settles in water.

Materials

- newspaper
- soil sample
- hand lens
- wide-mouth glass or plastic jar with lid
- water

Activity Procedure

1. Cover your work surface with newspaper.

2. Examine the soil sample with a hand lens. Look for differences in the particles that make up soil. **Record** your **observations**.

3. Add soil to the jar until it is about one-third full.

◄ Soil has formed in the crack of this rock. The soil gives the tree a place to grow.

Picture A

Picture B

4 Add water until the jar is almost full. (Picture A)

5 Tightly screw the lid onto the jar. Shake the jar for at least 15 seconds to mix the soil and water well.

6 Let the jar sit overnight.

7 **Observe** the soil and water in the jar. Use the hand lens to observe each soil part in the jar more closely. (Picture B) **Record** your observations.

Draw Conclusions

1. How did mixing and shaking change the soil?

2. **Compare** your **observations** of the soil before shaking and after settling. In which observation could you see soil parts more easily? Explain your answer.

3. **Scientists at Work** Scientists often use instruments, or tools, to **observe** details. How did the hand lens help you in this investigation?

Investigate Further Different soils have different-sized particles. Observe some different soils. Based on your knowledge of cause and effect, predict how particles in the soils will form layers. Repeat the activity twice with each different soil. How are your results related to your predictions?

Process Skill Tip

When you **observe**, look first for general characteristics, such as overall appearance. Then use a tool such as a hand lens to look more closely for details.

Soil Formation

FIND OUT ———

• why soil is important

• how soil forms

VOCABULARY

humus

The Importance of Soil

Think about the foods you've eaten and the objects you've used today. Maybe you had breakfast at a wooden table. You may have eaten toast and a banana. For lunch perhaps you had a glass of milk and an egg salad or bologna sandwich. Maybe you wore cotton jeans to school. You probably sat at a desk and wrote on paper.

Soil is needed to provide these things and other things you use every day. Fruits and vegetables grow in soil. Meat, milk, and eggs come from animals, of course. The animals, however, eat corn, wheat, and other plants that grow in soil. Houses, desks, and paper are made from wood. Wood comes from trees, which grow in soil. Cotton and other clothing materials come from plants that grow in soil. Because you buy many of these things in stores, it is easy to forget that they depend on soil.

✔ **What are some foods that depend on soil?**

This dairy cow feeds on grass and hay, which grow in soil. ▼

The wheat that grows in this rich farmland soil may become part of your favorite bread or breakfast cereal. ▼

Soil Begins with Rock

The processes that form soil occur all the time, little by little. Most of the soil you see today has been forming for thousands of years.

Weathering is the process that breaks up rocks. As the outsides of rocks warm and cool, they expand, or become larger, and contract, or become smaller. You don't notice these changes in size. But they are big enough over time to crack rocks. The cracks become larger and larger. Bits of rock break off. Water gets into the cracks. When the water freezes, it expands. This forces the rock to break up even faster.

Wind and moving water erode bits of rock and other material. These bits of rock are dropped in another area, where they may build up and become part of soil.

✔ **How does rock become soil?**

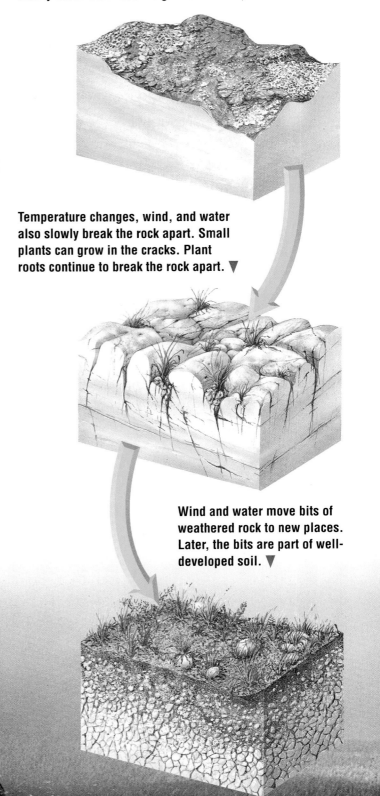

Lichens (LYK•uhnz), or tiny plantlike living things, grow on the outsides of rocks. They slowly break down rock to get nutrients. ▼

Temperature changes, wind, and water also slowly break the rock apart. Small plants can grow in the cracks. Plant roots continue to break the rock apart. ▼

Wind and water move bits of weathered rock to new places. Later, the bits are part of well-developed soil. ▼

Soil Forms Layers

In the investigation, you saw that soil forms layers when it settles in water. The layers form by the size of the particles. If you dug a hole in the ground, you would also see layers. As in the investigation, the particles in the top layers are smaller than those in the bottom layers. The three main layers of soil are topsoil, subsoil, and bedrock, sometimes called parent rock.

Topsoil is the top layer of soil. In most places it is only a few centimeters thick. Topsoil contains rotting plant and animal materials called **humus** (HYOO•muhs). It also contains bits of rock that come from the weathering of rocks above ground.

The second layer is called subsoil. It is made up mostly of small rocks. Subsoil forms as larger rocks are broken up. Because subsoil is near the surface, temperature changes help weather the rocks in this layer.

In fact, most weathering of rock takes place in this layer and the layer below. Tree roots also break up rocks in these layers.

The bottom layer, bedrock, is mostly solid rock. Cracks slowly widen and break up the top parts of the bedrock. Bits of rock break off. Over time, these rock bits become part of the upper layers of soil.

✔ **Where does most rock weathering happen?**

A - topsoil

B - subsoil

C - bedrock

Summary

Most products that we need, such as food, clothing, and building materials, depend on soil. Soil forms by the weathering and erosion of rocks. In weathering, plants and changes in weather cause rocks to break apart. In erosion, wind and moving water carry bits of rock to new places.

Review

1. Explain how a wool sweater depends on soil.

2. How does water freezing in a crack in a rock help break the rock apart?

3. What are the three layers of soil?

4. **Critical Thinking** Effects of weather, such as temperature changes, are greater on the surface than in deeper layers of soil. Why then does most weathering take place in the deeper layers?

5. **Test Prep** Which layer of soil contains the most dead plant and animal materials?

   A bedrock   **C** parent rock
   B subsoil   **D** topsoil

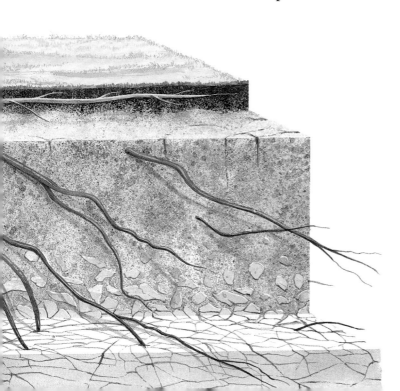

LINKS

MATH LINK

Graphing On your own, make a water and soil sample like the one in the investigation. Shake the container and then allow the soil parts to settle. Measure each layer with a metric ruler. Then make a bar graph to show how thick each layer is.

WRITING LINK

Expressive Writing — Poem Write a poem for a classmate describing how a tree root helps weather rocks to make soil. Begin your poem by describing how the tree seed comes to the spot where it sprouts and grows.

ART LINK

Clay Different kinds of clay are used to make dishes, pottery, sculpture, and other objects. Use the library to learn more about how artists use clay. Make a poster that shows sources of clay. For each source, include a picture of an artwork made of that clay.

TECHNOLOGY LINK

Learn more about how humus forms by visiting the National Museum of Natural History Internet site.
www.si.edu/harcourt/science

What Are Some Properties of Soil?

In this lesson, you can . . .

INVESTIGATE the ability of soils to hold water.

LEARN ABOUT soil properties.

LINK to math, writing, health, and technology.

◀ This terrarium is a habitat for plants. Its soil helps plants meet their needs for water and nutrients.

INVESTIGATE

The Ability of Soils to Hold Water

Activity Purpose Plants take in water mainly through their roots. Some plants need soil that holds plenty of water. Others need well-drained soil, which lets more water pass through it. In this investigation you will **control variables** to find out how well different soil types hold water.

Materials

- 3 clear plastic cups
- wax pencil
- metric ruler
- 2 large coffee filters
- 2 rubber bands
- $\frac{3}{4}$ cup potting soil
- measuring cup
- $\frac{1}{4}$ cup sand
- stir stick or spoon
- water
- stopwatch or watch with second hand

Activity Procedure

1. Make a chart like the one shown on the next page.

2. On each cup, mark lines 1 cm, 2 cm, 3 cm, and 4 cm from the bottom. Label one cup *Potting Soil*, label another cup *Sandy Soil*, and label the last cup *Water*.

3. Put a coffee filter over the top of the potting-soil cup. With your fingertips, push it about halfway into the cup. Fold the filter edge over the rim of the cup. Use a rubber band to hold the filter on the cup.

4. Repeat Step 3 for the sandy-soil cup. (Picture A)

Soil Types and Water Drainage

	Potting Soil	Sandy Soil
Time of first drop		
Time of last drop		
Amount of water drained		

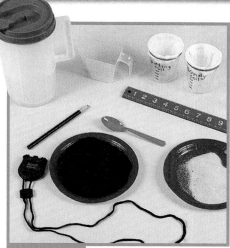

5. Pour $\frac{1}{2}$ cup of potting soil into the coffee filter of the potting-soil cup.

6. Pour the sand into the remaining potting soil. Stir it well to make sandy soil. Pour $\frac{1}{2}$ cup of sandy soil into the coffee filter of the sandy-soil cup.

7. **Predict** whether sandy soil or potting soil will drain water faster. **Record** your prediction.

8. Fill the water cup up to the 4-cm mark. Pour the water into the potting-soil cup. As you start to pour, have a partner start the stopwatch. (Picture B) **Record** the time when water begins dripping through the filter. Also record the time when the water stops dripping. Then record the amount of water in the cup.

9. Repeat Step 8 for the sandy soil.

Picture A

Draw Conclusions

1. Which soil type held water longer? Was your prediction correct?

2. Which soil type do you **infer** would be better for planting a cactus? Why?

Picture B

3. **Scientists at Work** When scientists **control variables**, they can find out the effect of one change. List the variables in this experiment. Which variable was changed? Which variables stayed the same?

Investigate Further Repeat this activity twice each for several soil types. You can use soils you can buy, soil from your yard, or your own soil mixes. How were your results and predictions related?

Process Skill Tip

When you **control variables** in an experiment, you change only one condition and keep all other conditions the same.

Soil Properties

Soil as a Habitat

FIND OUT

• what properties make soil good for supporting life

• how soil can be improved

VOCABULARY

fertile

Before studying soil, you may have thought that all soil was much alike. Scientists have classified more than 70,000 soil types around the world. The amounts of humus, clay, silt, and sand in a soil determine the soil type. Each soil type helps meet the needs of the living things that depend on it.

Soil is an important nonliving part of ecosystems. The plants, animals, and microorganisms that live in a soil meet their needs by using the soil around them. Remember the basic needs of living things. Soil must provide most of these needs for organisms that live in it. Soil with lots of humus provides plenty of nutrients for plants. Loosely packed soil has spaces between the particles. These spaces fill with water and air. Plants and animals in the soil use the water and air to meet their needs.

✔ **How does soil help living things meet their needs?**

Plants and animals that need little water can live in dry, sandy desert soil. ▼

Good farm soil has lots of humus. Such soil helps many kinds of plants and animals meet their needs. ▼

Rain-forest soil is mostly clay. It supports many kinds of life. That is because nutrients are always being recycled quickly. ▼

Water Absorption

Soil types differ in how well they hold water. In the investigation, you saw that potting soil absorbs, or takes in, more water than sandy soil. Potting soil contains a lot of humus. Clay soil absorbs more water than sandy soil but the water is hard for plants to use.

The ability of soil to absorb water affects how much water plants and animals have during dry periods. It also determines how much water runs off during rainstorms or as snow melts.

✔ **Which soil type best absorbs water?**

▲ Soil that contains a lot of humus absorbs water like a sponge. This water is then available to the plants that live in the soil. Only a little water runs off. Also, the plant roots make spaces where water can run into soil.

▲ Packed, dry clay soil with few plants causes a lot of runoff. It blocks water almost as well as brick or tile. Wet clay soil holds water so well that it is difficult for plants to get the water they need.

Sandy soil is usually light in color but can be any color. It is the coarsest form of soil. Sandy soil does not stick together well when wet. ▶

Soil rich in humus is dark in color because it has a lot of decaying plant and animal matter. It feels spongy and crumbles easily. ▶

Various minerals in clay give it color. For example, iron makes it red. Particles of clay are very fine. When wet, clay becomes sticky. ▶

Color and Texture

Two other properties of soil are color and texture. *Color* refers to the way a soil looks. *Texture* refers to the way the soil feels.

A soil's color tells a lot about the soil. It shows the presence of certain minerals or other substances. For example, red soil contains a lot of iron. Black soil contains a lot of humus. Color can also tell you how warm a soil will get. Dark soil is warmed a lot by the sun. Light-colored soil reflects more sunlight and is warmed less.

Texture describes the size of the particles that make up soil. Soil textures range from coarse to fine. A coarse soil is made up of large grains, like sand, which feel rough. A fine soil is made of dust or other powdery substances and feels smooth. Fine soil may feel sticky when wet.

✔ **Which property of soil can you discover by feeling the soil?**

◀ Fertilizers can add nutrients to soil.

◀ Adding sand to soil makes water flow through it more easily.

◀ Adding lime makes water dissolve nutrients more slowly. This can give plants time to absorb nutrients before they are washed away.

Soil Richness

A soil that can grow a lot of plants is said to be **fertile** (FERT•uhl). Fertile soil is rich in nutrients and provides the right conditions for plants to grow.

A soil can be made more fertile by changing it or adding to it. Fertilizers (FUHRT•uhl•eye•zerz) are products that make soil richer. Most fertilizers add decaying plant matter or minerals.

Farmers and soil scientists have found that soil containing an even mixture of sand, clay, and humus is best for growing most plants. Soil with this mixture absorbs just the right amount of water. It also provides enough nutrients. People can add a missing part to make a poor soil better.

Water dissolves nutrients in soil. Sometimes nutrients dissolve so quickly that they are washed away before plants can use them. Adding lime to the soil slows down the rate at which minerals dissolve. Less often, water dissolves nutrients too slowly. Adding sulfur to the soil increases the rate at which water dissolves nutrients.

✔ **What products make soil richer?**

This farmer is spraying the soil with ammonia. The ammonia adds nitrogen to the soil, helping the soil grow more plants. ▼

▲ You can help recycle soil nutrients by making a compost pile. Beneficial bacteria will rot raked leaves and grass clippings to form a rich humus. You can add the humus back to the soil.

Summary

Soil is important because it is a habitat for plants and animals. Soil properties such as color and texture, fertility, and ability to hold water make some soil types better than others for growing plants. Most soil can be improved by adding fertilizers, missing soil parts, or other minerals.

Review

1. Where are air and water found in soil?

2. Why is a soil's texture important in determining how the soil absorbs water?

3. What combination of soil parts is best for growing most plants?

4. **Critical Thinking** You start a vegetable garden and find that most of the soil is clay. What can you add to make the garden's soil better?

5. **Test Prep** Which of these soil parts has the largest particles?

   A silt

   B clay

   C humus

   D sand

LINKS

MATH LINK

Soil Temperature The temperature of soil affects how plants sprout and grow. Measure the temperature of soil outside that has been in direct sunlight for an hour. Then measure the temperature of soil that has been in shade for an hour. Find the difference between the two. Why do you think seeds are more likely to sprout in a warm place?

WRITING LINK

Informative Writing — How-To Find out which plants grow best in the soil types in your area. Make a gardening guide for students your age. Include in your guide a description of each soil type and pictures of the plants that grow in it.

HEALTH LINK

Good Nutrition Fresh fruits and vegetables are often rich in nutrients that they take from the soil. Find out which foods are rich in minerals and what the minerals are. Make a chart of your findings.

TECHNOLOGY LINK

Visit the Harcourt Learning Site for related links, activities, and resources.

www.harcourtschool.com/ca

What Are Some Ways to Conserve Soil?

In this lesson, you can . . .

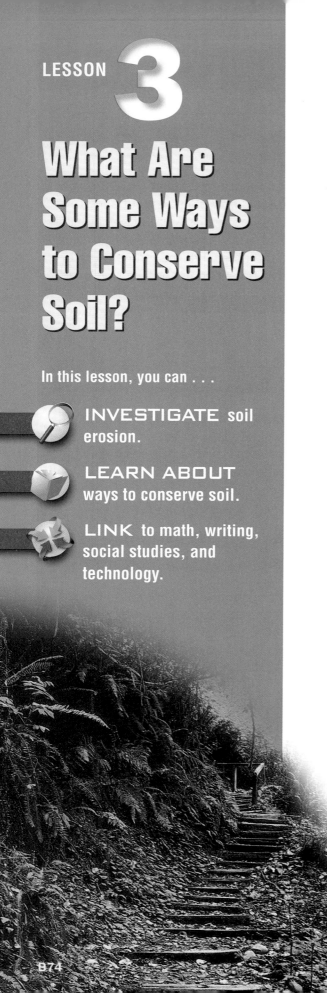

INVESTIGATE soil erosion.

LEARN ABOUT ways to conserve soil.

LINK to math, writing, social studies, and technology.

INVESTIGATE

Soil Erosion

Activity Purpose Sometimes there is more rain than the soil can hold. The extra water runs off. Runoff water can cause soil erosion, especially on hills. Because soil takes so long to form, it is important to keep it in place. In this investigation you will **build models** of two ways to plow a hill. You will compare the amounts of soil eroded in the two models.

Materials

- masking tape
- 2 wide-mouth jars
- flat board about 15 cm long
- sandy soil
- metric ruler
- craft stick
- roller-type paint tray
- plastic cup
- water
- watering can

Activity Procedure

1 Place a piece of masking tape on each jar. Label one jar *Down Rows*. Label the other *Across Rows*.

2 Cover the board with damp soil to a depth of about 2 cm.

3 Make rows that run down the board by pressing the craft stick into the soil. Make the rows about 2 cm apart. (Picture A)

4 Place the board in the paint tray. One end of the board should be slightly higher than the other end.

◄ The boards along this path hold soil in place. They prevent the soil from crumbling or from being washed away.

Picture A

Picture B

5. Put 2 cups of water into the watering can. Hold the can about 10 cm above the tray. Sprinkle the soil with water until the can is empty. (Picture B)

6. Carefully remove the board and set it aside. Pour the runoff from the paint tray into the *Down Rows* jar.

7. Smooth out the soil on the board. Add soil to make the depth about 2 cm. Make fresh rows in the soil, only this time make rows that run across the board.

8. Repeat Steps 4–6, but pour the runoff water into the *Across Rows* jar.

9. Allow the soil in both jars to settle for 30 minutes.

Draw Conclusions

1. **Observe** the material in each jar. Which jar has more runoff? Which jar has more soil?

2. Which model showed the better way to keep soil from eroding?

3. **Scientists at Work** Scientists **compare** results of tests to find the best answer. What did you compare in this activity?

Investigate Further Use cause and effect relationships to **predict** how covering soil affects the amount of soil erosion. Repeat the experiment, but this time cover the soil with shredded newspaper. Use different jars to collect runoff. Which material had the least runoff? Use your results to **draw a conclusion** about how soil cover affects the amount of runoff and soil erosion.

Process Skill Tip

When you **compare** things, you observe them to see how they are alike and how they are different. It is important to observe all the things in the same way. Otherwise, you may miss important differences. Or you may see false differences because you observed in different ways.

Soil Conservation

Soil Loss

Soil changes all the time. Weathering breaks up rock to form new soil. Erosion by wind and water moves soil from place to place. Because of these and other changes, some places gain soil. Other places lose soil.

Erosion most affects soil without a covering of plants. Farmlands and construction sites usually have lots of such bare soil. The soil soaks up some rainwater. During heavy rains, however, too much rain falls at one time to be soaked up. Water begins to run off. Runoff carries soil to a stream. The stream then drains into larger and larger rivers.

Eroded soil can be deposited anywhere along streams and rivers. However, much of the soil is carried downstream until a river enters the ocean. As the river flows into the ocean, it slows down. Eroded soil is deposited to form new land called a delta. As long as soil flows with the river, the delta grows farther and farther out into the ocean. The delta gets rich topsoil from the land the river flows through. But the land upriver loses soil.

FIND OUT

- how soil and nutrients from soil can be lost
- ways to protect soil

VOCABULARY

soil conservation
contour plowing
strip cropping
terracing

In the United States, about half of the land is used for agriculture. ▼

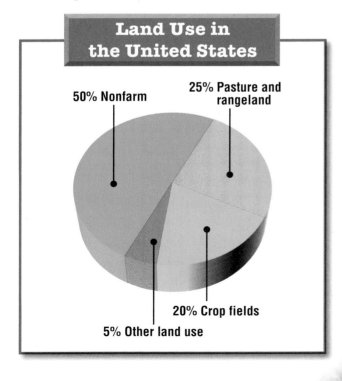

Land Use in the United States

50% Nonfarm

25% Pasture and rangeland

20% Crop fields

5% Other land use

The Mississippi River delta stretches 121 km (about 75 mi) farther into the Gulf of Mexico than it did 100 years ago. ▼

You can see evidence of water erosion. Runoff can dig deep gullies. This usually happens on steep hills. With each heavy rainfall, runoff makes the gullies wider and deeper.

Sometimes deposited soil blocks rivers or streams. There may be flooding, or a new flow path may result.

Land can also lose soil by wind erosion. Plants cover and protect soil. When people clear land to plant fields or build homes, they take away trees and other plants. Then there are no roots to hold soil and no plants to shelter soil from wind and rain. When the wind blows, it picks up dry topsoil and carries it away.

✔ **What happens to soil in a river when it enters the ocean?**

▲ This gully was formed as runoff water rushed to a lower area.

▲ When land cleared for farming is dry, wind can carry soil away.

One of these two rivers contains more eroded soil. Notice the different colors of water where they join. ▼

Controlling Soil Loss

Soil conservation (kahn•ser•VAY•shuhn) is saving soil. Farmers work hard to protect their valuable soil. One way farmers have found to control soil loss is to plow and plant around a hill rather than up and down the hill. Plowing around a hill is called **contour** (KAHN•toor) **plowing**. In the investigation, you saw reasons that contour plowing is good. The rows catch runoff and slow it down. They keep it from flowing quickly downhill.

Farmers also use strip cropping to save soil. In **strip cropping** one or more crops are planted between rows of other crops. For example, alfalfa is sometimes planted between rows of corn. The corn slows down the wind, which could erode soil that isn't covered. The roots of both plants help hold the soil in place.

A farming method used on steep hillsides is terracing. In **terracing** (TAIR•uhs•ing) a steep hill is cut to form broad, flat areas at different heights. A terraced hillside looks like a huge stairway. The steps

▲ Contour plowing protects soil on gentle, rolling hillsides.

▲ Strip cropping protects soil by planting strips of short and tall plants side by side. The tall plants help slow down the wind. The short plants provide good cover for the soil.

◄ Terracing changes a steep hillside into a series of flat steps. Crops are grown on the steps.

allow farmers to grow crops on hillsides that would otherwise have been too steep. The steps slow down water as it rushes down the hill.

Builders of roads, especially highways, look for ways to protect roadsides from erosion. Roads through mountains may have roadside terracing. Often trees, grass, and other plants are put along roads to reduce erosion.

Gardeners also want to conserve soil. At homes and in city parks, gardeners plant lawns and gardens that look good and protect the soil.

✔ **What are three farming methods that save soil?**

Landscaping to Control Soil Loss

Like farmland, a hillside garden can easily lose soil. A gardener must plan carefully and use several ways to control erosion. Using more than one way protects the garden and adds interest.

1 The roots of plants, such as these ornamental grasses, help hold soil in place.

2 Stones can be set in ways that slow the flow of water.

3 A retaining wall holds soil in place, keeping it from being washed away.

Controlling Nutrient Loss

Erosion is not the only way soil becomes less rich. Overuse and misuse can take nutrients from soil. Growing the same crop in a field year after year can take important minerals from the soil. For example, if a farmer planted just corn in a field for several years, the corn would use most of the nitrogen (NY•truh•jehn) in the soil. Eventually, there would not be enough nitrogen to grow corn.

Not every plant uses the same nutrients. Some plants even add nutrients to the soil. Farmers have found that if they plant a different crop in a field every year, they can control nutrient loss. This is called crop rotation. Chemical fertilizers can replace lost nutrients, but chemicals that run off can harm nearby ponds and streams. Crop rotation helps replace nutrients without using as much of these chemicals.

✔ **How can planting the same crop year after year harm the soil?**

▲ The next year, the farmer plants soybeans. Soybeans add nitrogen to the soil.

One spring a farmer plants corn in a field. The corn takes nitrogen from the soil. ▶

Some Important Soil Nutrients	
Nutrient	**How the Nutrient Helps Plants**
Nitrogen	Helps make up the green matter that absorbs the sun's energy
Phosphorus (FAHS•fuh•ruhs)	Helps plants change the sun's energy into food energy
Potassium (poh•TAS•ee•uhm)	Helps a plant keep the right amount of water in its stems, roots, and leaves
Calcium (KAL•see•uhm)	Helps allow water and gases to pass through plant cells
Magnesium (mag•NEE•zee•uhm)	Helps a plant use the food it makes

▲ In the fall, after the soybeans have been harvested, the farmer plants winter wheat. The field "rests" during the late summer and fall after the wheat is harvested. The dead plant parts decay and add nutrients to the soil.

Summary

Soil can be lost to wind and water erosion. Farmers use soil conservation techniques such as contour plowing, strip cropping, terracing, and crop rotation to reduce these problems. Nutrients in soil can be lost if the same crop is planted year after year.

Review

1. In what ways is soil always changing?

2. What are two things gardeners and road builders hope to do?

3. How does crop rotation keep soil from losing nutrients?

4. **Critical Thinking** If farmers didn't try to save soil, what could happen?

5. **Test Prep** Which way of planting can reduce water erosion on a steep hillside?

   A strip cropping   C contour plowing

   B terracing   D crop rotation

LINKS

MATH LINK

Calculating Soil Loss Suppose topsoil is 1 m deep. It is eroded at a rate of 5 cm a year. How long will the topsoil last? If new strip cropping reduces erosion by half, how long will the topsoil last?

WRITING LINK

Informative Writing—How-To Suppose you are in charge of helping the people in an area practice soil conservation. The area could include a construction site, a golf course being built, or a farm. Write a handout that tells ways people could change habits to conserve soil.

SOCIAL STUDIES LINK

Dust Bowl More than 70 years ago, dust clouds blew across many states. People had to wear scarves to keep grit out of their eyes and mouths. Investigate the Dust Bowl years to see the lessons people learned about misusing the land.

TECHNOLOGY LINK

Learn more about ways farmers control erosion by viewing *African Soil Erosion* on the **Harcourt Science Newsroom Video** in your classroom video library.

SOIL ENRICHMENT

People who grow a garden in the same place year after year quickly learn an important fact of soil science—plants take nutrients from the soil. For plants to grow well the next year, the nutrients must be put back in some way.

Ancient Soil Practices

People in China learned about putting nutrients back into soil hundreds of years ago. For more than 4000 years, some farms in China have been replanted every year. Chinese farmers kept their farmland fertile by adding organic material to the soil. One way they did this was by growing a crop of *legumes* (LEG•yoomz). Legumes include beans, soybeans, clover, alfalfa, and peanuts. These plants are rich in nitrogen, an impor-

tant soil nutrient. Farmers harvested the legumes and mixed them with rich soil from near a river. Then they spread this mixture over their fields.

The ancient Roman and Greek farmers added natural fertilizers to the soil, too. They also buried human and animal bones. Bones add nitrogen and potassium to the soil. Many other cultures also have used bones to enrich the soil. Even today you can find bags of bone meal, or ground-up animal bones, in garden supply stores.

Enhancing Soil in the Americas

Some Native Americans enriched their soil by burying fish with their corn seeds. Western Apache families each had several small farms. They would plant only some

The History of Soil Enrichment

Chinese 2,000 B.C.
Chinese use legumes to enrich soil. Romans and Greeks use natural fertilizers including bones.

Carver 1800s
George Washington Carver experiments with plants and soil.

2000 B.C.	300-900 A.D.	1600 A.D.	1700 A.D.	1800 A.D.

Mayans 300-900 A.D.
Mayan culture cuts and burns forest to provide farmland.

Americans 1600s
Native Americans teach colonists planting methods.

of the farms each year. Grasses and weeds grew on the unused farmland. These plants were a source of nutrients the next time crops were planted.

Modern Methods—Mix of Old and New

In the United States during the late 1800s, many farmers had soil problems. Planting the same crop, such as cotton, every year was taking nutrients from the soil. But, farmers couldn't afford to leave some fields unplanted each year. George Washington Carver did experiments with plants to solve these problems. Carver came up with a plan of *rotating crops* in the same field. His idea was to plant a crop of cotton one year and a crop of peanuts, a kind of legume, the next year.

Carver also recommended *composting* (KAHM•pohst•ing), which is now popular again. To make compost, people mix leaves, grass clippings, kitchen scraps, paper, and wood chips together. As the leaves and other materials rot, they form rich organic material that can be used to improve soil. If materials aren't composted,

they usually take up space in landfills. So composting is a wise way to reuse resources.

Fertilizers are materials that enrich soil. The United States produces a lot of chemical fertilizers. These are either artificial substances or substances taken out of mineral resources. Fertilizers are made to replace nitrogen, phosphorus, and potassium—the three substances most often missing from soil. Nitrogen fertilizers, for example, usually add some form of ammonia to the soil.

All these ways of improving the soil were developed because people know soil is a valuable resource. As the needs of the world increase, scientists keep looking for new ways to improve soil and to grow more and better crops.

Think About It

1. What are two ways to add needed nitrogen to soil?
2. How are the nonartificial ways of enriching soil alike?

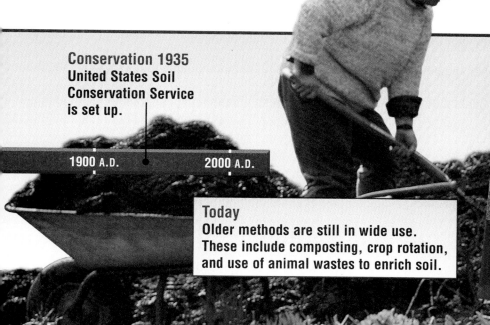

Conservation 1935
United States Soil
Conservation Service
is set up.

1900 A.D.   2000 A.D.

Today
Older methods are still in wide use. These include composting, crop rotation, and use of animal wastes to enrich soil.

BONE MEAL
5-11-0
NET WEIGHT 4 LBS. (1.8 kg)

Ignacio Rodriguez-Iturbe

HYDROLOGIST

"I always tell my students that to do good research it is necessary to be able to dream."

Dr. Ignacio Rodriguez-Iturbe thinks his ability to dream came from his father. "To see far and to see well, one needs the eyes of the heart," his father would tell him. Ignacio Rodriguez-Iturbe has applied the "eyes of the heart" to his scientific work.

Dr. Ignacio Rodriguez-Iturbe is from Venezuela, and has taught there and at the Massachusetts Institute of Technology. He now teaches at the Princeton Environmental Institute. In 1998 he received the Robert E. Horton Medal from the American Geophysical Union.

Like all hydrologists(hy•DRAHL•uh•jists), Rodriguez-Iturbe studies water. Some hydrologists look for sources of fresh water. Others study water pollution and floods. Rodriguez-Iturbe studies how water moves through river systems, soil, and underground rock. He hopes to understand how this part of nature works. With that understanding, he can solve the problems of flooding or of wells that are drying up.

Rodriguez-Iturbe enjoys working on scientific problems with his students. He has even been known to call a student late at night to discuss research ideas. The people he has been able to work with throughout the years are important to him. He has had friends and co-workers in both Venezuela and the United States who share his interest in water.

THINK ABOUT IT

1. How would it be helpful to have friends and co-workers who share your research interests?

2. What kinds of things about water might a hydrologist study?

Observing Soil Textures

How can you describe soils by their texture?

Materials

- 3 paper towels
- topsoil
- sandy soil
- clay soil
- 3 index cards
- hand lens
- water
- dropper

Procedure

1. Spread each soil type on a separate paper towel. Write the name of each soil type on a different index card.

2. Observe each soil sample with the hand lens. Describe each soil type on the index card for that sample.

3. Hold some of one sample in your hand, and add five drops of water to the soil. Then squeeze and work the soil for a few seconds. On the index card for that soil type, describe the texture of the soil.

4. Repeat Step 3 for the other two soil samples. **CAUTION** Be sure to wash your hands after handling soil.

Draw Conclusions

Which of these soil types do you think would work best for a houseplant? A cactus?

Soils as Life Support

How well do soil types support plant growth?

Materials

- 4 small flowerpots with saucers
- potting soil, clay, sand, sphagnum peat moss
- 4 small plants of the same type and size
- water
- spoon

Procedure

1. Fill each pot half way with a different soil.

2. Put a plant in each pot. Add more soil if needed. Give each plant the same amount of water. Put the pots in a sunny spot.

3. Test each pot for dryness daily. To do this, insert a spoon into the soil and then remove it. If little soil clings to it, add water.

4. Keep a daily log. Record when the plants received water. Also record general observations about the plants. Describe how each plant looks.

Draw Conclusions

After two weeks, compare the plants. How well did each soil type meet the needs of its plant?

Vocabulary Review

Use the terms below to complete the sentences. The page numbers in ( ) tell you where to look in the chapter if you need help.

humus (B66)

fertile (B72)

soil conservation (B78)

contour plowing (B78)

strip cropping (B78)

terracing (B78)

1. Planting a crop between rows of another crop is ____.

2. Plowing around a hill is ____.

3. Cutting broad, flat areas in the sides of a steep mountain to grow crops is called ____.

4. Soil that is ____ is capable of growing a lot of plants.

5. ____ means saving of soil.

6. The soil part ____ is made up of rotting plant and animal materials.

Connect Concepts

Use the terms in the Word Bank to complete the concept map.

crop rotation   **contour plowing**   **erosion**

fertile   **soil conservation**   **terracing**

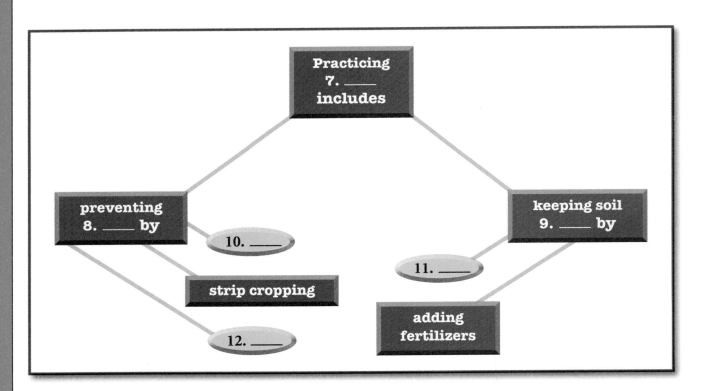

Practicing 7. ____ includes

preventing 8. ____ by

keeping soil 9. ____ by

10. ____

11. ____

strip cropping

adding fertilizers

12. ____

Check Understanding

Write the letter of the best choice.

13. The soil layer that is affected the most by erosion is —
    A topsoil   C bedrock
    B subsoil   D parent rock

14. When the temperature is high during the day and cold at night, rocks are likely to —
    F expand   H crack
    G contract   J harden

15. Cotton, which is grown to make clothing, depends mostly on ____ to grow.
    A topsoil   C bedrock
    B subsoil   D parent rock

16. ____ becomes richer as dead plants decay.
    F Topsoil   H Bedrock
    G Subsoil   J Parent rock

17. Terracing a hillside can slow —
    A weathering   C erosion
    B absorption   D soil formation

18. The soil at the top of a hill has a lot of the smallest type of soil particle. The soil is made up mostly of —
    F bedrock   H humus
    G sand   J clay

19. Tree roots reach down into the middle layer of soil, breaking up the rocks there. This soil layer is called —
    A bedrock   C subsoil
    B topsoil   D parent rock

Critical Thinking

20. You are planning a vegetable garden. You want your first year's harvest to be good. Name two important properties you want your soil to have. Tell how you could improve these soil properties.

21. You have two fields. One is on a gently sloping hillside, and the other is on flat ground. Tell what you would do to reduce soil erosion on each field.

Process Skills Review

22. You **observe** soil that is light in color and that doesn't hold together well when wet. What kind of soil is it likely to be? How well would it take up water?

23. You want to set up an experiment to compare the texture of soil types when they are wet. What are two **variables** you need to control?

24. How could you **compare** the runoff and erosion from two types of terracing?

Performance Assessment

Landscape Plan

Draw a plan for landscaping the schoolyard. Think of ways to make it look good and to prevent erosion. Include areas for games and sports you like to play. Label the parts of your design that are important for erosion control.

Unit Project Wrap Up

Here are some ideas for ways to wrap up your unit project.

Make a Book

Use index cards to make a book about your collection. Use one card for each sample. Draw a picture or attach a photo of the sample, identify it, and add information you have gathered.

Landscape with Rocks

Get permission to landscape a small outdoors area with your rocks. Use the rocks along with living and other nonliving things to make a landscape design that you like. Identify each rock with a label.

Display at a Science Fair

Display your earth-sample collection in a school science fair. Make maps, charts, or tables to help communicate what you learned.

Investigate Further

How could you make your project better? What other questions do you have about Earth's surface? Plan ways to find answers to your questions. Use the Science Handbook on pages R2-R9 for help.

Matter and Electricity

PHYSICAL SCIENCE

Matter and Electricity

Unit Project

Energy-Efficient Home

Make a model of a house. Use the model to test how well different kinds of materials insulate for sound and heat. Find ads for insulation, and insulate your house in ways that you think are most efficient. Then test the different materials.

Chapter 1

Physical Properties of Matter

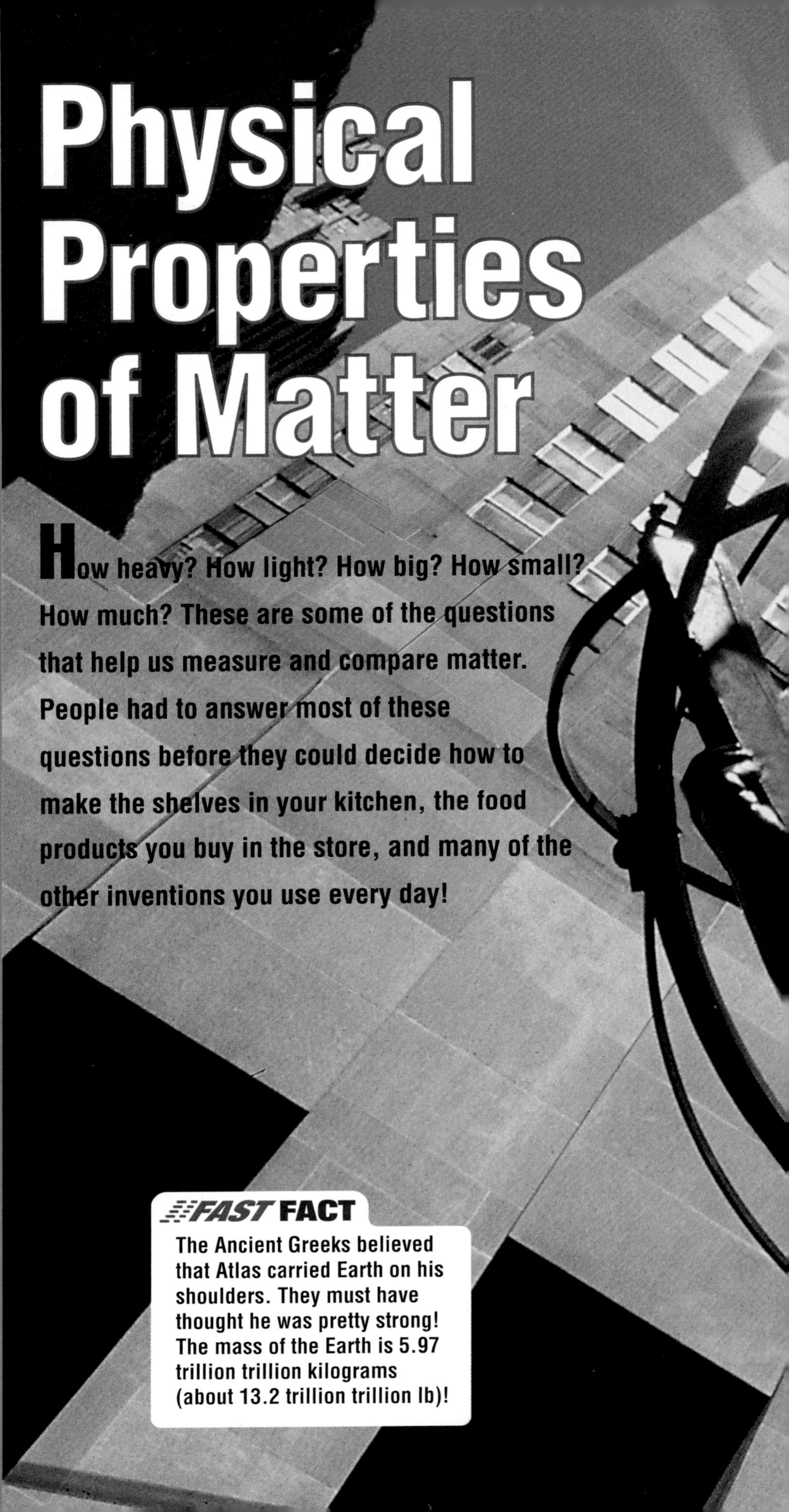

How heavy? How light? How big? How small? How much? These are some of the questions that help us measure and compare matter. People had to answer most of these questions before they could decide how to make the shelves in your kitchen, the food products you buy in the store, and many of the other inventions you use every day!

Vocabulary Preview

matter
mass
solid
liquid
gas
volume
density
solution
dissolve
solubility
buoyancy

FAST FACT

The Ancient Greeks believed that Atlas carried Earth on his shoulders. They must have thought he was pretty strong! The mass of the Earth is 5.97 trillion trillion kilograms (about 13.2 trillion trillion lb)!

If all the ice in the world melted (a volume of 60 million cubic kilometers or 14.3 million cubic miles), the oceans would rise 55–80 meters (180–262 ft or 18–27 stories)! In New York City's harbor, the entire Statue of Liberty would be under water except for her crown and torch!

Which is denser, gold or lead? To figure out how dense a material is, scientists compare an object's density to the density of water. Water has a density of 1 g/cubic centimeter. How dense are some other common materials?

Densities

Materials	Density (g/cm³)
Aluminum	2.7
Copper	9.0
Gold	19.3
Ice	0.9
Iron	7.9
Lead	11.3
Mercury	13.6

Atlas Statue in New York City

What Are Three States of Matter?

In this lesson, you can . . .

INVESTIGATE a physical property of matter.

LEARN ABOUT solids, liquids, and gases.

LINK to math, writing, technology, and other areas.

INVESTIGATE

Physical Properties of Matter

Activity Purpose You can't see it. Often you can't even feel it. But air is all around you. In this investigation you will **observe** one way air behaves and you will **infer** a property of matter.

Materials
- plastic bag
- plastic drinking straw
- book

Activity Procedure

1 Wrap the opening of the plastic bag tightly around the straw. Use your fingers to hold the bag in place. (Picture A)

2 Blow into the straw. **Observe** what happens to the bag.

3 Empty the bag. Now place a book on the bag. Again wrap the opening of the bag tightly around the straw and use your fingers to hold the bag in place.

◀ After a while this horse carving made of ice will melt into a puddle of water. How are the carving and a puddle alike? How are they different?

C4

Picture A

Picture B

4 **Predict** what will happen when you blow into the straw. Justify your prediction. Blow into it and **observe** what happens to the book.(Picture B)

Draw Conclusions

1. What happened to the bag when you blew air into it? What happened to the book?

2. What property of air caused the effects you observed in Steps 2 and 4?

3. **Scientists at Work** Scientists **draw conclusions** after they think carefully about observations and other data they have collected. What data supports your answer to Question 2 above?

Investigate Further Water changes as it freezes. Fill five small, clear cups half-full of water. Mark the level of water on the side of each cup. Put the cups on a flat, level surface in a freezer. Predict how the water will change. The next day, mark the ice levels. Measure any differences in level. Based on your observations and measurements, how do you infer water changes as it becomes ice? How did conducting multiple trials make you more confident about your results?

Process Skill Tip

When you **draw a conclusion,** you make a statement of what you know based on all the data you have collected. Unlike an inference, a conclusion is supported, or shown to be likely, by results of tests.

LEARN ABOUT

States of Matter

Solids

FIND OUT

- how atoms and molecules are arranged in matter
- how three states of matter are different

VOCABULARY

matter
mass
solid
liquid

One way you know about the world around you is from your sense of touch. A tree trunk stops your finger. Water changes its shape as you poke your finger into it. You feel the moving air of a breeze. By touch you know that wood, water, and air have different properties. Yet they are all matter. Everything in the universe that has mass and takes up space is classified as **matter**.

In the investigation you saw that air takes up space. Matter also has mass. **Mass** is the amount of matter something contains. A large, heavy object such as an elephant has a lot of mass. A small, light maple leaf has much less mass. Even though an elephant and a leaf are very different, each is matter.

All matter is made of extremely small particles called *atoms*, or groups of atoms called *molecules*. These tiny particles are always moving very quickly, faster when the temperature is high and more slowly when the temperature is low.

The arrangements of atoms and molecules give matter properties. Each arrangement is called a *state of matter*. A door key is an example of matter in the solid state. When you touch a door key, it stops your finger. A **solid** is matter that has a definite shape and takes up a definite amount of space. The atoms and molecules in a solid are close together, like neat and even stacks of tiny balls. Each moves back and forth in all directions but around one point. This arrangement gives a solid its definite shape.

✔ **How are atoms and molecules arranged in a solid?**

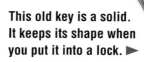

This old key is a solid. It keeps its shape when you put it into a lock. ▶

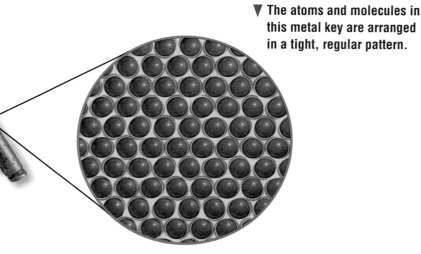

▼ The atoms and molecules in this metal key are arranged in a tight, regular pattern.

Liquids

A frozen ice cube keeps its shape. But when you heat the ice cube in a pan, the ice becomes liquid water. The water changes shape and fills the bottom of the pan. If you spill the water onto a table, the water will spread out to cover the tabletop. The water still takes up the same amount of space as in the pan. It just has a new shape. A **liquid** is matter that takes the shape of its container and takes up a definite amount of space.

When matter is a liquid, its atoms and molecules slip and slide around each other. They don't keep the same neighbors, as those in a solid do. They move from place to place. But they still stay close to each other.

As the atoms and molecules in a liquid move, they bump into the walls of their container. The solid walls of the container don't change shape. The atoms and molecules of the liquid can't move past the walls, and the liquid atoms and molecules stay close together. So, the liquid takes the shape of its container.

If you pour a liquid from one container into another, the amount of matter in the liquid stays the same. The amount of space the liquid takes up also stays the same.

✔ **Why does a liquid have the same shape as its container?**

▲ The atoms and molecules in a liquid move past each other easily. They are still close together but are not in a neat, even arrangement, as atoms and molecules in a solid are.

As these straws show, a liquid always takes the shape of its container. ▶

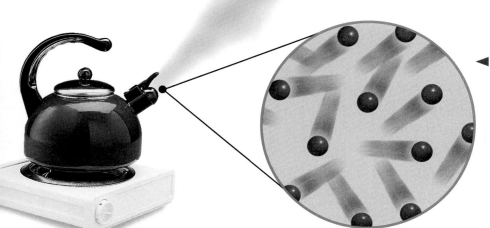

◄ Water vapor is a gas that you can't see. Its atoms and molecules fly out the whistling teakettle spout. Some cool and clump together to form tiny water drops. The drops are the white mist that you can see.

Gases

A **gas** is matter that has no definite shape and takes up no definite amount of space. Like atoms and molecules in liquids, the bits in gases are not arranged in any pattern. Unlike atoms and molecules in liquids, however, those in gases don't stay close together. This is because atoms and molecules in gases are moving much faster than those in liquids.

The amount of space a gas takes up depends on the amount of space inside its container. A gas always fills the container it is in. If the container is open, the gas atoms and molecules move out.

Most matter can change state from a solid to a liquid to a gas. You can see this when you leave an ice cube in a pan on a hot stove. In a few minutes, the cube changes from a solid to a liquid. Minutes later the liquid is gone—the water has become a gas called *water vapor*. The gas molecules have moved off in all directions.

Heating matter makes atoms and molecules move faster. When ice is heated, some molecules begin to move fast enough to break away from their neighbors. As the regular arrangement of molecules breaks down, the ice melts. Heated molecules of liquid water move faster and faster. After a while they move fast enough to bounce away from each other. The liquid boils, or changes quickly into a gas.

✔ **How does heating matter change its state?**

◄ A lot of air is squeezed into the tank carried by this diver. The tank valve is open. Atoms and molecules of gases move out of the tank as the diver breathes in.

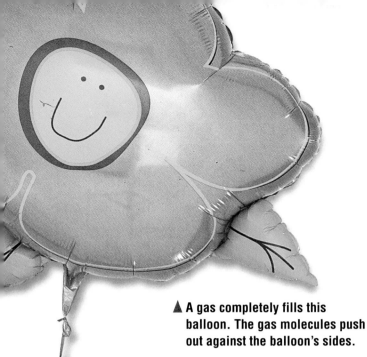

LINKS

MATH LINK

Liquid Mercury Mercury is a metal that becomes a solid at 39° *below* 0°C. It becomes a gas at 357° *above* 0°C. What is the total number of degrees Celsius at which mercury is a liquid?

WRITING LINK

Narrative Writing—Story Suppose that you are a molecule in a solid that melts and then becomes a gas. Write a story for your teacher about your experiences.

▲ A gas completely fills this balloon. The gas molecules push out against the balloon's sides.

HEALTH LINK

States of Matter in the Body Find out which organ in the body is a liquid. Name some of the organs that bring a gas into the body. Plan and make a model of one body system that uses a liquid or a gas.

Summary

Matter takes up space. Matter is made up of atoms and molecules. Those in solid matter stay close together and move back and forth in all directions but around one point. Atoms and molecules in liquid matter stay close together but move past each other. Those in a gas are spread far apart.

Review

1. What are three states of matter?
2. Which state of matter keeps its shape?
3. Which states of matter take the shapes of their containers?
4. **Critical Thinking** How can matter be changed from a liquid to a solid?
5. **Test Prep** Which sentence describes a liquid?

   A Atoms and molecules slide past each other.

   B Atoms and molecules stay near their neighbors.

   C Atoms and molecules are arranged in a pattern.

   D Atoms and molecules bounce away from each other.

ART LINK

Using Matter in Art Find and describe in your own words one example each of a work of art that uses a solid, a liquid, and a gas.

TECHNOLOGY LINK

Visit the Harcourt Learning Site for related links, activities, and resources.

WELCOME TO THE LEARNING SITE

www.harcourtschool.com/ca

C9

How Can Matter Be Measured and Compared?

In this lesson, you can . . .

 INVESTIGATE the densities of some types of matter.

 LEARN ABOUT measuring and comparing matter.

 LINK to math, writing, health, and technology.

 **INVESTIGATE**

Density

Activity Purpose Some objects have more matter packed into a smaller space than other objects. In this investigation you will **measure** the mass of raisins and of breakfast cereal. Then you will **compare** their masses and the amounts of space they take up.

Materials
- 3 identical plastic cups
- raisins
- breakfast cereal
- pan balance

Activity Procedure

1 Fill one cup with raisins. Make sure the raisins fill the cup all the way to the top. (Picture A)

2 Fill another cup with cereal. Make sure the cereal fills the cup all the way to the top.

3 **Observe** the amount of space taken up by the raisins and the cereal.

4 Adjust the balance so the pans are level. Place one cup on each pan. **Observe** what happens. (Picture B)

◄ A gold coin as small as a dime has more mass than a quarter.

C10

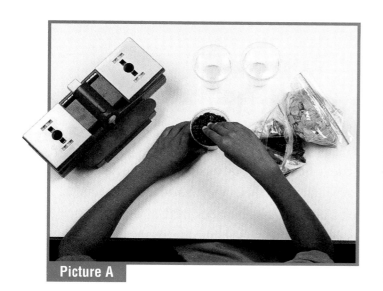

Picture A

Picture B

5 Fill the third cup with a mixture of raisins and cereal. **Predict** how the mass of the cup of raisins and cereal will compare with the masses of the cup of raisins and the cup of cereal. Justify your predictions. Use the pan balance to check your predictions.

Draw Conclusions

1. **Compare** the amount of space taken up by the raisins with the space taken up by the cereal.

2. Which has more mass, the cup of raisins or the cup of cereal? Explain your answer.

3. Which cup has more matter packed into it? Explain your answer.

4. **Scientists at Work** It is important to know the starting place when you measure. What would happen if you **measured** without making the balance pans equal? Explain your answer.

Investigate Further Write step-by-step directions to **compare** the masses of any two materials and the space they take up. Exchange sets of directions with a classmate. Test the directions and suggest revisions.

Process Skill Tip

A balance **measures** by comparing two masses. To make sure the comparison is accurate, you must make both sides of the balance equal before you measure. This is what you did in Step 4.

Measuring Matter

Measuring Mass

FIND OUT

• about mass and volume and how to measure them

• a way to use measurements of mass and volume to describe density

VOCABULARY

volume

density

When the pans of a balance are level, the pieces of matter on the two pans have the same mass. These cotton balls have the same mass as the wood block. ▼

You can compare the amount of matter in two objects by measuring the mass of each. The object with more mass has the greater amount of matter. Mass is measured in units called grams and kilograms (KIL•uh•gramz). Half a kilogram, or $\frac{1}{2}$ kg, is about the same mass as four sticks of margarine. A medium-sized paper clip masses about 1 gram, or 1 g.

One way to compare two masses is by using a pan balance. Put an object in each pan. When the pans of the balance are level, the matter in the two pans has the same mass. In the investigation, you used a pan balance to find out that a cup of raisins has more mass than a cup of cereal.

If you know the mass of the matter in one pan, you can find the mass of the matter in the other pan. This is one way scientists measure mass. They have objects with masses that are known—for example, 50 grams, 200 grams, and 1 kilogram. These objects are known as *standard masses*. Scientists put an object whose mass they don't know in one pan and put standard masses in the other pan. Then they add or remove standard masses until the two pans balance. The total of the standard masses equals the mass of the object.

✔ **Name one way you can measure mass.**

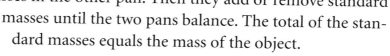
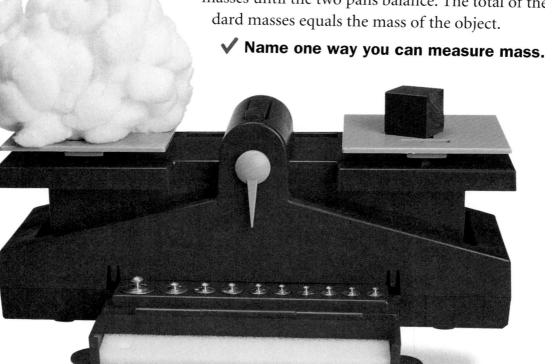

◀ It is easy to measure the volume of a liquid by using this container marked in milliliters, or mL. This container is called a beaker, and it has about 400 mL of red liquid.

Volume

Matter has mass and takes up space. The amount of space that matter takes up is called its **volume** (VAHL•yoom). You can measure the amount of space a solid or liquid takes up. You also can measure a container such as a box and calculate its volume. Volume often is measured in cubic centimeters. A *cubic centimeter* is the space taken up by a cube that has each side equal to 1 centimeter. A cubic centimeter is the same as a milliliter.

Cooks use measuring cups and measuring spoons to find the volume of ingredients for a recipe. Scientists measure volume with a beaker or a graduate, a tall cylinder with measuring marks on the side.

A solid keeps its shape, so it is easy to see that its volume stays the same. A liquid changes shape to match its container. But it does not change its volume. A gas has no definite volume. However, the mass of a gas sample doesn't change when the volume of the gas changes.

✔ **What is volume?**

▲ You can find the volume of odd-shaped solid objects, such as these marbles, by sinking them in water. They push away some of the water, and the water level rises. The change in water level gives the volume of the solids.

▲ The level in this graduate changed from 250 mL to 285 mL when the marbles were added. Therefore, the volume of the marbles is 285 mL – 250 mL = 35 mL.

To find the volume of a box, first measure its height, width, and length. Then multiply the three numbers together. This box is about 6 cm thick, 20 cm wide, and 30 cm tall. Its volume is 6 cm × 20 cm × 30 cm = 3600 cubic centimeters. ▶

Density

Some matter takes up a large space but has a small mass. A balloon filled with gas may take up 10,000 cubic centimeters. But it may have such a small mass that it floats in the air. Other matter takes up very little space and has a large mass. A brick is smaller than the balloon, but it has much more mass.

The property of matter that compares the amount of matter to the space taken up is called **density** (DEN•suh•tee). The gas in a balloon has a low density. The density of a brick is much higher.

You can find the density of an object by dividing the mass of the object by its volume. For example, an apple may have a mass of 200 grams and a volume of 200 cubic centimeters. Its density is 200 grams ÷ 200 cubic centimeters, or 1 gram per cubic centimeter.

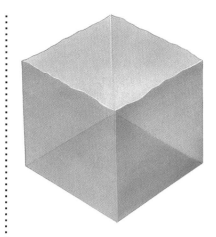

◄ One cubic centimeter of water has a mass of 1 gram. The density of water is 1 gram per cubic centimeter.

In the investigation you saw that cereal is less dense than raisins. You also found that a mixture of cereal and raisins is denser than cereal and less dense than raisins. Whenever you mix two kinds of matter, the density of the mixture is between the densities of the two separate materials.

✔ **Which material in the table has the greatest density?**

Density of Some Common Materials

Materials	Density (g per cubic centimeter)	Relative Size of 1-kg Disk
Pine	0.40	
Motor oil	0.90	
Plastic (HDPE)	0.96	
Lead	11.30	

◄ The disks show the volume needed to make up one kilogram of each material. Notice how the size of the disks compares to the density of the materials.

Summary

All matter has mass and volume. Mass is the amount of matter in an object. The space that matter takes up is called volume. Density compares the amount of matter in an object to the amount of space it takes up. You can find the density of an object by dividing its mass by its volume.

Review

1. What is one way to measure mass?
2. What word is used to describe the amount of space that matter takes up?
3. What property of matter compares the amount of matter to the space that the matter takes up?
4. **Critical Thinking** You are shopping for cereal. How does estimating density help you find a good buy?
5. **Test Prep** If a black ball is denser than a white ball of the same size, the black ball has —

   A less volume
   B more volume
   C more matter taking up the same space
   D less matter taking up the same space

LINKS

MATH LINK

Compare Volumes Use a pan balance and three cups to measure 100 g, 200 g, and 300 g of water. Use a beaker or a graduate to measure and compare the volumes of water.

WRITING LINK

Informative Writing—Narration You are making a short video for younger students. It will show how to measure volume and mass. Decide what you will show. Then, write a script to explain what you are showing.

HEALTH LINK

Your Density Find out how to measure and compare the mass of a person's muscles and body fat. Make a comic strip that shows how this is done.

TECHNOLOGY LINK

Learn more about measuring matter by visiting this Internet site.
www.scilinks.org/harcourt

What Are Some Useful Properties of Matter?

In this lesson, you can . . .

INVESTIGATE what happens to some solids in water.

LEARN ABOUT ways to group kinds of matter.

INVESTIGATE

Floating and Sinking

Activity Purpose Some solids sink in liquid water, and others float. But even solids that sink can be made to float. In this investigation you will see what happens to two solid materials when they are placed in water. Then you will make boats from the materials. You will **infer** some of the things that affect floating and sinking.

Materials

- plastic shoe box
- water
- sheet of aluminum foil
- modeling clay

Activity Procedure

1 Fill the plastic shoe box halfway with water.

2 Take a sheet of aluminum foil about 10 cm long and 10 cm wide. Squeeze it tightly into a ball. Before placing the ball in the shoe box, **predict** whether it will sink or float. Test your prediction and **record** your **observations.**

3 Take a thin piece of modeling clay about 10 cm long and 10 cm wide. Squeeze it tightly into a ball. Place the ball in the shoe box. **Observe** whether it sinks or floats.

LINK to math, writing, technology, and other areas.

◀ This sailing ship is made to float, but its black metal anchor is made to sink.

Picture A

Picture B

4 Uncurl the foil. Use it to make a boat. (Picture A) Before placing the boat on the water, **predict** whether it will sink or float. Test your prediction and **record** your **observations.**

5 Make a boat out of the modeling clay. Before placing the boat on the water, **predict** whether it will sink or float. Test your prediction and **record** your **observations.** (Picture B)

Draw Conclusions

1. Which objects floated? Which objects sank?

2. Which do you think has the greater density, the ball of aluminum foil or the ball of modeling clay? Explain.

3. **Scientists at Work** Scientists often look at two situations in which everything is the same except for one property. What property was the same in Step 3 as in Step 5? What property was different in Step 3 and Step 5? What can you **infer** about how that difference changed the results?

Investigate Further Poke a hole of the same size in the bottom of each boat. Put both boats in the water. What happens?

> **Process Skill Tip**
>
> Usually in an investigation, only one property is changed at a time. This makes it easier to **infer** the causes of the results. This is called controlling variables.

How Water Interacts with Other Matter

Water and Sugar

If you put a spoonful of solid sugar into a glass of liquid water and stir, what happens? The sugar seems to disappear. The glass still contains a clear liquid. Where did the sugar go?

The answer is that the sugar and the water formed a kind of mixture called a solution. A **solution** (suh•LOO•shuhn) is a mixture in which the atoms and molecules of different kinds of matter are mixed evenly with each other. In this case the sugar molecules mixed with the water molecules. You can't see the sugar, but you can tell it is there because the solution tastes sweet. Another way to show that the sugar is still there is to let the water evaporate, or dry up. After all the water is gone, solid sugar will be left at the bottom of the glass.

FIND OUT

• how solids dissolve in water

• why objects float or sink

VOCABULARY

solution
dissolve
solubility
buoyancy

When you mix sugar and water, they form a solution. What is happening to the sugar as you stir the water? ▼

Dissolving

1 When a lump of sugar dissolves in water, water molecules pull sugar molecules away from the solid sugar.

2 Moving water molecules spread sugar molecules to all parts of the solution.

3 After a while all the sugar molecules are pulled away by water molecules. The sugar is completely dissolved. It can't be seen because the molecules are too small and spread out.

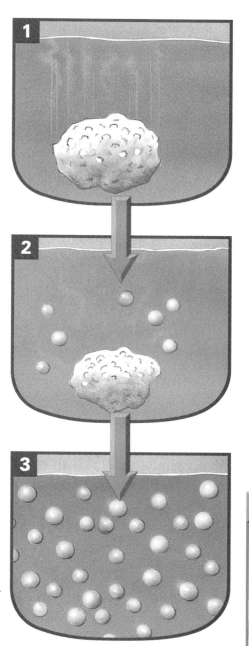

When one material forms a solution with another material, we say it **dissolves** (dih•ZAHLVZ). As sugar dissolves in water, molecules of solid sugar are pulled away from each other by water molecules. The water molecules bump into and move the sugar. Very quickly the sugar molecules spread to all parts of the solution. You can no longer see the sugar because the very small sugar molecules are mixed evenly with the water molecules.

If you add more and more sugar to a glass of water, at some point the sugar molecules can't mix evenly with the water molecules. The extra sugar doesn't dissolve. When you stop stirring, the extra sugar falls to the bottom of the glass.

Some solids dissolve in water. Other solids do not. Try stirring sand into water. While you are stirring, the sand mixes with the water but does not dissolve. When you stop stirring, the sand falls to the bottom of the jar. **Solubility** (sahl•yoo•BIL•uh•tee) is a measure of the amount of a material that will dissolve in another material. The solubility of sand in water is zero. No amount of sand dissolves in water.

✔ **What happens to a solid when it forms a solution with water?**

Solubility in Water		
Material	Volume of Water (mL)	Mass of Material That Can Be Dissolved in Water at 25˚C (g)
Sugar	100	105
Salt	100	36
Baking soda	100	7
Sand	100	0

Floating and Sinking

If you put a coin, such as a penny, into water, it doesn't dissolve. It sinks. A chip of wood doesn't dissolve in water, either. It floats. The ability of matter to float in a liquid or gas is called **buoyancy** (BOY•uhn•see).

A solid object denser than water sinks in water. Lead is more than 11 times as dense as water, so a lead fishing weight rapidly sinks. A solid object less dense than water floats in water. Pine wood is about half as dense as water. So a plank of pine floats.

▲ Most humans have a density that is a little less than 1 gram per cubic centimeter, so they float in water.

If you tied several pine planks together to form a raft, the raft would float because it is made of a material that is less dense than water.

Liquids can also float or sink. Have you ever seen rainbow streaks on puddles on a road or sidewalk? Motor oil floating on the water causes the streaks. The oil floats because it is less dense than water.

Some liquids sink in water. Maple syrup is mostly a sugar solution. It is denser than pure water. Maple syrup sinks to the bottom when you pour it into a glass of water.

Gases can also sink or float. All the gases in the air you breathe are much less dense than liquid water. When you blow through a drinking straw into water, air bubbles are pushed up, or buoyed up, by the water. They rise to the top of the glass. Helium is another gas that is less dense than air. When you fill a balloon with helium, it is buoyed up by the air and rises.

◀ A scuba diver wears a belt or vest with dense pieces of lead. This makes the diver's density about the same as that of water. With the belt on, the diver can swim up or down easily.

The density of the cup and air is less than water so the cup floats.

Most rocks sink. But pumice (PUHM•is) is a kind of rock that contains a lot of air, so pumice floats.

Diet soft drink is less dense than water, so a can of diet soft drink floats. A can of regular soft drink sinks.

Most wood floats, but most metal sinks.

Remember from Lesson 2 that you can change the density of a material by mixing it with material that has a different density.

Air is not very dense. A good way to lower the density of an object is to add air to it. If you add enough air, the object will become less dense than water. Then it will float. Clay is denser than water. In the investigation you got clay to float by making it into a boat. A boat contains air. The sides and bottom of a boat keep water out and hold air in. The clay boat floated because it contained a lot of air. Even a heavy metal boat will float if it contains enough air.

Most human bodies are a little less dense than water. So, most people float on water. Scuba divers don't want to float or sink. If they floated, they would have to swim hard to stay under water. If they sank, they would have to swim hard to get back to the water's surface. Scuba divers control their buoyancy by wearing a belt or vest loaded with dense lead pieces. While wearing the lead weights, a diver has about the same density as water.

✔ What is buoyancy?

Each liquid layer in this beaker has a different density. The densest layer is liquid mercury on the bottom. Even a steel bolt floats on mercury. The less dense materials float on the more dense materials. ▶

Floating Transportation

Humans use machines to control buoyancy and to move from place to place. Submarines, hot-air balloons, and blimps all use buoyancy to help move people. Hot-air balloons are buoyed up by air, so they rise. This is because hot air is less dense than cool air. Blimps are big, football-shaped balloons. They are filled with helium, a gas that is less dense than air. Submarines control their density to float and to sink in the water.

✔ **How is buoyancy used for travel?**

THE INSIDE STORY

How Submarines Work

Submarines can float on top of the ocean or dive down and travel deep under water. They do this by adding or removing water to control their density.

1. When a submarine floats on the surface of the water, it is like any other metal boat. It is filled with enough air to make it float.

2. Tanks inside the submarine have air in them when the submarine is at the surface. To make the submarine float just below the surface, some of the air is taken out and the tanks are partly filled with water. The combination of the submarine, the water, and the air has about the same density as water.

3. The submarine can dive to the bottom by squeezing air in its tanks into smaller tanks. Because the air's volume is now smaller, its density is greater. The original tanks are then filled with water. This makes the metal submarine denser than water. To allow the submarine to return to the surface, water is pumped out of the tanks. Air is allowed to expand back into them. The submarine becomes less dense than water. It is buoyed up and rises to the surface.

Summary

Solutions are mixtures in which the atoms and molecules are mixed evenly. Some matter dissolves in water and some does not. Matter that is less dense than water floats on water. Buoyancy can be controlled by changing density.

Review

1. What changes happen to sugar when it dissolves in water? What stays the same?
2. What happens when you add more of a material to water than the water will dissolve?
3. How can you float a piece of solid material that is denser than water?
4. **Critical Thinking** What could you do to make an object float in air?
5. **Test Prep** Any material that floats in water —
   A is denser than water
   B has the same density as water
   C is less dense than water
   D is made of metal

LINKS

MATH LINK

Solubility The greatest amount of sugar you can dissolve in 100 milliliters of water is 105 grams. How much sugar can you dissolve in 1000 milliliters of water?

WRITING LINK

Informative Writing—Explanation Find out what the ancient Greek scientist Archimedes discovered about density. Write an explanation of what you learn for a younger student.

PHYSICAL EDUCATION LINK

Floating and Swimming Find out what survival floating is. Use a model to demonstrate it for your class, or make a poster that explains it.

LITERATURE LINK

Submarine Predictions Read *20,000 Leagues Under the Sea* to find out what French science-fiction writer Jules Verne predicted about the modern submarine.

TECHNOLOGY LINK

Learn more about physical properties of matter by viewing *Peep Science* on the **Harcourt Science Newsroom Video** in your classroom video library.

Plastics You Can Eat

Plastics are artificial materials, or substances that are made by people. They can be shaped into different objects, such as bottles, chairs, or notebook covers. There are hundreds of different plastics, each with its own properties. One new type has an unusual property for a plastic. It dissolves in a special way, so it can be eaten!

Why Would Anyone Want to Eat Plastic?

You wouldn't want to eat regular plastic. It could be harmful. But the people who

The two inventors of edible plastic

invented plastic that can be eaten weren't thinking about making it edible. Two students were trying to make green slime in their high-school laboratory for a Halloween trick. But something went wrong. There was a small explosion. Green slime flew everywhere, covering the laboratory floor, ceiling, and walls. The students cleaned up the mess before anyone found out. But they missed a little bit of slime that landed in a jar.

The next day, their teacher found the green slime in the jar. It was stuck to a glass stirring rod. It looked like a lollipop. It even looked edible, and it really was.

Plastic Coated Medicine

It turned out that the green slime dissolves in the saliva in your mouth, but it doesn't dissolve in just water. This makes it perfect as a coating for pills. It protects the medicine in the pills from moisture in the air, but still is digested easily in the stomach. Other pill coatings take in moisture from the air. This can make the medicine less effective.

Green slime works well for coating medicine that can be absorbed in the stomach. But some medicines, such as the insulin needed by people who have diabetes, are destroyed by the digestive juices in the stomach. For that reason, these medicines are usually given as shots instead of pills. But no one likes to get shots.

Another Edible Plastic

Scientists have invented another kind of edible plastic that won't dissolve in the mouth, the stomach, or even the small intestine. Medicine that has been coated with this plastic gets all the way to the large

intestine. There, the plastic absorbs water and gets larger. Tiny holes in the plastic open up as that happens. The medicine gets out through the holes, and the patient gets the medicine without getting a shot.

Think About It

1. What other uses can you think of for edible plastic?

2. Do you know of any other medicines that can't be swallowed that edible plastic could be used for?

WEB LINK:
For Science and Technology updates, visit the Harcourt Internet site.
www.harcourtschool.com/ca

Careers Industrial Engineer

What They Do

Industrial engineers design and build machines for factories. They solve problems to help people make things and put things together easily and quickly. For example, they might design the machines to make pills and coat them with plastic. They also might decide what shapes work best for plastic or metal car parts.

Education and Training Industrial engineers need a college degree. They may be licensed as a professional engineer by the state they live in. For that, they will need four years of experience and a passing grade on a state test.

Shirley Ann Jackson

PHYSICIST

As a little girl in Washington, D.C., Shirley Jackson collected live hornets, bumblebees, and wasps to study. She kept the animals in old mayonnaise jars under the back porch. She also studied fungi and molds around her home. Her father helped her with these science projects. She won first place at a science fair with an experiment on how different environments affect the growth of bacteria.

Jackson graduated first in her class at Roosevelt High School. She won scholarships for college and decided to go to the Massachusetts Institute of Technology (MIT). She became the first African-American woman to receive a doctoral degree, or advanced degree, from MIT.

In 1995, President Clinton nominated her to the five-member U.S. Nuclear Regulatory Commission (NRC). She is now chairperson of that group. NRC makes sure nuclear reactors and radioactive materials are used safely. Dr. Jackson is also chairperson of the International Nuclear Regulators' Association. This group is made up of representatives from eight countries.

In 1998, Jackson was inducted into the National Women's Hall of Fame. She was included because of her work in education, science, and public policy.

THINK ABOUT IT

1. What areas of science first interested Jackson when she was young? What area of science most interests her now?
2. What skills and talents do you think a person needs to work for NRC?

◄ This is a view downward into the core of a nuclear reactor.

Liquid Layers

How does density help you predict which liquids float?

Materials

- 3 clear plastic cups
- water
- corn oil
- maple syrup

Material	Density
water	1 g/mL
corn oil	< 1 g/mL
maple syrup	> 1 g/mL

Procedure

1. Fill one cup about one-fourth full of water.

2. Repeat Step 1 for the corn oil and for the maple syrup.

3. Slowly pour the maple syrup down the inside of the cup containing water. Observe what happens.

4. Predict what will happen when you pour the corn oil into the same cup. Slowly pour the corn oil down the side of the cup. Observe what happens.

Draw Conclusions

What can you conclude about the buoyancy of these liquids?

Solubility

How can you determine solubility?

Materials

- safety goggles
- rubber gloves
- 200-mL beaker
- water
- balance
- 40 g alum
- small scrap of paper
- stirring stick

Procedure

1. Put on the goggles and gloves.

2. Fill the beaker to the 100-mL mark with cold tap water.

3. Measure 25 g of alum on the paper. Use the paper to pour the alum into the water.

4. Stir until the alum dissolves.

5. Measure 1 g of alum, and add it to the beaker. Stir. Observe the solution.

6. Repeat Step 5 until no more alum will dissolve.

Draw Conclusions

What is the solubility of alum? Repeat the activity with fresh water and alum. Is your result the same?

Chapter 1 Review and Test Preparation

Vocabulary Review

Use the terms below to complete the sentences. The page numbers in ( ) tell you where to look in the chapter if you need help.

matter (C6)
mass (C6)
solid (C6)
liquid (C7)
gas (C8)
volume (C13)

density (C14)
solution (C18)
dissolve (C19)
solubility (C19)
buoyancy (C20)

1. The _____ of a solid cube is the amount of space it takes up.

2. In a _____, the atoms and molecules are far away from each other and move quickly.

3. You can't see a solid when you _____ it, because its atoms and molecules become separated by water molecules.

4. The amount of matter in an object is its _____.

5. If the atoms and molecules of matter move back and forth around one point, the matter is in the _____ state.

6. _____ is a measure of whether an object floats or sinks in a gas or liquid.

7. When matter is in the _____ state, its atoms and molecules can slip and slide past each other.

8. When the atoms and molecules of a mixture are evenly mixed and can't be seen, the mixture is a _____.

9. Air and pine wood each have a _____ that is less than that of water.

10. _____ is a measure of the amount of a material that will dissolve in another material.

11. _____ is anything that takes up space and has mass.

Connect Concepts

Some of the substances and objects mentioned in the chapter are listed in the Word Bank. In the table below, list each substance or object under each of its properties. Use each item as often as necessary.

air   lead weight   water vapor   brick
wood   sugar cube   ice   water

Properties of Matter		
Dissolves in Water	**Floats in Water**	**Density About 1 g/mL**
12. _____	13. _____	15. _____
	14. _____	
Takes Shape of Container	**Sinks in Water**	**Has No Definite Volume**
16. _____	19. _____	21. _____
17. _____	20. _____	22. _____
18. _____		

Check Understanding

Write the letter of the best choice.

23. A boat made from matter that is denser than water can float on water if it is filled with enough —
    A water
    B air
    C salt
    D salt water

24. When two materials are mixed, the ____ of the mixture is between those of the separate materials.
    F mass
    G volume
    H density
    J state

25. Which of the following properties of sugar does **NOT** change when sugar dissolves in water?
    A color
    B shape
    C texture
    D taste

26. The volume of a ____ depends on the size of its container.
    F liquid
    G solid
    H gas
    J solution

27. A ____ has a definite shape.
    A solid
    B sugar-water solution
    C gas
    D liquid

Critical Thinking

28. Compare the relationships between molecules in ice, water, and water vapor.

29. When a solid dissolves completely in water, what happens to the atoms and molecules that made up the solid?

Process Skills Review

30. You measure the temperature of four pans of boiling water. Your measurements are 99°C, 100°C, 100°C, and 101°C. What **conclusion** can you **draw** about the temperature at which water boils? Explain your answer.

31. You use the same pan balance to **measure** the mass of a rock on two days. Your measurement is larger on the second day. The rock hasn't changed. How do you explain the difference in measurements?

32. You take a sip from a glass of clear water, and it tastes salty. What can you **infer** about what is in the glass?

Performance Assessment

Maximum Float

Use a piece of aluminum foil to make a shape that will float in water. Experiment to find the boat shape that will support the largest number of pennies. Explain the reasons you changed the boat's shape.

Chapter 2

Electricity and Magnetism

Snap! Crackle! Pop! Your socks crackle and spark when you separate them from your freshly dried sweater! This kind of electricity is called static electricity. You can become charged with static electricity just by dragging your feet when you walk across carpet. Then *ZAP!* you'll get a "charge" out of opening the next door you come to!

Vocabulary Preview

charge
static electricity
electric field
electric current
circuit
electric cell
conductor
insulator
resistor
series circuit
parallel circuit
magnet
magnetic pole
magnetic field
electromagnet

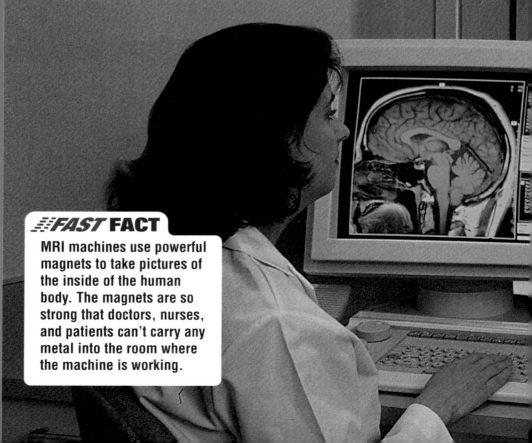

FAST FACT

MRI machines use powerful magnets to take pictures of the inside of the human body. The magnets are so strong that doctors, nurses, and patients can't carry any metal into the room where the machine is working.

Photocopiers make images by using static electricity! A large charged drum inside a photocopier pulls powdered ink to it. The ink goes to wherever dark spots on the original are reflected on the drum. The powder pattern is put on a piece of paper. Then the paper is heated and the ink melts, making a permanent copy.

Electricity use is measured in kilowatt-hours. Every home has a meter that measures how many kilowatt-hours have been used. A 60-watt light bulb uses 0.06 kilowatt-hours in one hour. Here's a list of the number of kilowatt-hours different appliances use in an hour:

Electricity Use

Appliance	Kilowatt-Hours Used in One Hour
Color television	0.23
Toaster	1.2
Hair dryer	1.5
Microwave oven	1.5
Clothes dryer	4.0
Refrigerator/freezer	5.0–7.0

What Is Static Electricity?

In this lesson, you can . . .

INVESTIGATE rubbing balloons with different materials.

LEARN ABOUT causes of static electricity.

LINK to math, writing, health, and technology.

◀ It's not the wind that's making this boy's hair stand on end. It's static electricity. You may be surprised to learn what else static electricity can do.

INVESTIGATE

Balloons Rubbed with Different Materials

Activity Purpose Have you ever opened a package that had something breakable inside? There may have been little foam pieces in the box, and you may have noticed the strange way they acted. They jumped away from each other but stuck to almost everything else. You can make balloons act this way, too. In this investigation you will rub balloons with different materials. Then you'll **compare** your **observations** to **infer** why the balloons behaved the way they did.

Materials

- two small, round balloons
- string
- tape
- scrap of silk cloth
- scrap of wool cloth
- paper towel
- plastic wrap

Activity Procedure

1. Blow up the balloons, and tie them closed. Use string and tape to hang one balloon from a shelf or table.

2. Rub the silk all over each balloon. Slowly bring the free balloon near the hanging balloon. **Observe** the hanging balloon. **Record** your observations. (Picture A)

Picture A

Picture B

3 Again rub the silk all over the hanging balloon. Move the silk away. Then slowly bring the silk close to the balloon. **Observe** the hanging balloon, and **record** your observations. (Picture B)

4 Repeat Steps 2 and 3 separately with the wool, a paper towel, and plastic wrap. **Record** your **observations.**

5 Rub the silk all over the hanging balloon. Rub the wool all over the free balloon. Slowly bring the free balloon near the hanging balloon. **Observe** the hanging balloon. **Record** your observations.

Draw Conclusions

1. **Compare** your observations in Step 2 with your observations in Steps 3 and 4.

2. **Compare** your observations of the hanging balloon in Step 2 with your observations of it in Step 5.

3. **Scientists at Work** Which of your observations support the **inference** that a force acted on the balloons and materials? Explain your answer.

Investigate Further Rubbing a balloon caused a charge to build up. Like charges repel. Opposite charges attract. Collect different materials. **Predict** whether pairs of materials will cause like or opposite charges on balloons. **Plan and conduct** multiple trials to test your predictions. How do your results relate to your predictions?

Process Skill Tip

A force is a push or a pull. You can **infer** a force between two objects by observing whether the objects are pulled toward each other or pushed away from each other.

Static Electricity

Two Kinds of Charge

Remember that matter is made of particles that have mass and volume. Particles of matter also have a property called *electric charge*. A particle can have a positive (+) charge, a negative (−) charge, or no charge at all.

Matter in an object normally has equal numbers of positive and negative particles. It is *neutral*. Rubbing two objects together, however, can move negative particles from one object to the other. In the investigation, rubbing made the number of positive charges different from the number of negative charges. **Charge** is a measure of the extra positive or negative particles that an object has. Rubbing gave one object an overall *positive charge*, and it gave the other an overall *negative charge*.

The charge that stays on an object is called **static electricity** (STAT•ik ee•lek•TRIS•ih•tee). *Static* means "not moving." Even though the charges moved to get there, they stay on the charged object.

✔ **What are the two types of charges?**

FIND OUT

- about a property of matter called charge
- how charges move from one piece of matter to another
- how electric fields cause forces

VOCABULARY

charge
static electricity
electric field

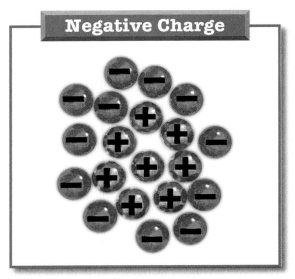

▲ A single positive charge is labeled +. A single negative charge is labeled −. When an object has more positive charges than negative charges, its overall charge is positive.

▲ If an object has more negative charges than positive charges, its overall charge is negative. How many extra negative charges are shown here?

Separating Charges

Most of the time, you, a balloon, and a doorknob have neither an overall negative charge nor an overall positive charge. You and the objects are neutral. To see the effects of forces between charges, you must separate negative charges from positive charges.

Only the negative charges move. When you rubbed the balloons, only the negative particles were pulled away. Combing dry hair is another example of separating charges. As you comb, the teeth of the comb rub negative charges from your hair. The comb gets extra negative charges, so it has an overall negative charge. Your hair loses some negative charges. It now has an overall positive charge.

✔ **Which kind of charge moves to make a static charge?**

As clothes tumble in a dryer, different fabrics rub against each other. Negative charges move from one piece of clothing to another. When this happens the clothes stick together. ▼

▲ If you hold a piece of wool next to a balloon, nothing happens. So you know that neither the wool nor the balloon is charged. The numbers of positive and negative charges on the balloon are equal. The charges are also equal on the wool. Both items have a neutral charge.

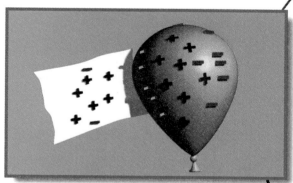

▲ Rubbing wool on a balloon separates charges. Negative charges move from the wool to the balloon. The balloon now has more negative charges than positive charges. The balloon is negatively charged. The wool loses negative charges. Now it has more positive charges than negative charges. It is positively charged.

Electric Forces

In the investigation you saw how a charged balloon pushed or pulled another charged balloon. The push or pull between objects with different charges is an *electric force*. The electric force causes two objects with opposite charges to *attract*, or pull, each other. The electric force also causes two objects with like charges to *repel* (rih•PEL), or push away from, each other.

The space where electric forces occur around an object is called an **electric field**. The electric field of a positive charge attracts a nearby negative charge. The electric field of a positive charge repels a nearby positive charge.

In diagrams, arrows are used to show an electric field. They point the way one positive charge would be pulled by the field. The pictures here show the electric fields of two pairs of balloons. One pair has opposite charges. The other pair has the same charges.

✔ **What is an electric field?**

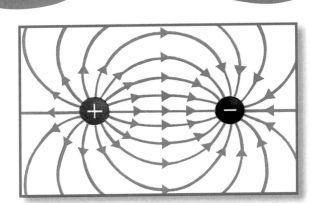

▲ One balloon has a positive charge. The other has a negative charge. Their electric fields form a closed pattern of field lines. Balloons with opposite charges attract each other.

Both balloons have negative charges. Their electric fields do not form a closed pattern of field lines. Balloons with the same type of charge repel each other.

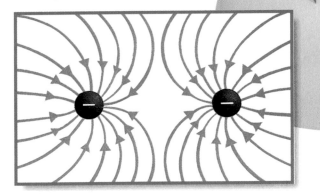

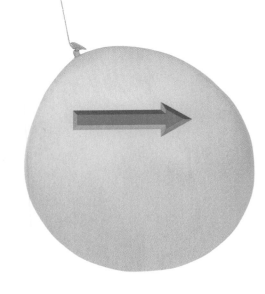

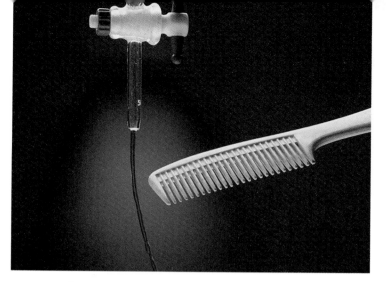

▲ After you comb your hair, your comb has a negative charge. Its electric field repels the negative particles in the stream of water. Negative particles are pushed to the opposite side of the stream. That leaves extra positive charges on the side near the comb. The stream bends toward the comb.

Summary

Objects become electrically charged when they gain or lose negative charges. A charge causes an electric field. The electric fields of charged objects interact to produce electric forces. Objects with like charges repel each other. Objects with unlike charges attract each other.

Review

1. What is static electricity?
2. What is charge?
3. What is an electric field?
4. **Critical Thinking** How can you make a piece of rubber that has an overall positive charge neutral again?
5. **Test Prep** A plastic ruler can get a positive charge by —
   A gaining a single negative charge
   B losing a single negative charge
   C gaining a single positive charge
   D losing a single positive charge

LINKS

MATH LINK

Charge Count The two pictures on page C34 show charges. How many single negative charges must each object gain or lose to become neutral? Use numbers and math symbols to show how you found your answer.

WRITING LINK

Informative Writing—Description Suppose you are a balloon. Write a paragraph for a classmate describing what happens to you as you gain a negative charge from a piece of wool.

HEALTH LINK

Lightning Safety Lightning is a big movement of charged particles. It can kill people and animals, and it can start fires. Find out the safety rules you should follow during a thunderstorm. Make a poster illustrating the rules.

TECHNOLOGY LINK

Learn more about early use of electricity by visiting the National Museum of American History Internet site.
www.si.edu/harcourt/science

What Is an Electric Current?

In this lesson, you can . . .

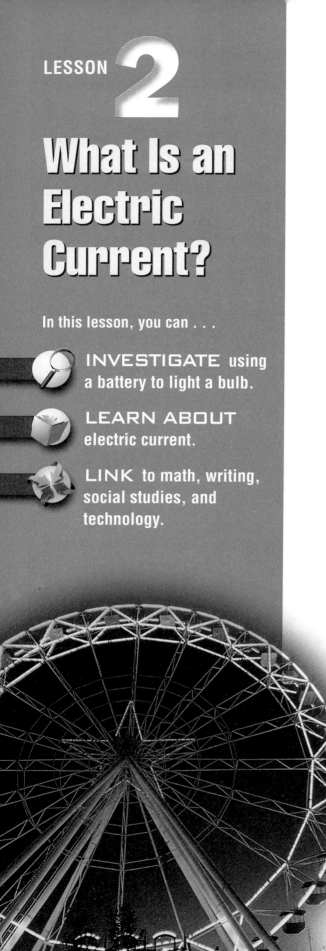

INVESTIGATE using a battery to light a bulb.

LEARN ABOUT electric current.

LINK to math, writing, social studies, and technology.

INVESTIGATE

Making a Bulb Light Up

Activity Purpose Can a flashlight work without batteries? You would be right if you said *no*. The batteries produce the electricity that makes the bulb shine. But how does the electricity get from the batteries to the bulb? You can **plan and conduct a simple investigation** to find out how materials need to be arranged to convert electricity into light.

Materials
- D-cell battery
- insulated electrical wire
- miniature light bulb
- masking tape

Activity Procedure

1 Make a chart like the one shown on the next page. You will use it to **record** your **observations**.

2 **Predict** a way to arrange the materials you have been given so that the bulb lights up. Make a drawing to **record** your prediction. (Picture A)

3 Test your prediction. **Record** whether or not the bulb lights up. (Picture B)

◄ The lights of a Ferris wheel shine in the night as the wheel goes round and round. The electricity that makes the bulbs glow and moves the wheel also goes round and round.

Picture A

Picture B

Predictions and Observations

Arrangement of Bulb, Battery, and Wire	Drawing	Observations

4 Continue to work with the bulb, the battery, and the wire. Try different arrangements to get the bulb to light. **Record** the results of each try.

Draw Conclusions

1. What did you **observe** about the arrangement of materials when the bulb lighted?

2. What did you **observe** about the arrangement of materials when the bulb did NOT light?

3. **Scientists at Work** To find out more about bulbs and batteries, you could **plan and conduct an investigation** of your own. To do that, you need to decide the following: What question do you want to answer? What materials will you need? How will you use the materials? What will you observe?

Investigate Further **Plan and conduct your investigation.**

Process Skill Tip

When you **plan and conduct a simple investigation**, you work to find the answer to a question or to solve a problem. By doing many tests and observing their outcomes, you can draw conclusions about how something works.

Electric Currents

Moving Charges

FIND OUT

- **how electric charges can move**
- **ways different materials control electric current**
- **differences between series and parallel circuits**

VOCABULARY

electric current
circuit
electric cell
conductor
insulator
resistor
series circuit
parallel circuit

You know that a static charge stays on an object. But even a static charge will move if it has a path to follow. The snap and crackle of a static electric shock are the result of a moving charge.

Have you ever gotten a small electric shock from touching a doorknob? Here's how it happens. Walking on a carpet rubs negative charges off the carpet and onto your feet. The charges spread out on your body. Your whole body becomes negatively charged. When you touch the doorknob, all the extra negative charges move at once from your hand to the doorknob. You get a small "zap." The static, or unmoving charge, has become a *current*, or moving charge. A flow of electric charges is called an **electric current**.

In the investigation you arranged a wire, a bulb, and a battery to make a path in which negative charges could flow. A path that is made for an electric current is called a **circuit** (SER•kit). The battery was an important part of the circuit you made. A battery is an **electric cell**, which supplies energy to move charges through a circuit.

✔ **What does an electric current need in order to flow?**

◀ An electric current in a circuit moves like a bike wheel. When you pedal, you give energy of motion to the whole wheel at once. When you connect a circuit, a battery moves energy to all parts of the circuit at the same time.

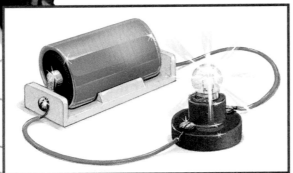

◀ Use your finger to trace the path of the current through each part of the circuit. What do you notice?

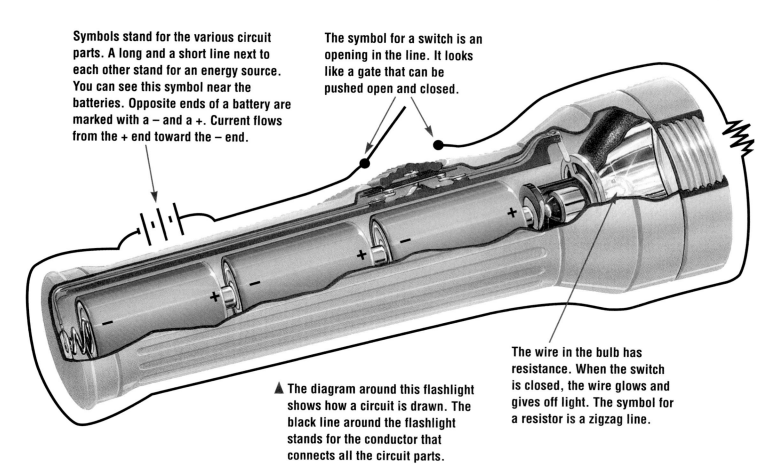

Symbols stand for the various circuit parts. A long and a short line next to each other stand for an energy source. You can see this symbol near the batteries. Opposite ends of a battery are marked with a − and a +. Current flows from the + end toward the − end.

The symbol for a switch is an opening in the line. It looks like a gate that can be pushed open and closed.

The wire in the bulb has resistance. When the switch is closed, the wire glows and gives off light. The symbol for a resistor is a zigzag line.

▲ The diagram around this flashlight shows how a circuit is drawn. The black line around the flashlight stands for the conductor that connects all the circuit parts.

Controlling Current

A circuit with a battery, bulb, and wires contains different materials such as copper and plastic. You can classify these materials by the way they control the flow of charges through them.

A **conductor** is a material that current can pass through easily. Most metals are good conductors of electric current. Electric wires are made of metal, often copper. The base of a light bulb is made of metal because it must conduct an electric current.

A material that current cannot pass through easily is called an **insulator** (IN•suh•layt•er). The black band between the metal tip and the screw-in part of a light bulb is an insulator. A plastic covering insulated the wire you used in the investigation. Plastic keeps the metal of the wire from touching other metal.

A flashlight has a switch to turn it on and off. A *switch* uses conductors and insulators to make and break a circuit. When the switch is on, two conductors touch. When they touch, the path is complete. Current flows through the circuit. When the switch is off, air separates the two conductors, breaking the path. No current can flow.

Some materials cut down, or resist, the flow of charges. A material that resists but doesn't stop the flow of current is called a **resistor** (rih•ZIS•ter). A flashlight bulb contains a tiny coil of metal. The coil is a resistor. As charges move through the resistor, they transfer thermal energy to it. The metal becomes hot. The glowing coil transfers some of its thermal energy to the air as radiation. It gives off light.

✔ **What does a switch do in a circuit?**

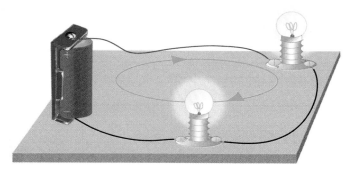

▲ The arrow shows how current flows in a series circuit. It flows through each circuit element, one after the other, or in *series*. If the circuit is broken anywhere, it will not work.

The two arrows show two paths where current can flow in this parallel circuit. If one path were broken, the other part of the circuit would still work. ▼

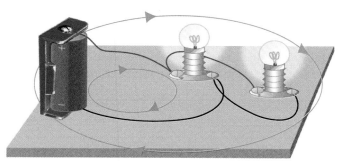

Series and Parallel Circuits

When you turn on a flashlight, there is one path for the current to follow through the circuit. A circuit that has only one path for the current is called a **series circuit**. The pictures below show a series circuit. Note that the current runs from the battery to one bulb, then to the next bulb, and then back to the battery. What happens if you remove one bulb or a bulb burns out? The single path is broken. No current moves through the circuit. The second bulb will go out.

Series Circuits

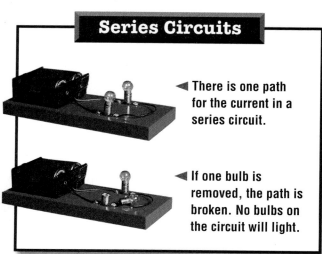

◀ There is one path for the current in a series circuit.

◀ If one bulb is removed, the path is broken. No bulbs on the circuit will light.

Parallel Circuits

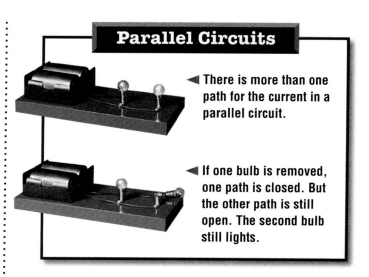

◀ There is more than one path for the current in a parallel circuit.

◀ If one bulb is removed, one path is closed. But the other path is still open. The second bulb still lights.

A **parallel** (PAIR•uh•lel) **circuit** has more than one path for current to travel. With your finger, trace the path of the current in the parallel circuit shown above. Part of the current moves through each path of the circuit. What happens when a bulb is removed from this circuit? The current still moves through the other path. The second bulb stays lit. If one bulb in a parallel circuit burns out, the other bulbs will stay on.

✔ **Which type of circuit has more than one path for current?**

Summary

Electric current is a flow of charges through a path called a circuit. A material in a circuit can be classified as a conductor, an insulator, or a resistor. If a circuit has one path for current, it is a series circuit. A parallel circuit has more than one path for current.

Review

1. What is an electric current?
2. Describe what has to be in place for a circuit to work.
3. Contrast conductors and insulators.
4. **Critical Thinking** Most wall outlets in your home have places for two plugs. Infer which type of circuit an outlet is part of. How do you know?
5. **Test Prep** What supplies energy in an electric circuit?
   A conductors
   B electric cells
   C resistors
   D switches

LINKS

MATH LINK

Current Costs Electric energy is measured in a unit called a kilowatt-hour, or kWh. Suppose a utility company charges 10 cents for each kWh of energy. A family uses 900 kWh of energy a month. How much does the energy cost?

WRITING LINK

Informative Writing—Compare and Contrast Write a paragraph for a younger student explaining why it would be easier to decorate a home with strings of lights in a parallel circuit instead of strings of lights in a series circuit.

SOCIAL STUDIES LINK

Inventing the Light Bulb The invention of the first practical electric light bulb is a good example of not giving up. Research the story of the light bulb's invention. When was it invented? Who invented it? How many materials were tried and set aside before a light bulb that worked well was made?

TECHNOLOGY LINK

Learn more about controlling large circuits by viewing *L.A. Traffic Control* on the **Harcourt Science Newsroom Video** in your classroom video library.

What Is a Magnet?

In this lesson, you can . . .

 INVESTIGATE how a compass works.

 LEARN ABOUT the ways magnets interact.

 LINK to math, writing, social studies, and technology.

◄ The compass is an important tool that helps sailors find their way across the oceans.

 **INVESTIGATE**

A Compass

Activity Purpose If you are like most people, you have papers stuck with magnets to your refrigerator. A *magnet* is an object that attracts certain materials, mainly iron and steel. The material in your refrigerator magnet attracts the steel in your refrigerator door. The attraction is strong enough that it works through paper. In this investigation you will make your own magnet and, based on your **observations, infer** how a compass works.

Materials
- safety goggles
- small bar magnet
- small objects made of iron or steel, such as paper clips
- large sewing needle or straight pin (4–5 cm long)
- small piece of cork
- glue
- cup of water

CAUTION

Activity Procedure

1 **CAUTION** **Put on your safety goggles.** Hold the bar magnet near a paper clip. **Observe** what happens. Now hold the needle near the paper clip. Observe what happens.

2 **CAUTION** **Be careful with sharp objects.** Hold the needle by its eye and drag its entire length over the magnet 20 times, always in the same direction. (Picture A)

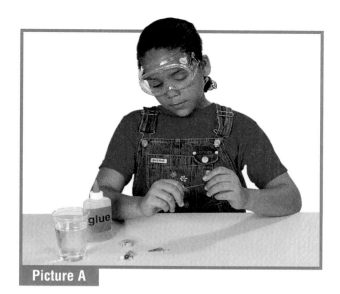

Picture A

Picture B

3 Repeat Step 1. **Observe** what happens.

4 Hold the needle on top of the cork. Then check to be sure that the needle will be parallel to the surface of the water when the cork floats. Glue the needle to the top of the cork. (Picture B)

5 Move the bar magnet at least a meter from the cup. Float the cork in the water. **Observe** what happens to the needle.

6 Carefully and slowly turn the cup. **Observe** the needle.

7 Hold one end of the bar magnet near the cup. **Observe** the needle. Switch magnet ends. What happens?

Draw Conclusions

1. Describe what happened when you floated the cork with the needle in water. What happened when you turned the cup?

2. What happened when you brought the bar magnet near the floating needle?

3. **Scientists at Work** What **hypothesis** can you make based on your observations of the needle? What predictions can you make by using your hypothesis?

Investigate Further **Plan and carry out a simple investigation** to test one of your predictions from Question 3, above. Conduct multiple trials. Are your results the same for each trial?

Process Skill Tip

When you **hypothesize**, you carefully explain all your observations. A hypothesis is more detailed than an inference. Unlike an inference, a hypothesis can be used to make predictions that you can test.

Magnets

Two Poles

FIND OUT

- about magnetic poles
- how magnetic fields cause magnetic forces
- how to use Earth's magnetic field to find directions

VOCABULARY

magnet
magnetic pole
magnetic field

In the investigation you made a needle into a magnet. You could tell it was a magnet because it attracted metal paper clips, just as other magnets do. A **magnet** is an object that attracts certain materials, usually objects made of iron or steel. A needle isn't a natural magnet. You changed it into a magnet by dragging it along the bar magnet.

A magnet has two ends called **magnetic poles**, or just *poles* for short. A magnet's pull is strongest at the poles. If a bar magnet can swing freely, one end, called the *north-seeking pole*, will always point north. The opposite end, called the *south-seeking pole*, will always point south. A magnet's north-seeking pole is usually marked *N*. Its south-seeking pole is marked *S*.

✔ **What is each end of a magnet called?**

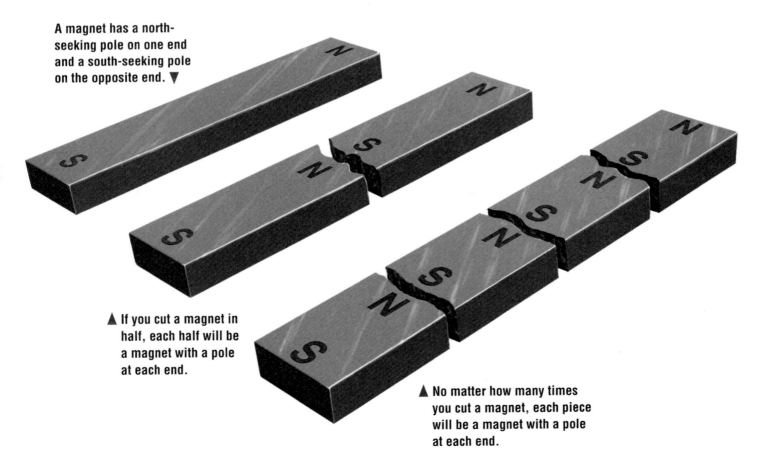

A magnet has a north-seeking pole on one end and a south-seeking pole on the opposite end. ▼

▲ If you cut a magnet in half, each half will be a magnet with a pole at each end.

▲ No matter how many times you cut a magnet, each piece will be a magnet with a pole at each end.

C46

Magnetic Forces

If you've ever played with magnets, you've probably felt them pull toward each other. At other times they seem to push away from each other. The forces you felt are magnetic forces caused by magnetic fields.

A **magnetic field** is the space all around a magnet where the force of the magnet can act. You can't see the field. However, a magnet can move iron filings into lines. The pattern made by the iron filings shows the shape of the magnet's field.

Forces between magnetic poles are like forces between electric charges. Opposite magnetic poles attract, and like poles repel. If the N pole of one magnet is held toward the S pole of another magnet, their fields form a closed pattern. This closed pattern of lines shows a force that pulls the magnets together.

If two magnets are held with their N poles near each other, their magnetic fields form an open pattern of lines. Just as with electric charges, this pattern shows a force that pushes the magnets away from each other.

✔ Where is the pull of a magnet strongest?

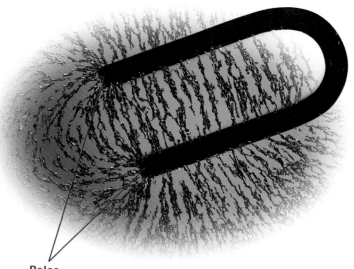

Poles

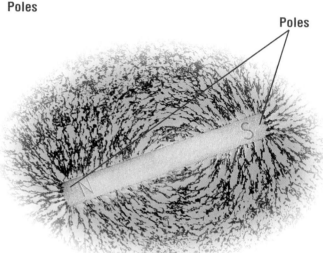

Poles

▲ The shape of a magnetic field depends on the shape of the magnet. The bunching of iron filings on the end of a magnet shows that the magnetic force is strongest at a magnet's poles.

▲ Opposite poles of two magnets attract. The pattern of iron filings is closed. This shows a magnetic force that attracts, or pulls, the magnets together.

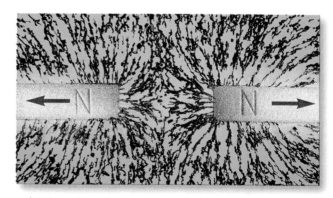

▲ Like poles of two magnets repel. The field lines are open, showing lines of force that push the magnets apart.

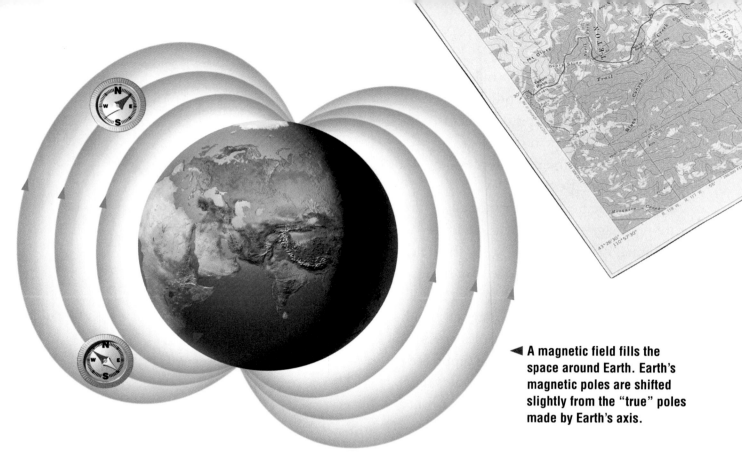

◀ A magnetic field fills the space around Earth. Earth's magnetic poles are shifted slightly from the "true" poles made by Earth's axis.

Compasses

The north-seeking and south-seeking property of magnets is useful. For hundreds of years, people have used magnets to find direction. The first magnets used were made of a heavy natural material called *lodestone*. Today geologists know this material as the mineral magnetite.

A compass today uses a lightweight magnetic needle that is free to turn. This is much like the needle you made into a magnet in the investigation. A compass needle points along an imaginary line connecting the North and South Poles. This is because Earth is like a giant magnet.

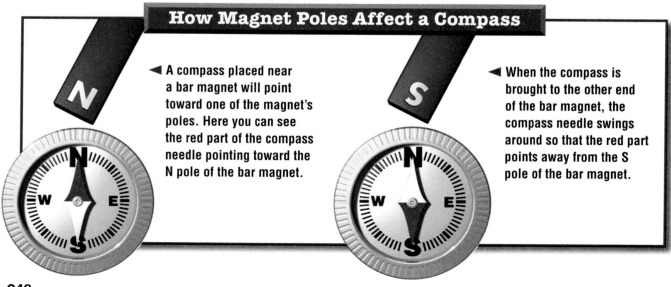

How Magnet Poles Affect a Compass

◀ A compass placed near a bar magnet will point toward one of the magnet's poles. Here you can see the red part of the compass needle pointing toward the N pole of the bar magnet.

◀ When the compass is brought to the other end of the bar magnet, the compass needle swings around so that the red part points away from the S pole of the bar magnet.

◀ When there are no landmarks you know, a map and a compass can help you find your way.

The field lines of Earth's magnetic field come together close to the planet's North and South Poles. This pattern is like the one shown by the iron filings around the bar magnet on page C47. Indeed, Earth's magnetic field is like the field of a giant bar magnet.

✔ **How does a compass work?**

Summary

Magnets are objects that attract materials such as iron. Every magnet has two magnetic poles. Magnetic forces are caused by the interaction of magnetic fields. Earth's magnetic field is like the field of a bar magnet. A compass needle interacts with Earth's magnetic field.

Review

1. How can you find the poles of a magnet?
2. What is a magnetic field?
3. Which type of magnet has a field that is about the same shape as Earth's magnetic field?
4. **Critical Thinking** Describe the field lines formed if the south poles of two magnets are brought close together.
5. **Test Prep** How many poles does a magnet have?
   - **A** none
   - **B** one
   - **C** two
   - **D** four

LINKS

MATH LINK

Magnet Strengths Decide on a way to measure the strength of different bar magnets. Test some magnets. Then use a computer program such as *Graph Links* to make a bar graph to show what you measured. Which magnet is strongest?

WRITING LINK

Informative Writing—How-To Write a paragraph telling a classmate how to use a compass to find the direction in which he or she is traveling.

SOCIAL STUDIES LINK

Earth's Moving Magnetic Poles Earth's north magnetic pole is constantly moving. Find out how the pole's location is shown on topographical (tahp•uh•GRAF•ih•kuhl) maps, which show the land's surface features, and on navigational charts. Find the current location of the north magnetic pole on a globe. Measure the distance between the true North Pole and the magnetic north pole.

TECHNOLOGY LINK

Learn more about Earth's magnetic field by visiting the National Air and Space Museum Internet site.
www.si.edu/harcourt/science

What Is an Electro-magnet?

In this lesson, you can . . .

INVESTIGATE the magnetic field around a wire that carries current.

LEARN ABOUT uses of electromagnets.

LINK to math, writing, language arts, and technology.

Strong magnetic forces lift this train slightly from the tracks and push it forward. ▼

INVESTIGATE

How Magnets and Electricity Can Interact

Activity Purpose The pictures at the bottom of page C48 show how a bar magnet affects a nearby compass. Have you ever tried this yourself? In this investigation you will **observe** how a bar magnet affects a compass needle. You'll **compare** it with the way a current in a wire affects a compass needle. You can then **infer** some things about electricity moving through wires.

Materials

- bar magnet
- small compass
- sheet of cardboard
- tape
- insulated wire, about 30 cm long, with stripped ends
- D-cell battery

Activity Procedure

1 Try several positions of the magnet and compass. **Record** your **observations** of how the magnet affects the compass needle.

2 Place the compass flat on the cardboard so the needle is lined up with north. Tape the middle third of the insulated wire onto the cardboard in a north-south line.

3 Tape one end of the wire to the flat end of a D-cell battery. Tape the battery to the cardboard. (Picture A)

4 Without moving the cardboard, put the compass on the taped-down part of the wire.

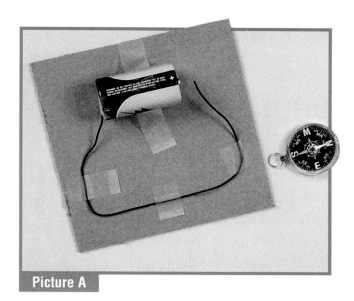

Picture A

Picture B

5 Touch the free end of the wire to the (+) end of the battery for a few seconds. (Picture B) **Observe** the compass needle. Repeat this step several more times. **Record** your observations.

6 Carefully remove the taped wire. Place the compass underneath the wire so that both line up along a north-south line. **Predict** what will happen if you repeat Step 5.

7 Repeat Step 5. **Record** your observations.

Draw Conclusions

1. **Compare** your observations in Step 5 with those in Step 7. Was your prediction accurate? Explain.

2. Using what you know about compasses in magnetic fields, what can you **infer** about currents in wires?

3. **Scientists at Work** Just as you predicted what would happen in Step 7, scientists often **predict** the outcome of an experiment based on their observations and inferences. Based on your observations of causes and effects, what would you predict will happen in this experiment if the current is made to move in the opposite direction?

Investigate Further Wrap the wire several times around a pencil and repeat the activity. Predict how the wire will affect the compass. Conduct multiple trials with different compass positions. How are your results related to your prediction?

Process Skill Tip

When you **predict**, you tell what you expect to happen. A prediction is based on patterns of observations. If you think you know the cause of an event, you can predict when it will happen again. Predictions aren't always correct.

Electromagnets

Currents Make Magnets

FIND OUT

- how electricity and magnetism are related
- ways to change the strength of an electromagnet
- uses of motors and generators

VOCABULARY

electromagnet

In the past, scientists wondered if electric charge and magnetism were related. They knew that charged objects and magnets both produce a force that can pull or push without touching. The discovery that an electric current can turn a compass needle proved that the two forces are related.

A current in a wire produces a magnetic field around the wire. You saw evidence of this in the investigation. The magnetic field produced by current moved the compass needle.

If you could see them, the field lines around a wire that carries current would look different from those around a bar magnet. They circle around the wire instead of looping out from the wire ends. A compass needle moves to point along magnetic field lines. So, it moves to point at right angles to the wire.

When current flows in the wire, it produces a circular magnetic field. The compass needle lines up with the field lines by turning at right angles to the wire. ▶

When the switch is open, current no longer flows and the magnetic field goes away. The compass needle swings back to its original position. ▶

This coil of wire is carrying an electric current. Iron filings show the shape of the magnetic field inside the coil. The lines of filings are closest together where the field is strongest. ▶

Compared with bar magnets, current-carrying wires produce weak magnetic fields. But there's a way to put a lot of wire in one place. When a current-carrying wire is coiled, the fields of the loops overlap. The strengths of the fields add up. The more loops you put together, the stronger the field gets.

The fields produced by many wire coils add up to make a field like that of a bar magnet. Iron filings line up along the middle of the coil. Outside the coil, the magnetic field lines loop out from one open end and back to the other.

Alone, a coil of wire easily bends. To make it stiffer and easier to use, the coil is wrapped around a solid material called a

core. This arrangement of wire wrapped around a core is called an **electromagnet** (ee•LEK•troh•mag•nit). An electromagnet is a temporary magnet. There is a magnetic field only when there is an electric current in the wire.

If the core of an electromagnet is made of iron, the core also becomes a magnet when there is current in the wire. This makes the electromagnet stronger.

✔ **Why is an electromagnet a temporary magnet?**

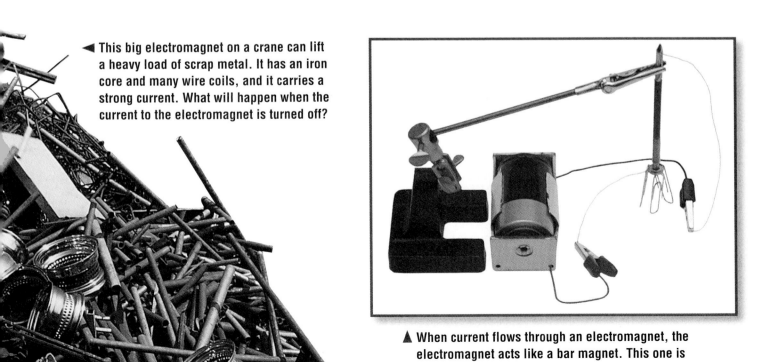

◀ This big electromagnet on a crane can lift a heavy load of scrap metal. It has an iron core and many wire coils, and it carries a strong current. What will happen when the current to the electromagnet is turned off?

▲ When current flows through an electromagnet, the electromagnet acts like a bar magnet. This one is strong enough to hold three paper clips.

Controlling Electromagnets

A magnet and an electromagnet have one main difference. An electromagnet is a temporary magnet. You can turn it on and off with a switch. A bar magnet is a permanent magnet. It doesn't have an *off* switch. Electromagnets are a useful tool because you can control them. You can learn how one is used in The Inside Story.

Turning an electromagnet on and off is one way to control it. You can also control the strength of an electromagnet. One way to do this is to add or remove coils of wire. The more coils an electromagnet has, the stronger it is.

The amount of current also affects the strength of an electromagnet. The more current that is flowing, the stronger the electromagnet is.

Electromagnets today are made to use large amounts of current to lift large amounts of weight. Smaller and weaker ones are also made. Small electromagnets work out of sight inside computer disk drives, video players, television screens, and other electronic devices.

✔ **What is the main difference between a bar magnet and an electromagnet?**

THE INSIDE STORY

Alarm Bell

The bells used in fire alarms, doorbells, and telephones work because electromagnets can be turned off and on very quickly. The picture and diagram on the right show you how an electric bell works.

❶ When the bell is turned on, current flows in the electromagnet. The electromagnet pulls the long iron rod into the coils.

❷ The hammer is connected to the rod. It moves and strikes the bell, making a sound.

❸ The strip of metal with the hammer acts like a switch. As the hammer moves to strike the bell, the switch opens. No current flows in the circuit. The electromagnet is turned off. The hammer returns to its original position.

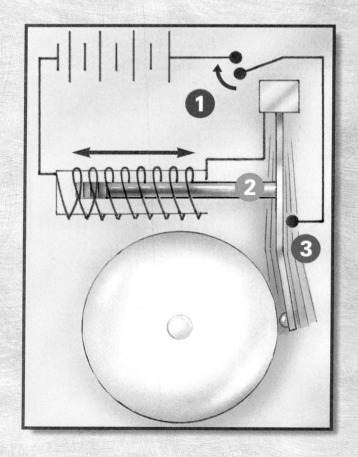

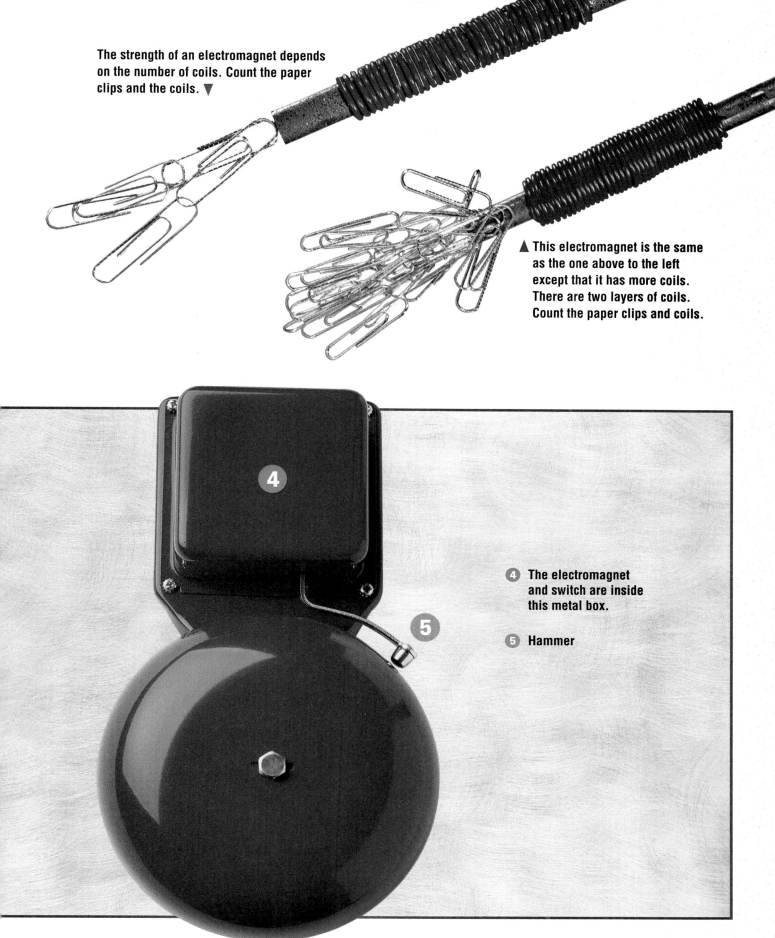

The strength of an electromagnet depends on the number of coils. Count the paper clips and the coils. ▼

▲ This electromagnet is the same as the one above to the left except that it has more coils. There are two layers of coils. Count the paper clips and coils.

4 The electromagnet and switch are inside this metal box.

5 Hammer

Motors and Generators

If electricity can produce a magnetic field, can a magnetic field produce electricity? Yes! If you move a coil of wire near a magnet, current flows in the wire. Current flows as long as the wire is moving through magnetic field lines. This is how an electric generator works.

A coil of wire, a magnet, and electricity can also be used to cause motion. That's how an electric motor works. The coil of an electromagnet is pushed and pulled by the poles of other magnets. The coil turns. This turning motion is used in machines such as kitchen appliances, toys, and tools.

✔ **What things do generators and motors have in common?**

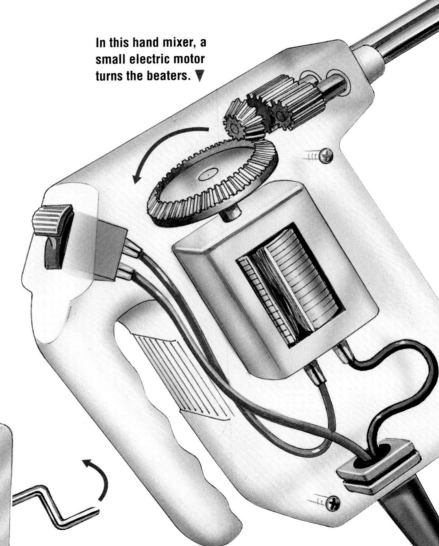

In this hand mixer, a small electric motor turns the beaters. ▼

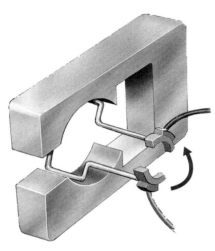

▲ One simple electric motor contains an electromagnet and a permanent magnet. When the motor is on, the direction of current is changed in a pattern. As it changes, the coil is pushed and then pulled by the permanent magnet. The coil turns. Electrical energy is converted into motion.

◀ A small, simple generator uses a hand crank to turn a magnet around a loop of wire. Generators that supply electric power for homes and factories are much bigger, about the size of a bus. They usually use steam or water power to turn a coil.

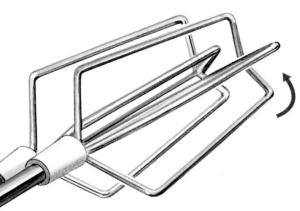

Summary

Wires carrying an electric current become magnets. An electromagnet is a core wrapped with wires that carry current. The ends of the electromagnet coil are its poles. An electromagnet is magnetic only when there is a current in the wire. Generators use electromagnets to produce current from motion. Motors use electromagnets to convert electricity to motion.

Review

1. What do magnets and electric charges have in common?
2. Name two ways that you can make an electromagnet stronger.
3. What is a motor?
4. **Critical Thinking** Why is it useful to have a magnet that can be turned on and off?
5. **Test Prep** The ends of an electromagnet that are useful are called —
   A cores
   B loops
   C poles
   D wires

LINKS

MATH LINK

Strength of an Electromagnet An electromagnet with 10 loops of wire can pick up 5 paper clips. With 20 loops it can pick up 10 paper clips. Make a line graph of the data. Interpret the graph to predict how many paper clips the electromagnet can pick up if it has 40 loops.

WRITING LINK

Informative Writing—Description Think of an appliance in your home that has an electric motor. Write a description for a younger child, telling what the appliance does. If there were no electric motors, how would you do what the appliance does?

LANGUAGE ARTS LINK

Making Words The word *electromagnet* was made by joining two words. What are they? Research these two words to find out where they came from and how old they are. Why do you think this word is used to describe the device you learned about in this lesson?

TECHNOLOGY LINK

Visit the Harcourt Learning Site for related links, activities, and resources.
www.harcourtschool.com/ca

WELCOME TO **THE LEARNING SITE**

Discovering Electromagnetism

Have you used a computer today? Answered the telephone or the doorbell? Watched television? These are just a few examples of everyday machines that work because of electromagnetism.

The First Discoveries

The early Greeks were the first people to observe and describe static electricity. They noticed that rubbing amber, a yellowish gemstone, with a cloth caused the amber to attract bits of straw or feathers. The Greek word for amber is *elektron*. Our words *electron* and *electricity* come from this Greek word.

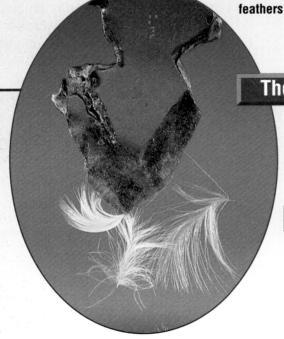

Amber and feathers

The Greeks were also the first to observe and describe magnetism. Thales (THAY•leez), a Greek philosopher, lived in a town called Magnesia. Some of the rocks near his town seemed to pull at the shepherds' walking sticks, which had iron tips. Thales noted that the rocks also pulled toward each other and toward all iron objects that were close to them. These rocks were magnetite, a natural magnet. Later, people in Europe called this natural magnet *lodestone* (LOHD•stohn), which means *leading stone*.

The Chinese may have been the first to use magnets as compasses. Sailors and other travelers found that lodestone always turns to point along a north-south line. Compasses could be made by putting a thin piece of lodestone on a piece of wood floating in

The History of Electricity and Magnetism

Chinese 2300 B.C.
Chinese invent magnetic compass.

2300 B.C. ➤ 600 B.C. ➤

Thales 600 B.C.
Thales studies magnetism.

water. Later, lodestone was used to magnetize iron compass needles.

Learning More About Electricity

In the 1700s scientists began experimenting with electricity and magnetism, which they thought might be related. One scientist, Alessandro Volta (ah•leh•SAHN•droh VOHL•tah), discovered that he could make electricity by using pieces of two different metals. He made the first battery, which he called a voltaic (vohl•TAY•ik) pile. Using this battery moved electricity steadily through a conductor, such as a salt solution, instead of giving off the electricity all at once, like a lightning bolt or a spark caused by static electricity.

The key to understanding the connection between electricity and magnetism came from a chance observation. While giving a demonstration for a class, Hans Oersted (HAHNZ ER•stuhd) noticed that when he put a compass over a wire carrying electricity, the compass needle moved. He went on to prove that an electric current always produces a magnetic field.

Other scientists built on Oersted's discovery. Michael Faraday invented a generator, a machine that produces electricity. The generator makes electricity from a moving magnet and a coil of wire.

James Clerk Maxwell also studied Oersted's work. Maxwell hypothesized that electric and magnetic fields work together to make radiant energy, or light. About 20 years after Maxwell's experiments, Heinrich (HYN•rik) Hertz proved Maxwell was right.

Superconductors

In 1911 Dutch scientist Heike Onnes (HY•kuh AW•nuhs) discovered superconductors. At very low temperatures, near $^-273°C$ ($^-459°F$), these metals or mixtures of metals conduct electric current without any resistance. Superconductors are part of MRI machines, which are used by doctors to make images of the inside of the human body. In the late 1990s, trains that float above their tracks using superconducting magnets were being built and tested in Japan!

Think About It

1. How did observation and curiosity help Oersted?

2. How has the research of Thales, Volta, Faraday, and others affected your life?

Faraday 1830
Faraday builds a generator and transformer.

Onnes 1911
Onnes discovers superconductors.

1800 A.D.   1900 A.D.   2000 A.D.

Oersted 1820
Oersted finds connection between electricity and magnetism.

Maxwell 1864
Maxwell studies light and electromagnetism.

Mag-lev 1999
Mag-lev (magnetic levitating) trains scheduled to be ready for passenger use in Japan.

Raymond V. Damadian

INVENTOR

"I think the thing that matters is not so much what you are doing but the spirit in which you are doing it."

Dr. Raymond Damadian had many interests besides science as he was growing up. He was an accomplished violinist by the time he was eight. He attended The Juilliard School of Music before becoming a doctor. He also was a professional tennis player.

Dr. Damadian and his co-workers invented the magnetic resonance imaging machine (MRI). An MRI machine uses very strong magnets to take pictures of the inside of the body. When certain atoms are in a strong magnetic field, they can be made to put out radio waves. Healthy cells and cancerous cells give off different radio waves. This allows doctors to detect cancer.

Damadian spent eight years building the first MRI machine, which he named *Indomitable*. The project had little money. He and the others working with him often had to buy equipment at electronics surplus stores.

Testing the first model took many years. First, the team tested mice who had cancer. Finally, they tried to test it on Damadian himself, but he

Dr. Damadian and *Indomitable*

was too big for the machine! They found a smaller man to test the machine, and produced the first human body MRI scan in 1977.

MRI has many good qualities. It is safer than many other tests. No surgery is needed. A patient gets no dangerous radiation. MRI "sees" through bone and can produce a clearer picture than X rays.

In 1989 Damadian was inducted into the National Inventors Hall of Fame in Washington, D.C. His first MRI model, *Indomitable*, is now housed at the Smithsonian Institution.

THINK ABOUT IT

1. What sort of magnets do you think Dr. Damadian's MRI machine used? Explain your answer.

2. Why do you think new methods in medicine must be tested on animals before being tested on humans?

MRI machine

Parallel and Series Circuits

How do lights work in different circuits?

Materials

- D-cell battery
- 3 bulb holders
- 6 wire pieces, ends stripped
- 3 flashlight bulbs
- masking tape

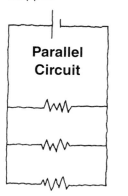
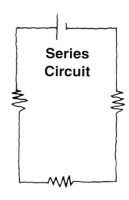

Parallel Circuit

Series Circuit

Procedure

❶ Follow the diagram to build a working parallel circuit using the materials. Observe the bulbs. Unscrew a bulb and again observe the bulbs.

❷ Repeat Step 1 using the series circuit diagram.

❸ Plan, build, and observe two similar circuits, using just two bulbs each.

Draw Conclusions

How are series and parallel circuits alike? How are they different? How do three-bulb circuits differ from two-bulb circuits?

Electrical Heat and Light

How can electricity be converted to heat and light?

Materials

- steel wool, long strand
- D-cell battery
- two wires, ends stripped
- tape
- index card

Procedure

❶ **CAUTION** **Be careful. Steel wool can cut you.** Tape the steel wool strand lengthwise on the card as shown.

❷ Tape the wires to the battery as shown.

❸ Touch one wire end to one end of the steel wool strand. Touch the other wire to the opposite end of the strand. Slowly slide one wire toward the other. Observe the wire carefully.

Draw Conclusions

What happened to the wire? How is the steel wool like a working light bulb? How is it different?

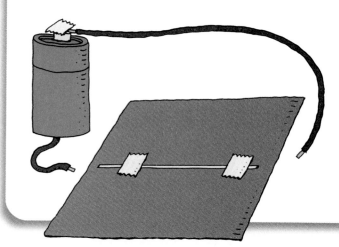

Chapter **2** Review and Test Preparation

Vocabulary Review

Use the terms below to complete the sentences. The page numbers in ( ) tell you where to look in the chapter if you need help.

charge (C34)
static electricity (C34)
electric fields (C36)
electric current (C40)
circuit (C40)
electric cell (C40)
conductor (C41)
insulator (C41)
resistor (C41)
series circuit (C42)
parallel circuit (C42)
magnet (C46)
magnetic pole (C46)
magnetic fields (C47)
electromagnet (C53)

1. A pathway for current is called a ____.

2. ____ and ____ are similar because they are both areas where forces can act without objects touching.

3. Current passes easily through a ____ but doesn't pass easily through an ____.

4. A core wrapped in a wire that is carrying current is called an ____.

5. A measure of the extra charges that are on an object is called ____.

6. A material that resists the flow of current is called a ____.

7. An ____ is a flow of charges.

8. In a ____, taking out one light does not turn off the whole circuit.

9. The charge that stays on an object is called ____.

10. A ____ attracts objects made of iron or steel.

11. A ____ has only one path for the current.

12. Energy to move current through a circuit is supplied by an ____.

13. A ____ is where a magnet's pull is strongest.

Connect Concepts

Use the terms in the Word Bank to complete the concept map.

poles
negative
charges
attract
north
repel
positive
south

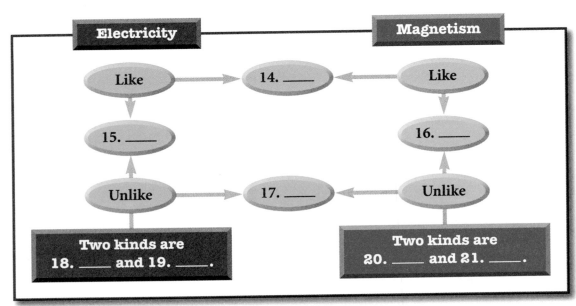

Electricity

Like → 14. ____ ← Like

15. ____

Unlike → 17. ____ ← Unlike

Magnetism

Like

16. ____

Unlike

Two kinds are 18. ____ and 19. ____.

Two kinds are 20. ____ and 21. ____.

Check Understanding

Write the letter of the best choice.

22. An object has a ____ charge if it has extra positive charges.
    A large   C negative
    B neutral   D positive

23. If the electric fields of two charged objects form a closed pattern of field lines, the objects are ____ charged.
    F negatively   H neutrally
    G positively   J oppositely

24. If one bulb is removed from a series circuit, the other bulbs will —
    A dim   C flicker
    B get brighter D go out

25. The strip of material that glows in a light bulb is —
    F a charge   H a conductor
    G an insulator J a resistor

26. A device that produces motion energy from electrical energy is —
    A a compass   C an electromagnet
    B a generator D a motor

Critical Thinking

27. Look at the circuit below. What will happen to each bulb if Switch 1 is off and Switch 2 is on?

28. Why will chalk dust sprinkled on a plastic sheet placed over a bar magnet **NOT** show the shape of the magnetic field?

Process Skills Review

29. You **observe** that the north pole and south pole of two magnets attract each other when there is a piece of paper between them. What can you **infer** about magnetic fields and paper?

30. **Plan a simple investigation** to show the results of wrapping more coils of wire around a magnet. Be sure to include a description of the observations you would make and the conclusions you might draw. Use the following materials: a battery, a long piece of insulated copper wire with the ends stripped, an iron nail, a pile of paper clips.

31. You observe in the investigation you planned for Question 30 that the magnet picks up 5 paper clips with 10 coils of wire, 10 paper clips with 20 coils of wire, and 15 with 30 coils of wire. What would you **predict** will happen when you test the electromagnet with 40 coils of wire? How could you test your prediction?

Performance Assessment

Make a Circuit

Make a diagram of a parallel circuit with wires, three light bulbs, and two batteries. Show where to put a switch to turn all the lights off and on. Explain why you chose that switch location. Build and test the circuit.

C63

Unit Project Wrap Up

Here are some ideas for ways to wrap up your unit project.

Write an Advertising Campaign

Make a series of ads that tell how energy-efficient your house is. Be sure you have evidence for your claims.

Display at a Science Fair

Display your model house in a school science fair. Prepare a written report describing the procedure you used and your results. You may want to add examples of energy-saving products to your display.

Build a Generator

Plan and install a device that will generate energy for your house. Show others how your device works.

Investigate Further

How could you make your project better? What other questions do you have about matter and energy? Plan ways to find answers to your questions. Use the Science Handbook on pages R2–R9 for help.

Extension Chapters

California Science Standards

Extension Chapters

CALIFORNIA SCIENCE STANDARDS

Vocabulary Preview

cell
tissue
organ
cardiac muscle
smooth muscle
striated muscle
lungs
capillary
heart
artery
vein
brain
neuron
nerve
spinal cord
esophagus
stomach
intestine

Human Body Systems

Your body is made up of many different parts that work together. Think about all the parts you are using right now. Your eyes are sending messages to your brain. Your lungs are moving gases, your heart is pumping blood, and your muscles are keeping you sitting straight in your chair. You may also be digesting your breakfast or lunch! You probably didn't realize you were so busy!

⣿⣿FAST FACT

You don't have the same body you had a few weeks ago. Each day, your body replaces millions of cells that have worn out. Some cells are replaced every couple of days. Other cells must last your entire lifetime.

When Cells Are Replaced

Stomach cells	2–3 days
Skin cells	19–34 days
Red blood cells	120 days
Brain cells	Never

These red blood cells
are shown magnified
about 25,000 times.

 **FAST FACT**

Your intestines are tubes inside
your abdomen. They're about
twice as long as you are tall.
Think about coiling a heavy
rope that long inside of you!

FAST FACT

You may have a whale of an
appetite, but you don't have a
whale's stomach. Your stomach
holds about $1\frac{1}{2}$ L. A right
whale's stomach holds 760 L!

How Do the Skeletal and Muscular Systems Work?

In this lesson, you can . . .

INVESTIGATE types of muscle tissue.

LEARN ABOUT the skeletal and muscular systems.

LINK to math, writing, technology, and other areas.

INVESTIGATE

Muscle Tissues

Activity Purpose The muscles you probably know most about are the ones you use to play or do work. There are also muscle types that you may not know you use, such as those in the digestive system and the heart. In this investigation you will **observe** and **compare** three types of muscles.

Materials

- Microslide Viewer
- Slide A—skeletal muscle tissue
- Slide B—smooth muscle tissue
- Slide C—heart muscle tissue

Skeletal muscle

▲ Slide A

Smooth muscle

▲ Slide B

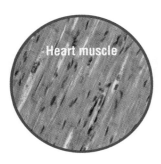

Heart muscle

▲ Slide C

◄ This boy uses the muscles in his leg to kick the soccer ball.

Activity Procedure

Type of Muscle	Observations	Ways Like Other Types of Muscle	Ways Different from Other Types of Muscle
Slide A			
Slide B			
Slide C			

1. Make a chart like the one shown.

2. Use the Microslide Viewer to carefully **observe** the muscle tissue on microslide 1 or the picture of Slide A on page E4. (Picture A)

3. Take notes to describe the way the tissue looks. What shapes do you see? Are there any colors or patterns?

4. **Record** your observations on your chart.

5. Repeat Steps 2–4 for microslides 2 and 3, or Slides B and C on page E4.

Picture A

Draw Conclusions

1. Describe each type of muscle tissue.

2. How do the tissues look the same? How do they look different?

3. **Scientists at Work** Many scientists use microscopes in their work. What does a microscope do that makes it possible to **observe** and **compare** muscle tissues?

Investigate Further If you have access to a microscope, use one to **observe** prepared slides of different kinds of tissue. See page R5 for help in using a microscope. Cells from different kinds of tissue in your body look different. Find pictures of other kinds of tissue, such as nerve tissue, bone tissue, and blood tissue. **Compare** these tissues to the muscle tissue you looked at.

Process Skill Tip

Observing and comparing are two skills you often use together. To **observe**, you may need to use a tool, such as a microscope. Comparing uses information gained from observations. When you **compare**, you look for ways things are alike and ways things are different.

The Skeletal and Muscular Systems

Structures of the Body

VOCABULARY

cell
tissue
organ
cardiac muscle
smooth muscle
striated muscle

The body is like a wonderful machine that needs very little help to keep running smoothly. When it does go wrong, it often can repair itself. The more the body is used, the stronger it gets. Have you ever wondered how this "machine" is put together?

Your body is made up of the basic building blocks of life—**cells**. Every cell in your body has a certain job. There are many types of cells, including bone cells, muscle cells, blood cells, and nerve cells.

Cells of the same type work together to form **tissue**. Bone cells make up bone tissue. Muscle cells make up muscle tissue.

Tissues of different kinds work together in **organs**. Organs are body parts that do special jobs. Bone tissue and other tissues form organs called bones. Muscle tissue and other tissues form organs called muscles.

Groups of organs that work together form *systems*. Your body has many systems. Bones working together make up the skeletal system. Muscles working together make up the muscular system.

✔ **What are organs made up of?**

Bone cells form bone tissue. ▼

Bone tissues form bones, one of the organs in the body. ▶

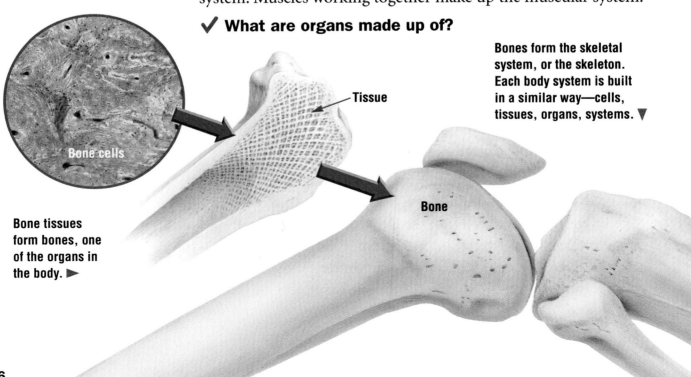

Bone cells

Tissue

Bone

Bones form the skeletal system, or the skeleton. Each body system is built in a similar way—cells, tissues, organs, systems. ▼

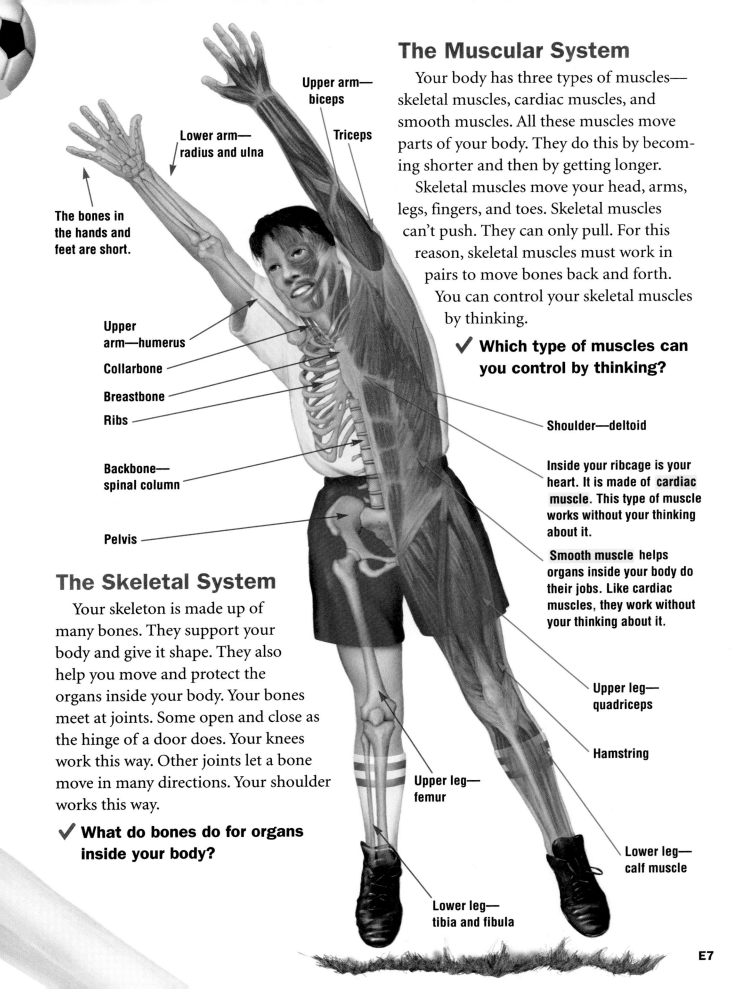

Upper arm—biceps

Triceps

Lower arm—radius and ulna

The bones in the hands and feet are short.

Upper arm—humerus

Collarbone

Breastbone

Ribs

Backbone—spinal column

Pelvis

The Muscular System

Your body has three types of muscles—skeletal muscles, cardiac muscles, and smooth muscles. All these muscles move parts of your body. They do this by becoming shorter and then by getting longer.

Skeletal muscles move your head, arms, legs, fingers, and toes. Skeletal muscles can't push. They can only pull. For this reason, skeletal muscles must work in pairs to move bones back and forth. You can control your skeletal muscles by thinking.

✔ **Which type of muscles can you control by thinking?**

Shoulder—deltoid

Inside your ribcage is your heart. It is made of cardiac muscle. This type of muscle works without your thinking about it.

Smooth muscle helps organs inside your body do their jobs. Like cardiac muscles, they work without your thinking about it.

Upper leg—quadriceps

Hamstring

Lower leg—calf muscle

The Skeletal System

Your skeleton is made up of many bones. They support your body and give it shape. They also help you move and protect the organs inside your body. Your bones meet at joints. Some open and close as the hinge of a door does. Your knees work this way. Other joints let a bone move in many directions. Your shoulder works this way.

✔ **What do bones do for organs inside your body?**

Upper leg—femur

Lower leg—tibia and fibula

A Closer Look at Muscles

As you saw in the investigation skeletal muscles have light and dark stripes. They are called **striated** (STRY•ayt•uhd) **muscles**. The stripes are patterns made by the working parts of the muscle cells. The fibers in a skeletal muscle can be up to 30 centimeters (12 in.) long. Some muscles have more than 2000 fibers packed tightly together.

Smooth muscle does not have stripes. It is found in the walls of organs such as the stomach, intestines, blood vessels, and bladder. Smooth muscle works by squeezing and relaxing slowly and smoothly. Its fibers are shorter than the fibers in skeletal muscle.

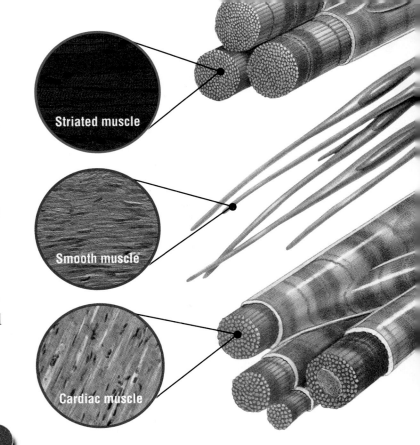

Striated muscle

Smooth muscle

Cardiac muscle

THE INSIDE STORY

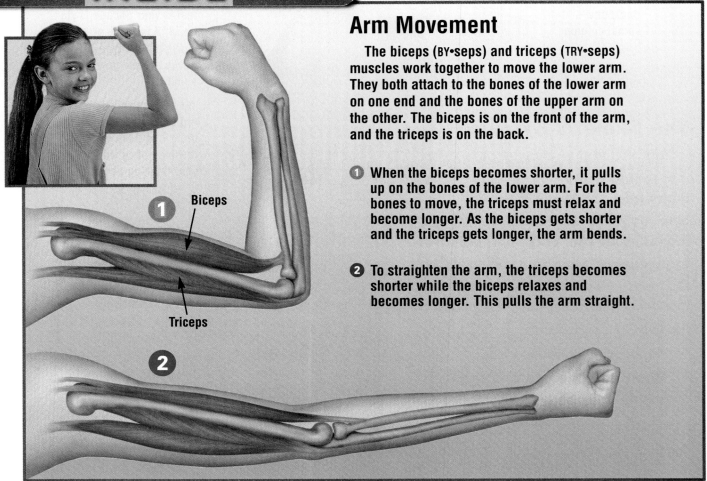

Biceps

Triceps

1

2

Arm Movement

The biceps (BY•seps) and triceps (TRY•seps) muscles work together to move the lower arm. They both attach to the bones of the lower arm on one end and the bones of the upper arm on the other. The biceps is on the front of the arm, and the triceps is on the back.

1 When the biceps becomes shorter, it pulls up on the bones of the lower arm. For the bones to move, the triceps must relax and become longer. As the biceps gets shorter and the triceps gets longer, the arm bends.

2 To straighten the arm, the triceps becomes shorter while the biceps relaxes and becomes longer. This pulls the arm straight.

◀ Muscles are made up of muscle fibers bundled together.

Cardiac muscle has stripes, but not as many as skeletal muscle. Cardiac muscle makes up the walls of the heart. Although cardiac muscle squeezes and relaxes without stopping, it never gets tired.

✓ **Which type of muscle doesn't have stripes?**

Summary

The body is made up of basic parts called cells. Cells make up tissues, tissues make up organs, and organs make up body systems. The skeletal and muscular systems work together to help the body move.

Review

1. What are the basic building blocks of life?

2. How do the skeletal and muscular systems work to move the body?

3. Which type of muscle works without ever stopping?

4. **Critical Thinking** Why is it good that people don't have to think about smooth muscles doing their jobs?

5. **Test Prep** _____ move bones in different directions.
   A Muscle pairs
   B Smooth muscles
   C Cardiac muscles
   D Cells

LINKS

MATH LINK

Calculating with Heartbeats Count the number of times your heart beats in one minute. This is your heart rate. Use this number to figure about how many times your heart beats in an hour and in a day.

WRITING LINK

Narrative Writing—Story Suppose you take a long hike. Write a story from the point of view of the muscles you would use. Describe for another classmate what it is like to walk and climb.

LITERATURE LINK

Let's Exercise Exercise is important for muscles and bones. Learn about exercise by reading *Staying Healthy: Let's Exercise* by Alice B. McGinty.

HEALTH LINK

Nutrition Find out what kinds of foods are important for building strong bones and muscles. Which ones would you like to try? Prepare a menu of meals and snacks for a day. Include foods that help build strong bones.

TECHNOLOGY LINK

Learn more about ways to keep your bones healthy by viewing *Bone Health* on the **Harcourt Science Newsroom Video** in your classroom video library.

How Do the Respiratory and Circulatory Systems Work?

In this lesson, you can . . .

INVESTIGATE breathing rates.

LEARN ABOUT the respiratory and circulatory systems.

LINK to math, writing, and technology.

INVESTIGATE

Breathing Rates

Activity Purpose Your breathing rate when you are active is different from the rate when you are sitting quietly. It may change even as you walk across the classroom or down the street. In this investigation you will **measure** your breathing rate after you do three different activities.

Materials

- stopwatch, timer, or clock with second hand

Activity Procedure

1 Make a chart like the one on the next page.

2 While you are sitting, count the number of times you breathe out in one minute. **Record** the number on your chart.

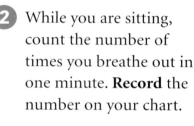

◄ Swimming is healthful exercise for both the respiratory and circulatory systems.

3. Stand up and march in place for one minute. Raise your knees as high as you can. As soon as you stop marching, begin to count the number of times you breathe out. Count your breaths for one minute. **Record** the number of breaths on your chart.

4. Rest for a few minutes, and then run in place for one minute. As soon as you stop running, begin to count the number of times you breathe out. Count your breaths for one minute. **Record** the number on your chart. (Picture A)

5. Make a bar graph to show how your breathing changed for each activity.

Picture A

Activity	Number of Breaths
Sitting	
After marching for 1 minute	
After running for 1 minute	

Draw Conclusions

1. Which activity needed the fewest breaths? Which needed the most breaths?

2. What can you **infer** about breathing from what happened in this investigation?

3. **Scientists at Work** Scientists don't usually **measure** something just once. What could you do to be sure your breathing rate measurements were correct?

Investigate Further Does your breathing rate increase if you exercise longer? March in place for two minutes, and then count your breaths. Run in place for two minutes, and then count your breaths. Add two new rows to your chart and **record** the numbers.

Process Skill Tip

Measuring should be repeated. Scientists often measure more than once to be sure their measurements are correct. They compare the sets of measurements to look for patterns and possible mistakes.

The Respiratory and Circulatory Systems

The Respiratory System

FIND OUT

- **what breathing does for the body**
- **why blood is important to the body's cells**

VOCABULARY

lungs
capillary
heart
artery
vein

Your body's cells need oxygen to work. When you breathe in, you take in oxygen your cells need. As your cells do work, they give off carbon dioxide. When you breathe out, you get rid of carbon dioxide that cells give off.

You saw in the investigation that your breathing rate goes up as your body works harder. That's because as muscles do more work, they need more oxygen. They also give off more carbon dioxide. You breathe in and out faster to bring in more oxygen and to get rid of more carbon dioxide.

The main organs of the respiratory system are the **lungs**. Air enters your body through your nose and mouth. It goes down your *trachea* (TRAY•kee•uh) to your lungs. As you breathe in, your chest gets bigger and your lungs fill with air.

Your trachea divides to form a system of tubes in your lungs. These tubes look like the branches of a tree. The branches get smaller and smaller until they end in air sacs. All around the air sacs are tiny blood vessels called **capillaries** (KAP•uh•lair•ees). The walls of the air sacs and the capillaries are very thin. Oxygen passes easily through these walls, moving from the air sacs into blood in the capillaries. Carbon dioxide passes the other way, from blood in capillaries into the air in the air sacs.

✔ **What are the main organs of the respiratory system?**

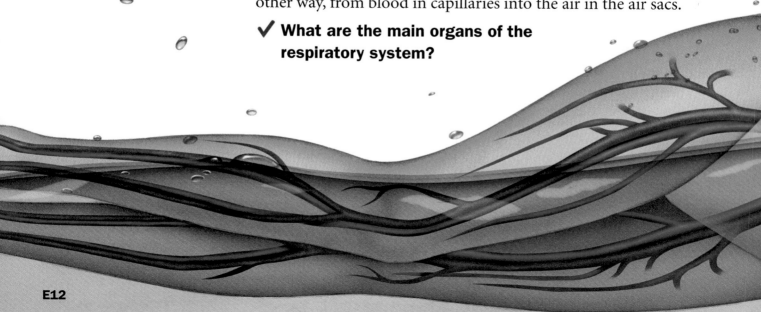

The Circulatory System

The capillaries around the air sacs in your lungs are part of your circulatory system. Your circulatory system includes your heart and all of your blood vessels, the tubes blood flows through. The job of the circulatory system is to take blood to all of your body's cells.

The **heart** is the muscle that pumps blood through your blood vessels to all parts of your body. It is only as big as your fist. It is very strong and works all the time, resting only between beats.

Blood leaves the heart through blood vessels called **arteries**. Arteries branch out to all parts of your body. They become smaller and smaller until they become tiny capillaries.

The capillaries carry blood to every cell in your body. There, oxygen passes from the blood into the cells. Carbon dioxide passes from cells into the blood. Capillaries

Capillaries

Blood leaves the heart through arteries. Arteries branch to become capillaries. Then blood returns to the heart through veins.

Artery

Vein

then become veins. **Veins** are the large blood vessels that return the blood to your heart.

✔ **Which part of the circulatory system pumps blood to all body parts?**

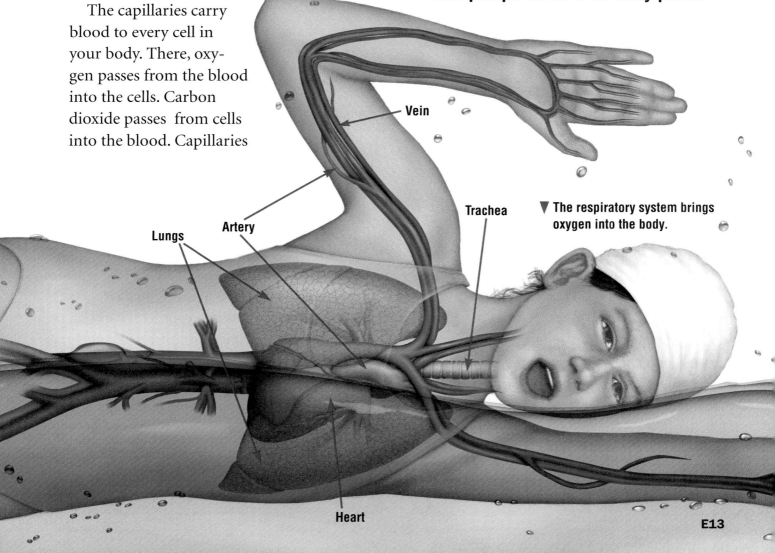

Vein

Lungs

Artery

Trachea

▼ The respiratory system brings oxygen into the body.

Heart

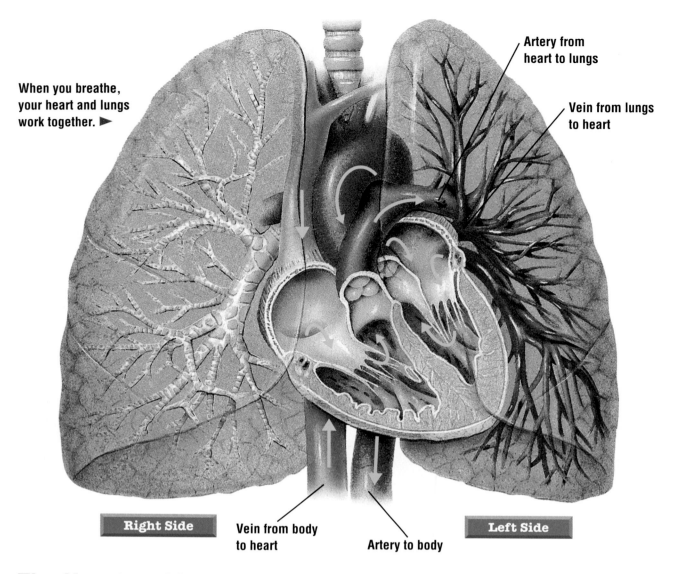

When you breathe, your heart and lungs work together. ▶

Artery from heart to lungs

Vein from lungs to heart

Right Side

Left Side

Vein from body to heart

Artery to body

The Heart and Lungs Work Together

The heart and lungs work together to bring oxygen into your body and to take away carbon dioxide. Each time you breathe in, the blood in your lungs gets fresh oxygen. This blood then travels to the heart, which pumps it to other parts of the body.

The heart has four sections called *chambers.* Each chamber acts as a pump. The chambers keep blood that enters the heart from mixing with blood that leaves the heart. The chambers are connected by openings. Each opening is covered by a valve that opens in only one direction. Each valve closes when its chamber is full.

Blood follows a one-way path through the heart. Blood from the lungs enters the top left chamber. The muscles of the chamber then shorten. This makes the space smaller, forcing the blood out. The only place it can go is into the lower left chamber.

This chamber is the main pump. It pushes blood through the whole body. When this chamber is full, it pushes the blood out of the heart and into the body's largest artery. The blood goes to all of the body, carrying oxygen to cells and picking up carbon dioxide. Then it returns to the heart.

Blood returning to the heart goes into the top right chamber. The muscles of this chamber force the blood into the chamber below.

The lower right chamber pumps the blood to the lungs. Here carbon dioxide leaves the blood and more oxygen enters. The blood is ready for another trip to the heart. It will be pumped around the body once again.

✓ **What makes blood follow a one-way path through the heart?**

Summary

Lungs are the organs the body uses to breathe. Breathing trades carbon dioxide, a waste cells give off, for oxygen, which cells need. Blood carries gases to and from cells through blood vessels. The heart pumps blood through the body.

Review

1. Why is it easy for gases to pass between air sacs and blood?

2. Which blood vessels take blood away from the heart?

3. Which blood vessels in the lungs help your body take in and give off gases?

4. **Critical Thinking** What do you think would happen if blood entering the heart mixed with blood leaving the heart?

5. **Test Prep** Which is a waste product of cells?

   A blood

   B water

   C oxygen

   D carbon dioxide

LINKS

MATH LINK

Interpret Data Knowing your target heart rate helps you exercise at a safe and healthful level. When you exercise, keep your heart rate between the maximum and minimum rates.

Exercise Heart Rate

Age	Minimum	Maximum
8	127	180
9	$126\frac{1}{2}$	179
10	126	$178\frac{1}{2}$
11	125	178

Do you think a 13-year-old would have a higher or lower maximum exercise heart rate than an 11-year-old? Why?

WRITING LINK

Expressive Writing—Song Lyrics Write a funny song for a younger student. Tell about a molecule of oxygen that enters the lungs. Explain what happens when it refuses to go to just any cell because it wants only to visit the big toe.

TECHNOLOGY LINK

Learn more about keeping heart beats regular by visiting the Smithsonian Institution Internet site.
www.si.edu/harcourt/science

How Do the Nervous and Digestive Systems Work?

In this lesson, you can . . .

INVESTIGATE the sense of touch.

LEARN ABOUT the nervous and digestive systems.

LINK to math, writing, health, and technology.

INVESTIGATE

The Sense of Touch

Activity Purpose To protect itself, the body must notice things that touch it. Some parts of the body have a better sense of touch than others. In this investigation you will first **predict** which of three areas of your body is the most sensitive to touch. Then you will **compare** how sensitive the areas are.

Materials
- index card
- ruler
- 8 toothpicks
- tape
- blindfold (optional)

Activity Procedure

1 Make a copy of the chart on the next page.

2 Look at the areas of the body listed on the chart. **Predict** which one has the best sense of touch. Write your prediction on the chart. Explain your choice.

3 Measure a space 1 cm wide on one edge of the index card. Mark each end of the space, and write the distance between the marks. Tape a toothpick to each mark so that one end of each toothpick sticks out about 1 cm past the edge of the card. Make sure the toothpicks point straight out from the edge of the card.

◄ This baseball catcher needs alert senses to catch the ball.

	Prediction: Distance Between Toothpicks When Two Toothpicks First Felt		
	Palm	Lower Arm	Upper Arm
Prediction			
Actual			

4 Repeat Step 3 for the other three sides of the index card. However, use spaces 2 cm, 5 cm, and 8 cm wide, one for each side.

5 Have a partner test your sense of touch. Ask him or her to lightly touch one body area listed on the chart with the toothpicks on each edge of the index card. Begin with the 1-cm side, and then use each side in turn with 2 cm apart, 5 cm apart, and 8 cm apart. Don't watch as your partner does this. (Picture A)

Picture A

6 For each area, tell your partner when you first feel two separate toothpicks touching your skin. Have your partner write the distance between these toothpicks on the chart.

7 Switch roles and test your partner.

Draw Conclusions

1. Which of the body parts felt the two toothpicks the shortest distance apart?

2. Based on this test, which of these body parts would you **infer** has the best sense of touch? Explain.

3. **Scientists at Work** Using what you observed in this investigation, which part of your body do you **predict** to be more sensitive, your fingertip or the back of your neck?

Investigate Further Have your partner use the toothpicks to test your fingertip and the back of your neck to check the **prediction** you just made.

Process Skill Tip

When you **predict**, you say or write what you think will happen. To make a prediction, you think about what you know. Then you use what you know in the new situation.

The Nervous and Digestive Systems

FIND OUT

• how the nervous system controls all the body's systems

• what the digestive system does for the body

VOCABULARY

brain
neuron
nerve
spinal cord
esophagus
stomach
small intestine
large intestine

The Nervous System

None of your body systems could work without the help of your nervous system. It controls all parts of your body. Your nervous system is always receiving messages from your body and sending out responses.

Your **brain** is the control center of your nervous system. It and all other parts of the system are made up of nerve cells, or **neurons** (NOO•rahns). The brain uses information it gets from your body to direct how each body system works.

Your brain gets a lot of information from the sense organs in your head—your eyes, ears, tongue, and nose. Your brain also gets information from other parts of your body. In the investigation, you tested the sense of touch in different parts of your arm. Your brain told you what you felt.

Your body has **nerves**, or groups of neurons, that pass along information. The sense organs in your head have nerves that connect directly to your brain. Your spinal cord connects the nerves in the rest of your body to your brain. Your **spinal** (SPY•nuhl) **cord** is a tube of nerves that runs through your spine, or backbone.

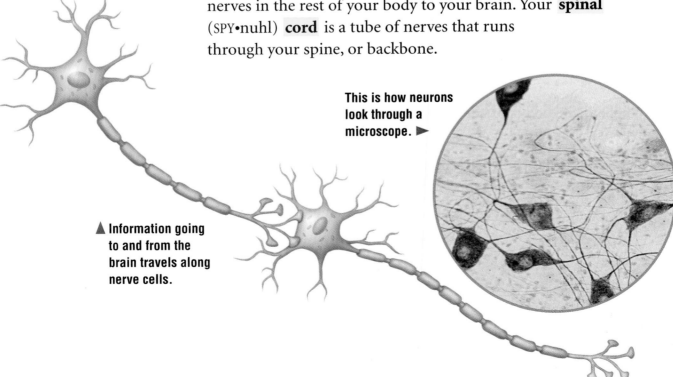

This is how neurons look through a microscope. ▶

▲ Information going to and from the brain travels along nerve cells.

E18

Information from your body goes up your spinal cord to your brain. Your brain acts on the information and sends a message back. For example, if you are at bat in a baseball game, your eyes watch the ball. They send information to your brain about the speed and direction of the ball. In less than a second, your brain decides whether or not to swing at the pitch.

If you decide to swing, your brain will send information down your spinal cord to nerves in your arms. The message will tell your arm muscles when and how hard to swing. If you hit the ball, your brain will tell your leg muscles to run. The more you practice, the better your brain will get at telling your muscles just how to hit the ball.

✔ **Which body part tells a batter whether or not to swing at a ball?**

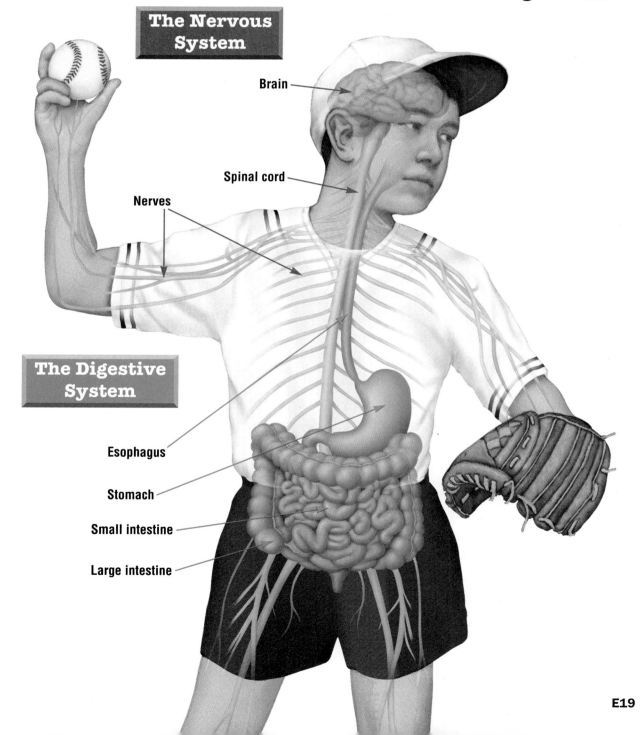

The Nervous System

The Digestive System

Brain

Spinal cord

Nerves

Esophagus

Stomach

Small intestine

Large intestine

E19

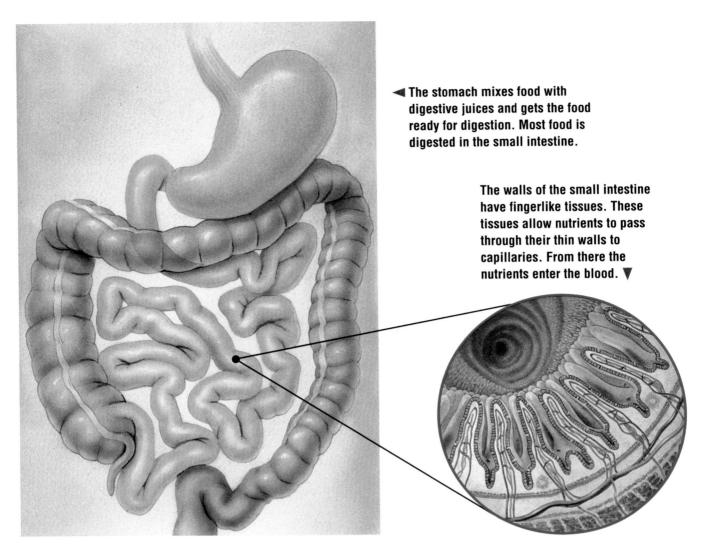

◄ The stomach mixes food with digestive juices and gets the food ready for digestion. Most food is digested in the small intestine.

The walls of the small intestine have fingerlike tissues. These tissues allow nutrients to pass through their thin walls to capillaries. From there the nutrients enter the blood. ▼

The Digestive System

The digestive system also does an important job for the whole body. It provides nutrients to all the body's systems. It does this by breaking down, or digesting, the food you eat into nutrients your body's cells can use.

Digestion begins in your mouth. When you chew, your teeth grind up food into smaller pieces. Saliva (suh•LY•vuh) softens the food and begins to digest it.

After you swallow, the food enters your **esophagus** (ih•SOF•uh•guhs), a tube that connects your mouth with your stomach. The actions of smooth muscles in your esophagus move the food down to your stomach.

The **stomach** is a bag made up of smooth muscles. The stomach muscles squeeze the food and mix it with digestive juices. The juices digest some parts of the food. The food is mixed and squeezed until it becomes mostly liquid.

The liquid food then passes into the **small intestine** (ihn•TES•tuhn), a long tube of muscle. Different digestive juices are added, and other parts of the food are digested. The small intestine does more than any part of the digestive system to digest food.

The nutrients from the digested food pass through the walls of the small intestine into capillaries. Blood carries these nutrients to the body's cells.

The last part of the digestive system is the **large intestine**. Most food that reaches the large intestine can't be broken down any more. The large intestine removes water from this food. What is left of the food travels through the large intestine until it passes out of the body.

✓ **What part of the digestive system does the most to digest food?**

Summary

The brain sends messages to and from all parts of the body through the spinal cord and nerves. It controls the way all other body systems work. The digestive system breaks down food to provide nutrients for all the body's cells. The blood carries these nutrients to every cell in the body.

Review

1. How does the brain connect with other parts of the body?
2. What gives information to the brain?
3. Where does digestion begin?
4. **Critical Thinking** Why would not chewing food enough make it harder for the digestive system to do its job?
5. **Test Prep** Which part of the digestive system makes food mostly liquid?
   A stomach
   B esophagus
   C small intestine
   D large intestine

LINKS

MATH LINK

Calculator Challenge Nerves can send messages back and forth at the amazing speed of 430 kilometers per hour. Find two things that travel faster than nerve messages and two that travel more slowly. Make a bar graph to show and compare all five speeds.

WRITING LINK

Informative Writing—Explanation You have seen how the nervous system controls your muscles. Write a paragraph for your school newspaper. Explain what your nervous system does when you score a point in your favorite sport.

HEALTH LINK

Nutrition Find information about the Food Guide Pyramid. Make your own model of the pyramid. Draw or cut out pictures of foods for each food group. Glue them to your model.

TECHNOLOGY LINK

Visit The Harcourt Learning Site for related links, activities, and resources.
www.harcourtschool.com/ca

WELCOME TO THE LEARNING SITE

Skin Adhesive

Almost everyone is badly cut at some time and has to get the cut stitched closed in an emergency room. Now, researchers are trying to make such stitches a thing of the past!

This cut is being glued closed with skin adhesive.

Super Surgical Glue

Stitches are used 86 million times a year all over the world. Doctors predict that half of the cuts will soon be repaired by skin adhesive (ad•HEE•siv), or artificial glue. It is like other "super" glues. But it is made to stick together living layers of skin!

Now, This Won't Hurt!

There are lots of good reasons to use this product. It takes less time than stitches. Doctors simply squeeze it out of a tube, much like rolling on lip gloss. Stitching a cut takes an average of $12\frac{1}{2}$ minutes. Using adhesive takes only about $3\frac{1}{2}$ minutes.

Stitched wounds are three times as likely to become infected as are wounds closed by adhesive. And adhesive stretches with the skin, so cuts don't break open when the patient stretches or moves. The skin adhesive comes off with dead skin cells. As a result, no visit to the doctor is needed to remove it, unlike stitches. Best of all, applying skin adhesive doesn't hurt, so skin doesn't have to be "numbed" first. For these reasons, the adhesive is comfortable for the patient and easier for the doctor. An added bonus is that it usually costs less than stitches.

Still to Come

Other companies are working to make adhesives for other medical work. One company has made an adhesive that also kills germs. Scientist are working to find adhesives to glue bone grafts, to close spinal fluid leaks, and to seal holes in the digestive tract. A spray adhesive may be used for burns. The adhesive would protect tender new skin as the new skin grows.

Don't Try This at Home!

CAUTION If you have a cut or wound, do *not* try to glue it closed. Get help from an adult. Surgical adhesives are **NOT** just like the glues at school or home. Only surgical adhesives are for use on skin.

Think About It

1. Why would a spray type of skin adhesive be helpful for burn patients?
2. What other medical uses can you think of for skin adhesives? Are there nonmedical ways it might be used?

WEB LINK:
For Science and Technology updates, visit the Harcourt Internet site.
www.harcourtschool.com/ca

Careers   Surgical Nurse

What They Do
Surgical nurses help patients before, during, and after surgery. They may help the surgeon during an operation. They also may stay with a patient in the recovery room after surgery.

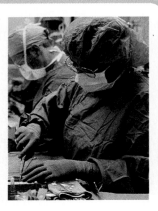

Education and Training   Many nurses have college degrees in nursing. Some learn in programs offered through hospitals. Some take two-year community college programs. Surgical nurses must take courses in surgical nursing. They must also study and train during their career. All nursing programs require practice on the job. All states require nurses to pass a national exam.

Rosalyn Sussman Yalow

MEDICAL PHYSICIST

"You won't all win Nobel Prizes, but the important thing is that you set goals for yourself and then live up to them."

Dr. Rosalyn Yalow knows about setting goals. By the time she was a teenager, she knew she wanted to have a career in science, marry, and raise a family. At that time, it was unusual for a woman to plan to have both a career and a family.

Yalow valued education and was especially good at math. She attended Hunter College and the University of Illinois at Urbana-Champaign.

While at the University of Illinois, Yalow later became interested in radioactive particles. These are given off when atoms break apart. Yalow later set up a laboratory in what had been a janitor's closet at the Veteran's Administration Hospital in the Bronx. Dr. Solomon Berson became her research partner. They worked together for over 20 years.

Berson and Yalow found that radioactive particles could help measure antibodies in the blood. They could also detect the level of certain

hormones. Their method is called radioimmuno-assay (ray•dee•oh•im•yoo•noh•AS•ay), or RIA. It takes only a small amount of blood. This was important because earlier methods required almost a cup of blood! RIA measures very precisely. It can detect amounts as small as one billionth of a gram. This precision helps doctors diagnose and treat many different diseases.

Dr. Berson died in 1972, and Yalow continued her work with a new research partner. Yalow was the first woman to receive the Albert Lasker Basic Medical Research Award. In 1977 she received the Nobel Prize for Medicine and Physiology.

THINK ABOUT IT

1. How are science and detective work alike?
2. Why is it sometimes helpful for scientists to work together on a large project?

RIA test equipment

Muscle Model

How does the biceps muscle work?

Materials

- 2 boards (about 5 cm × 25 cm)
- duct tape
- scissors
- long balloon
- string

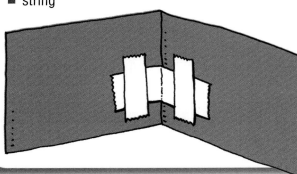

Procedure

1. Place the boards end to end. Use duct tape to make a hinge connecting the boards.

2. Blow up the balloon about one-fourth full.

3. Using the string, tie the two ends of the balloon to the outside ends of the boards.

4. Open and close the model you made.

5. Record your observations.

Draw Conclusions

Explain how this model is like the biceps muscle and the upper and lower bones of the arm.

Reaction Time

How does practice affect the nervous system?

Materials

- meterstick

Procedure

1. Work with a partner. Put your forearm flat on your desktop with your hand extending over the edge.

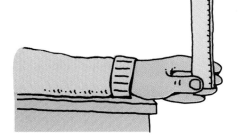

2. Have your partner hold the meterstick above your hand so that the zero mark is between your index finger and your thumb.

3. Have your partner drop the meterstick without giving you any warning. Catch the meterstick as quickly as you can.

4. Record the number that was between your fingers when you caught the stick. This is the distance the meterstick fell before you caught it.

5. Repeat the test ten times. Record the distance the stick fell each time.

Draw Conclusions

Make a line graph of your results. Did your reaction times change? In what way?

Chapter 1 Review and Test Preparation

Vocabulary Review

Use the terms below to complete the sentences. The page numbers in ( ) tell you where to look in the chapter if you need help.

cell (E6)
veins (E13)
tissue (E6)
brain (E18)
organ (E6)
neurons (E18)
cardiac muscle (E7)
nerves (E18)
smooth muscle (E7)
arteries (E13)

spinal cord (E18)
striated muscle (E8)
esophagus (E20)
lungs (E12)
stomach (E20)
capillaries (E12)
small intestine (E20)
heart (E13)
large intestine (E21)

1. Two long tubes of muscle that lead from the stomach and help absorb food are the ____ and the ____.

2. Your ____ is a bag made up of muscles that churns food.

3. Three main parts of your nervous system are the ____, ____, and ____.

4. From your heart, blood first flows away through ____ to the body, then through ____, and back to the heart through ____.

5. Your ____ is the organ that pumps blood.

6. The ____ is the major building block of life.

7. The ____ are the main organs of the respiratory system.

8. The cells that form nerves are ____.

9. A group of cells of the same type is a ____.

10. The ____ connects your mouth to your stomach.

11. An ____ is made up of different tissues that work together to do a certain job in the body.

12. The three types of muscles in your body are ____, or heart muscle; ____; and ____.

Connect Concepts

Use concepts from the chapter to complete the concept map.

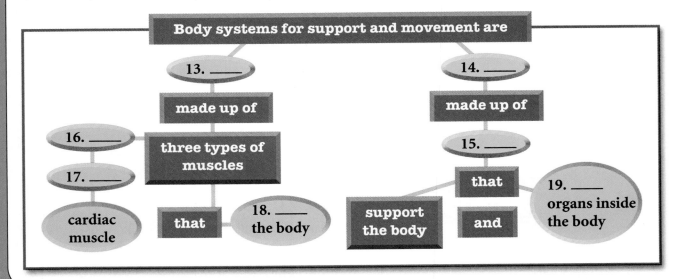

Body systems for support and movement are

13. ____

14. ____

made up of

made up of

16. ____

17. ____

three types of muscles

15. ____

cardiac muscle

that

18. ____ the body

support the body

that

and

19. ____ organs inside the body

Check Understanding

Write the letter of the best choice.

20. Leg muscles that you use when you lift a box are —

   A smooth muscles

   B striated muscles

   C cardiac muscles

   D heart muscles

21. The brain is an ＿＿ that is part of your nervous system.

   F organ

   G leg

   H cell

   J system

22. When you exercise, your body needs more ＿＿, so you breathe faster.

   A oxygen

   B water

   C carbon dioxide

   D speed

23. When blood passes through ＿＿, it exchanges oxygen and carbon dioxide.

   F arteries

   G veins

   H the heart

   J capillaries

24. Which body system tells you when to reach for and catch a falling book?

   A muscular

   B skeletal

   C nervous

   D respiratory

Critical Thinking

25. Why isn't the heart made up of smooth muscles like other organs inside your body?

26. Which body system would smoking cigarettes affect most directly? Explain.

27. How might a serious injury to your spinal cord affect the rest of your body?

Process Skills Review

28. What features would you look for if you wanted to **compare** bones in the human body?

29. How would you **measure** the number of times students dropped pencils during class?

30. To **predict** who would win a race, what would you want to know?

Performance Assessment

Digestion Model

With a partner, make a small model or a poster showing how your digestive system would digest an apple.

Chapter 2

Vocabulary Preview
energy
thermal energy
temperature
heat
conduction
convection
radiation
infrared radiation
fuel
solar energy

Heat— Energy on the Move

You push and shove! Finally the door opens! In summer, doors often stick. This is because materials expand and contract as they get hot and cold. For the same reason, if you put a jar with a stuck lid under hot water, the lid will loosen!

FAST FACT

If you add enough heat, almost anything will boil. If you take away enough heat, things freeze. Water freezes at 0°C (32°F) and boils at 100°C (212°F). Substances freeze and boil at different temperatures.

Freezing and Boiling

Substance	Freezes at °C (°F)		Boils at °C (°F)	
Iron	1538	(2800)	2862	(5184)
Mercury	-39	(-38)	357	(675)
Nitrogen	-209	(-344)	-196	(-321)
Oxygen	-218	(-360)	-183	(-297)

Molten iron

When a light bulb is on, the temperature of the glowing wire inside is a sizzling 2500°C (about 4500°F). That's why the outside of a light bulb gets hot while the bulb is on. The empty space around the wire keeps the bulb from melting and the wire from burning up.

The temperature of a lightning bolt is estimated to be 30,000°C (54,000°F)! If people could harness the energy from a single lightning bolt, they could light up an average-size town for a year.

How Does Heat Affect Matter?

In this lesson, you can . . .

 INVESTIGATE how heat affects air in a balloon.

 LEARN ABOUT thermal energy.

 LINK to math, writing, social studies, and technology.

 **INVESTIGATE**

Changes in a Heated Balloon

Activity Purpose Have you ever wondered why a hot-air balloon rises? Or how a thermometer measures temperature? The answers have something in common—a property of matter. In this investigation you will **measure** changes in a balloon as it is heated. Then you'll **infer** what caused the changes.

Materials

- desk lamp
- bulb
- safety goggles
- 3 rubber balloons
- balloon clamps
- ruler

CAUTION

Activity Procedure

1 Turn on the lamp, and let the light bulb get warm.

2 **CAUTION** **Put on your safety goggles.** Blow up a rubber balloon just enough to stretch it. Clamp the end.

3 **Measure** the length of the balloon with the ruler. **Record** the measurement. (Picture A)

4 Carefully hold the balloon by its clamped end about 3 cm above the lamp. Hold it there for two minutes. (Picture B) **CAUTION** **The light bulb is hot. Do not touch it with your hands or with the balloon. Observe** what happens to the balloon. **Record** your observations.

◄ Icicles form when water melts, flows, and freezes again.

E30

Picture A

Picture B

5 **Measure** the length of the balloon while it is still over the lamp. **Record** the measurement.

6 Repeat Steps 2 through 5 using a new balloon each time.

Draw Conclusions

1. What did you **observe** as you warmed the balloons?

2. **Compare** the lengths of the heated balloons with the lengths of the unheated balloons.

3. What can you **infer** happened to the air inside the balloons as you heated it?

4. **Scientists at Work** Scientists often **measure** several times to make sure the measurements are accurate. In this investigation you measured the lengths of three different balloons. Were the measurements all the same? Explain.

Investigate Further Fill a balloon with water that is at room temperature. Put the balloon on a desk and **measure** its length. Heat the balloon by putting it in a bowl of hot tap water for 15 minutes. Take the balloon out of the bowl and measure its length. **Compare** these lengths with those you measured with the air-filled balloons in the investigation.

Process Skill Tip

Scientists often observe and **measure** an object or an event several times. Patterns among measurements may show something important in an investigation.

Matter and Energy

Thermal Energy

Have you ever thrown a ball? Pushed a grocery cart? Run in a race? All these activities need energy. **Energy** is the ability to cause a change. In each of these cases, the thing that changed was the position of an object. You threw the ball from one place to another. You pushed the grocery cart through the store. You moved yourself along the racetrack. Moving anything from one place to another takes energy.

The particles in matter are always moving from one place to another. The particles in a solid jiggle back and forth like balls on a spring. The particles in a liquid slide past each other. The particles in a gas move quickly in many directions. All of this movement requires energy. The energy of the motion of particles in matter is called **thermal energy**. The word *thermal* means "heat." We feel the thermal energy of the particles in matter as heat.

✔ What is thermal energy?

FIND OUT

• what thermal energy is

• the difference between thermal energy and temperature

VOCABULARY

energy
thermal energy
temperature

Water boils when its particles are moving so fast that many begin to fly away from its surface. This happens when the water's temperature is 100°C (212°F). ▼

When liquid water freezes, its particles settle into an arrangement as a solid. This happens when the temperature of the water is 0°C (32°F). The ice cubes and lemonade are 0°C. ▼

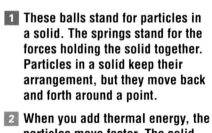

1 These balls stand for particles in a solid. The springs stand for the forces holding the solid together. Particles in a solid keep their arrangement, but they move back and forth around a point.

2 When you add thermal energy, the particles move faster. The solid gets hotter.

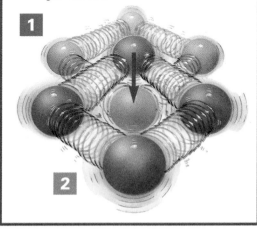

▲ The water in this cup is the same temperature as the nearly boiling water in the hot spring. But the water in the spring has more thermal energy because it has more water and, therefore, more moving particles of matter.

Temperature

Most people think that temperature is a measure of heat. Actually, **temperature** is a measure of the average energy of motion of the particles in matter. At 50°F (about 10°C) the particles in the air move more slowly than they do at 80°F (about 27°C). They have less thermal energy.

In the investigation you heated a balloon and observed how its volume changed. You can measure temperature by observing how the volume of a liquid changes as it is heated or cooled. One kind of thermometer has liquid in a narrow tube. When the liquid gets hotter, its volume changes and it moves up the tube. When it gets colder, it moves back down the tube.

✔ **What does temperature measure?**

Temperature and Thermal Energy

Two pieces of matter can be at the same temperature but not have the same amount of thermal energy. Temperature measures the *average* amount of motion of the particles in a piece of matter. Thermal energy is the *total* energy of motion of the particles in a piece of matter. More matter equals more particles. More particles equals more energy of motion.

When a drop of cold water falls into a hot pan or skillet, the water boils away in a second or two. Its particles speed up and fly off. Little thermal energy is needed to warm the drop to 100°C (212°F). A pan full of cold water has many more particles. It takes much more thermal energy to boil the water.

✔ **What is the difference between temperature and thermal energy?**

E33

Adding Thermal Energy

Adding Thermal Energy

▲ When thermal energy is added to frozen water, the water slowly changes from a solid to a liquid and then from a liquid to a gas. When thermal energy is removed from water vapor, this process is reversed.

Adding Thermal Energy

When thermal energy is added to matter, the particles in the matter move faster. Below 0°C (32°F) water is solid ice. The particles move back and forth around one point. As you add thermal energy, the particles move faster and faster. At 0°C (32°F) the particles begin to move past and around each other. The ice melts.

After ice melts, adding energy causes the particles of liquid water to move faster and faster. The temperature of the liquid water rises. After a while, particles begin to fly away from the water's surface. The water boils, or rapidly becomes a gas.

✔ **What happens to matter when you add thermal energy?**

Water vapor in the air loses energy to the cold air outside the window. First, it becomes small water droplets on the glass. Then, it becomes a solid and forms these ice crystals. ▼

Summary

Energy is the ability to cause change. Energy is needed to move something from one place to another. The total energy of motion of the particles in matter is thermal energy. Temperature is a measure of the average motion of these particles. Adding thermal energy causes the particles of matter to move faster. More matter equals more particles. More particles mean more total thermal energy.

Review

1. What does temperature measure?
2. If all particles in a metal spoon start moving faster, how has the spoon's temperature changed?
3. When you add thermal energy to matter, what happens?
4. **Critical Thinking** The water in two glasses has the same average energy of motion. One glass holds 250 mL, and one holds 400 mL. Which glass of water has more thermal energy? Why?
5. **Test Prep** The particles in two pieces of chocolate have the same average energy of motion. One piece has more mass than the other. Which piece is at a higher temperature?

    A the piece with more mass

    B the piece with less mass

    C the piece with more thermal energy

    D They are the same temperature.

LINKS

MATH LINK

Thermometers On a Fahrenheit temperature scale, water freezes at 32°F and boils at 212°F. How many Fahrenheit degrees are between the two temperatures? Now think about the boiling and freezing temperatures in Celsius degrees. Are degrees Celsius bigger or smaller units of measure than degrees Fahrenheit?

WRITING LINK

Expressive Writing—Poem Write a poem for your family that describes a hot day and a cold day. You could describe how your neighborhood looks, things people do, and how you feel.

SOCIAL STUDIES LINK

Early Thermometers Find out who invented the first thermometers and temperature scales and how the thermometers worked. Make a time line that shows what you learned.

TECHNOLOGY LINK

Visit the Harcourt Learning Site for related links, activities, and resources.
www.harcourtschool.com/ca

LESSON 2

How Can Thermal Energy Be Transferred?

In this lesson, you can . . .

 INVESTIGATE one way thermal energy is transferred.

 LEARN ABOUT the three ways thermal energy is transferred.

 LINK to math, writing, art, and technology.

◄ A glass blower uses a tube to blow air into hot glass. The long tube keeps heat from the glass away from his face. How can you tell the glass is hot?

E36

INVESTIGATE

Hot Air

Activity Purpose Have you ever watched a hawk soaring high in the sky? The hawk rides on air that is moving up. But what makes the air move up? In this investigation you will **observe** the effects of air moving up and **infer** why the air is moving up.

Materials
- sheet of construction paper
- scissors
- straight pin
- 20-cm piece of thread
- desk lamp
- bulb

Activity Procedure

1. **CAUTION** **Be careful when using scissors.** Cut out a spiral strip about 2 cm wide from the sheet of construction paper. (Picture A)

2. **CAUTION** **Be careful with the pin.** With the pin, carefully make a small hole through the center of the paper spiral. Tie the thread through the hole.

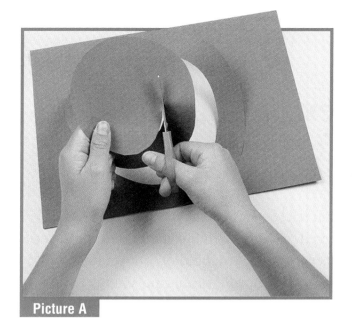

Picture A

Picture B

3 Hold the spiral above your head by the thread. Blow upward on it. **Observe** the spiral.

4 Carefully hold the spiral a few centimeters above the unlighted desk lamp. **Observe** the spiral.

5 Turn on the desk lamp. Let the bulb warm up for a few minutes.

6 Carefully hold the spiral a few centimeters above the lighted desk lamp. **Observe** the spiral. (Picture B)

Draw Conclusions

1. What did you **observe** in Steps 3, 4, and 6?

2. What caused the result you **observed** in Step 3?

3. What was different about Steps 4 and 6?

4. **Scientists at Work** Scientists often **infer** from **observations** a cause that they can't see directly. What do you think caused the result you observed in Step 6?

Investigate Further Hold the spiral a few centimeters away from the side of the lighted desk lamp. **Observe** the spiral. What can you **infer** from your observation?

Process Skill Tip

You need to **observe** what an object does in different situations before you can **infer** the causes of what it does.

E37

How Thermal Energy Is Transferred

FIND OUT

- what heat is
- three ways thermal energy is transferred

VOCABULARY

heat
conduction
convection
radiation
infrared radiation

Heat

When you touch an icicle, some of the thermal energy in your hand is transferred, or moved, to the icicle. Your hand gets colder. The icicle gets warmer. If you hold on long enough, the icicle melts completely. This transfer of thermal energy from one piece of matter to another is called **heat**.

Thermal energy is transferred naturally from hot matter to cold matter. When you walk in warm sand, some of the thermal energy from the sand moves to your feet. The soles of your feet get warmer. When your lips touch a cold can of soft drink, thermal energy is transferred from your lips to the can. Your lips lose thermal energy and get cooler. The can gains thermal energy and gets warmer.

Thermal energy is transferred in three ways—conduction, convection, and radiation. You will learn more about these processes on the next pages.

✔ **What is heat?**

◀ The burning gases from the artist's torch are very hot. A large amount of thermal energy moves to the metal where the gases touch it. The metal glows and quickly melts.

Conduction

You can tell if tap water is hot by touching the metal faucet it is running through. This works because the hot particles of water bump into the particles of the faucet and transfer some of their thermal energy. Soon the particles of the faucet have the same temperature as the particles of water. The transfer of thermal energy by particles of matter bumping into each other is called **conduction** (kuhn•DUHK•shuhn).

Thermal energy moves from an electric stove burner to a metal pot by conduction. Conduction happens every time you grab something hot or cold. Conduction can cause a painful burn from a hot pan.

Some kinds of matter don't conduct thermal energy well. A plastic-foam cup full of cocoa does not conduct well. The plastic foam's particles take a long time to speed up when the particles of hot cocoa bump

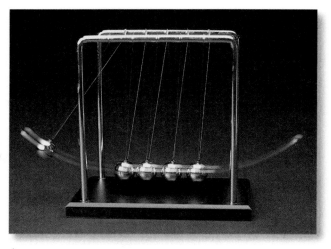

▲ A moving ball transfers motion energy when it bumps into its neighbor. A particle in matter transfers motion energy when it bumps into a nearby particle.

into them. Materials that don't conduct thermal energy well are called *insulators*. Materials that easily conduct thermal energy are called *conductors*. Most metals are good conductors.

✔ **What is conduction?**

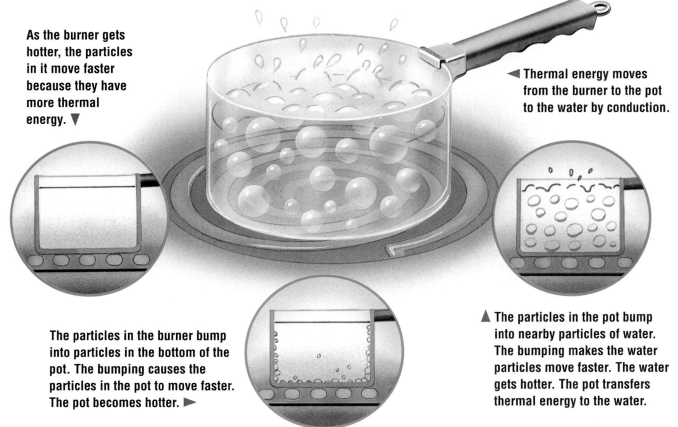

As the burner gets hotter, the particles in it move faster because they have more thermal energy. ▼

◄ Thermal energy moves from the burner to the pot to the water by conduction.

The particles in the burner bump into particles in the bottom of the pot. The bumping causes the particles in the pot to move faster. The pot becomes hotter. ▶

▲ The particles in the pot bump into nearby particles of water. The bumping makes the water particles move faster. The water gets hotter. The pot transfers thermal energy to the water.

E39

Convection

Unlike particles in solids, particles in liquids and gases move from one place to another. A large group of hot particles can move and transfer thermal energy. This type of energy transfer in a liquid or a gas is called **convection** (kuhn•VEK•shuhn).

In the investigation you held a paper spiral above a lighted bulb. The heated air above the light bulb moved enough to cause the spiral to twirl. Convection caused that movement.

As the air near a hot object gets hot, it takes up more space, or expands. You saw a balloon expand in the investigation on pages E30–E31. Because the hot air is less dense, it is forced up by the cooler, denser air around it.

As the hot air is forced up, it warms the air around it. The hot air cools. Its density increases, and it sinks. This process can repeat. The air can move in a circle—warming, being pushed up, cooling, sinking, and then warming again. This pattern of movement is called a *convection current*.

✔ **What is convection?**

The air above the stove gets warm. Cool air pushes in and forces the warm air up. The warm air moves through the room and transfers energy to the things around it.

◀ As cooler air pushes up air warmed by a campfire, sparks, smoke, and soot are pushed up also.

The warm air slowly cools and sinks to the floor.

Cool air moves toward the stove and forces up the warm air near the stove. Then the cool air is heated. This cycle of convection currents transfers thermal energy from the stove to the rest of the room.

A Hot-Air Balloon

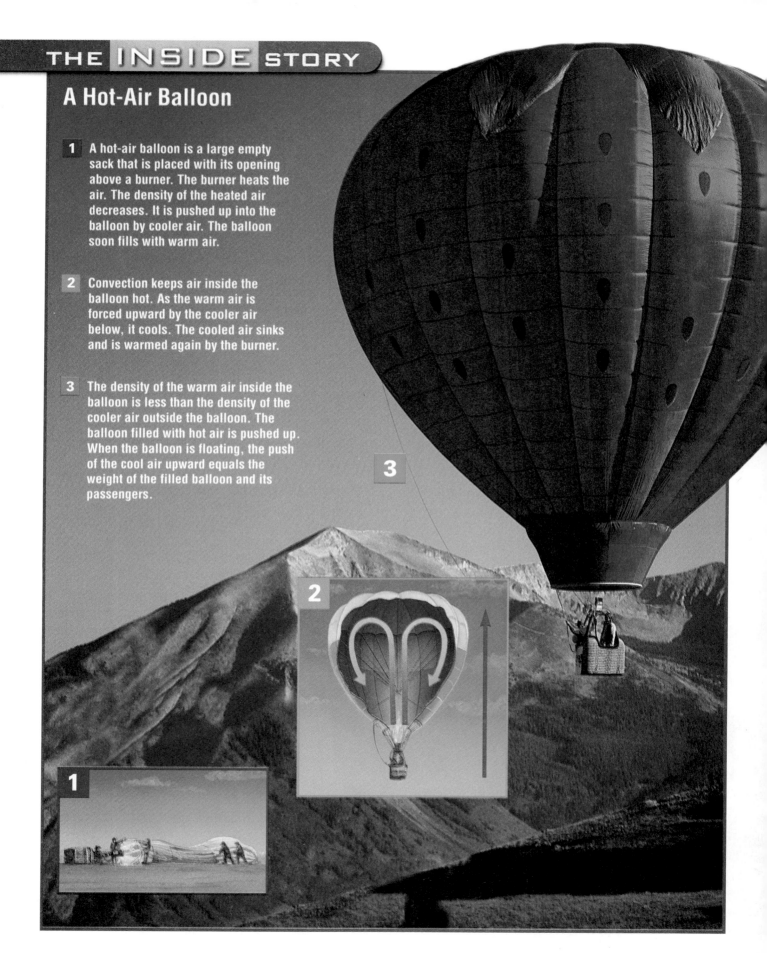

1 A hot-air balloon is a large empty sack that is placed with its opening above a burner. The burner heats the air. The density of the heated air decreases. It is pushed up into the balloon by cooler air. The balloon soon fills with warm air.

2 Convection keeps air inside the balloon hot. As the warm air is forced upward by the cooler air below, it cools. The cooled air sinks and is warmed again by the burner.

3 The density of the warm air inside the balloon is less than the density of the cooler air outside the balloon. The balloon filled with hot air is pushed up. When the balloon is floating, the push of the cool air upward equals the weight of the filled balloon and its passengers.

Radiation

The sun produces great amounts of thermal energy. But there's no matter between Earth and the sun to which it can transfer that energy. So energy can't reach Earth by conduction or convection. The sun transfers bundles of energy that can move through matter and empty space. Bundles of energy that move through matter and empty space are called **radiation** (ray•dee•AY•shuhn).

You sense some bundles of energy with your eyes. This radiation is visible light. You sense other bundles of energy with your skin. These bundles of energy are transferring heat. Bundles of energy that transfer heat are called **infrared** (in•fruh•RED) **radiation**. Outside on a sunny day, your skin feels warm because of infrared radiation from the sun.

Some things can transfer thermal energy by conduction, convection, and radiation at the same time. For example, the air above a

campfire is warmed by convection. This hot air quickly warms your hands by conduction. You can warm your hands around the sides of a campfire, too. But it is radiation, not hot air, that is warming them.

✔ **How is thermal energy transferred from the sun?**

▼ A gila (HEE•luh) monster warms its body by moving to a sunny place where its skin absorbs infrared radiation.

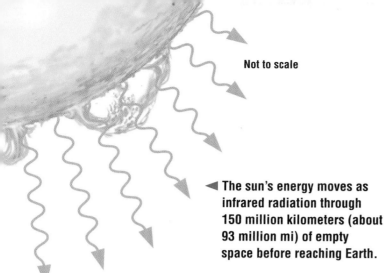

Not to scale

The sun's energy moves as infrared radiation through 150 million kilometers (about 93 million mi) of empty space before reaching Earth.

Summary

Heat is the transfer of thermal energy from one piece of matter to another. Thermal energy naturally moves from warm matter to cool matter. Conduction and convection need moving particles of matter to transfer thermal energy. Thermal energy is transferred as infrared radiation through matter and empty space.

Review

1. Which type of thermal-energy transfer requires moving liquids and gases?

2. How is thermal energy transferred through empty space?

3. How is thermal energy transferred when particles are touching?

4. **Critical Thinking** Which type of thermal-energy transfer is prevented when a baker uses a potholder to remove hot cookie sheets from an oven?

5. **Test Prep** What property must be different between two pieces of matter for thermal energy to be transferred between them?
   A density
   B mass
   C temperature
   D volume

LINKS

 MATH LINK

Figuring Cooling The ability of air conditioners to cool air is rated in British thermal units (Btus). It takes about 12,000 Btus to cool a room that measures 500 square feet. How many Btus are needed to cool a room with 100 square feet of floor space?

 WRITING LINK

Persuasive Writing—Business Letter Imagine that you are selling a furnace for a house to a homeowner. Write a letter describing the furnace and giving reasons for the homeowner to buy it.

ART LINK

Icons A "don't walk" sign that shows a walking person inside a circle with a slanted line across it is an icon. So is a smiley face. Design icons that show (1) heating by conduction, (2) heating by convection, and (3) heating by radiation.

 TECHNOLOGY LINK

Learn more about how thermal energy is used to shape glass by viewing *Glass Blowing* on the **Harcourt Science Newsroom Video** in your classroom video library.

How Is Thermal Energy Produced and Used?

In this lesson, you can . . .

INVESTIGATE temperatures in a solar cooker.

LEARN ABOUT ways to produce and use thermal energy.

LINK to math, writing, literature, and technology.

◄ Most people like pizza best when it is crisp and fresh from the oven. This pizza oven burns wood to produce thermal energy for baking. In what other ways is thermal energy produced and used?

INVESTIGATE

Temperatures in a Solar Cooker

Activity Purpose You know that heat from a campfire can cook hot dogs. Heat from the sun can cook them, too. A solar cooker uses a mirror to reflect, or bounce, infrared radiation from the sun to the food. In this activity you will make a mirror to reflect infrared radiation onto a thermometer. You will then **gather, record, display,** and **interpret data** about the temperatures in the cooker.

Materials

- 2 sheets of graph paper
- shoe-box lid
- aluminum foil
- tape
- thermometer
- clock or watch
- scissors
- poster board
- glue
- string

Activity Procedure

1. Label the two sheets of graph paper like the one shown on page E45.

2. Tape a piece of foil into the shoe-box lid. Place the thermometer in the lid. (Picture A)

3. Place the lid in sunlight. **Record** the temperature immediately. Then record the temperature each minute for 10 minutes.

4. In the shade, remove the thermometer from the shoe-box lid.

Temperature Change

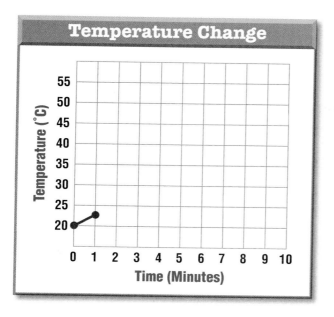

Picture A

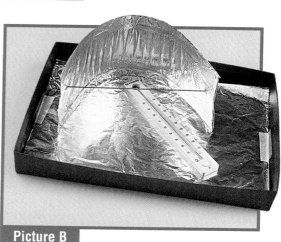

Picture B

5 Cut a rectangle of poster board 10 cm by 30 cm. Glue foil to one side. Let the glue dry for 10 minutes.

6 **CAUTION** Be careful when using scissors. Use scissors to punch a hole about 2 cm from each end of the rectangle. Make a curved reflector by drawing the poster board ends toward each other with string until they are about 20 cm apart. Tie the string.

7 Put the curved reflector in the shoe-box lid. Put the thermometer in the center of the curve. Repeat Step 3. (Picture B)

8 Make a line graph of the measurements in Step 3. Make another line graph of the measurements in Step 7.

Draw Conclusions

1. Describe the temperature changes shown on each graph.

2. **Compare** the temperature changes shown on the two graphs.

3. **Infer** what may have caused the differences in the temperatures on the two graphs.

4. **Scientists at Work** How does **displaying the data** in a graph help you **interpret** what happened to the temperature in Steps 3 and 7?

Process Skill Tip

When scientists **interpret data** in graphs, they look at the slants of the lines on the graphs. In your graphs a line with a steep slant means a fast change in temperature. A line with a less steep slant means a slower temperature change.

E45

Using Thermal Energy

Burning Fuel

FIND OUT

- ways to produce thermal energy
- uses of the sun's energy
- examples of wasted thermal energy

VOCABULARY

fuel
solar energy

When something burns, it gets hot. Burning releases thermal energy. Many homes are heated by furnaces that burn oil or natural gas. Some cooking stoves burn natural gas. Any material that can burn is called a **fuel**. Wood was the first fuel people used, and it is still used today. Wood contains a substance called carbon. When wood burns, the carbon combines with oxygen from the air. Together they form a new substance called carbon dioxide. As the wood burns, energy stored in the wood is released as thermal energy and light.

Many fuels contain carbon. Coal is mainly carbon. Fuel oil and natural gas both contain carbon. Much of the thermal energy people use today comes from burning fuels that contain carbon.

✔ **What happens when a fuel burns?**

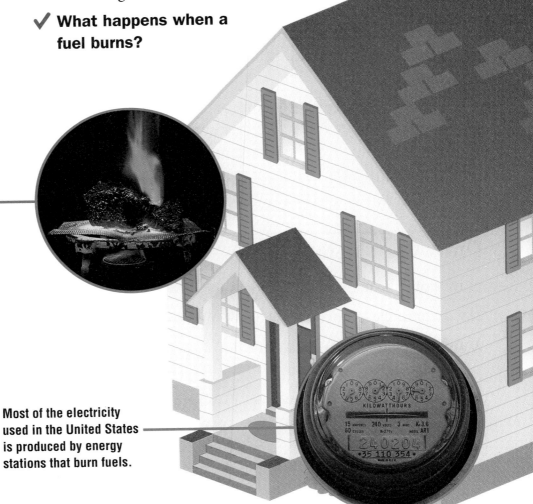

Burning coal releases thermal energy. In some houses the energy is used to warm air directly. In others it is used to heat water in radiators. Like the burner below the coal, a gas stove burns natural gas. The thermal energy released from the flame is used for cooking and baking.

Most of the electricity used in the United States is produced by energy stations that burn fuels.

Solar Energy

The energy given off by the sun is called **solar energy**. People use solar energy to heat water. They put solar panels on top of their roofs. The panels absorb infrared radiation from the sun. The radiation heats water flowing through the panels. The hot water can be used for washing. Solar energy also heats some homes and businesses.

Solar energy can also be used to cook. A solar cooker gathers infrared radiation from the sun and reflects it onto food. You know this works because you measured temperature change in a solar cooker in the investigation.

The sun is the source of most energy on Earth. Even the thermal energy in fossil fuels, such as coal and oil, came from the sun. These fuels have stored energy from plants and animals that lived long ago. The plants used the sun's energy to make food by photosynthesis. The animals got their energy by eating plants or other animals.

✔ **What is solar energy?**

Rooftop solar panels like these are used to heat water.

An electric water heater contains a tank of water. Under the tank is an electric heating coil.

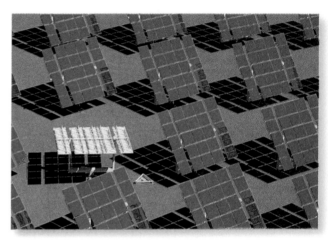

▲ These mirrors focus the sun's thermal energy on a target. The thermal energy gathered in the target is used to produce electricity.

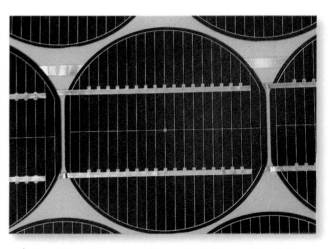

▲ Small appliances such as calculators and watches often use solar cells to supply electricity. Solar cells can also keep batteries charged.

Waste Heat

Using fuel for energy has a side effect. It often makes thermal energy that no one wants or needs. This unneeded thermal energy is called *waste heat*. For example, a campfire produces thermal energy even if the campers need it only for light. Even a campfire used for warmth sends most of its thermal energy straight up, where it is not useful to campers.

Common light sources such as candles and bulbs also make waste heat. So do car engines, electric energy stations, computers, and people. Almost any time energy is produced or used, thermal energy is a part of the process. Much of that thermal energy is not useful, and it can even be harmful. It must be gotten rid of. For example, cars have radiators to carry thermal energy that is not needed away from the engine.

✔ **What is waste heat?**

▲ Light bulbs give off both light and heat. But most of the thermal energy from light bulbs in your home is waste heat.

A candle produces less light than a light bulb but can produce more thermal energy. Most of the thermal energy from candles is not used. ▶

Electric energy stations can't change all thermal energy from fuel into electricity. There is always some waste heat produced. One way to remove this waste heat is to let it heat water. The hot water then cools in towers or ponds. ▼

Fans and radiators carry waste heat away from a car engine. If either the fan or the radiator stops working, the engine soon overheats and stops working as well. ▼

Radiator

▲ Large, very fast computers need special cooling systems such as this one to get rid of waste heat from wiring and circuits.

Summary

Much of the thermal energy used by people today comes from burning fuels that contain carbon. Energy given off by the sun is called solar energy. Solar energy can be used to heat homes and businesses, heat water, and cook food. Most processes that use energy also produce thermal energy. If this thermal energy isn't useful, it is waste heat.

Review

1. What is a fuel?
2. What happens when a fuel burns?
3. What do we call energy given off by the sun?
4. **Critical Thinking** What happens to most waste heat?
5. **Test Prep** Which of the following removes waste heat?
   A car radiator
   B solar cell
   C stove burner
   D windmill

LINKS

MATH LINK

Waste Heat A water heater produces a total of 500 Btus of thermal energy each hour. Only 400 Btus go to heat water. How much waste heat is produced per hour? How much waste heat is produced in a 24-hour day?

WRITING LINK

Persuasive Writing—Opinion A new kind of light bulb, called a compact fluorescent bulb, produces less waste heat than an incandescent light bulb. Write an ad telling consumers why you think they should use this new bulb.

LITERATURE LINK

A Cold Time in the North In Jack London's short story "To Build a Fire," a man lost in the wilderness has a lot of trouble getting thermal energy. Read the story and suggest other ways the man might have kept warm.

TECHNOLOGY LINK

Learn more about fossil fuels and thermal energy by visiting this Internet site.
www.scilinks.org/harcourt

Refrigerants

Hot weather and high humidity can be unpleasant. For some people, such as older people or those with lung diseases, heat can even be dangerous. Their bodies don't work well enough to stay cool. They need to be kept cool by air conditioning.

Air Conditioning

You already know that when thermal energy moves from one place to another, the place it moves *to* gets hotter. The place it moves *from* gets colder. That's part of what makes air conditioners work.

An air conditioner is a machine that uses energy to move heat in the opposite direction from where it would flow on its own. An air conditioner moves heat from inside a house to the outdoors, where it's hotter. To do this, an air conditioner uses a material called a *refrigerant* (ree•FRIJ•er•uhnt).

In an air conditioner, liquid refrigerant is pumped under pressure through tubes. In the part of the air conditioner that is inside

Outdoors

Refrigerant tube

Indoors

the house, the refrigerant gets thermal energy from the air. This causes it to boil. The refrigerant, which is now a gas, is pumped to the part of the air conditioner that is outside the house. There the gas is squeezed and changed back to a liquid. It must lose thermal energy to do this. The thermal energy moves to the outside air.

The first refrigerant used was ammonia (uh•MOHN•yuh). It's still used for large refrigerators in factories. It has an unpleasant smell, however, and it is a poison. Leaks of ammonia, common in the first air conditioners, can cause breathing problems for any people nearby. The second refrigerant used was methyl chloride (METH•uhl KLOR•eyed). But when methyl chloride leaked into the air, it exploded.

Freon

Freon (FREE•ahn) is a colorless, tasteless, odorless gas that doesn't explode and does not make people ill. It also boils at a temperature that works best for refrigerants. So when Thomas Midgley discovered Freon, he thought he'd found the perfect refrigerant.

Freon made home air conditioners and modern refrigerators possible. From its discovery in the 1930s until the 1990s, Freon was almost the only refrigerant used. In the 1970s, however, scientists discovered that Freon and similar refrigerants harm Earth's protective ozone layer. So the use of Freon as a refrigerant was banned in the United States. Scientists started looking for other materials to use.

Old and New Refrigerants

Ammonia and other "old" refrigerants may be used to replace Freon in refrigerators and home air conditioners. New

machines use less ammonia and are sealed more tightly. Other substances that are like Freon but are less damaging are being developed. However, none of these materials work very well in cars, where refrigerants sometimes must both heat and cool the air. Scientists at the University of Illinois are testing ordinary carbon dioxide gas as a refrigerant for cars. So, some of the gas that you breathe out may end up cooling you off!

Think About It

1. Why do you think refrigerant leaks were so common in early air conditioners?
2. Where does the thermal energy that leaves an air-conditioned home go?

WEB LINK:
For Science and Technology updates, visit the Harcourt Internet site.
www.harcourtschool.com/ca

Careers   HVAC Technician

What They Do
HVAC (heating, ventilation, and air conditioning) technicians install, repair, and maintain heating and cooling systems. These systems may be in buildings, vehicles, or machinery such as the refrigerator in your home.

Education and Training   Most HVAC technicians need a high-school education that includes math, electricity, and technical drawing. Most employers prefer technicians to have also finished either a two-year apprenticeship or a technical program.

Frederick McKinley Jones

INVENTOR

Frederick Jones was an orphan by the age of nine and quit school after sixth grade. He was sent to live with a Catholic priest in Kentucky. As an older teenager, he moved to Minnesota and began a job fixing farm machinery. He studied electricity and mechanical engineering when he wasn't working.

Jones served in World War I. When he came back from the war, he built a radio transmitter in his town. He also invented machine parts so that movies with sound could be run on small projectors. During the early 1930s, he heard a man who owned trucks telling his boss that a whole shipment of chicken had spoiled because of the heat. Jones began to design a refrigeration unit for trucks.

Earlier ways to keep trucks cold took up too much room. Most also fell apart quickly because of being shaken during travel. Jones built his first refrigeration unit by using odds and ends of machine parts. It was small, shake-proof, and lightweight. But it was made to go beneath the truck and broke down often because mud and dirt from roads got inside.

After a time, Jones designed and made a unit that went on top of a truck. He and his boss formed a partnership to build the trucks. Jones was vice-president of the company.

The refrigerated trucks could ship more than food. During World War II, Jones's invention saved lives. Because the units were portable, badly needed blood and medicine could be shipped safely to battlefields.

Jones continued to work on his inventions. He eventually received more than 60 patents. More than 40 of them were for refrigeration products.

THINK ABOUT IT

1. What were some design problems that Jones solved to make a working truck-refrigerator?

2. What foods do you eat that might be shipped in a refrigerated truck?

Modern refrigerated truck

Compare Conductors

Which material conducts thermal energy fastest?

Materials

- 3 thermometers
- warm tap water
- tape
- jar

- plastic, wood, and metal spoons of about the same size

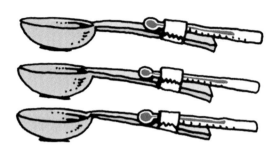

Procedure

1. Carefully tape the bulb of a thermometer to the handle of each spoon.

2. Fill the jar with warm tap water to a level that will cover only the bottoms of the spoons. Carefully place the spoons in the jar.

3. Measure and record the temperature of each spoon every minute for 5 minutes.

Draw Conclusions

Which spoon conducted thermal energy most quickly? How do you know?

Thermal Energy

How do different amounts of water affect melting?

Materials

- warm tap water
- 2 jars, 1 large and 1 small
- 4 ice cubes that are the same size
- clock or watch

Procedure

1. Fill each container almost full with warm tap water.

2. Put two ice cubes in each container.

3. Measure the time it takes for each pair of cubes to melt completely.

Draw Conclusions

Did one pair melt faster than the other pair? Why were the times different?

Chapter ② Review and Test Preparation

Vocabulary Review

Use the terms below to complete the sentences. The page numbers in ( ) tell you where to look in the chapter if you need help.

energy (E32)
thermal energy (E32)
temperature (E33)
heat (E38)
conduction (E39)
convection (E40)
radiation (E42)
infrared radiation (E42)
fuel (E46)
solar energy (E47)

1. ____ is the transfer of thermal energy.

2. The ability to cause a change is ____.

3. A material that is burned to produce thermal energy is ____.

4. ____ is a measure of the average energy of motion of particles in matter.

5. The total energy of motion of particles of matter is ____.

6. ____ is the transfer of heat by particles bumping into each other.

7. Radiation that transfers heat is called ____.

8. ____ is bundles of energy that can travel through empty space.

9. Energy given off by the sun is called ____.

10. ____ is the heat transfer that can occur only in a liquid or gas.

Connect Concepts

Fill in the blanks in the diagram below to correctly describe some of the main concepts of this chapter.

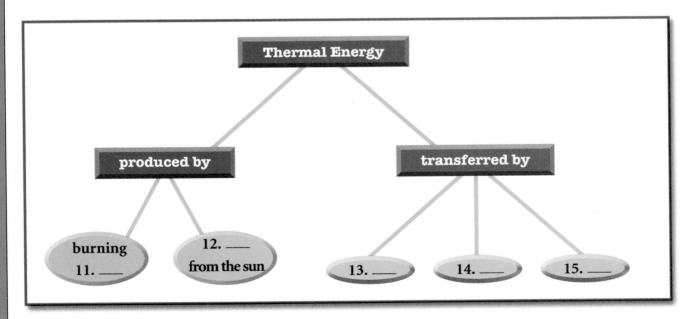

Thermal Energy

produced by   transferred by

burning   11. ____

12. ____ from the sun

13. ____   14. ____   15. ____

Check Understanding

Write the letter of the best choice.

16. Most thermometers work because matter ____ when it is heated.
    A disappears
    B collects radiation
    C expands
    D loses mass

17. A thermometer measures the ____ energy of motion of particles of matter.
    F total   H solar
    G long-term   J average

18. Two pieces of the same kind of matter have the same temperature. The one with the larger mass has more —
    A conduction
    B thermal energy
    C convection
    D solar energy

19. When thermal energy moves from one piece of matter to another, the transfer is called —
    F solar energy H temperature
    G heat   J fuel

20. Thermal energy can be transferred by conduction from one piece of matter to another only if the two pieces are —
    A liquids   C solids
    B touching   D fuel

21. Convection takes place only in liquids and —
    F gases   H solids
    G energies   J states

22. Thermal energy that travels from the sun to Earth is being transferred by —
    A conduction C convection
    B fuel   D radiation

Critical Thinking

23. You put a pot of water on the burner of an electric stove and turn the burner on high heat. The water soon boils. Describe how the heat from the stove gets to the water in the pot.

24. A solar panel on a roof collects solar energy to warm water for a house. Describe how the heat is transferred from the sun to the panel, and then from the panel to the water.

Process Skills Review

25. What property of particles of matter do you **measure** with a thermometer?

26. Suppose a thermometer is hanging from a thread inside a jar completely empty of gases or liquids. You **infer** that infrared radiation is falling on the thermometer. What observation would lead you to this inference? Explain.

27. A line graph has the temperature scale on the left and the time scale on the bottom. If the line is level, what can you conclude by **interpreting** the temperature **data** shown?

Performance Assessment

Temperature Balance

Your teacher will give you a thermometer, a straw, a full glass of warm water, a full glass of cool water, and an empty glass. Your goal is to use the materials to end up with a glass that is half full of water that is about room temperature. You can't wait for the two full glasses to cool and warm naturally. Explain what you did and why it worked.

References

Planning an Investigation

When scientists observe something they want to study, they use the method of scientific inquiry to plan and conduct their study. They use science process skills as tools to help them gather, organize, analyze, and present their information. This plan will help you use scientific inquiry and process skills to work like a scientist.

Step 1—Observe and ask questions.

Which soil works best for planting marigold seeds?

- Use your senses to make observations.

- Record a question you would like to answer.

Step 2—Make a hypothesis.

My hypothesis: Marigold seeds sprout best in potting soil.

- Choose one possible answer, or hypothesis, to your question.

- Write your hypothesis in a complete sentence.

- Think about what investigation you can do to test your hypothesis.

Step 3—Plan your test.

I'll put identical seeds in three different kinds of soil.

- Write down the steps you will follow to do your test. Decide how to conduct a fair test by controlling variables.

- Decide what equipment you will need.

- Decide how you will gather and record your data.

Step 4 — Conduct your test.

I'll make sure to record my observations each day. Each flowerpot will get the same amount of water and light.

- Follow the steps you wrote.
- Observe and measure carefully.
- Record everything that happens.
- Organize your data so that you can study it carefully.

Step 5 — Draw conclusions and share results.

Hmm. My hypothesis was not correct. The seeds sprouted equally well in potting soil and sandy soil. They didn't sprout at all in clay soil.

- Analyze the data you gathered.
- Make charts, graphs, or tables to show your data.
- Write a conclusion. Describe the evidence you used to determine whether your test supported your hypothesis.
- Decide whether your hypothesis was correct.

Investigate Further

I wonder if a combination of soils would work best. Maybe I'll try...

Using Science Tools

Using a Hand Lens

A hand lens magnifies objects, or makes them look larger than they are.

1. Hold the hand lens about 12 centimeters (5 in.) from your eye.

2. Bring the object toward you until it comes into focus.

Using a Thermometer

A thermometer measures the temperature of air and most liquids.

1. Place the thermometer in the liquid. Don't touch the thermometer any more than you need to. Never stir the liquid with the thermometer. If you are measuring the temperature of the air, make sure that the thermometer is not in line with a direct light source.

2. Move so that your eyes are even with the liquid in the thermometer.

3. If you are measuring a material that is not being heated or cooled, wait about two minutes for the reading to become stable, or stay the same. Find the scale line that meets the top of the liquid in the thermometer, and read the temperature.

4. If the material you are measuring is being heated or cooled, you will not be able to wait before taking your measurements. Measure as quickly as you can.

Caring for and Using a Microscope

A microscope is another tool that magnifies objects. A microscope can increase the detail you see by increasing the number of times an object is magnified.

Caring for a Microscope

- Always use two hands when you carry a microscope.
- Never touch any of the lenses of a microscope with your fingers.

Using a Microscope

1. Raise the eyepiece as far as you can by using the coarse-adjustment knob. Place your slide on the stage.

2. Always start by using the lowest power. The lowest-power lens is usually the shortest. Start with the lens in the lowest position it can go without touching the slide.

3. Look through the eyepiece, and begin adjusting it upward with the coarse-adjustment knob. When the slide is close to being in focus, use the fine-adjustment knob.

4. When you want to use a higher-power lens, first focus the slide under low power. Then, watching carefully to make sure that the lens will not hit the slide, turn the higher-power lens into place. Use only the fine-adjustment knob when looking through the higher-power lens.

You may use a Brock microscope. This is a sturdy microscope that has only one lens.

1. Place the object to be viewed on the stage.

2. Look through the eyepiece, and begin raising the tube until the object comes into focus.

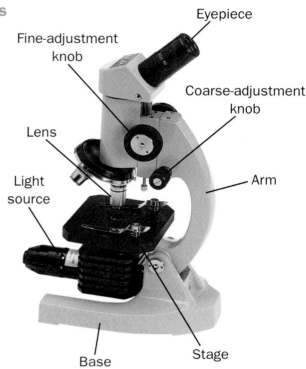

Eyepiece
Fine-adjustment knob
Coarse-adjustment knob
Lens
Arm
Light source
Base
Stage

A Light Microscope

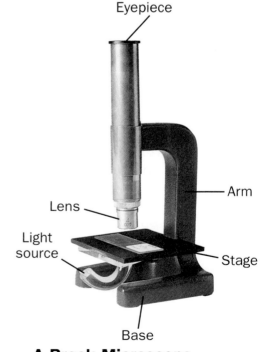

Eyepiece
Arm
Lens
Light source
Stage
Base

A Brock Microscope

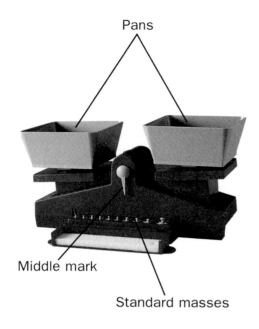

Pans

Middle mark

Standard masses

Using a Balance

Use a balance to measure an object's mass. Mass is the amount of matter an object has.

1. Look at the pointer on the base to make sure the empty pans are balanced.
2. Place the object you wish to measure in the left-hand pan.
3. Add the standard masses to the other pan. As you add masses, you should see the pointer move. When the pointer is at the middle mark, the pans are balanced.
4. Add the numbers on the masses you used. The total is the mass in grams of the object you measured.

Using a Spring Scale

Use a spring scale to measure forces such as the pull of gravity on objects. You measure weight and other forces in units called newtons (N).

Measuring the Weight of an Object

1. Hook the spring scale to the object.
2. Lift the scale and object with a smooth motion. Do not jerk them upward.
3. Wait until any motion of the spring comes to a stop. Then read the number of newtons from the scale.

Measuring the Force to Move an Object

1. With the object resting on a table, hook the spring scale to it.
2. Pull the object smoothly across the table. Do not jerk the object.
3. As you pull, read the number of newtons you are using to pull the object.

Measuring Liquids

Use a beaker, a measuring cup, or a graduate to measure liquids accurately.

1. Pour the liquid you want to measure into a measuring container. Put your measuring container on a flat surface, with the measuring scale facing you.

2. Look at the liquid through the container. Move so that your eyes are even with the surface of the liquid in the container.

3. To read the volume of the liquid, find the scale line that is even with the surface of the liquid.

4. If the surface of the liquid is not exactly even with a line, estimate the volume of the liquid. Decide which line the liquid is closer to, and use that number.

Beaker   **Graduate**

Using a Ruler or Meterstick

Use a ruler or meterstick to measure distances and to find lengths of objects.

1. Place the zero mark or end of the ruler or meterstick next to one end of the distance or object you want to measure.

2. On the ruler or meterstick, find the place next to the other end of the distance or object.

3. Look at the scale on the ruler or meterstick. This will show the distance you want or the length of the object.

Using a Timing Device

Use a timing device such as a stopwatch to measure time.

1. Reset the stopwatch to zero.

2. When you are ready to begin timing, press *Start*.

3. As soon as you are ready to stop timing, press *Stop*.

4. The numbers on the dial or display show how many minutes, seconds, and parts of seconds have passed.

Using a Computer

A computer can help you communicate with others and can help you get information. It is a tool you can use to write reports, make graphs and charts, and do research.

Writing Reports

To write a report with a computer, use a word processing software program. After you are in the program, type your report. By using certain keys and the mouse, you can control how the words look, move words, delete or add words and copy them, check your spelling, and print your report.

Save your work to the desktop or hard disk of the computer, or to a floppy disk. You can go back to your saved work later if you want to revise it.

There are many reasons for revising your work. You may find new information to add or mistakes you want to correct. You may want to change the way you report your information because of who will read it. Computers make revising easy. You delete what you don't want, add the new parts, and then save. You can save different versions of your work if you want to.

For a science lab report, it is important to show the same kinds of information each time. With a computer,

you can make a general format for a lab report, save the format, and then use it again and again.

Making Graphs and Charts

You can make a graph or chart with most word processing software programs. You can also use special software programs such as *Data ToolKit* or *Graph Links*. With *Graph Links* you can make pictographs and circle, bar, line, and double-line graphs.

First, decide what kind of graph or chart will best communicate your data. Sometimes it's easiest to do this by sketching your ideas on paper. Then you can decide what format and categories you need for your graph or chart. Choose that format

for the program. Then type your information. Most software programs include a tutorial that gives you step-by-step directions for making a graph or chart.

Doing Research

Computers can help you find current information from all over the world through the Internet. The Internet connects thousands of computer sites that have been set up by schools, libraries, museums, and many other organizations.

Get permission from an adult before you log on to the Internet. Find out the rules for Internet use at school or at home. Then log on and go to a search engine, which will help you find what you need. Type in keywords, words that tell the subject of your search. If you get too much information that isn't exactly about the topic, make your keywords more specific. When you find the information you need, save it or print it.

Harcourt Science tells you about many Internet sites related to what you are studying. To find out about these sites, called Web sites, look for Technology Links in the lessons in this book. If you need to contact other people to help in your research, you can use e-mail. Log into your e-mail program, type the address of the person you want to reach, type your message, and send it. Be

sure to have adult permission before sending or receiving e-mail.

Another way to use a computer for research is to access CD-ROMs. These are discs that look like music CDs. CD-ROMs can hold huge amounts of data, including words, still pictures, audio, and video. Encyclopedias, dictionaries, almanacs, and other sources of information are available on CD-ROMs. These computer discs are valuable resources for your research.

How to Use a Table of Diagnostic Properties

Use this table to identify minerals in the Investigate Further on page B35 and in the Performance Assessment on page B59. The table lists some common minerals and their properties. The minerals are separated into two groups by luster—metallic or nonmetallic. In each group, minerals are listed in order of increasing hardness (Mohs' scale).

To identify an unknown mineral sample, first observe its luster, hardness, color, and streak. Choose the group for the correct luster. Then use the hardness of the sample to narrow down your choices. Finally, use the color and streak of the sample to select the correct mineral name.

Minerals with Metallic Luster				
Mineral	**Color**	**Streak**	**Hardness**	**Uses and other properties**
silver	silvery white, tarnishes to black	light gray to silver	2.5	coins, fillings for teeth, jewelry, silver plate, wires; malleable and ductile
galena	gray	gray to black	2.5	source of lead, used in pipes, shields for X rays, fishing equipment sinkers
gold	pale to golden yellow	yellow	2.5–3	jewelry, money, gold leaf, fillings for teeth, medicines; does not tarnish
chalcopyrite	brassy to golden yellow	greenish black	3.5–4	main ore of copper
chromite	black or brown	brown to black	5.5	ore of chromium, stainless steel, metallurgical bricks
hematite	black or reddish brown	red or reddish brown	6	source of iron; roasted in a blast furnace, converted to "pig" iron, made into steel
magnetite	black	black	6	source of iron, naturally magnetic, called lodestone
pyrite	light brassy yellow	greenish black	6.5	source of iron, "fool's gold," alters to limonite

Minerals with Nonmetallic Luster

Mineral	Color	Streak	Hardness	Uses and other properties
talc	white, greenish	white	1	easily cut with fingernail; used for talcum powder; soapstone; is used in paper and for table tops
bauxite	gray, red, white, brown	gray	1–3	source of aluminum; used in paints, aluminum foil, and airplane parts
gypsum	colorless, gray, white, brown	white	2	used extensively in the preparation of plaster of paris, alabaster, and drywall for building construction
sphalerite	brown	pale yellow	3.5–4	main ore of zinc; used in paints, dyes, and medicine
muscovite	white, light gray, yellow, rose, green	colorless	2.5	occurs in large flexible plates; used as an insulator in electrical equipment, lubricant
biotite	black to dark brown	colorless	2.5	occurs in large flexible plates
calcite	colorless, white, pale, blue	colorless, white	3	fizzes when HCl is added; used in cements and other building materials
fluorite	colorless, white, blue, green, red, yellow, purple	colorless	4	used in the manufacture of optical equipment; glows under ultraviolet light
hornblende	green to black	gray to white	5–6	will transmit light on thin edges; 6-sided cross section
feldspar (orthoclase)	colorless, white to gray, green, and yellow	colorless	6	insoluble in acids; used in the manufacture of porcelain
feldspar (plagioclase)	gray, green, white	colorless	6	used in ceramics; striations present on some faces
quartz	colorless, various colors	colorless	7	used in glass manufacture, electronic equipment, radios, computers, watches, gemstones
topaz	white, pink, yellow, pale blue, colorless	colorless	8	valuable gemstone
corundum	colorless, blue, brown, green, white, pink	colorless	9	gemstones; ruby is red, sapphire is blue; industrial abrasive

Measurement Systems

SI Measures (Metric)

Temperature
Ice melts at 0 degrees Celsius (°C)
Water freezes at 0°C
Water boils at 100°C

Length and Distance
1000 meters (m) = 1 kilometer (km)
100 centimeters (cm) = 1 m
10 millimeters (mm) = 1 cm

Force
1 newton (N) = 1 kilogram ×
   1 meter/second/second (kg-m/s^2)

Volume
1 cubic meter (m^3) = 1m × 1m × 1m
1 cubic centimeter (cm^3) =
   1 cm × 1 cm × 1 cm
1 liter (L) = 1000 milliliters (mL)
1 cm^3 = 1 mL

Area
1 square kilometer (km^2) =
   1 km × 1 km
1 hectare = 10 000 m^2

Mass
1000 grams (g) = 1 kilogram (kg)
1000 milligrams (mg) = 1 g

Rates (Metric and Customary)
kmh = kilometers per hour
m/s = meters per second
mph = miles per hour

Customary Measures

Volume of Fluids
8 fluid ounces (fl oz) = 1 cup (c)
2 c = 1 pint (pt)
2 pt = 1 quart (qt)
4 qt = 1 gallon (gal)

Temperature
Ice melts at 32 degrees
   Fahrenheit (°F)
Water freezes at 32°F
Water boils at 212°F

Length and Distance
12 inches (in.) = 1 foot (ft)
3 ft = 1 yard (yd)
5,280 ft = 1 mile (mi)

Weight
16 ounces (oz) = 1 pound (lb)
2,000 pounds = 1 ton (T)

Health Handbook

Good Nutrition

The Food Guide Pyramid

No one food or food group supplies everything your body needs for good health. That's why it's important to eat foods from all the food groups. The Food Guide Pyramid can help you choose healthful foods in the right amounts. By choosing more foods from the groups at the bottom of the pyramid and fewer foods from the group at the top, you will eat the foods that provide your body with energy to grow and develop.

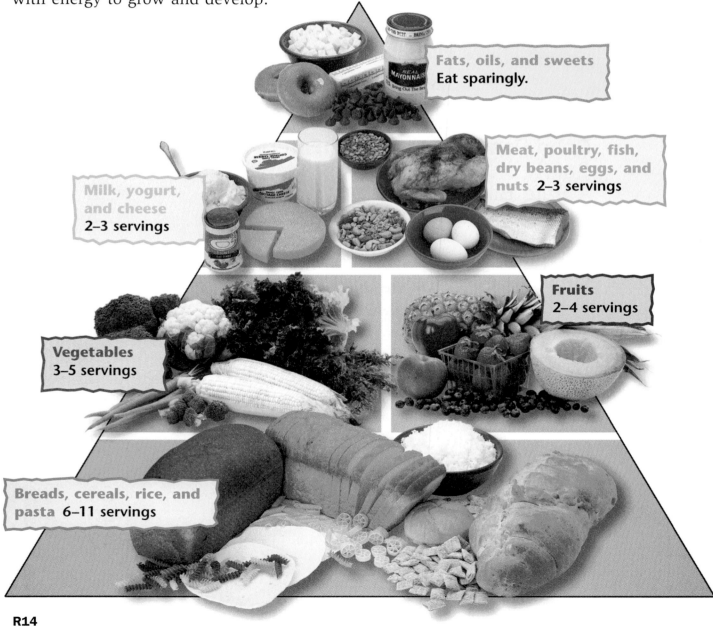

Fats, oils, and sweets
Eat sparingly.

Meat, poultry, fish, dry beans, eggs, and nuts 2–3 servings

Milk, yogurt, and cheese
2–3 servings

Fruits 2–4 servings

Vegetables 3–5 servings

Breads, cereals, rice, and pasta 6–11 servings

Estimating Serving Sizes

Choosing a variety of foods is only half the story. You also need to choose the right amounts. The table below can help you estimate the number of servings you are eating of your favorite foods.

Food Group	Amount of Food in One Serving	Some Easy Ways to Estimate Serving Size
Bread, Cereal, Rice, and Pasta Group	1 ounce ready-to-eat (dry) cereal	large handful of plain cereal or a small handful of cereal with raisins and nuts
	1 slice bread, $\frac{1}{2}$ bagel	
	$\frac{1}{2}$ cup cooked pasta, rice, or cereal	ice cream scoop
Vegetable Group	1 cup of raw, leafy vegetables	about the size of a fist
	$\frac{1}{2}$ cup other vegetables, cooked or raw, chopped	
	$\frac{3}{4}$ cup vegetable juice	
	$\frac{1}{2}$ cup tomato sauce	ice cream scoop
Fruit Group	medium apple, pear, or orange	a baseball
	$\frac{1}{2}$ large banana or one medium banana	
	$\frac{1}{2}$ cup chopped or cooked fruit	
	$\frac{3}{4}$ cup of fruit juice	
Milk, Yogurt, and Cheese Group	$1\frac{1}{2}$ ounces of natural cheese	two dominoes
	2 ounces of processed cheese	$1\frac{1}{2}$ slices of packaged cheese
	1 cup of milk or yogurt	
Meat, Poultry, Fish, Dry Beans, Eggs, and Nuts Group	3 ounces of lean meat, chicken, or fish	about the size of your palm
	2 tablespoons peanut butter	
	$\frac{1}{2}$ cup of cooked dry beans	
Fats, Oils, and Sweets Group	1 teaspoon of margarine or butter	about the size of the tip of your thumb

Preparing Foods Safely

Fight Bacteria

You probably already know to throw away food that smells bad or looks moldy. But food doesn't have to look or smell bad to make you ill. To keep your food safe and yourself from becoming ill, follow the steps outlined in the picture below. And remember—when in doubt, throw it out!

FIGHT BAC!

Keep Food Safe From Bacteria

CLEAN Wash hands and surfaces often.

SEPARATE Don't cross-contaminate.

CHILL Refrigerate promptly.

COOK Cook to proper temperatures.

BAC

™

Food Safety Tips

Tips for Preparing Food

- Wash hands in warm, soapy water before preparing food. It's also a good idea to wash hands after preparing each dish.

- Defrost meat in the microwave or the refrigerator.

- Keep raw meat, poultry, fish, and their juices away from other food.

- Wash cutting boards, knives, and countertops immediately after cutting up meat, poultry, or fish. Never use the same cutting board for meats and vegetables without washing the board first.

Tips for Cooking Food

- Cook all food completely, especially meat. Complete cooking kills the bacteria that can make you ill.

- Red meats should be cooked to a temperature of 160°F. Poultry should be cooked to 180°F. When done, fish flakes easily with a fork.

- Never eat food that contains raw eggs or raw egg yolks, including cookie dough.

Tips for Cleaning Up the Kitchen

- Wash all dishes, utensils, and countertops with hot, soapy water. Use a soap that kills bacteria, if possible.

- Store leftovers in small containers that will cool quickly in the refrigerator. Don't leave leftovers on the counter to cool.

Being Physically Active

Planning Your Weekly Activities

Being active every day is important for your overall health. Physical activity helps you manage stress, maintain a healthful weight, and strengthen your body systems. The Activity Pyramid, like the Food Guide Pyramid, can help you choose a variety of activities in the right amounts to keep your body strong and healthy.

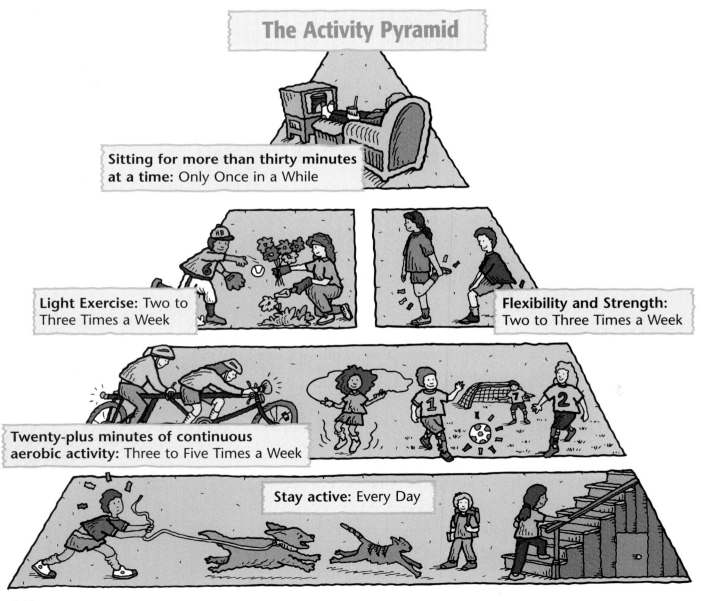

The Activity Pyramid

Sitting for more than thirty minutes at a time: Only Once in a While

Light Exercise: Two to Three Times a Week

Flexibility and Strength: Two to Three Times a Week

Twenty-plus minutes of continuous aerobic activity: Three to Five Times a Week

Stay active: Every Day

Guidelines for a Good Workout

There are three things you should do every time you are going to exercise—warm up, work out, and cool down.

Warm-Up When you warm up, your heart rate, breathing rate, and body temperature increase and more blood flows to your muscles. As your body warms up, you can move more easily. People who warm up are less stiff after exercising, and are less likely to have exercise-related injuries. Your warm-up should include five minutes of stretching, and five minutes of low-level exercise.

Workout The main part of your exercise routine should be an aerobic exercise that lasts 20 to 30 minutes. Aerobic exercises make your heart, lungs, and circulatory system stronger.

You may want to mix up the types of activities you do. This helps you work different muscles, and provides a better workout over time.

Cool-Down When you finish your aerobic exercise, you need to give your body time to cool down. Start your cool-down with three to five minutes of low-level activity. End with stretching exercises to prevent soreness and stiffness.

Using a Computer Safely

Good Posture at the Computer

Good posture is important when using the computer. To help prevent eyestrain, stress, and injuries, follow the posture tips shown below. Also remember to grasp the mouse lightly and take frequent breaks for stretching.

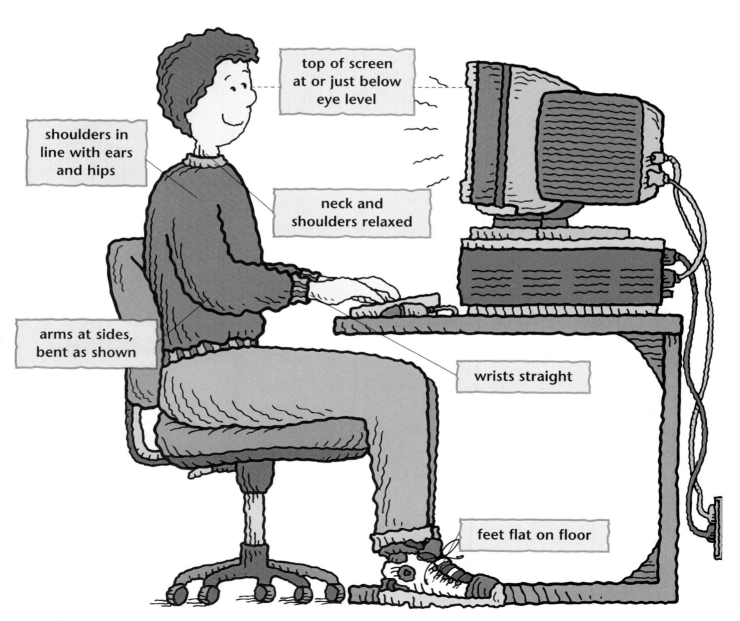

top of screen at or just below eye level

shoulders in line with ears and hips

neck and shoulders relaxed

arms at sides, bent as shown

wrists straight

feet flat on floor

Safety on the Internet

You can use the Internet for fun, education, research, and more. But like anything else, you should use the Internet with caution. Some people compare the Internet to a real city—not all the people there are people you want to meet and not all the places you can go are places you want to be. Just like in a real city, you have to use common sense and follow safety rules to protect yourself. Below are some easy rules to follow to help you stay safe on-line.

Rules for On-line Safety

- Talk with an adult family member to set up rules for going on-line. Decide what time of day you can go on-line, how long you can be on-line, and appropriate places you can visit. Do not access other areas or break the rules you establish.

- Don't give out information like your address, telephone number, your picture, or the name or location of your school.

- If you find any information on-line that makes you uncomfortable, or if you receive a message that is mean or makes you feel uncomfortable, tell an adult family member right away.

- Never agree to meet anyone in person. If you want to get together with someone you meet on-line, check with an adult family member first. If a meeting is approved, arrange to meet in a public place and take an adult with you.

Bicycle Safety

A Safe Bike

You probably know how to ride a bike, but do you know how to make your bike as safe as possible? A safe bike is the right size for you. When you sit on your bike with the pedal in the lowest position, you should be able to rest your heel on the pedal. Your body should be 2 inches (about 5 cm) above the support bar that goes from the handlebar stem to the seat support when you are standing astride your bike with both feet flat on the ground. After checking for the right size, check your bike for the safety equipment shown below. How safe is *your* bike?

headlight

horn

white front reflector

red rear reflector

clear reflector

pedal reflectors

clear reflector

Your Bike Helmet

About 400,000 children are involved in bike-related crashes every year. That's why it's important to *always* wear your bike helmet. Wear your helmet flat on your head. Be sure it is strapped snugly so that the helmet will stay in place if you fall. If you do fall and strike your helmet on the ground, replace it, even if it doesn't look damaged. The padding inside the helmet may be crushed, which reduces the ability of the helmet to protect your head in the event of another fall. Look for the features shown here when purchasing a helmet.

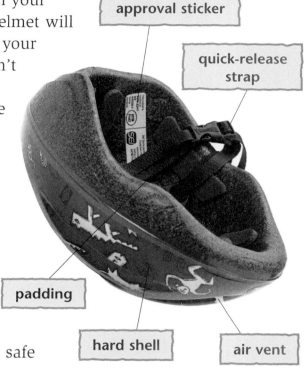

approval sticker

quick-release strap

padding

hard shell

air vent

Safety on the Road

Here are some tips for safe bicycle riding.

- Check your bike every time you ride it. Is it in safe working condition?

- Ride in single file in the same direction as traffic. Never weave in and out of parked cars.

- Before you enter a street, **STOP. Look** left, then right, then left again. **Listen** for any traffic. **Think** before you go.

- Walk your bike across an intersection. **Look** left, then right, then left again. Wait for traffic to pass.

- Obey all traffic signs and signals.

- Do not ride your bike at night without an adult. Be sure to wear light-colored clothing and use reflectors and front and rear lights for night riding.

Safety in Emergencies

Fire Safety

Fires cause more deaths than any other type of disaster. But a fire doesn't have to be deadly if you prepare your home and follow some basic safety rules.

- Install smoke detectors outside sleeping areas and on every other floor of your home. Test the detectors once a month and change the batteries twice a year.

- Keep a fire extinguisher on each floor of your home. Check them monthly to make sure they are properly charged.

- Make a fire escape plan. Ideally, there should be two routes out of each room. Sleeping areas are most important, as most fires happen at night. Plan to use stairs only, as elevators can be dangerous in a fire.

- Pick a place outside for everyone to meet. Choose one person to go to a neighbor's home to call 911 or the fire department.

- Practice crawling low to avoid smoke.

- If your clothes catch fire, follow the three steps shown here.

1. STOP

2. DROP

3. ROLL

Earthquake Safety

An earthquake is a strong shaking or sliding of the ground. The tips below can help you and your family stay safe in an earthquake.

Before an Earthquake	During an Earthquake	After an Earthquake
• Attach tall, heavy furniture, such as bookcases, to the wall. Store the heaviest items on the lowest shelves. • Check for fire risks. Bolt down gas appliances, and use flexible hosing and connections for both gas and water lines. • Strengthen and anchor overhead light fixtures to help keep them from falling.	• If you are outdoors, stay outdoors and move away from buildings and utility wires. • If you are indoors, take cover under a heavy desk or table, or in a doorway. Stay away from glass doors and windows and from heavy objects that might fall. • If you are in a car, drive to an open area away from buildings and overpasses.	• Keep watching for falling objects as aftershocks shake the area. • Check for hidden structural problems. • Check for broken gas, electric, and water lines. If you smell gas, shut off the gas main. Leave the area. Report the leak.

Storm Safety

- **In a Tornado** Take cover in a sheltered area away from doors and windows. An interior hallway or basement is best. Stay in the shelter until the danger has passed.

- **In a Hurricane** Prepare for high winds by securing objects outside or bringing them indoors. Cover windows and glass with plywood. Listen to weather bulletins for instructions. If asked to evacuate, proceed to emergency shelters.

- **In a Winter Storm or Blizzard** Stock up on food that does not have to be cooked. Dress in thin layers that help trap the body's heat. Pay special attention to the head and neck. If you are caught in a vehicle, turn on the dome light to make the vehicle visible to search crews.

First Aid

For Choking . . .

The tips on the next few pages can help you provide simple first aid to others and yourself. Always tell an adult about any injuries that occur.

If someone else is choking . . .

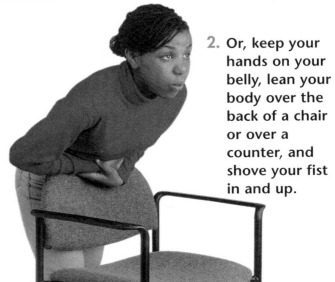

1. Recognize the Universal Choking Sign—grasping the throat with both hands. This sign means a person is choking and needs help.

2. Put your arms around his or her waist. Make a fist and put it above the person's navel. Grab your fist with your other hand.

3. Pull your hands toward yourself and give five quick, hard, upward thrusts on the choker's belly.

If you are choking when alone . . .

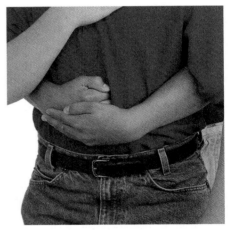

1. Make a fist and place it above your navel. Grab your fist with your other hand. Pull your hands up with a quick, hard thrust.

2. Or, keep your hands on your belly, lean your body over the back of a chair or over a counter, and shove your fist in and up.

For Bleeding . . .

If someone else is bleeding . . .

Wash your hands with soap, if possible.

Put on protective gloves, if available.

Wash small wounds with soap and water. Do *not* wash serious wounds.

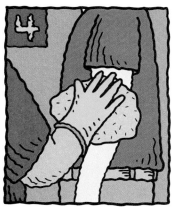

Place a clean gauze pad or cloth over the wound. Press firmly for ten minutes. Don't lift the gauze during this time.

If you don't have gloves, have the injured person hold the cloth in place with his or her own hand.

If after ten minutes the bleeding has stopped, bandage the wound. If the bleeding has not stopped, continue pressing on the wound and get help.

If you are bleeding . . .

- Follow the steps shown above. You don't need gloves to touch your own blood.

- Be sure to tell an adult about your injury.

First Aid

For Nosebleeds . . .

- Sit down, and tilt your head forward. Pinch your nostrils together for at least ten minutes.

- You can also put an ice pack on the bridge of your nose.

- If your nose continues to bleed, get help from an adult.

For Burns . . .

Minor burns are called first degree burns and involve only the top layer of skin. The skin is red and dry and the burn is painful. More serious burns are called second or third degree burns. These burns involve the top and lower layers of skin. Second degree burns cause blisters, redness, swelling, and pain. Third degree burns are the most serious. The skin is gray or white and looks burned. All burns need immediate first aid.

Minor Burns

- Run cool water over the burn or soak it in cool water for at least five minutes.

- Cover the burn with a clean, dry bandage.

- Do *not* put lotion or ointment on the burn.

More Serious Burns

- Cover the burn with a cool, wet bandage or cloth. Do *not* break any blisters.

- Do *not* put lotion or ointment on the burn.

- Get help from an adult right away.

For Insect Bites and Stings . . .

▲ deer tick

- Always tell an adult about bites and stings.

- Scrape out the stinger with your fingernail.

- Wash the area with soap and water.

- Ice cubes will usually take away the pain from insect bites. A paste made from baking soda and water also helps.

- If the bite or sting is more serious and is on the arm or leg, keep the leg or arm dangling down. Apply a cold, wet cloth. Get help immediately!

- If you find a tick on your skin, remove it. Crush it between two rocks. Wash your hands right away.

- If a tick has already bitten you, do not pull it off. Cover it with oil and wait for it to let go, then remove it with tweezers. Wash the area and your hands.

For Skin Rashes from Plants . . .

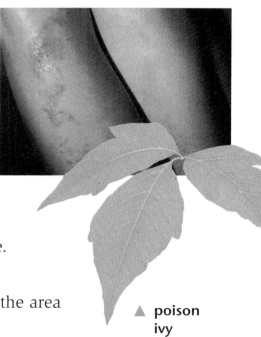

▲ poison ivy

Many poisonous plants have three leaves. Remember, "Leaves of three, let them be." If you touch a poisonous plant, wash the area. Put on clean clothes and throw the dirty ones in the washer. If a rash develops, follow these tips.

- Apply calamine lotion or a baking soda and water paste. Try not to scratch. Tell an adult.

- If you get blisters, do *not* pop them. If they burst, keep the area clean and dry. Cover with a bandage.

- If your rash does not go away in two weeks or if the rash is on your face or in your eyes, see your doctor.

Sense Organs

Eyes

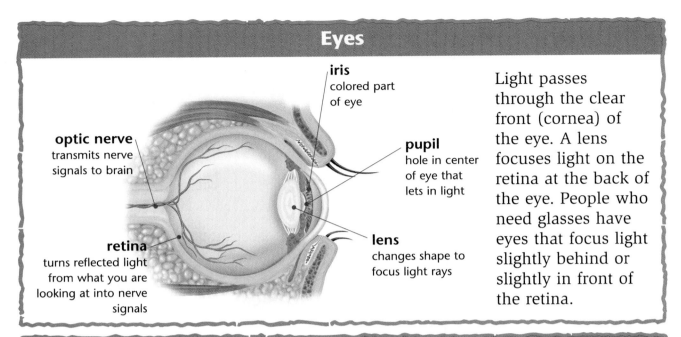

iris
colored part of eye

optic nerve
transmits nerve signals to brain

pupil
hole in center of eye that lets in light

retina
turns reflected light from what you are looking at into nerve signals

lens
changes shape to focus light rays

Light passes through the clear front (cornea) of the eye. A lens focuses light on the retina at the back of the eye. People who need glasses have eyes that focus light slightly behind or slightly in front of the retina.

Ears

Sounds make the eardrum move back and forth. The small bones in the middle ear send waves to the fluid in the inner ear. Hairs in the inner ear then move, passing signals to a nerve. Your brain reads the signals, and you hear the sound.

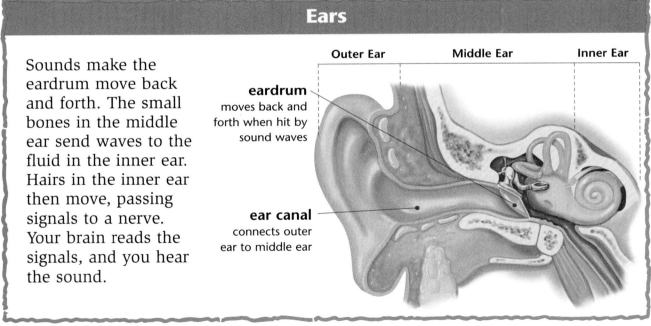

Outer Ear   Middle Ear   Inner Ear

eardrum
moves back and forth when hit by sound waves

ear canal
connects outer ear to middle ear

Caring for Your Eyes and Ears

• Wear safety glasses when participating in activities where you can get hit or where a foreign object can hit an eye, such as sports and mowing grass.

• Avoid listening to very loud sounds for long periods of time. Loud sounds destroy the delicate hairs in the inner ear. You can lose your hearing little by little.

Nose

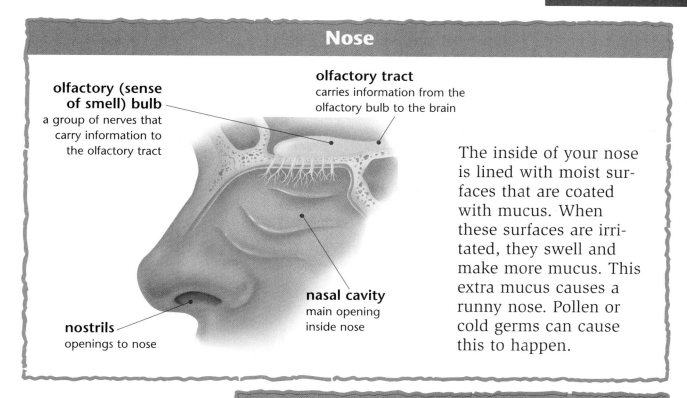

olfactory (sense of smell) bulb
a group of nerves that carry information to the olfactory tract

olfactory tract
carries information from the olfactory bulb to the brain

nostrils
openings to nose

nasal cavity
main opening inside nose

The inside of your nose is lined with moist surfaces that are coated with mucus. When these surfaces are irritated, they swell and make more mucus. This extra mucus causes a runny nose. Pollen or cold germs can cause this to happen.

Caring for Your Nose, Tongue, and Skin

- If you have a cold or allergies, don't blow your nose hard. Blowing your nose hard can force germs into your throat and ears.

- When you brush your teeth, brush your tongue too.

- Always wear sunscreen when you are in the sun.

Tongue

Germs live on your tongue and in other parts of your mouth. Germs can harm your teeth and give you bad breath.

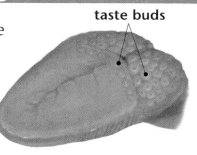

taste buds

Skin

protective outer layer

strong, springy middle layer

fatty lower layer

Your skin protects your insides from the outside world. Your skin has many touch-sensitive nerves. Because your skin can feel temperature, pain, and pressure, you can avoid cuts, burns, and scrapes.

Skeletal System

Each of your bones has a particular shape and size that allow it to do a certain job. You have bones that are tiny, long, wide, flat, and even curved. The job of some bones is to protect your body parts.

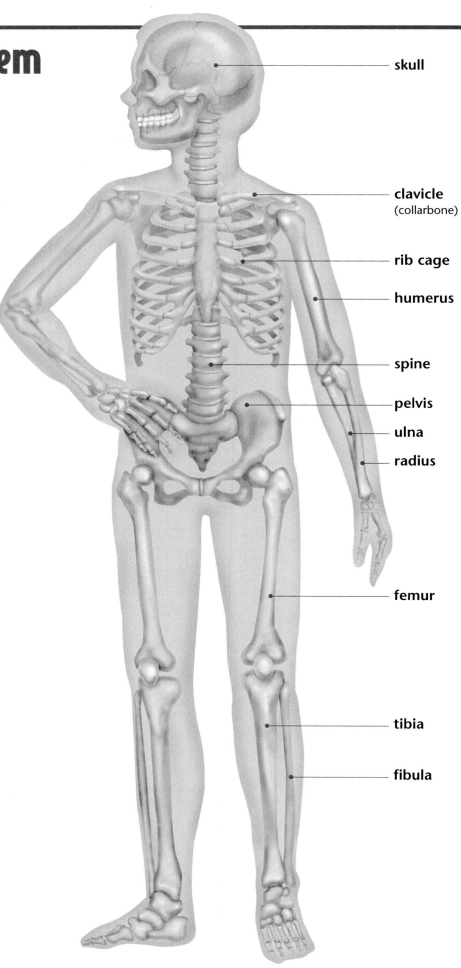

skull

clavicle
(collarbone)

rib cage

humerus

spine

pelvis

ulna

radius

femur

tibia

fibula

Spine, Skull, and Pelvis

Spine Your spine, or backbone, is made up of small bones called vertebrae that protect your spinal cord. Each vertebra has a hole in it, like a doughnut. These bones fit together, one on top of the other, and the holes line up to form a tunnel. Cartilage disks sit like cushions between the vertebrae. Your spinal cord runs from your brain down your back inside this tunnel.

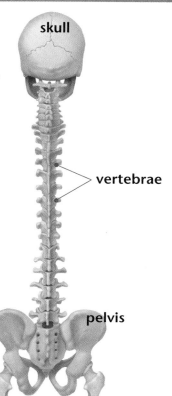

skull

vertebrae

pelvis

Skull The bones in your head are called your skull. Some of the bones in your skull protect your brain. The bones in your face are part of your skull too.

Pelvis Your spine connects to your hipbone, or pelvis. Your pelvis connects to your thighs. Your flexible spine, pelvis, and legs are what let you stand up straight, twist, turn, bend, and walk.

Caring for Your Skeletal System

- Calcium helps bones grow and makes them strong. Dairy products like milk, cheese, and yogurt contain calcium. Have two to three servings of dairy products every day. If you can't eat dairy products, dark green, leafy vegetables such as broccoli and collard greens or canned salmon with bones are also sources of calcium.

- Sit up straight with good posture. Sitting slumped over all the time can hurt muscles around your spine.

Activities

1. Make a stack of hard candy rings and run a string down through it. This is how your spinal cord runs through your spine.

2. Stand facing a wall. Without moving your feet, how far can you twist your body? How far can you see behind you?

3. Find the bony part of your hipbone that sticks out near your waist. Pick up one leg. Where does the thigh bone connect to your pelvis? How far is it from the bony part?

Muscular System

L ike your bones, each muscle in your body does a certain job. Muscles in your thumb help you hold things. Muscles in your neck help you turn your head. Your heart muscle pumps blood through your body. Small muscles control your eyes.

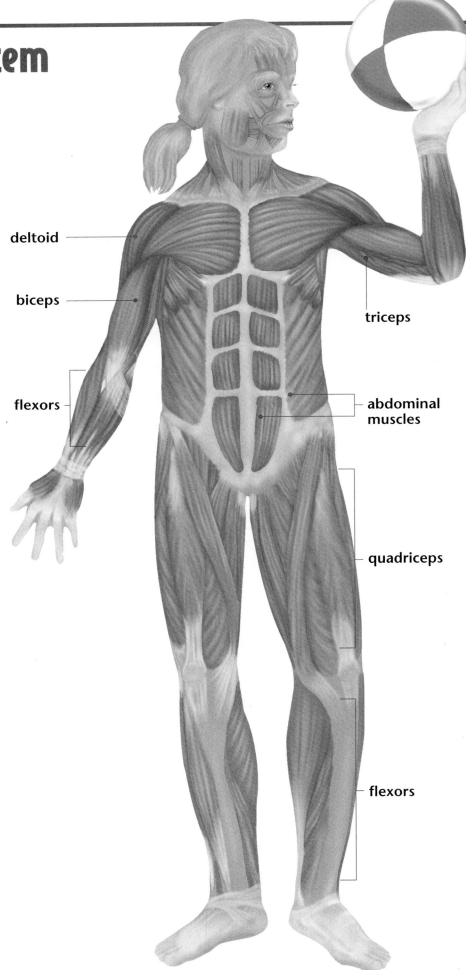

deltoid

biceps

flexors

triceps

abdominal muscles

quadriceps

flexors

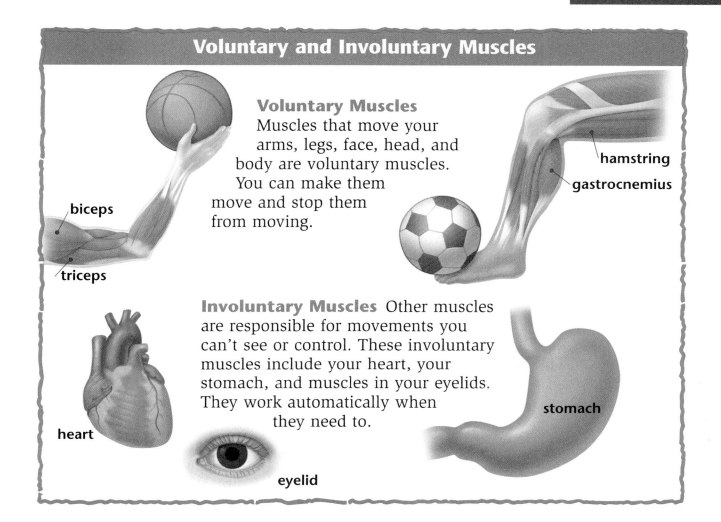

Voluntary and Involuntary Muscles

Voluntary Muscles
Muscles that move your arms, legs, face, head, and body are voluntary muscles. You can make them move and stop them from moving.

biceps

triceps

hamstring

gastrocnemius

Involuntary Muscles Other muscles are responsible for movements you can't see or control. These involuntary muscles include your heart, your stomach, and muscles in your eyelids. They work automatically when they need to.

heart

eyelid

stomach

Caring for Your Muscular System

- Exercise makes your muscles stronger and larger.
- Warming up by moving all your big muscles for five to ten minutes before you exercise helps prevent injury or pain.

Activities

1. Look into a mirror and cover one eye. Watch the pupil in the other eye. How does it change? Did you change it?

2. Try not to blink for as long as you can. What happens?

3. Without taking off your shoes, try moving each of your toes one at a time. Can you move each of them separately?

Digestive System

Food is broken down and pushed through your body by your digestive system. Your digestive system is a series of connected parts that starts with your mouth and ends with your large intestine. Each part helps your body get different nutrients from the food you eat.

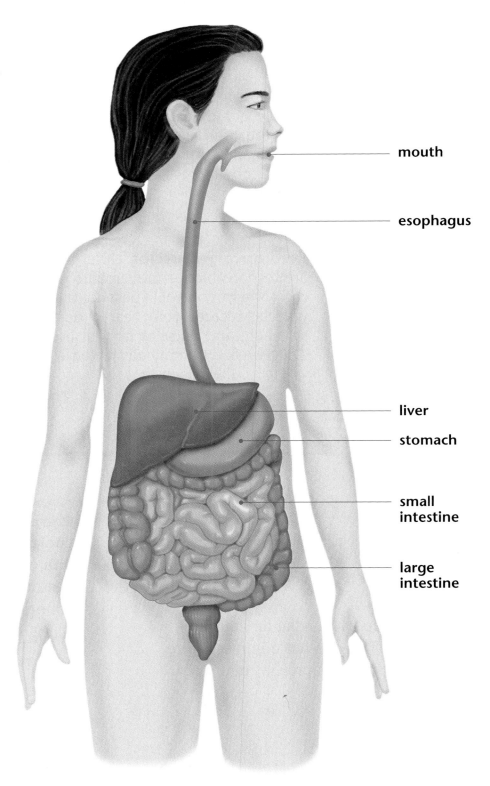

mouth

esophagus

liver

stomach

small intestine

large intestine

Small and Large Intestines

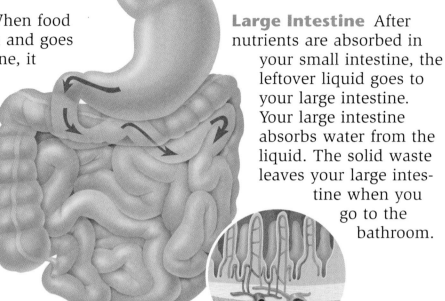

Small Intestine When food leaves your stomach and goes to your small intestine, it is a thick liquid. The walls of the small intestine are lined with many small, finger-shaped bumps. Tiny blood vessels in the bumps absorb nutrients from the liquid.

Large Intestine After nutrients are absorbed in your small intestine, the leftover liquid goes to your large intestine. Your large intestine absorbs water from the liquid. The solid waste leaves your large intestine when you go to the bathroom.

Caring for Your Digestive System

- Fiber helps your digestive system work better. Eat foods with fiber, such as fresh vegetables, beans, lentils, fruits, cereals, and breads, every day.

- Eat a balanced diet so that your body gets all the nutrients it needs.

Activities

1. Find the small and large intestines on the diagram of the digestive system. About how far is it from your belly button to where the small intestine starts?

2. On the diagram of the digestive system, trace the path that food takes through your body.

3. Draw a long line on a sheet of notebook paper. Fold the paper like an accordion. The line is like the path of food over the bumps in the small intestine.

R37

Circulatory System

Food and oxygen are carried by your blood through your circulatory system to every cell in your body. Blood moves nutrients throughout your body, fights infection, and helps control your body temperature. Your blood is mostly made up of a watery liquid called plasma. It also contains three kinds of cells.

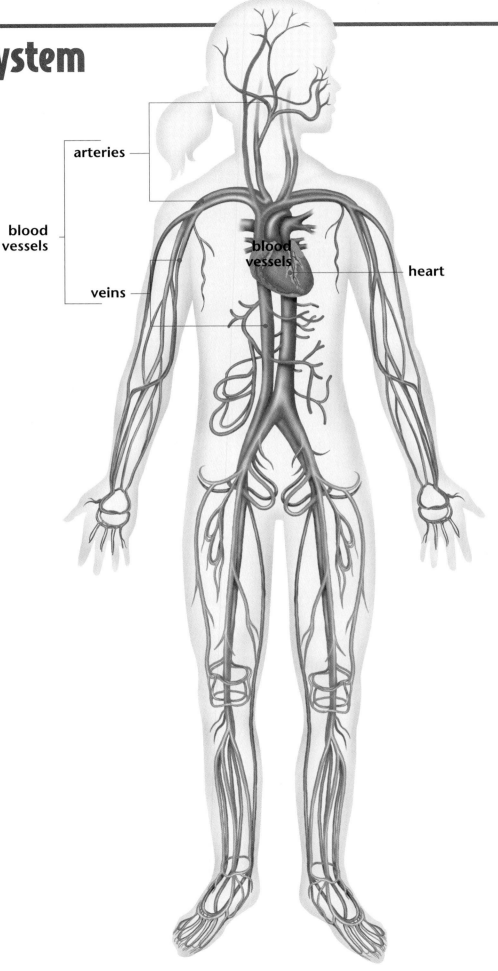

arteries

blood vessels

blood vessels

veins

heart

Blood Cells

Red Blood Cells Red blood cells carry oxygen from your lungs to the rest of your body. They also carry carbon dioxide from your body back to your lungs, so you can breathe it out.

Platelets Platelets help clot your blood, which stops bleeding. Platelets clump together as soon as you get a cut. The sticky clump traps red blood cells and forms a blood clot. The blood clot hardens to make a scab and seals the cut.

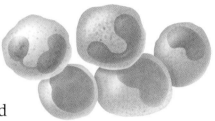

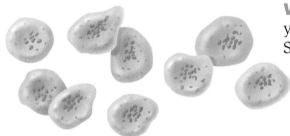

White Blood Cells When you are ill, your white blood cells come to the rescue. Some types of white blood cells identify what is making you ill. Some organize an attack. Others kill the invading germs or infected cells.

Caring for Your Circulatory System

- Never touch another person's blood.
- Don't pick scabs. If you pick a scab, you might make it bleed and the clotting process must begin again.

Activities

1. On the diagram of the circulatory system, trace the path of blood from the heart to the knee.

2. Red blood cells are medium-size and are the most common cells in your blood. White blood cells are larger and are the least common. Platelets are the smallest blood cells. Draw a picture of what a drop of blood might look like under a microscope.

Respiratory System

Your body uses its respiratory system to get oxygen from the air. Your respiratory system is made up of your nose and mouth, your trachea, your two lungs, and your diaphragm.

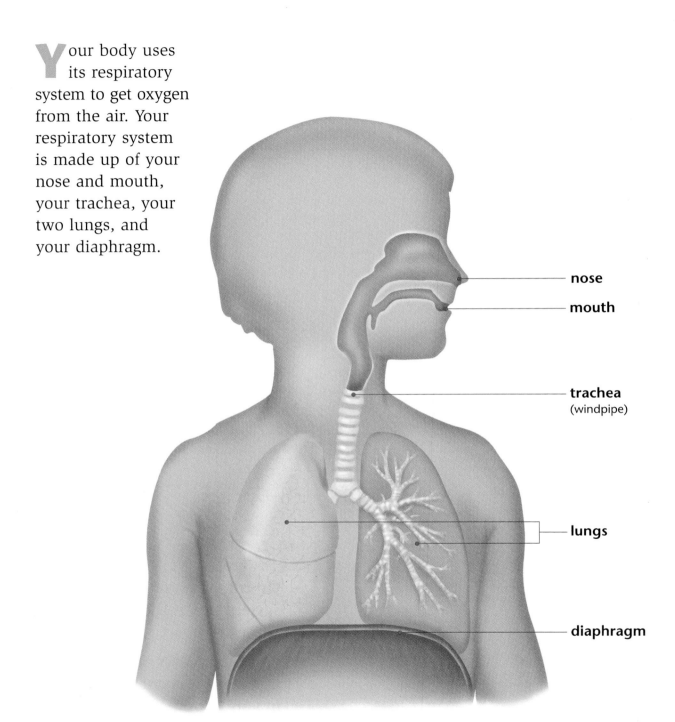

nose

mouth

trachea
(windpipe)

lungs

diaphragm

Functions of the Lungs

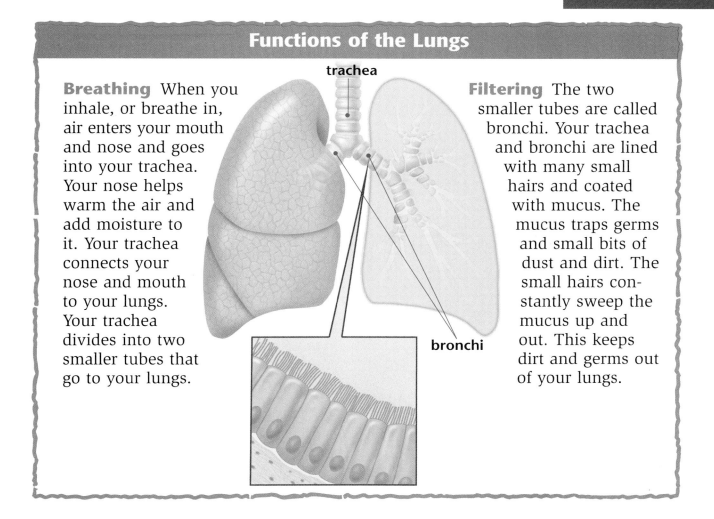

trachea

bronchi

Breathing When you inhale, or breathe in, air enters your mouth and nose and goes into your trachea. Your nose helps warm the air and add moisture to it. Your trachea connects your nose and mouth to your lungs. Your trachea divides into two smaller tubes that go to your lungs.

Filtering The two smaller tubes are called bronchi. Your trachea and bronchi are lined with many small hairs and coated with mucus. The mucus traps germs and small bits of dust and dirt. The small hairs constantly sweep the mucus up and out. This keeps dirt and germs out of your lungs.

Caring for Your Respiratory System

- Avoid smoke and other air pollution. They can paralyze the tiny hairs and cause you to become ill.
- Get plenty of exercise to keep your heart and lungs strong.

Activities

1. Take several breaths through your nose. Notice how the inside of your nose feels when you breathe in. Moisten a paper towel and take several breaths through the towel. Does your nose feel different?

2. Take a deep breath and hold it. Have someone measure your chest with a tape measure. Breathe the air out, and have someone measure your chest again. Is your chest bigger when you breathe in or when you breathe out?

Nervous System

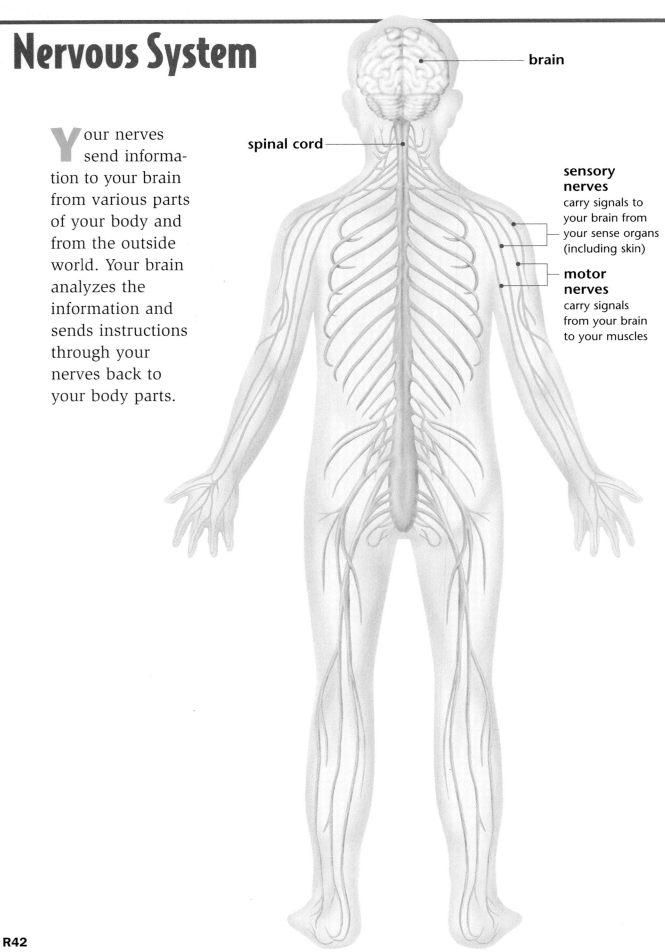

Your nerves send information to your brain from various parts of your body and from the outside world. Your brain analyzes the information and sends instructions through your nerves back to your body parts.

brain

spinal cord

sensory nerves carry signals to your brain from your sense organs (including skin)

motor nerves carry signals from your brain to your muscles

Messages to and from the Brain

Incoming Messages Your sensory nerves send signals to your brain from your sense organs. Every minute your brain receives millions of these signals. Your brain has to decide how to deal with each piece of information. For example, your brain might decide to deal with a barking dog nearby before it deals with a person calling to you from a distance.

Outgoing Messages Every minute, millions of nerve signals also leave your brain. Your motor nerves carry these messages. Your motor nerves connect to your muscles and tell them what to do. When you ride your bike, your brain helps you maintain balance and sends instructions to all the muscles you use to ride a bike.

Caring for Your Nervous System

- Eat a healthful, balanced diet. Your brain needs energy and nutrients to work well.

- Always wear a helmet when you ride your bike, skate, or use a skateboard.

Activities

1. **Balance on one foot for as long as you can. Close your eyes and try again. Was it easier or harder the second time?**

2. **Pick up five pennies. Try it again wearing a glove. Why was it harder?**

3. **Hold a ruler at one end and dangle it just above a partner's open index finger and thumb. Drop the ruler through the gap. Where on the ruler does your partner grab? Try it several times, and then switch roles.**

Glossary

This Glossary contains important science words and their definitions. Each word is respelled as it would be in a dictionary. When you see the ′ mark after a syllable, pronounce that syllable with more force than the other syllables. The page number at the end of the definition tells where to find the word in your book. The boldfaced letters in the examples in the Pronunciation Key that follows show how these letters are pronounced in the respellings after each glossary word.

PRONUNCIATION KEY

a	**a**dd, m**a**p	m	**m**ove, see**m**	u	**u**p, d**o**ne		
ā	**a**ce, r**a**te	n	**n**ice, ti**n**	û(r)	b**ur**n, t**er**m		
â(r)	**c**are, **air**	ng	ri**ng**, so**ng**	yo͞o	**f**use, **few**		
ä	p**a**lm, f**a**ther	o	**o**dd, h**o**t	v	**v**ain, e**v**e		
b	**b**at, ru**b**	ō	**o**pen, s**o**	w	**w**in, a**w**ay		
ch	**ch**eck, cat**ch**	ô	**o**rder, j**aw**	y	**y**et, **y**earn		
d	**d**og, ro**d**	oi	**oi**l, b**oy**	z	**z**est, mu**s**e		
e	**e**nd, p**e**t	ou	p**ou**t, n**ow**	zh	vi**si**on, plea**s**ure		
ē	**e**qual, tr**ee**	o͝o	t**oo**k, f**u**ll	ə	the schwa, an		
f	**f**it, hal**f**	o͞o	p**oo**l, f**oo**d		unstressed vowel		
g	**g**o, lo**g**	p	**p**it, sto**p**		representing the sound		
h	**h**ope, **h**ate	r	**r**un, poo**r**		spelled		
i	**i**t, g**i**ve	s	**s**ee, pa**ss**		*a* in **a***bove*		
ī	**i**ce, wr**i**te	sh	**s**ure, ru**sh**		*e* in *sick***e***n*		
j	**j**oy, le**dg**e	t	**t**alk, si**t**		*i* in *poss***i***ble*		
k	**c**ool, ta**k**e	th	**th**in, bo**th**		*o* in *mel***o***n*		
l	**l**ook, ru**l**e	t̶h̶	**th**is, ba**th**e		*u* in *circ***u***s*		

Other symbols:
- separates words into syllables
- ′ indicates heavier stress on a syllable
- ′ indicates light stress on a syllable

acid rain [as′id rān′] Precipitation resulting from pollution condensing into clouds and falling to Earth **(A139)**

adaptation [ad′əp·tā′shən] A body part or behavior that helps an animal meet its needs in its environment **(A14)**

artery [är′tər·ē] A blood vessel that takes blood away from the heart **(E13)**

biome [bī′ōm′] A large-scale ecosystem **(A104)**

brain [brān] The control center of your nervous system **(E18)**

buoyancy [boi′ən·sē] The ability of matter to float in a liquid or gas **(C20)**

camouflage [kam′ə·fläzh′] An animal's color or pattern that helps it blend in with its surroundings **(A18)**

capillary [kap′ə·ler′ē] A tiny blood vessel that allows gases and nutrients to pass from blood to cells **(E12)**

carbon dioxide [kär′bən dī·ok′sīd′] A gas breathed out by animals **(A40)**

cardiac muscle [kär′dē·ak mus′əl] A type of muscle that works the heart **(E7)**

cell [sel] The basic building block of life **(E6)**

charge [chärj] A measure of the extra positive or negative particles that an object has **(C34)**

circuit [sûr′kit] A path that is made for an electric current **(C40)**

climate [klī′mit] The average temperature and rainfall of an area over many years **(A7)**

climate zone [klī′mit zōn′] A region throughout which yearly patterns of temperature, rainfall, and amount of sunlight are similar **(A104)**

climax community [klī′maks′ kə•myōō′nə•tē] The last stage of succession **(A133)**

community [kə•myōō′nə•tē] All the populations of organisms living together in an environment **(A68)**

competition [kom′pə•tish′ən] The contest among organisms for the limited resources of an ecosystem **(A82)**

conduction [kən•duk′shən] The transfer of thermal energy caused by particles of matter bumping into each other **(E39)**

conductor [kən•duk′tər] A material that electric current can pass through easily **(C41)**

conserving [kən•sûr′ving] The saving or protecting of resources **(A144)**

consumer [kən•sōō′mər] An organism in a community that must eat to get the energy it needs **(A74)**

continental drift [kon′tə•nen′təl drift′] A theory of how Earth's continents move over its surface **(B22)**

contour plowing [kon′to͞or plou′ing] Plowing around a hill to reduce erosion **(B78)**

convection [kən•vek′shən] The transfer of thermal energy by particles of a liquid or gas moving from one place to another **(E40)**

core [kôr] The center of the Earth **(B14)**

crust [krust] The thin, outer layer of Earth **(B14)**

decomposer [dē′kəm•pōz′ər] A consumer that breaks down the tissues of dead organisms **(A75)**

density [den′sə•tē] The property of matter that compares the amount of matter to the space it takes up **(C14)**

deposition [dep′ə•zish′ən] The process of dropping, or depositing, sediment in a new location **(B7)**

dissolve [di•zolv′] When one material forms a solution with another material **(C19)**

earthquake [ûrth′kwāk′] A shaking of the ground caused by the sudden release of energy in Earth's crust **(B18)**

ecosystem [ek′ō•sis′təm] A community and its physical environment together **(A68)**

electric cell [i•lek′trik sel′] A device that supplies energy to move charges through a circuit **(C40)**

electric current [i•lek′trik kûr′ənt] A flow of electric charges **(C40)**

electric field [i•lek′trik fēld′] The space around an object in which electric forces occur **(C36)**

electromagnet [i•lek′trō•mag′nit] An arrangement of wire wrapped around a core producing a temporary magnet **(C53)**

endangered [en•dān′jərd] A population of organisms that is likely to become extinct if steps are not taken to save it **(A91)**

energy [en′ər•jē] The ability to cause a change **(E32)**

energy pyramid [en′ər•jē pir′ə•mid] Shows the amount of energy available to pass from one level of a food chain to the next **(A78)**

environment [in•vī′rən•mənt] Everything that surrounds and affects an animal, including living and nonliving things **(A6)**

erosion [i•rō′zhən] The process by which wind and moving water carry away bits of rock **(B7)**

esophagus [i•sof′ə•gəs] The tube that connects your mouth with your stomach **(E20)**

estuary [es′cho͞o•er′ē] The place where a freshwater river empties into an ocean **(A120)**

extinct [ik•stingkt′] No longer in existence; the result when the last individual of a population dies and that organism is gone forever **(A91)**

fault [fôlt] A break or place where pieces of Earth's crust move **(B18)**

fertile [fûr′təl] Soil that has the nutrients to grow many plants **(B72)**

fibrous root [fī′brəs rōōt′] A long root that grows near the surface **(A47)**

food chain [fōōd′ chān′] The way in which the organisms in an ecosystem interact with one another according to what they eat **(A75)**

food web [fōōd′ web′] Shows the interactions among many different food chains in a single ecosystem **(A76)**

fossil [fos′əl] The remains or a trace of past life usually found in sedimentary rock **(B23)**

fuel [fyōō′əl] A material that can burn **(E46)**

gas [gas] The state of matter that has no definite shape and takes up no definite amount of space **(C8)**

germinate [jûr′mə•nāt′] To sprout; said of a seed **(A52)**

habitat [hab′ə•tat′] A place in an ecosystem where a population lives **(A69)**

hardness [härd′nis] A mineral's ability to resist being scratched **(B37)**

heart [härt] The muscle that pumps blood through your blood vessels to all parts of your body **(E13)**

heat [hēt] The transfer of thermal energy from one piece of matter to another **(E38)**

hibernation [hī′bər•nā′shən] A period when an animal goes into a long, deep "sleep" **(A25)**

humus [hyōō′məs] The rotting plant and animal materials in topsoil **(B66)**

igneous rock [ig′nē•əs rok′] A rock that forms when completely melted rock hardens **(B42)**

individual [in′də•vij′ōō•əl] A single organism in an environment **(A68)**

infrared radiation [in•frə•red′ rā′dē•ā′shən] The bundles of light energy that transfer heat **(E42)**

instinct [in′stingkt] A behavior that an animal begins life with **(A22)**

insulator [in′sə•lāt′ər] A material that current cannot pass through easily **(C41)**

intertidal zone [in′tər•tīd′əl zōn′] An area where the tide and churning waves provide a constant supply of oxygen and nutrients to living organisms **(A117)**

landforms [land′fôrmz′] The physical features on Earth's surface **(B6)**

large intestine [lärj′ in•tes′tən] The last part of the digestive system where water is removed from food **(E21)**

liquid [lik′wid] The state of matter that takes the shape of its container and takes up a definite amount of space **(C7)**

lungs [lungz] The main organs of the respiratory system **(E12)**

luster [lus′tər] A way that the surface of a mineral reflects light **(B37)**

magma [mag′mə] A hot, soft rock from Earth's lower mantle **(B16)**

magnet [mag′nit] An object that attracts certain materials, such as iron or steel **(C46)**

magnetic field [mag•net′ik fēld′] The space all around a magnet where the force of the magnet can act **(C47)**

magnetic pole [mag•net′ik pōl′] The end of a magnet **(C46)**

mantle [man′təl] The layer of rock beneath Earth's crust **(B14)**

mass [mas] The amount of matter something contains **(C6)**

mass movement [mas′ mōōv′mənt] The downhill movement of rock and soil because of gravity **(B9)**

matter [mat′ər] Everything in the universe that has mass and takes up space **(C6)**

metamorphic rock [met′ə•môr′fik rok′] A rock changed by heat or pressure, but not completely melted **(B46)**

metamorphosis [met′ə•môr′fə•sis] The process of change; for example, from an egg to an adult butterfly **(A10)**

migration [mī•grā′shən] The movement of a group of one type of animal from one region to another and back again **(A23)**

mimicry [mim′ik•rē] An adaptation in which an animal looks very much like another animal or an object **(A18)**

mineral [min′ər•əl] A natural, solid material with particles arranged in a repeating pattern **(B36)**

near-shore zone [nir′shôr′ zōn′] The area beyond the breaking waves that extends to waters that are about 180 m deep **(A117)**

nerve [nûrv] A group of neurons that carries signals from the brain to the body and from the body to the brain **(E18)**

neuron [no͞or′on′] A nerve cell **(E18)**

niche [nich] The role each population has in its habitat **(A69)**

nutrient [no͞o′trē•ənt] A substance, such as a mineral, which all living things need in order to grow **(A40)**

open-ocean zone [ō′pən•ō′shən zōn′] The area that includes most deep ocean waters; most organisms live near the surface **(A117)**

organ [ôr′gən] A group of tissues of different kinds working together to perform a task **(E6)**

oxygen [ok′si•jən] One of the many gases in air **(A7)**

Pangea [pan•jē′ə] A supercontinent that existed about 225 million years ago containing all of Earth's land **(B22)**

parallel circuit [par′ə•lel sûr′kit] A circuit that has more than one path along which current can travel **(C42)**

photosynthesis [fōt′ō•sin′thə•sis] The process by which a plant makes its own food **(A41)**

pioneer plants [pī′ə•nir′ plants′] The first plants to invade a bare area **(A132)**

plate [plāt] A rigid block of crust and upper mantle rock **(B15)**

pollution [pə•lo͞o′shən] A waste product that damages an ecosystem **(A139)**

population [pop′yə•lā′shən] All the individuals of the same kind living in the same environment **(A68)**

producer [prə•do͞os′ər] An organism that makes its own food **(A74)**

radiation [rā′dē•ā′shən] The bundles of energy that move through matter and through empty space **(E42)**

reclamation [rek′lə•mā′shən] The process of restoring a damaged ecosystem **(A150)**

recycle [rē•sī′kəl] To recover a resource from an item and use the recovered resource to make a new item **(A145)**

reduce [ri•do͞os′] To cut down on the use of resources **(A144)**

resistor [ri•zis′tər] A material that resists the flow of current but doesn't stop it **(C41)**

reuse [ri′yo͞oz′] To use items again; sometimes for a different purpose **(A145)**

rock [rok] A material made up of one or more minerals **(B42)**

rock cycle [rok′ sī′kəl] The slow, never-ending process of rock changes **(B52)**

S

sedimentary rock [sed′ə•men′tər•ē rok′] A rock formed by layers of sediments squeezed and stuck together over a long time **(B44)**

series circuit [sir′ēz sûr′kit] A circuit that has only one path for current **(C42)**

shelter [shel′tər] A place where an animal is protected from other animals or from the weather **(A9)**

small intestine [smôl′ in•tes′tən] A long tube of muscle where most food is digested **(E20)**

smooth muscle [smōōth′ mus′əl] A type of muscle found in the walls of some organs such as the stomach, intestines, blood vessels, and bladder **(E7)**

soil conservation [soil′ kon′sər•vā′shən] The saving of soil **(B78)**

solar energy [sō′lər en′ər•jē] The energy given off by the sun **(E47)**

solid [sol′id] The state of matter that has a definite shape and takes up a definite amount of space **(C6)**

solubility [sol′yə•bil′ə•tē] A measure of the amount of a material that will dissolve in another material **(C19)**

solution [sə•lōō′shən] A mixture in which the particles of different kinds of matter are mixed evenly with each other and particles do not settle out **(C18)**

spinal cord [spī′nəl kôrd′] The tube of nerves that runs through your spine, or backbone **(E18)**

spore [spôr] A tiny cell that ferns and fungi use to reproduce **(A53)**

static electricity [stat′ik ē′lek•tris′i•tē] An electric charge that stays on an object **(C34)**

stomach [stum′ək] A bag made up of smooth muscles that mixes food with digestive juices **(E20)**

streak [strēk] The color of the powder left behind when you rub a mineral against a white tile called a streak plate **(B37)**

striated muscle [strī′āt•ed mus′əl] A muscle with light and dark stripes; a muscle you can control by thinking **(E8)**

strip cropping [strip′ krop′ing] The practice of planting one or more crops between rows of other crops to control erosion **(B78)**

succession [sək•sesh′ən] A gradual change in an ecosystem, sometimes occurring over hundreds of years **(A132)**

symbiosis [sim′bī•ō′sis] A long-term relationship between different kinds of organisms **(A85)**

symmetry [sim′ə•trē] The condition in which each feature on one half of an object has a matching feature on the other half **(A46)**

taproot [tap′ro͞ot′] A plant's single main root that goes deep into the soil **(A47)**

temperature [tem′pər•ə•chər] A measure of the average energy of motion of the particles in matter **(E33)**

terracing [ter′əs•ing] A farming method used on steep hillsides to control erosion in which the hillside is cut to form broad, flat areas at different heights **(B78)**

thermal energy [thûr′məl en′ər•jē] The energy of the motion of particles in matter **(E32)**

threatened [thret′ənd] Describes a population of organisms that are likely to become endangered if they are not protected **(A91)**

tissue [tish′o͞o] A group of cells of the same type **(E6)**

transpiration [tran′spə•rā′shən] The giving off of water vapor by plants **(A46)**

tuber [to͞o′bər] A swollen underground stem **(A55)**

vein [vān] A blood vessel that returns blood to the heart **(E13)**

volcano [vol•kā′nō] A mountain formed by lava and ash **(B16)**

volume [vol′yəm] The amount of space that matter takes up **(C13)**

weathering [we͟th′ər•ing] The process by which rocks are broken down into smaller pieces **(B7)**

wetlands [wet′landz′] The water ecosystems that include saltwater marshes, mangrove swamps, and mud flats **(A151)**

A

Abdominal muscles, R34
Acid rain (map), A139
Activity pyramid, planning weekly, R18
Adaptation(s), A14, A83
    animal, A14–19
    defined, A14
    in desert, A109
    in estuaries, A120
    in freshwater ecosystem, A118
Adhesives, medical, E22
African plate, B16
Air conditioning, E50–51
Air pollution, A139
Air sacs, E12
Alarm bell, workings of, C54–55
Aldabra tortoise, A3
Algal bloom, A138
Alligators, A18
Amber, C58
American Geophysical Union, B84
Ammonia, B72, B83, E51
Anchorage, AK, B18
Animal behaviorist, A30
Animal(s)
    African, A8
    behavior of, A22–27
    body coverings of, A16–17
    color and shape of, A18
    needs of, A6–11
    speed of, A2
    what they eat, A8
    young of, A10–11
Ant(s), A85
Apache families, B82–83
Aphids, A85
Arcata, CA, wetlands, A151
Arches National Park, UT, B40
Arp, Alissa J., A124
Arteries, E13, E14, R38

Ash, B16, B17
Athabasca Glacier, B8
Attini ants, B61
Attraction, C36

B

Backbone, E7
Bacteria and food safety, R16
Balance, measuring, R6
Bald eagles, A92, A155
Baptist, Kia K., B28
Basalt, B43, B50
Bat(s), North American, A25
Battery, invention of, C59
Beach crossovers, A142
Beaker, C13
Beaks, bird, A14
Bedrock, B66
Behaviors, learned, A26–27
Berson, Solomon, E24
Beta carotene, A57
BetaSweet carrot, A57
Biceps, E7, E8, R34
Biome(s), A104–105
    comparing, A112–113
    differences within, A105
    land, A104–113
    world, A104–105
Biosphere 2 (AZ), A102
Bird(s) adaptations of, A14–15
Bison, American, A17
Blood, paths of, E14
Blood vessels, R38
Blowtorch, E38
Bluebonnet, Texas, A47, A152
Boiling, C8, E32
Bone meal, B82–83
Bones
    bird, A15
    human, E6
Botanist, A58
Brackish-water ecosystem, A116, A120–121
Brain, E18
    messages to and from, R43
Breastbone, E7
Breathing, R41

Brilliant luster, B37
Brock microscope, R5
Bronchi, R41
Brown bear, A8
Buds, A54
Bulbs, A54
Bullhorn acacia, A36
Buoyancy, C20–21
Burning fuels, E46
Burrowing owl, A108
Butterfly, metamorphosis of, A10

C

Cactus, A38, A42, A43, A47
Calcite, B36, B44
Calf muscle, E7
California condor, A92
Camouflage, A18, A82
Canada lynx, A110
Capillaries, E12, E13
Carbon, E46
Carbon dioxide, A40, A41, A69, A155, E12, E14, E46
Carbonic acid, B9
Cardiac muscle, E7, E8, E9
Caribou, A68
Carnivores, A75
Carson, Rachel, A154–155
Cartilage, R33
Carver, George Washington, B82–83
Cascade Mountains, B16
Casts, fossil, B24
Catalytic converter, A144
Caterpillars, A10
Cells, E6
    human, E6
    plant, A53
    replacement of, E2
Chalcopyrite, B37
Chambers, heart, E14
Chameleon, A8
Charges, electric, C34
    moving, C40
    separating, C35
Chase, Agnes, A58

Photography Credits: Page Placement Key: (t)-top (c)-center (b)-bottom (l)-left (r)-right (fg)-foreground (bg)-background (i)-inset

Cover: Tim Flach/Tony Stone Images; (bg) Richard Price/FPG International

Table of Contents: Page: i, ii Tim Flach/Tony Stone Images; (bg) Richard Price/FPG International

Unit A: A1 (fg) Steinhart Aquarium/Tom McHugh/Photo Researchers; A1 (bg) Mark Lewis/Photo Researchers; A2-A3 Manoj Shah/Tony Stone Images; A3 (t) Rudie Kuiter/Innerspace Visions; A3 (b) Peter Weimann/Animals Animals; A4 Corel; A6 (bg) Rich Reid/Earth Scenes; A6 (li) Larry Minden/Minden Pictures; A6 (ri) Renee Lynn/Photo Researchers; A6 (ci) John Cancalosi/DRK; A7 Daniel J. Cox/Natural Exposures; A8 (t) T. Kitchen/Natural Selection Stock Photography; A8-A9 (b) Bios/Peter Arnold, Inc. A8 (bl) Daniel J. Cox/Natural Selection Stock Photography; A9 (l) Osolinski, S. OSF/Animals Animals; A9(r) David E. Myers/Tony Stone Images; A9 (li) Stephen Krasemann/Tony Stone Images; A9 (ri) E. & P. Bauer/Bruce Coleman, Inc.; A10 B.& C. Alexander/Photo Researchers; A10 (ti) Ralph Clevenger/Westlight; A10 (bi) Dan Suzio Photography; A11 (t) Ben Simmons/The Stock Market; A11 (i) D. Parer & E. Parer-Cook/Auscape; A12 (b) Joe McDonald/Bruce Coleman, Inc.; A14 (l) Robert Lankinen/The Wildlife Collection; A14(r) Martin Harvey/The Wildlife Collection; A14(c) Zefa Germany/The Stock Market; A15 (t) Fritz Polking/Dembinsky Photo Associates; A15 (b) Tui De Roy/Minden Pictures; A15 (i) Zig Leszczynski/Animals Animals; A16 (l) Tom & Pat Leeson; A16 (r) Zig Leszczynski/Animals Animals; A16 (c) Fred Bavendam/Peter Arnold, Inc.; A16-A17 (b) Stuart Westmorland/Tony Stone Images; A17(t), A17 (ti) Bruce Wilson/Tony Stone Images; A17 (c) Wolfgang Kaehler Photography; A17 (bl) Martin Harvey/The Wildlife Collection; A17 (br) Bruce Davidson/Animals Animals; A18 (t) Art Wolfe/Tony Stone Images; A18 (bl) Stephen Krasemann/Tony Stone Images; A18 (br) Stouffer Prod./Animals Animals; A19 Joan Baron/The Stock Market; A20 C. Bradley Simmons/Bruce Coleman, Inc.; A22-A23 Mike Severns/Tony Stone Images; A24 (t) Grant Heilman Photography; A24-A25 (b) Daniel J. Cox/Tony Stone Images; A25 (t) Joe McDonald/Animals Animals; A25 (bl) Darrell Gulin/Tony Stone Images; A25 (br) J. Foott/Bruce Coleman, Inc.; A26 (t) Tom Brakefield/The Stock Market; A26-A27(b) Mark Petersen/Tony Stone Images; A27 (t) Darryl Torckler/Tony Stone Images; A28 Katsumi Kasahara/Associated Press; A29 Phil McCarten/PhotoEdit; A30 Michael K. Nichols/NGS Image Collection; A35 (l) Ralph Clevenger/Westlight; A35 (li) Dan Suzio Photography; A36-A37 Bertram G. Murray, Jr./Animals Animals; A37 (l) Gilbert S. Grant/Photo Researchers; A37 (r) J. A. Kraulis/Masterfile; A38 Christi Carter/Grant Heilman Photography; A40 H. Mark Weidman; A41 Porterfield-Chickering/Photo Researchers; A41 (i) Dr. Jeremy Burgess/SPL/Photo Researchers; A42 (t) Frans Lanting/Minden Pictures; A42 (b) Patti Murray/Earth Scenes; A43 C. K. Lorenz/Photo Researchers; A44 Dr. E. R. Degginger/Color-Pic; A46 (t), A46 (bl) Runk/Schoenberger/Grant Heilman Photography; A46 (br) Dr. E. R. Degginger/Earth Scenes; A47 (tl) John Kaprielian/Photo Researchers; A47 (tr), A47 (br), Runk/Schoenberger/Grant Heilman Photography; A47 (bl) Lefever/Grushow/Grant Heilman; A48 (r) Bill Lea/Dembinsky Photo Associates; A48 (tl), A48 (bl) Kim Taylor/Bruce Coleman, Inc.; A50 Runk/Schoenberger/Grant Heilman Photography; A52 Gregory K. Scott/Photo Researchers; A53 (t) Ed Reschke/Peter Arnold, Inc.; A53 (bl) Gay Bumgarner/Tony Stone Images; A53 (br) Laura Riley/Bruce Coleman, Inc.; A54 (l) Runk/Schoenberger/Grant Heilman Photography; A54 (r), A55 Heather Angel/Biofotos; A56 James Lyle/Texas A&M University; A57 Chris Rogers/The Stock Market; A58 Hunt Institute for Botanical Documentation/Carnegie Mellon University; A63 (t) Bruce Coleman, Inc.; A63 (b) Breck P. Kent/Animals Animals; A64-A65 P.& R. Hagan/Bruce Coleman, Inc.; A65 (l) Mitsuaki Iwago/Minden Pictures; A65 (r) Tomas del Amo/Pacific Stock; A66 Tim Davis/Photo Researchers; A68-A69 (bg) J. A. Kravlis/Masterfile; A68 (li) Michael Giannechini/Photo Researchers; A68-A69 (i) Ted Kerasote/Photo Researchers; A69 (bi) Mitsuaki Iwago/Minden Pictures; A69 (ti) SuperStock; A70 (tl) David Muench Photography, Inc.; A70 (tr), A70 (bl) Barry L. Runk from Grant Heilman Photography; A70 (br) David Muench Photography, Inc.; A72 SuperStock; A74-A75 (bg) Larry Ditto/Bruce Coleman, Inc. A74 (tli) V.P. Weinland/Photo Researchers; A74 (tri) Parviz M. Pour/Photo Researchers; A74-A75 (bi) David M. Phillips/Visual Unlimited; A75 (tli) Tom McHugh/Photo Researchers; A75 (tri) Tom & Pat Leeson/Photo Researchers; A76-A77 Woods, Michael J./NGS Image Collection; A79 Bruce Coleman, Inc.; A80, A80 (i) Joe McDonald/McDonald Wildlife Photography; A82 (bg) Stuart Westmorland/Tony Stone Images; A82 (li) Roger Rickel/New England Stock Photo; A82 (ri) Bruce Coleman, Inc.; A83 (l) Kevin Schafer/Peter Arnold, Inc.; A83 (r) Mitsuaki Iwago/Minden Pictures; A84 (t) John Shaw/Bruce Coleman, Inc.; A84 (c) Hal H. Harrison/Photo Researchers; A84 (b) Wayne Lankinen/Bruce Coleman, Inc.; A85 (t) M. & C. Photography/Peter Arnold, Inc.; A85 (b) Denise Tackett/Tom Stack & Associates; A86 (t) J.H. Robinson/Photo Researchers; A86 (b) Tom Stack/Tom Stack & Associates; A87 Dwight Kuhn/Bruce Coleman, Inc.; A88 Bryan & Cherry Alexander/Masterfile; A90 (t) Tim Davis/Photo Researchers; A90 (bl) Johnny Johnson/Tony Stone Images; A90 (br) Malcolm Boulton/Photo Researchers; A91 Tom McHugh/Photo Researchers; A92-A93 (t) Galen Rowell/Mountain Light; A92 (b) Roy Toft/Tom Stack & Associates; A94 Gunter Ziesler/Peter Arnold, Inc.; A95 (t) Doug Cheeseman/Peter Arnold; A95 (b) Bonnie Kamin/PhotoEdit; A96 (t) Louisiana State University Chemistry Library Website; A 96 (b) Meckes/Ottawa Photo Researchers; A100-A101 Craig Tuttle/The Stock Market; A101 (l) Earth Satellite Corporation/SPL/Photo Researchers; A101 (r) Jake Rajs/Tony Stone Images; A102 Chromosohm/Sohm/Tony Stone Images; A104 (b) Gary Braasch/Tony Stone Images; A104 (t) David Muench Photography, Inc.; A105 (tl) SuperStock; A105 (tr) Steve Kaufman/Peter Arnold, Inc.; A105 (br) Colin Prior/Tony Stone Images; A105 (bl) Joseph Van Os/The Image Bank; A106 Wolfgang Kaehler Photography; A106 (i) Mark Moffett/Minden Pictures; A107 SuperStock; A107 (i) Roger Bickel/New England Stock Photo; A108 David Muench Photography, Inc.; A108 (i) William Manning/The Stock Market; A109 Darrell Gulin/Tony Stone Images; A109 (i) T. Eggers/The Stock Market; A110 David Muench Photography, Inc.; A110 (i) Joseph Van Os/The Image Bank; A111 (t) Kennan Ward Photography; A111 (b) Carr Clifton/Minden Pictures; A112 (l) Nicholas DeVore, III/Bruce Coleman, Inc.; A112 (r) Tui De Roy/Minden Pictures; A114 Stan Osolinski/The Stock Market; A120 (t) Jim Brandenburg/Minden Pictures; A120 (b) David Muench Photography, Inc.; A122 NASA GSFC/SPL/Photo Researchers; A123 (t) Manfred Kage/Peter Arnold, Inc.; A123 (b) Pete Saloutos/The Stock Market; A124 (t) Romberg Tiburon Center; A124 (b) Emory Kristof/NGS Image Collection; A126 Jim Brandenburg/Minden Pictures; A128-A129 Gary Brettnacher/Tony Stone Images; A129 (t) Jonathan Wallen; A129 (b) Argus Fotoarchiv/Peter Arnold, Inc.; A130 Frans Lanting/Minden Pictures; A132 Runk/Schoenberger/Grant Heilman Photography; A133 (t) Kennan Ward Photography; A133 (b) Ed Reschke/Peter Arnold, Inc.; A134 (t) Larry Nielsen/Peter Arnold, Inc.; A134 (c) John Marshall/Tony Stone Images; A134 (b) Jeff & Alexa Henry/Peter Arnold, Inc.; A136 Art Wolfe/Tony Stone Images; A138 Mark E. Gibson; A138 (i) Dr. E. R. Degginger/Color-Pic; A139 J. H. Robinson/Photo Researchers; A140 Francois Gohier/Photo Researchers; A141 Tony Arruza/Bruce Coleman, Inc.; A144 (c) Jim Corwin/Tony Stone Images; A146 Tim Davis/Photo Researchers; A150 Mark E. Gibson; A151 (l) Bernard Boutrit/Woodfin Camp & Associates; A151 (r) Bill Tiernan/The Virginian-Pilot; A152 Wolfgang Kaehler Photography; A152 (i) Key Sanders/Tony Stone Images; A154 (tl) SuperStock; A154 (tr) Tom Bean/The Stock Market; A 155 John Hyde/Bruce Coleman, Inc.; A156 (t) Centre For Ecological Studies; A156 (b) E. Hanumantha/Photo Researchers; A160 (fg) Steinhart Aquarium/Tom McHugh/Photo Researchers; A160 (bg) Mark Lewis/Photo Researchers.

Unit B: B1 (fg) Francois Gohier/Photo Researchers; B1 (bg) Kunio Owaki/The Stock Market; B2-B3 Roger Werth/Woodfin Camp & Associates; B3 (t) John Livzey/Tony Stone Images; B3 (b) Royal Observatory, Edinburgh/SPL/Photo Researchers; B4 Tom Bean/Tom & Susan Bean, Inc.; B6-B7 Eric Neurath/Stock, Boston; B6 (tl) Helen Paraskevas Photography; B6 (tr) Tom Bean/Tom & Susan Bean, Inc.; B6 (bi) Mark E. Gibson; B7 NASA Photo/Grant Heilman Photography; B8, B8 (i) Mark E. Gibson; B9 M. T. OiKeefe/Bruce Coleman, Inc.; B10-B11 Michael Collier/Stock, Boston; B12 Soames Summerhays/Photo Researchers; B16 G. Gualco/Bruce Coleman, Inc.; B17 (t) Gregory G. Dimijian/Photo

Researchers; B17 (c) Krafft/Explorer/Science Source/Photo Researchers; B17 (b) Tom & Pat Leeson/Photo Researchers; B18 UPI/Corbis-Bettmann; B20 M.P.L. Fogden/Bruce Coleman, Inc.; B23 Tom Bean/Tom & Susan Bean, Inc.; B24 (t), B24 (b) The Natural History Museum, London; B24 (ct) Martin Land/SPL/Photo Researchers; B24 (cb) A. Kerstitch/Bruce Coleman, Inc.; B25 R. T. Nowitz/Photo Researchers; B26 Walter H. F. Smith & David T. Sandwell/NOAA National Data Centers; B27 (t) NASA; B27 (b) David Young-Wolff/PhotoEdit; B28 (t) Santa Fabio/Black Star/Harcourt; B28 (b) Tom Bean/Tom & Susan Bean, Inc.; B31 (l) Dr. E. R. Degginger/Color-Pic; B31 (r) Joyce Photographics/Photo Researchers; B32-B33 Dan Suzio/Photo Researchers; B33 (l) Sam Ogden/SPL/Photo Researchers; B33 (br) Breck P. Kent/Earth Scenes; B34 The Natural History Museum, London; B36 (tl), B36 (r) Dr. E. R. Degginger/Color-Pic; B36 (bl) E. R. Degginger/Bruce Coleman, Inc.; B36 (c) Joy Spurr/Bruce Coleman, Inc.; B37 (c1), B37 (c5), B37 (c6) B37 (c8) Dr. E.R. Degginger/Color-Pic; B37 (c2), B37 (c3), B37 (c10) E. R. Degginger/Bruce Coleman, Inc.; B37(c9) Mark A. Schneider/Dembinsky Photo Associates; B38 (tl), B38 (bl) Dr. E. R. Degginger/Color-Pic; B38 (cl)Biophoto Associates/Photo Researchers; B38 (cr) Andy Sacks/Tony Stone Images; B38 (br) B. Daemmrich/The Image Works; B40 Joe McDonald/Bruce Coleman, Inc.; B42 (t) Dr. E. R. Degginger/Color-Pic; B42 (b) Phillip Hayson/Photo Researchers; B43 (tl), B43 (tcl) Dr. E. R. Degginger/Color-Pic; B43 (tr) Breck P. Kent/Earth Scenes; B43 (tcr) Robert Pettit/Dembinsky Photo Associates; B43 (b) Martha McBride/Unicorn Stock Photos; B44, B45 (tl), B45 (tr), B45 (tcl), B45 (tcr) Dr. E. R. Degginger/Color-Pic; B45 (bg) David Bassett/Tony Stone Images; B46 (t) G. R. Roberts Photo Library; B46 (b), B46-B47 (ti), B47 Dr. E. R. Degginger/Color-Pic; B48 Tom Till/Auscape; B50, B51 (t), B51 (b), B52 (l), B52 (r), B52-B53 (t) Dr. E. R. Degginger/Color-Pic; B54-B55 James P. Blair & Victor Boswell/NGS Image Collection; B55 (b) Mark Richards/PhotoEdit; B56 (t) Photo Courtesy of Mrs. Alma G. Gipson; B56 (b) Stuart McCall/Tony Stone Images; B60-B61 Wolfgang Kaehler Photography; B61 (t) Jeff Foott/Bruce Coleman, Inc.; B61 (b) Mark W. Moffett/Minden Pictures; B62 Rod Planck/Photo Researchers; B64-B65 Holt Studios International (Inga Spence)/Photo Researchers; B64 (i) Lynn M. Stone/Natural History Photography; B68 Dr. E. R. Degginger/Color-Pic; B70 (l) Rob Boudreau/Tony Stone Images; B70 (c) Willard Clay/Tony Stone Images; B70 (r) Gary Braasch/Tony Stone Images; B72 (b) Grant Heilman/Grant Heilman Photography; B73 Martha McBride/Unicorn Stock Photos; B74 Kent & Donna Dannen; B76-B77 (b) C. C. Lockwood/DRK; B76 (i) Grant Heilman/Grant Heilman Photography; B77 (t) Simon Fraser/SPL/Photo Researchers; B77 (c) Jim Richardson/Woodfin Camp & Associates; B78 (t) Earl Roberge/Photo Researchers; B78 (c) Grant Heilman/Grant Heilman Photography; B78 (b) Hilarie Kavanagh/Tony Stone Images; B79 (t) Heather Angel/Biofotos; B79 (c) Mark E. Gibson; B79 (b) G. R. Roberts/G. R. Roberts Photo Library; B80 (t) Norman O. Tomalin/Bruce Coleman, Inc.; B80 (b) H. P. Merten/The Stock Market; B81 Mark E. Gibson; B82 (l) Roy Morsch/The Stock Market; B82 (c) Boltin Picture Library; B82 (r) Norm Thomas/Photo Researchers; B83 Hans Reinhard/Bruce Coleman, Inc.; B84 (r) James Lyle/Texas A&M University; B84 (b) Gary Meszaros/MESZA/Bruce Coleman, Inc.; B88 (fg) Francois Gohier/Photo Researchers; B88 (bg) Kunio Owaki/The Stock Market.

Unit C: C1 (fg) Steve Taylor/Tony Stone Images; C1 (bg) Michael Abbey/Photo Researchers; C2-C3 Jon Riley/Tony Stone Images; C3 (l), C3 (r) Dr. E. R. Degginger/Color-Pic; C4 SuperStock; C6 Michael Denora/Liaison International; C8 (b) Bob Abraham/The Stock Market; C10 Robert P. Carr/Bruce Coleman, Inc.; C14-C15 Richard R. Hansen/Photo Researchers; C16 Tony Stone Images; C20 (t) Kathy Ferguson/PhotoEdit; C20 (b) Doug Perrine/Innerspace Visions; C20 (i) Felicia Martinez/PhotoEdit; C21 (b) Chip Clark; C22-C23 Richard Pasley/Stock, Boston; C24 Courtesy of J. G.ís Edible Plastic; C25 David R. Frazier; C26 (t) United States Nuclear Regulatory Commission; C26 (b) Tom Carroll/Phototake; C30-C31 Pete Saloutos/The Stock Market; C32 Doug Martin/Photo Researchers; C37 Charles D. Winters/Photo Researchers; C38 Cosmo Condina/Tony Stone Images; C44 National Maritime Museum Picture Library; C47 Richard Megna/Fundamental Photographs; C48-C49 (t) Phil Degginger/Color-Pic; C50 Gamma Tokyo/Liaison International; C52-C53 Spencer Grant/PhotoEdit; C53 (t), C53 (br) Tom Pantages;

C54-C55 (bg) W. Cody/Corbis Westlight; C55 (t), C55 (c) Phil Degginger/Color-Pic; C55 (b) Bruno Joachin/Liaison International; C58 (l) Phil Degginger/Color-Pic; C58 (r) Corbis-Bettmann; C59 (t) William E. Ferguson; C59 (b) Phil Degginger/Color-Pic; C60 (t) Fonar Corporation; C60 (b) Jean Miele/The Stock Market; C64 (fg) Steve Taylor/Tony Stone Images; C64 (bg) Michael Abbey/Photo Researchers.

Extension Chapters: E1 (fg) Nance Trueworthy/Liaison International; E1 (bg) Simon Fraser/Science Photo Library/Photo Researchers; E2-E3 Dr. Dennis Kunkel/Phototake; E3 (b) Doug Perrine/Auscape; E4 (tr) Al Lamme/Len/Phototake; E4 (cr) M. Abbey/Photo Researchers; E4 (br) Astrid & Hanns-Frieder Michler/SPL/Photo Researchers; E6 Biophoto Associates/Science Source/Photo Researchers; E8 (t) Al Lamme/Len/Phototake; E8 (c) M. Abbey/Photo Researchers; E8 (b) Astrid & Hanns-Frieder Michler/SPL/Photo Researchers; E18 Biophoto Associates/Photo Researchers; E22 Courtesy of DERMABOND* Topical Skin Adhesive, trademark of Ethicon, Inc.; E23 Owen Franken/Tony Stone Images; E24 (t) UPI/Corbis; E24 (b) Will & Deni McIntyre/Photo Researchers; E28-E29 Ray Ellis/Photo Researchers; E29 (t) Peter Steiner/The Stock Market; E29 (b) Murray & Assoc./The Stock Market; E30 Craig Tuttle/The Stock Market; E33 (bg) Jim Zipp/Photo Researchers; E34 Ted Horowitz/The Stock Market; E38 D. Nabokov/Gamma Liaison; E40 L.West/Bruce Coleman, Inc.; E40 (i) Jonathan Wright/Bruce Coleman, Inc.; E41 Gary Milburn/Tom Stack & Associates; E42-E43 (b) Jeff Foott/Bruce Coleman, Inc.; E46 (t) Craig Hammell/The Stock Market; E46 (b) Russell D. Curtis/Photo Researchers; E47 (tl) Stu Rosner/Stock, Boston; E47 (tr) John Mead/SPL/Photo Researchers; E47 (br) John Cancalosi/Stock, Boston; E48 (t) Telegraph Colour Library/FPG International; E48 (c) Charles D. Winters/Photo Researchers; E48 (b) David Falconers & Associates; E48 (bi) Montes De Oca & Associates; E49 Paul Shambroom/Science Source/Photo Researchers; E51 Danny Daniels/The Picture Cube; E52 (t) Minnesota Historical Society; E52 (b) Peter Vadnai/The Stock Market.

Health Handbook: R25 Palm Beach Post; R29 (t) Andrew Spielman/Phototake; R29 (c) Martha McBride/Unicorn Stock; R29 (b) Larry West/FPG International.

All other photographs by Harcourt photographers listed below, © Harcourt: Weronica Ankarorn, Bartlett Digital Photography, Victoria Bowen, Eric Camden, Digital Imaging Group, Charles Hodges, Ken Karp, Ken Kinzie, Ed McDonald, Sheri O'Neal, Terry Sinclair.

Illustration Credits: Mike Dammer A31, A32, A33, A59, A60, A61, A125, B29, B57, B85, C27, C32, C61, E25, E53; John Dawson A78, A118 - A119; Eldon Doty A97, B29; Jean Calder E7, E8, E12 - E13, E18, E19; Susan Carlson A23; Pat Foss A97, A125, A157; George Fryer B44, B46; Patrick Gnan C3, C31, E50; Terry Hadler C14, C19, E39; Roger Kent A84; Mike Lamble B7, B16, B17; Joe LeMoniier A30, A58; Ruth Lindsay A132 - A133; Alan Male A83; Janos Marffy B22; Colin Newman A116 - A117; Sebastian Quigley C6, C7, C8, C22, C34, C35, C48, C52; Mike Saunders A41, A52, B9, B10, B14 - B15, B18 -B19, B24, B31, B50 -B51; Steve Seymour C36, C40, C41, E33, E34, E41; Andrew Shiff A157; Eberhand Reinmann E6, E8 - E9, E13(t), E14, E20; Steve Westin B40 - B41, B42, B45, C46.

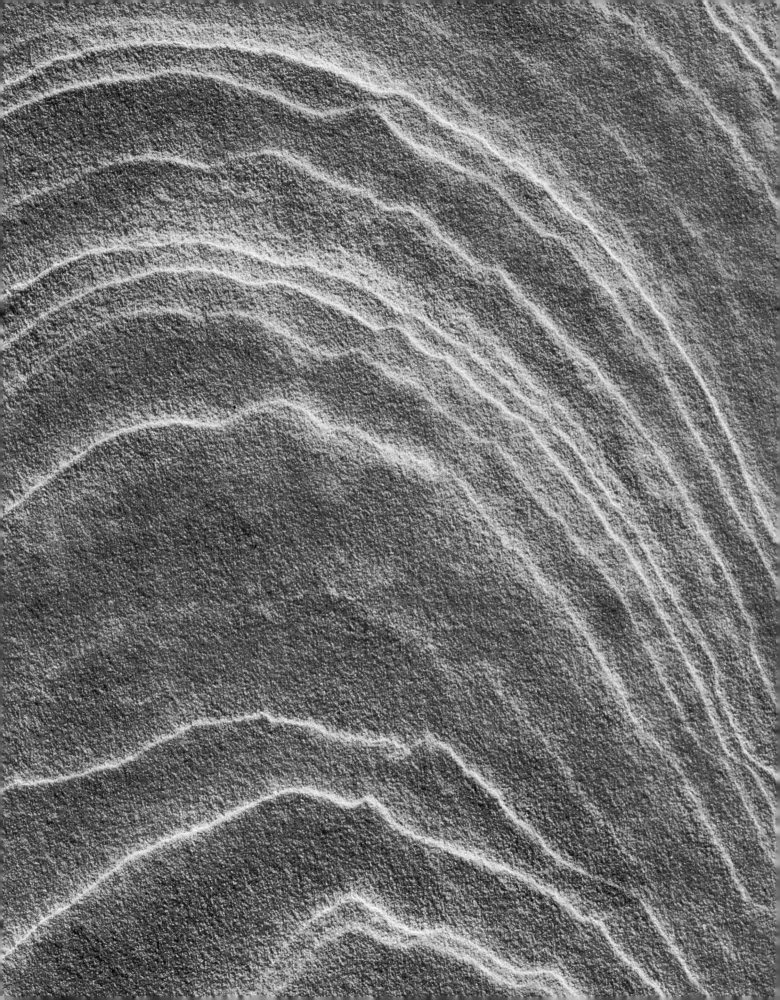

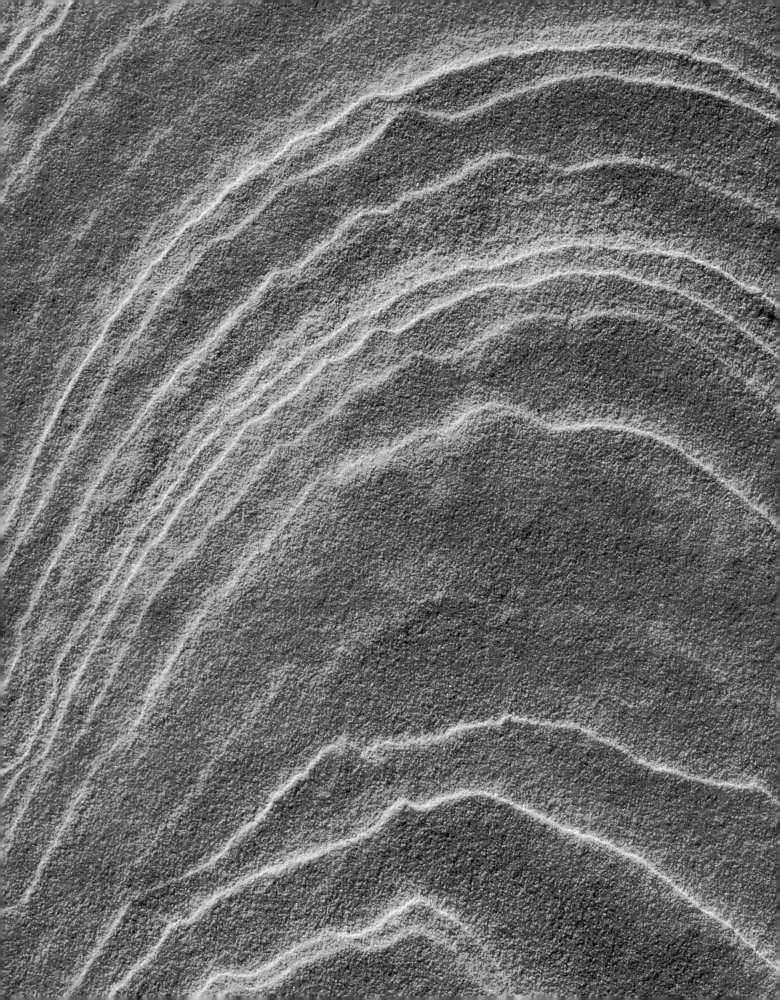